James S. Jackson, Ph.D., was named Associate Dean of the University of Michigan's Rackham School of Graduate Studies in 1987. He has been at the University of Michigan since 1971 and is currently a Professor of Psychology, Research Scientist at the Institute for Social Research, and Faculty Associate at the Center for Afro-American and African Studies and the Gerontology Institute. In 1986–87 he was a National Research Council/ Ford Foundation Senior Postdoctoral Fellow at the Groupe D'Études en Sciences Sociales, Paris, France. Dr. Jackson received his undergraduate degree in psychology from Michigan State University, his M.A. degree in psychology from the University of Toledo in 1970, and his Ph.D. in social psychology from Wayne State University in 1972. Since 1977 he has been the Director of the Program for Research on Black Americans of the Research Center for Group Dynamics, Institute for Social Research. He is currently a member of several scientific review panels, including the National Academy of Sciences Committee on the Status of Black Americans: 1940–1980, the National Cancer Institute's study on black/white cancer survival differences, the European Economic Community Study on Immigration and Racism, and chairs the Gerontological Society Task Force on Racial Minority Groups.

THE BLACK AMERICAN ELDERLY
Research on Physical and Psychosocial Health

James S. Jackson, Ph.D.
Editor

Patricia Newton, M.D.
Adrian Ostfield, M.D.
Daniel Savage, M.D., Ph.D.
Edward L. Schneider, M.D.
Associate Editors

SPRINGER PUBLISHING COMPANY
New York

Springer Publishing Company, Inc.
536 Broadway
New York, NY 10012

90 91 92 / 5 4 3 2

LIBRARY OF CONGRESS
Library of Congress Cataloging-in-Publication Data

The Black American elderly: research on physical and psychosocial
   health/James S. Jackson, editor; Patricia Newton . . . [et al.],
   associate editors.
      p.   cm.
   Collection of papers presented during a workshop held at the
National Institutes of Health on Sept. 25–26, 1986.
   Workshop was co-sponsored by the National Institute on Aging, the
American Association of Retired Persons, and the Dept. of Health and
Human Services' Minority Health Office.
   Includes bibliographies and index.
   ISBN 0-8261-5810-2
   1. Afro-American aged—Health and hygiene—Congresses.   2. Afro-
American aged—Diseases—Congresses.   3. Afro-American aged—
Psychology—Congresses.   4. Aging—Social aspects—Congresses.
I. Jackson, James S. (James Sidney), 1944-   . II. National
Institute on Aging.   III. American Association of Retired Persons.
IV. United States. Office of Minority Health.
   [DNLM: 1. Aging—physiology—congresses. 2. Aging—psychology—
congresses.   3. Blacks—United States—congresses.   WT 150 B627
1986]
RA448.5.N4B56 1988
362.1'9897'00973—dc19
DNLM/DLC
for Library of Congress   88-4922
                                                                               CIP

Printed in the United States of America

Contents

Foreword by T. Franklin Williams   *ix*
Preface by Vivian A. Betton   *xi*
Editor's Preface   *xiii*
Contributors   *xv*

PART I   Introduction

1   Growing Old in Black America: Research   3
    on Aging Black Populations
    James S. Jackson

2   The Role of Black Universities in Research   17
    on Aging Black Populations
    David Satcher

PART II   Demography and Epidemiology of Older Black Adults

3   The Demography of Older Blacks   25
    in the United States
    Ron C. Manuel

4   Cancer Prevention and Control in the Black   50
    Population: Epidemiology and Aging Implications
    Claudia R. Baquet

5   Social Determinants of the Health of Aging   69
    Black Populations in the United States
    Jacquelyne Johnson Jackson

6   Social Participation in Later Life: 99
    Black-White Differences
    Linda K. George

PART III   Biological and Health Status of Older Black Adults

7   Dietary Intake and Nutritional Status of Older   129
      U.S. Blacks: An Overview
    Norge W. Jerome

8   Diabetes and Obesity in Elderly   150
      Black Americans
    Leslie Sue Lieberman

9   Aging and Hypertension among Blacks: 190
      A Multidimensional Perspective
    Norman B. Anderson

10   Dementing Illness and Black Americans   215
     F. M. Baker

PART IV   Social and Behavioral Processes among Older Black Adults

11   Subjective Well-Being among Older Black   237
       Adults: Past Trends and Current Perspectives
     Linda M. Chatters

12   Aging and Supportive Relationships   259
       among Black Americans
     Robert Joseph Taylor

13   Health-Seeking Behavior of Elderly Blacks   282
     Tyson Gibbs

14   Health Attitudes/Promotions/Preventions: 292
       The Black Elderly
     James H. Carter

15   The Work, Retirement, and Disability of Older   304
       Black Americans
     Rose C. Gibson

PART V   Methodological Issues in Research
on Older Black Adults

16   Survey Research on Aging Black Populations   327
      James S. Jackson

17   The Design and Conduct of Case-Control Studies   347
      in Research on Aging Black Populations
      Jerome Wilson

18   Clinical Trials and the Black Elderly: Issues   354
      and Considerations
      Bettie Nelson Knuckles and Camilla A. Brooks

PART VI   Conclusion

19   Future Directions in Research on Aging   369
      Black Populations
      James S. Jackson

Index   373

Foreword

It is indeed rewarding and satisfying to see the fruition, in this book, of the efforts of a number of scholars (most of whom are themselves black) to assemble what is currently known as well as to identify gaps in our knowledge about older black persons in America. A broad range of demographic, biological, medical, and social aspects are examined, in each instance by experts in the relevant field.

It would be both impossible and presumptuous to attempt to summarize in a few words the varied and rich contents of this book. But certain outstanding themes seem to me to be reinforced again and again. First is the importance of the contributions of better understanding of race-specific and culture-specific findings to the overall understanding of biological, medical, and clinical phenomena; that is, through study of specific characteristics related to race and culture, we can and should enlighten our understanding not only of the special needs and potentialities of blacks, for example, but also our understanding of phenomena that affect all races and cultures through the comparative and distinguishing knowledge obtained.

Second, there is the overriding message of the need for more research related to older black persons (and those of other ethnic and cultural groups). Our relative neglect of such research is a major obstacle to the advancement of both understanding aging and aging-related problems, needs, and potentialities of older black persons as well as of our society at large. Third, in order to address the research challenges, we clearly need more training of investigators, scholars, and teachers, including, in particular, blacks, but also others who will address these challenges. We need to strengthen our support for such research training and research efforts in predominantly black academic institutions and also in other settings.

The National Institute on Aging was honored to be one of the sponsoring agencies for the conference which resulted in this book. We encourage other similar activities which aim to stimulate further research on aging in minority populations, as well as to recruit new investigators to the field. I would like to express our appreciation to the editor and authors of the chapters for the contributions they are making.

T. FRANKLIN WILLIAMS, M.D.
Director, National Institute on Aging

Preface

The purpose of this book is to present current knowledge on a relatively unexamined scientific subject—the black aging process—and to explore where future research efforts should be directed. It is hoped that the information contained in these chapters will enlighten scientific and lay readers and encourage further research on the subject of aging among blacks, as well as other ethnic and racial groups.

This book is a compilation of papers that were presented during a two-day workshop, "Research on Aging Black Populations," held at the National Institutes of Health on September 25 and 26, 1986. The National Institute on Aging (NIA), the American Association of Retired Persons (AARP), and the Department of Health and Human Services' Minority Health Office served as co-sponsors. It marked the first time that a large group of minority researchers, behavioral scientists, geriatric fellows, nursing home administrators, epidemiologists, internists, and medical students gathered to examine and explore aging processes among black adult populations.

Contributors to this volume, representing a number of major universities, presented critical reviews and empirical research findings on the cultural, behavioral, economic, social, and biomedical aging processes among blacks. Each chapter examines an important facet of aging among black adults, showing the myriad ways in which blacks are both similar to and different from their elderly counterparts in other racial and ethnic groups.

In summary, this book should be of great value to anyone interested in biological, psychological, and social aging processes among black populations.

VIVIAN A. BETTON
Equal Employment Opportunity Manager
National Institute on Aging

Editor's Preface

The "Research on Aging Black Populations" workshop evolved from a series of meetings convened by the National Institute on Aging (NIA) in 1984 and 1985 to discuss the need for increased empirical research on older black adults. Included in these planning meetings were a number of NIA administrators and scientists, Shirley Bagley, Vivian Betton, Kathleen Bond, Alfred Burke, Mary Farmer, Richard Sprott, Edward Schneider, Alice Thomas, and Huber Warner, and several university-based scientists, including Adrian Ostfield, Patricia Newton, Tyson Gibbs, and myself. It was decided that a research workshop designed to examine the current state of knowledge would best highlight the issues of aging among black adults.

Vivian A. Betton, Equal Employment Opportunity Manager of the National Institute on Aging, was the originator of the idea for the workshop. She assumed the administrative responsibility as the workshop coordinator, and I agreed to serve as the workshop chair. Ms. Betton's contribution to the success of the workshop cannot be overstated. It was her interest and dedication in securing the funding and logistic support that resulted in a successful meeting. I would also like to gratefully acknowledge the financial and substantive contributions of Dr. T. Franklin Williams, Director of the National Institute on Aging, Dr. Herbert Nickens, Director of the Minority Health Office, Department of Health and Human Services, and Marie W. Phillips, Director of the Minority Affairs Initiative, the American Association of Retired Persons.

Since all the potential topics could not possibly be covered within one workshop, four major areas were selected. These were demography and epidemiology, biomedical research, social and behavioral research, and research design issues. Within these broad domains specific scientific problems and authors were selected by the planning group. Because of their expertise in these areas and contribution to the planning of the workshop, Patricia Newton, Adrian Ostfield, Daniel Savage, and Edward Schneider agreed to chair specific sessions of the workshop. They also participated in the process of editing this volume and are listed as Associate Editors.

There are many other problems and specific authors that could have been selected, including exciting new research on the boundaries of the substantive areas included. The chosen topics, however, were considered to represent both well-researched scientific domains and areas of little previous study, and to be of importance to future research on health and aging in black populations. In addition, while the number of invitees to the workshop had to be limited, our aim was to attract a balance of established and new researchers in the field and to highlight the work of black researchers. The contents of this volume reflect the success in meeting these objectives.

JAMES S. JACKSON
The University of Michigan

Contributors

Norman B. Anderson, Ph.D., Department of Psychiatry, Duke University Medical Center, Duke University, Durham, North Carolina

F. M. Baker, M.D., Department of Psychiatry, University of Texas Medical School Health Science Center at San Antonio, San Antonio, Texas

Claudia R. Baquet, M.D., Cancer Control Science Program, Division of Cancer Prevention and Control, National Cancer Institute, Bethesda, Maryland

Vivian A. Betton, Equal Employment Opportunity Manager, National Institute on Aging, Bethesda, Maryland

Camilla A. Brooks, Ph.D., Division of Sexually Transmitted Diseases, Center for Disease Control, Atlanta, Georga

James H. Carter, M.D., Department of Psychiatry, Duke University, Durham, North Carolina

Linda M. Chatters, Ph.D., Florence Heller Graduate School, Brandeis University, Waltham, Massachusetts

Linda K. George, Ph.D., Department of Gerontology, Duke University Medical Center, Durham, North Carolina

Tyson Gibbs, Ph.D., Department of Gerontology, Meharry Medical College, Nashville, Tennessee

Rose C. Gibson, Ph.D., School of Social Work, The University of Michigan, Ann Arbor, Michigan

Jacquelyne Johnson Jackson, Ph.D., Department of Psychiatry, Duke University, Durham, North Carolina

James S. Jackson, Ph.D., Institute for Social Research, The University of Michigan, Ann Arbor, Michigan

Norge W. Jerome, Ph.D., University of Kansas Medical Center, University of Kansas, Kansas City, Missouri

Bettie Nelson Knuckles, Ph.D., Gerontology Center, Meharry Medical College, Nashville, Tennessee

Leslie Sue Lieberman, Ph.D., Department of Anthropology, University of Florida, Gainesville, Florida

Ron C. Manuel, Ph.D., Department of Sociology and Anthropology, Howard University, Washington, DC

Patricia Newton, M.D., Department of Psychiatry, Johns Hopkins University, Baltimore, Maryland

Adrian Ostfield, M.D., School of Public Health, Yale University, New Haven, Connecticut

David Satcher, M.D., Meharry Medical College, Nashville, Tennessee

Daniel Savage, M.D., Health Examination Field Operations Branch, National Center for Health Statistics, Hyattsville, Maryland

Edward L. Schneider, M.D., Andrus Gerontology Center, University of Southern California, Los Angeles, California

Robert Joseph Taylor, Ph.D., Graduate School of Social Work, Boston College, Chestnut Hill, Massachusetts

Jerome Wilson, Ph.D., Epidemiology and Biostatistics, Howard University Cancer Center, Howard University, Washington, DC

PART I
Introduction

1

Growing Old in Black America: Research on Aging Black Populations

James S. Jackson

The focus on black aging populations assumes that there is sufficient variability in the aging process between blacks and whites, and within the black population itself, to warrant serious scientific attention (1–3). Some research suggests that black Americans may experience a very different process of development and aging (1–6). McLoyd and Randolph (6), in their review of the developmental psychology literature, suggested that differences within racial minority groups may be accounted for better by different sets of variables than those that explain between-race group differences.

Levine (5) and Krauss (7) both proposed that variability within race and sex are important sources of information that are often disregarded in aging research (3). Levine (5) suggested that these characteristics need to be considered as essential, substantive aspects of research on aging and human development. Empirical evidence exists suggesting that black Americans respond differently from whites in research situations (6, 8). This may be even more true for older cohorts of blacks born or reared in the South, who possess distinctive language and cultural patterns in comparison to whites and later cohorts of black Americans (9).

This chapter was written while the author was a Ford Foundation Senior Postdoctoral Fellow at the Groupe D'Etudes Et Recherches Sur La Science, Ecole Des Hautes Etudes En Sciences Sociales, Paris, France.

3

The failure to attend to the variability among black population subgroups may result in biased and distorted research perspectives on the black aging experience (3, 8). If recognized and systematically understood, the source of this variability could be empirically investigated (5, 7, 10).

THE AGING OF BLACK AMERICA

Recent data from the United States Census Bureau indicate that a greater proportion of the population is living longer and that persons over the age of 65 actually constitute a larger proportion of the total population than ever before (11). Siegel (12) reported that over the next 20 to 40 years an even larger proportion of the total population will be constituted by those over the age of 65 than is true at present.

The aging of America is also being experienced by ethnic and racial minorities, particularly blacks, at an increasingly faster rate than in the general population (11). Demographic trends over the last four decades, as well as projections for the next few decades, indicate a significant upward shift in the mean age of the black population and greater concentrations of blacks in all age ranges over 45. In 1980 blacks comprised some 11.5% of the total U.S. population. Approximately 8% of the black population was 65 years of age and older. This 8% figure was a 40.3% increase over 1970. This contrasts with a 25.2% increase within the aged white population. This growth in both the black and white populations over age 65 is substantially greater than the 11.5% increase in the total population.

Most projections are for a continuing increase in the proportions and numbers of both black and white elderly through the year 2020. These projections show that the white elderly population should increase by 22.7% by the year 2000, while the black aged population should increase by 45.6%. The largest proportional increase of older adults is predicted to occur in the over-75 age group, at least through the year 2000, with a gradual tapering off through 2020. This increase will be slightly more accelerated for blacks than for whites. These latter increases undoubtedly reflect the greater material and social advantages of these black cohorts in comparison to past ones. This change in the composition of the population has resulted in much speculation regarding the implications of an aging society (13) and the individual health needs of a population with a larger proportion of long-lived individuals (14–17).

Among blacks over 55 years of age, those aged 75 and older constitute approximately 7% of the older black population. Projected increases in this older group are based largely on expected decreased mortality among black females over the age of 65 (15). In fact, blacks and whites in the oldest-old category have, since 1950, enjoyed a decided advantage in terms of their constituting increasing proportions of their respective populations. These increases suggest that the black oldest-old will constitute a sizable proportion of the black population in the near future and over the next few decades. Across all demographic categories, however, older black adults show relatively poorer status in comparison to their white counterparts: greater poverty, less formal educational attainment, a lower proportion of marriage for both both males and females, and a more unfavorable sex ratio in all age groups over 65 (11).

In summary, both the black and white populations over the age of 65 have grown over the preceding decades. This growth will show no appreciable abatement over the next several decades. For whites, the median age will also rise, but not quite as steeply as for blacks. The greatest proportionate growth over the next several decades is predicted to be in the oldest-old categories, raising many policy issues regarding the support of large numbers of frail elderly (18).

BLACK LIFE-COURSE CONTINUITIES AND DISCONTINUITIES

There has been little theoretical work regarding lifespan continuity and discontinuity of ethnic and racial minority groups (1). It is highly probable, however, that life circumstances at younger years have significant influences on the quality (and quantity) of life for blacks in the latter stages of the life course. Some have labeled this the multiple-jeopardy hypothesis (1). This hypothesis holds that negative environmental, social, and economic conditions early in the life course of blacks have deleterious effects on later social, psychological, and biological growth. These accumulate over the individual lifespan and when combined with the negative consequences of old age itself result in higher levels of morbidity and mortality at earlier years in old age for blacks than for whites.

The shortened life expectancy of blacks compared to whites suggests, but does not prove (1), the accuracy of this theory. At every stage of the lifespan blacks have greater rates of mortality, disability, and morbidity. In infancy this is marked by the higher incidence of mortality as well as higher accident and disease rates. Adolescence and young adulthood are characterized by more homicides and accidental deaths. Middle age and early old age show increased disability, early retirement, and ultimately higher death rates. It is only after the age of 75 to 80 that blacks tend to show increased longevity in comparison to whites (19–24).

It has been suggested that this racial crossover phenomenon at older ages is an artifact of age misreporting in older black cohorts (1). Others have argued strongly that this crossover is consistent with findings in other cultures (1, 20, 25). It has been hypothesized that genetic and environmental factors act in tandem on a heterogeneous black population to produce hardier older blacks (16, 19). One implication of this hypothesis is the existence of differential aging processes within the black and white populations (20). As noted by Jackson (1), however, no research findings yet support such a claim. This issue is being investigated in the recent research on effective functioning in the oldest-old groups (14, 16, 18).

Concern with the growing numbers of both white and other oldest-old members of the population focuses largely on issues of frail health and public policy—who is to care for these large numbers of dependent individuals (14, 16–18). Research by Gibson and Jackson (16) on a national sample of black elderly, however, suggests that the emergent black oldest-old group is a very heterogeneous one. They reported that 65% indicate no or only mild functional limitations. Rather than increasing with age, physical limitations are more concentrated in the younger-old groups, those 65 to 74. The data also suggest that the oldest-old blacks may be psychologically better off than younger-old blacks and to have more effective and helpful informal networks to depend on. These survey data on the black oldest-old are consistent with Manton's (19–20) conclusions, which view black survivors in older age groups as perhaps aging differently from their white counterparts.

Most gerontologists conceive of individual aging in biological, psychological, and social terms (26–27). These systems differentially affect the nature and makeup of the population. Biological aging refers to basic processes involved in cell physiology, including factors that influence the physical health status of the whole organism. Psychological aging generally refers to issues of cognitive and mental functioning. Social aging generally refers to changes in role positions and social functioning with increased chronological age.

Some researchers have argued that blacks and whites may age differently in this society due to both genetic and environmental influences (1, 19). Because chronological age is an imprecise measure of human growth and development, and individual human biological systems do age differentially, it is difficult to assess the meaning of racial differences in physical functioning across chronological age (28). Several attempts to develop functional markers of human growth and development have not proven particularly effective or useful.

The use of chronological age as a definitive, independent variable is particularly problematic in scientific and health-policy comparisons between any ethnic or racial minority group and the general population. Events from birth, such as infant mortality rates and childhood poverty, reflect the fact that the lifespans of individual ethnic and racial minority group members are divergent from those of the general population. Thus the use of an arbitrary age as an indication of entry into the later parts of the lifespan can be highly questionable—perhaps more so for blacks than whites (19). Because of general policy concerns, however, most data regarding the social, economic, and health status of the older adult population are presented in relationship to age 60 or 65 and older. Functionally, some other age in the lifespan may provide a more appropriate transition point. For example, it has been suggested (21) that age 55 is a more appropriate marker for old age for black adults because of accumulated deficits, health disabilities, and early retirement.

HEALTH OF AGING BLACKS

The most striking positive health statistic over the last 50 years has been the increased life expectation of blacks at birth (11). In 1940 the life expectation for black males was just over 50 years; this had increased to approximately 65 years in 1985. This is contrasted with white males, who had a life expectancy of 62 years in 1940 and nearly 73 years in 1985. The rate of change for black and white males is approximately the same, although the level is different and has been maintained over the 40-year interval. For black females, the rate of increased life expectancy has been somewhat steeper, rising from 55 years of age in 1940 to nearly 73 years of age in 1985. This is contrasted with white females, who had a life expectancy of approximately 67 years in 1940 and now have a life expectancy of 79 years at birth. The average remaining years of life at 65 years of age has also shown an increase for black males and females over the years. If black males survive to age 65, they have a slight advantage over white males. There still remains, however, a major discrepancy in life expectancy between white and black males at birth.

In the over-65 age group a small number of disease categories account for the majority of deaths (11). In 1980 diseases of the heart accounted for 44% of all deaths. Diseases of the heart, malignant neoplasms, and cerebral vascular diseases accounted for three-quarters of all deaths. The rates for remaining causes of death were so low that each cause taken separately accounted for less than 5% of the total number. Examining these major causes of death for blacks over the age of 65, Jackson (1) reported that from 1950 to 1976 the rates of deaths among blacks from diseases of the heart were usually much higher than for whites. Although there was a decrease for both black males and females from 1950 to 1976, this decrease was not as steep as for white males.

Baquet and Ringen (29) reported that between 1978 and 1981 blacks had the highest overall incident rates for cancer, followed by native Hawaiians and then whites. After age 35 to 39, blacks had higher age-specific incidence rates than whites for all cancer sites combined. This difference increased at age 55 to 59 and then decreased until age 70 to 74, where it began to increase again. If relative survival rates are examined, blacks had the lowest five-year relative survival rates for cancer of the cervix, uterus, cervix uteri, corpus uteri, and esophagus. The relative survival rates for all cancer sites remained virtually unchanged from 1973–1975 to 1976–1981. Whites, however, had slightly higher survival rates in 1976–1981 than in 1973–1975.

Another significant cause of death in the elderly, suicide, shows a different, almost opposite pattern. Over the age of 65, black females have the lowest rate, 1.6 per 100,000, while white males have the highest rate, 38.1. Black males and white females, at 10.9 and 9.3 respectively, form the middle two groups.

Brody and Brock (30) reported that data on morbidity for the older population is much more sporadic and difficult to obtain than mortality data. In terms of the burden of illness, black morbidity is of critical importance to the family and community. Manuel and Read (31) reported a number of selected morbidity factors for older blacks. In 1977, 27% of blacks, in comparison to 23% of whites, reported poor subjective health status. In terms of functional health status, 28% of blacks, in comparison to 23% of whites, reported eight or more bed days for the year; 46% of blacks, compared to 34% of whites, reported some limitations in their activities. Gibson (15) found a large increase, from 27.4% in 1969 to 41.1% in 1981, in the number of restricted activities in black adults over the age of 55. This is in comparison to a smaller, though parallel, increase in whites, from 19.3% to 26.0%. Gibson's (15) findings are particularly important for the cohorts younger than age 65, since they suggest entry into older ages by individuals who are in relatively poor health. Differential rates and restrictions on health, as well as perceptions of health between blacks and whites, may reflect the presence of significantly different environmental conditions.

This concern with morbidity does not diminish the burden of death on the individual or the immediate family (32). An increased burden of illness across the lifespan, however, can have important consequences not only for the individual but also for the nature and constitution of the family and others in social and economic support networks. Not only are individual blacks at increased risk for death, but these losses, along with added morbidity burdens, may require unbearable levels of familial and social-network resources for health care, as well as continued economic support. For example, the death and disability of black men early in the life course have negative consequences for the black family structure, family interaction, and childrearing; subsequently, they have important implications for individual and family productivity, schooling, career choices, marital stability, and the availability of tangible resources and affective supports.

THE STATUS OF BLACK AGING POPULATIONS

Both the demographic and health-status data for older blacks suggest that they are in a disadvantaged position relative to older whites. The data, however, also point to tremendous variability among blacks on these same dimensions. Not all older blacks reside in the inner city, live in poverty, have low education, are female, are spouseless, or are disabled. Major concerns of the workshop and this volume are what this variation among the older black populations may portend for (1) theories of black aging and human development, (2) health-related research on aging black populations, and (3) the implications of this work for the more practical issues of improved health and effective functioning for individual blacks across the life course. The remaining chapters in this volume address these concerns.

In Chapter 2 David Satcher provides a brief overview of aging issues as seen from the vantage point of the president of one of America's four black medical training institutions. He draws our attention to the importance of studying aging among blacks, the need for new research designs, the need for horizontal integration among disciplines, and the value of a life-course perspective. He concludes with a call for greater involvement of biomedical professionals and the National Institute on Aging in the problems of aging among blacks.

The remainder of the volume is organized into four sections: research on demography and epidemiology, research on biological and health status, research on social and behavioral processes, and methodological issues in designing research on older black adults.

Demography and Epidemiology of Older Black Adults

This section includes four chapters that examine the demographic make-up of black aging populations, their vital statistics, socioeconomic predictors of health in later years, and the nature of informal and formal social participation.

Ron C. Manuel, in Chapter 3, presents the current numbers and projected increases of black aging populations and their distribution across major status dimensions such as sex, age, income, and education. He also briefly examines data revealing the poor health and high disability status among older black adults. He concludes that the demographics indicate little improvement in the situation of black older adults relative to whites.

In Chapter 4, Claudia Baquet provides descriptive information on cancer, one of the major debilitating and fatal diseases among the black elderly. Using data from the national Surveillance, Epidemiology, and End Results (SEER) program, she examines the excesses of incidence and mortality for the black population. She notes that even though the black population has a younger age structure than the white population, older adult blacks to the eighth decade have a particularly severe cancer experience for a number of sites. She discusses the differential cancer experience among blacks, particularly for age and sex. Baquet concludes with a presentation of current knowledge regarding the major contributing factors to the excessive cancer rates among certain subgroups of the black population.

Jacquelyne J. Jackson discusses the important role that socioeconomic status may have as a health determinant among the black elderly in Chapter 5. Drawing on her considerable expertise in this area, she focuses attention on the validity of current measures of health and effective functioning among black aging populations. Jackson concludes that there are major problems in our assessment and measurement of this important construct, making it difficult to ascertain the contribution that socioeconomic status may make to health status and functioning among aging black populations. She particularly takes issue with the concept of excess death among older black adults and the lack of attention to the social determinants of health status.

Linda K. George, in Chapter 6, draws upon her considerable background in gerontology to examine differences in informal and formal social groups among the black and white elderly. She notes the importance of studying intraracial variability, drawing a distinction between racial differences due largely to voluntary factors (e.g., culturally determined behaviors) and involuntary factors (e.g., socioeconomic status). She indicates the difficulty in making clear distinctions between formal and informal social groups, citing the family as a major case in point. George reports that there is a serious lack of suitable data meeting minimal quality criteria on black social participation, hampering the drawing of firm conclusions. She summarizes by describing two major ongoing research activities, the Epidemiologic Catchment Area and the Established Populations for Epidemiologic Studies of the Elderly, that may soon provide better data for examining social participation among aging black populations.

Biological and Health Status of Older Black Adults

This section focuses on issues of biological and physiological functioning among aging black populations. The four authors discuss basic differences between black and white older adults in nutrition, obesity and diabetes, hypertension, and dementing illnesses.

In Chapter 7, Norge W. Jerome discusses current knowledge regarding the food consumption and nutritional intake among blacks. She notes the lack of concerted research effort on this topic and the cultural differences in food selection and preparation that make understanding of black diets difficult. She concludes by outlining an approach to the study of nutrition among older black adults, with specific recommendations for its implementation.

Leslie S. Lieberman, in Chapter 8, draws on her extensive research background to review the epidemiology of obesity and diabetes, emphasizing the status of the black elderly. She notes that older black adults are particularly at risk for obesity, which is a primary risk factor for noninsulin-dependent diabetes mellitus. The older black adult female is shown to be particularly at risk. Lieberman concludes by suggesting that while much is known about obesity and diabetes among older black adults, much remains to be done. She lists major research questions in five domains, ranging from basic research to patient education. The most pressing questions, she suggests, are those involved in access to health care, patient education, and the prevention of morbidity and mortality resulting from obesity and diabetes.

In Chapter 9, Norman B. Anderson begins from the observation that the incidence of essential hypertension in blacks is approximately twice that in whites and increases with age. From this epidemiologic base he proceeds to discuss essential hypertension as the leading contributor to cardiovascular and cerebrovascular disease morbidity and mortality in blacks. He reviews the literature in the biological, behavioral, social, nutritional, and treatment dimensions related to essential hypertension. He concludes that while our knowledge of essential hypertension in blacks is substantial, there are major gaps. He identifies six research questions within each of the five dimensions. These questions include the need to understand normative developmental changes in blacks, the possible existence of different pathological mechanisms between elderly and younger blacks and the possibility that such changes and differences are more pronounced for blacks at risk for essential hypertension.

F. M. Baker, in Chapter 10, highlights the lack of good epidemiological data on dementing illnesses in older black adults. Since the prevalence rates are not known in adult black populations, several important questions regarding causes and the existence of specific risk factors in cognitive impairment have never been addressed. She reviews the few available studies in the context of general problems of studying cognitive impairment with increased age. Baker concludes that recent data, notably from the Durham, North Carolina, and New Haven, Connecticut, Epidemiologic Catchment Area studies, will provide important screening information on differences between blacks and whites in potential dementing illnesses by age. She notes, however, that even this information will leave many important questions unanswered.

Social and Behavioral Processes Among Older Black Adults

In this section some of the more well developed areas of scientific knowledge about older black adult populations are reviewed. The general questions addressed by these five authors relate to the role of social factors in the well-being, health, and effective behavioral functioning of older black adults. These issues range from such disparate topics as psychological well-being and the correlates of family and social support to outcomes of the retirement process. While all the authors note a surfeit of research literature in comparison to the authors in prior sections, the quality and value of this existing work is questioned.

In Chapter 11, Linda M. Chatters reviews the voluminous literature on subjective well-being (SWB) in blacks and whites. She notes the emphasis of prior work on simple race comparisons and the relatively scant attention to the intragroup distribution of SWB and processes that may account for observed differences among older black populations. Chatters highlights the importance of social status, cultural values and traits, and lifespan conceptions of adaptation as important themes in theorizing about the nature of SWB in older black adults. She concludes with the important contributions that research on older black adults has made to general theorizing and a summary of selected research investigating underlying mechanisms that potentially contribute to variations in SWB among older black adults.

Robert J. Taylor, in Chapter 12, examines the previous literature on inter- and intraracial kin and nonkin support within a theoretical model that views sociodemographic and family factors as having causal roles in the amount and quality of support given and received. He notes that much of the previous literature regarding kin and nonkin support was based largely on small qualitative studies and that it is only recently that larger, representative population studies have become available. In the nonkin area he focuses attention on the role of the church in fostering major support networks for older black adults. Taylor concludes with an outline of needed ethnographic and survey research on aging black populations. These research areas include correlates of support from nonkin, the nature of intergenerational support networks, and the type and amount of support given and received among older black adults.

Tyson Gibbs, in Chapter 13, uses an in-depth ethnographic study of rural elderly as a basis for examing the general literature on the health-seeking behavior of older black adults. He concludes that current models of health-seeking behavior may be appropriate for older black populations but that prior research does not permit an unambiguous interpretation. He proposes the need for new studies that explore the role of social norms, health habits, health delivery program characteristics, and pathways of health behavior. These types of studies, Gibbs suggests, may provide more definitive understanding of health-seeking behavior among older black adults.

In Chapter 14, James H. Carter draws on his extensive experience as a primary-care physician in the rural South to examine a number of myths about health and mental health attitudes and behaviors of older black adults. He argues that the health attitudes of older blacks reflect complex cultural and socioeconomic conditions. Carter suggests that health programs for the black elderly are fragmented and often too crisis-oriented to provide effective services. He concludes that quality health care for the ambulatory black aged can best be provided through an accessible neighborhood comprehensive health care system.

Rose C. Gibson reviews the major research on retirement related to older black adults in Chapter 15. She indicates that a new type of retired black person is emerging—the "unretired-retired." These are older individuals who are not working but who identify themselves as disabled rather than retired. Based on the identification of this group of older blacks she proposes that they form a sizable number of older black adults and that they have been systematically excluded from previous research and policy decisions. She discusses the need for new research in the context of the role of gender, the nature of current retirement policies, and the social aspects of black intraindividual aging. She concludes that there is a need for longitudinal, theory-driven research. This research should permit race and class comparisons and an examination of the role of disability and prior work experiences on the labor-force participation and nonparticipation of older black adults.

Methodological Issues in Research on Older Black Adults

The three chapters in this section focus on the importance of methodological considerations in social, clinical, and epidemiological research on aging black populations. All three conclude that these approaches, when properly conducted, can be of great utility in studying substantive problems among black older adults.

In Chapter 16, James S. Jackson examines the application of survey research methods in black populations, concluding that they have rarely been conducted appropriately in previous studies. He provides examples of the large numbers of poor survey studies in the past, particularly problems in drawing adequate samples, designing appropriate instruments, coding difficulties, and problems of analysis and interpretation. He concludes that recent work on sampling and survey design can contribute to the better planning and execution of future survey research projects on black elderly populations.

Jerome Wilson, in Chapter 17, concisely outlines the basic elements of case-control designs in epidemiological research. He suggests that it is a method that has been greatly underutilized in prior research on blacks. He concludes that it is well suited to studying health issues related to aging in black populations because of efficiencies of personnel costs and time, its applicability to particular health problems of blacks, and the availability of potential data sources.

Bettie N. Knuckles and Camilla A. Brooks review the past use of clinical trials in black aging populations in Chapter 18. They note the lack of inclusion of adequate numbers of blacks in most of the prior research. They discuss reasons for this underrepresentation and indicate the necessity and importance of including greater numbers of blacks in future studies. Knuckles and Brooks conclude with specific suggestions outlining how larger and better clinical trials can be conducted on aging black populations. They note particularly that the cooperation of large research projects and black institutions could contribute to obtaining adequate numbers of older black adults.

In a brief concluding chapter, major themes related to future research on aging black populations are presented. These themes emerged from interactions among participants at the workshop and from the literature and suggestions for future research presented in each of the chapters.

REFERENCES

1. Jackson JJ. Race, national origin, ethnicity, and aging. In: Binstock RH, Shanas E, eds. *Handbook of Aging and the Social Sciences* (2nd ed.). New York: Van Nostrand Reinhold; 1985:264–303.
2. Jackson JS. The program for research on black Americans. In: Jones RL, ed. *Advances in Black Psychology*. Berkeley, CA: Cobb and Henry Publishers. In Press.
3. Jackson JS. Science, values and research on ethnic and racial groups. Unpublished manuscript. The University of Michigan. 1986.
4. Spencer MB, Brookens GR, Allen WR, eds. *Beginnings: The Social and Affective Development of Black Children*. Hillsdale, NJ: Lawrence Erlbaum Associates; 1985.
5. Levine EK. Old people are not alike: social class, ethnicity/race, and sex are bases for important differences. In: Sieber JE, ed. *The Ethics of Social Research*. New York: Springer-Verlag; 1982:127–144.
6. McLoyd VC, Randolph SM. Secular trends in the study of Afro-American children: a review of *Child Development*, 1936–1980. In: Smuts AB, Hagen JW, eds. History and research in child development. *Monographs of the Society for Research in Child Development*. 1985; 50:78–92.
7. Krauss IK. Between- and within-group comparisons in aging research. In: Poon LW, ed. *Aging in the 1980's*. Washington, DC: American Psychological Association; 1980:542–551.
8. Jackson JS, Tucker MB, Bowman PB Conceptual and methodological problems in survey research on black Americans. In: Liu WT, ed. *Methodological Problems in Minority Research*. Chicago: Pacific/Asian American Mental Health Center; 1982:11–40.
9. Burton LM, Bengtson VL. Research in elderly minority communities: Problems

and potentials. In: Manuel RC, ed. *Minority Aging: Sociological and Social Psychological Issues.* Westport, CT: Greenwood Press; 1982:215–222.

10. Labouvie EW. Identity versus equivalence of psychological measures and constructs. In: Poon LN, ed. *Aging in the 1980's.* Washington, DC: American Psychological Association; 1980:493–502.
11. U.S. Bureau of the Census. *Demographic and Socioeconomic Aspects of Aging in the United States* (Current Population Reports, Series P–23, No. 138). Washington, DC: U.S. Government Printing Office; 1984.
12. Siegel JS. Recent and perspective trends for the elderly population and some implications for health care. In: Haynes SG, Feinleib M. eds. *Epidemiology of Aging* (NIH Publication No. 80–969). Washington, DC: U.S. Department of Health and Human Services; 1980: 289–343.
13. Pifer A, Bronte, DL. Introduction: squaring the pyramid. *Daedalus* 1986; 115:1–12.
14. Suzman R, Riley MW. Introducing the "oldest old." In: Suzman R, Riley MW, eds. The oldest old. *Milbank Memorial Fund Quarterly* (Supplement) 1985; 63:177–186.
15. Gibson RC. Blacks in an aging society. *Daedalus* 1986; 115:349–372.
16. Gibson RC, Jackson JS. The black aged. In: Willis R, ed. Currents of health policy and impact on black Americans. *The Milbank Memorial Fund Quarterly (Supplement)* In Press.
17. Manton KG, Soldo BJ. Dynamics of health changes in the oldest old: new perspectives and evidence. In: Suzman G, Riley MW, eds. The oldest old. *Milbank Memorial Fund Quarterly (Supplement)* 1985; 63:206–285.
18. Suzman R, Willis D. eds. *The Oldest Old.* New York: Oxford University Press; in press.
19. Manton KG, Poss SS, Wing S. The black/white mortality crossover: investigation from the perspectives of the components of aging. *The Gerontologist* 1979; 19:291–299.
20. Manton KG. Differential life expectancy: Possible explanations during the later years. In: Manuel RC, ed. *Minority Aging: Sociological and Social Psychological Issues.* Westport, CT: Greenwood Press, 1982:63–70.
21. Jackson JS, Gibson RC. Work and retirement among the black elderly. In: Blau ZS, ed. *Current Perspectives on Aging and the Life Cycle* (Vol. 1). Greenwich, CT: JAI Press; 1985: 193–222.
22. Burton L, Bengtson VL. Research in elderly minority communities: problems and potentials. In: Manuel RC, ed. *Minority Aging: Sociological and Social Psychological Issues.* Westport, CT: Greenwood Press; 1982:215–222.
23. Jackson JJ. *Minorities and Aging.* Belmont, CA: Wadsworth Publishing Co.; 1980.
24. Markides KS. Mortality among minority populations: a review of recent patterns and trends. *Public Health Reports* 1983; 98:252–260.
25. Omran AR. Epidemiologic transition in the U.S. *The Population Bulletin* 1977; 32.
26. Adelman RC. Definition of biological aging. In: Haynes SG, Feinleib M, eds. *Epidemiology of Aging* (NIH Publication No. 80–969). Washington, DC: U.S. Department of Health and Human Services; 1980:9–14.

27. Butler RN. Current definitions of aging. In: Haynes SG, Feinleib M, eds. *Epidemiology of Aging* (NIH Publication No. 80–969). Washington, DC: U.S. Department of Health and Human Services 1980:7–8.
28. Costa PT, McCrae RR. Functional age: a conceptual and empirical critique. In: Haynes SG, Feinleib M, eds. *Epidemiology of Aging* (NIH Publication No. 80–969). Washington, DC: U.S. Department of Health and Human Services; 1980:23–46.
29. Baquet CR, Ringen K. *Cancer Among Blacks and Other Minorities: Statistical Profiles* (NCI Publication No. 86-2785). Washington, DC: U.S. Department of Health and Human Services; 1986.
30. Brody JA, Brock DB. Epidemiologic and statistical characteristics of the United States elderly population. In: Finch CE, Schneider E., eds., *The Handbook of the Biology of Aging* New York: Van Nostrand Reinhold; 1985:3–26.
31. Manuel RC, Reid J. A comparative demographic profile of the minority and nonminority aged. In: Manuel RC, ed. *Minority Aging: Sociological and Social Psychological Issues*. Westport, CT: Greenwood Press; 1982:31–52.
32. Kastenbaum R. Dying and death: a life-span approach. In: Birren JE, Schaie KW, eds. *Handbook of the Psychology of Aging*. New York: Van Nostrand Reinhold; 1985:619–646.

2

The Role of Black Universities in Research on Aging Black Populations

David Satcher

We have recently realized that persons over the age of 65 are becoming an increasingly important segment, numerically and sociopolitically, of this society. It is generally agreed that, as a group, the elderly deserve the best that our society has to offer. Yet as a society we are very poorly prepared and perhaps poorly motivated to deal with the needs of the elderly. In fact, with all of our sophistication, we still have a poor understanding of those needs. Nowhere is this more evident than in the health care field.

We pride ourselves as a nation on having the most highly sophisticated health care system in the world. The strengths of that system, we claim, are its diversity, its specialization, and its technology. Yet when confronting the perspectives of the elderly and their needs, the weaknesses of our system become apparent: fragmentation, lack of coordination, and lack of integration. It is clear that if we are able to respond to the challenges the elderly present to our health delivery system, we will have much improved health care for everyone.

Inherent in these systemic problems facing health needs of the elderly are the biases of health care professionals that affect their experiences. Rarely are the elderly popular with young physicians looking to make exotic diagnoses. In that context, when I was in medical training the elderly were often referred to in very negative terms. In addition, because we often expected the elderly to be "naturally sick," we did not vigorously look for treatable causes.

THE NEED FOR DISCIPLINARY INTEGRATION

Aging research starts with the questions of what aging is and how we separate it from other life processes and pathology. What determines diversity in the qualities and characteristics that we associate with aging? How do we optimize the aging process for any individual or group, and how do we reduce pathology? How do we better organize services within the health care system to meet the needs of the elderly? Do we have the researchers to address these kinds of questions? Certainly we have outstanding biochemists, physiologists, immunologists, and pathologists. We have outstanding internists and practitioners of every specialty in clinical medicine. We have outstanding behavioral and social scientists. But what we do not have is the kind of integration and communication among these various specialties that allow us to answer questions we have posed, questions that can only be answered by an integrated effort with maximum communication among disciplines.

We lack horizontal integration of researchers and health care providers within our institutions and society. But even if we had this horizontal integration, how would we assess the time-related process of aging long enough to answer the basic questions? That requires vertical integration and communication even between the generations. It requires quality longitudinal research, and longitudinal research is all too rare at institutions in our country. It does not have the short-term payoff or gratification that has become so important in our society. It does not respond to the need to "publish or perish." And yet it is clear that longitudinal research is critical to progress in knowledge about aging. Thus in order to respond to the needs of the elderly in the health care system, I suggest the following changes:

1. More positive attitudes on the part of all concerned.
2. Better communication and integration of effort among biomedical scientists, behavioral scientists, and clinicians.
3. Increased longitudinal studies with vertical integration of research and services.
4. Extended coordination of services, including home care, ambulatory care, inpatient care, and long-term care.

AGING RESEARCH IN BLACK POPULATIONS

What about aging research in black populations? Are the issues different? Are the challenges different? Some data, of course, are very revealing. Blacks constitute approximately 15% of the population under the age of 15 in our country. Over the age of 65, blacks constitute about 8% of the population.

Those data are very telling. In life expectancies, blacks overall average about 5.6 years less than whites. What do these data say about aging in blacks? We really do not know. Only if the burden of environmental challenges and onslaughts were randomly distributed throughout society would these data tell us anything about aging in blacks. The Department of Health and Human Services Task Force on the Health Status of Blacks and Other Minorities made it quite clear that the burdens are not randomly distributed horizontally or vertically. Infant mortality is twice as common in blacks. Cardiovascular disease and cancer affect blacks at a much greater rate. In fact, prior to the age of 70, more than 42% of black deaths are excess deaths—deaths that would not have occurred if blacks had the same life expectancy, age- and sex-adjusted, as whites. In addition to cardiovascular disease and cancer, more common causes of deaths in blacks include homicide, accidents, and substance abuse. In fact, poverty is more common in blacks at every age. Many blacks today over the age of 65 have survived the same burdens that have led to the deaths of the bulk of their cohorts, but in many cases they bear the scars, including the poverty.

One goal of aging research must be to minimize the burdens and to maximize the outcome of the aging process for all people, including blacks. The black elderly are victims historically and currently are excessively burdened by poverty, crime, and discrimination based on race and age. Aging research on black Americans certainly deserves special consideration and priority.

In addition to the challenges facing aging research in general (including attitudes, lack of communication, integration and coordination of resources), we currently face several serious problems. There is a paucity of well-trained investigators with special interests in the problems of aging in blacks. Less than 3% of physicians, pharmacists, dentists, and other health care professionals in this country are black, while approximately 2% of all biomedical scientists are black.

Even for those blacks interested in research on aging in black populations there are serious barriers. These include (1) research experience and discipline; (2) peer support for starting research; (3) difficulty in obtaining the resources needed for research, including skills and negotiating the system; and (4) bias within the system of support at every level.

THE CHALLENGES FACING HISTORICALLY BLACK INSTITUTIONS

It is important to place in perspective the challenges facing historically black institutions. As a rule, these institutions were founded with a special commitment to provide unique opportunities for health-professional education for minorities and the disadvantaged and access to health care for the underserved. For many years, these institutions stood virtually alone in providing access to health-professional education for blacks in this country. In fact, almost 90% of the black veterinarians today are alumni of the Tuskegee School of Veterinary Medicine. Seventy percent of the black pharmacists are graduates of the one of the four black schools of pharmacy, and more than 50% of the black physicians and dentists are graduates of Howard University or Meharry Medical College. One of the major challenges facing black institutions today is to continue our unique commitment to the underserved, since the needs of the underserved are still paramount in this country. There are three major areas of concern: (1) the health status of blacks and other minorities, (2) the underrepresentation of blacks and other minorities in the health professions and the biomedical sciences, and (3) the need to strengthen our institutions to respond to these challenges.

In order to deal with these concerns adequately, there are several themes that must be emphasized. First, we must underline the need to cultivate the relationship we have with the black community, including the black elderly, through our institutions and our alumni throughout the country. The access we have to the black community provides a special opportunity for us to contribute to problem solutions. We also need to increase our emphasis on research, even in the face of the demands for teaching and delivering health services with limited faculties and resources. We need to continue to improve the environment of our institutions, so that research can more easily flourish.

A good example of this environmental improvement is the Plan for Academic Renewal (PAR) at Meharry Medical College started in July 1982. This is both a financial and an academic plan. It is a plan to significantly strengthen our faculty, with special emphasis on research skills. It is a plan to develop centers of excellence for research in areas such as geriatrics, nutrition, and tropical diseases. It is a plan to provide more educational support in terms of student scholarships, as well as support for the library. It is a plan to revitalize our facilities. All of these efforts as they come about are strengthening our institution as one that contributes significantly to research in various areas. As a part of this effort we have also had to increase significantly the performance expectations of our faculty and students. In fact, there is an increasing demand for faculty to become more involved in research and for students to take advantage of opportunities to develop and prepare for research careers.

Another challenge to our institutions is to develop more cooperative efforts with majority institutions in research benefiting black populations. For example, in addition to sharing the Nashville-General Hospital, Meharry Medical College and Vanderbilt University have found new ways to cooperate. It is now not unusual for members of our faculty and members of the Vanderbilt faculty to submit joint proposals, such as the Training Program in Tropical Diseases headed by Dr. George Hill at Meharry Medical College or the Alcoholism Control Project headed by Andy Spickard at Vanderbilt, a project involving several Meharry faculty members. Especially at our institution, we must maximize the role of teams in research internally and with consortia externally. It is important to our institutions that basic scientists, behavioral scientists, clinicians, and social scientists involved in applied community interventions collaborate to address problems facing the black elderly.

Our students have special needs. They need more information and greater understanding of the plight of the elderly. They need more appreciation for research on black aging populations, more role models in gerontology and geriatrics. Our students need more experience with good researchers and good clinicians. They need more opportunities to become involved with research on aging and comprehensive health care models in black populations.

SUMMARY

In summary, I make the following recommendations. First, it is clear that there needs to be greater concerted commitment to funding research on aging in this country, and especially aging in black populations. Second, there need to be more opportunities for horizontal and vertical integration in our approaches to research on aging, especially in black populations. More effort should be directed to initiating longitudinal research on aging, and those studies should be securely funded. The longitudinal research study of hypertension at Meharry is an excellent opportunity. I am very pleased that it is now supported by the National Institute on Aging.

Third, there needs to be more involvement of black scientists in aging research. Just as the black aging population carries heavy burdens from past experiences, blacks in research carry their own burdens. If we are serious about expediting research, we will make efforts to lighten those burdens as blacks attempt to become involved in research. Fourth, there needs to be more involvement of black institutions in aging research. This needs to be encouraged by the National Institute on Aging and other agencies within the National Institutes of Health. Just as the National Institutes of Health made special efforts in the late 1950s and early 1960s to enhance the research capabilities of institutions like Vanderbilt and the University of Virginia, efforts must now be made to enhance research opportunities and activities at historically black institutions.

PART II
Demography and Epidemiology of Older Black Adults

3

The Demography of Older Blacks in the United States

Ron C. Manuel

Seemingly the problems of the aged have been solved, or, at least, one might surmise as much when reading or listening to current popular news media. In 1982, for example, an article in the *New York Times* (1) began by noting that "old doesn't mean poor any more." Or consider a more recent *Times* headline—"More gold in the golden years" (2). Speaking directly to the point, Jane Seaberry, writing in the *Washington Post* in 1985 and summarizing the annual report of the President's Council of Economic Advisors, observed that: "elderly Americans have achieved basic economic parity with the rest of the population and no longer are a disadvantaged group" (3). One rather easily deduced implication is that, indeed, the problems of the aged have been solved.

By what evidence or, more appropriately, by what failure of observation does one so optimistically conclude that the older population is no longer disadvantaged, when one frequently hears of situations like Ruth Mellott's? Ruth Mellott has been bedridden since 1975. She complains she does not get enough to eat. Knowing that the two of them have only $654 a month to

The data utilized in this paper were made available, in part, through the Inter-university Consortium for Political and Social Research and the National Center for Health Statistics. The data were originally collected during various surveys by the (1) U.S. Department of Commerce, Bureau of the Census and (2) U.S. Department of Health and Human Services, National Center for Health Statistics. Neither the collectors of the original data nor the Consortium bear any responsibility for the analyses or interpretations presented here.

live on, her husband observes: "I starve myself to feed her; I still owe Safeway because the checks bounce. . . . I cook, I clean, I bathe her; I need help some way. . . . We're gonna go down the drain and we don't have long to go" (4).

The Mellotts are not unique. They were among 99,000 elderly residents in the nation's capital in 1983—the year Ms. Mellott was interviewed—who lived on inadequate incomes; they are among approximately 4 million elderly persons nationwide who continue to cope with impoverished incomes and the attendant gamut of health, legal, and socioemotional problems. In short, if the problems of the aged have been solved, why are cases like the Mellotts' so frequent?

The answer to this question, in part, must be traced to the longstanding tendency to treat the older population (aged 65 and over) as one statistical conglomerate.[1] To conclude that all is well with the older population simply because, for example, the per capita family income for the population aged 65 and over was $9,080 in 1983, compared with $8,960 for nonaged families, fails to consider that the aged are not a homogeneous group. It is rather easy to conclude or deduce that the problems of the older population have been addressed if one accepts that all older persons experience the same conditions of aging. Observing a more complete set of data that reflect the heterogeneity in the older population, one cannot escape the conclusion that there are pockets of significant need that continue to characterize uniquely the older population.

This chapter directs attention to one dimension—racial and ethnic diversity—by which it is possible to document this simple conclusion. Specifically, the objective is to present an array of sociodemographic data to show that substantial variations continue to exist in the older population and that these variations have important implications for (1) conclusions about the level and nature of the needs that remain in the older population and (2) directions for research in gaining a clearer understanding of the factors producing, and consequent of, the unique patterning of the data. The discussion begins by emphasizing differences in the size, growth, and projected growth and distribution of the older black or minority population and the older white population (or nonminority population).[2] Next, several health-related indicators are analyzed, followed by a study of income circumstances. The discussion is placed in historical context as much as possible. Data from 1960 are frequently discussed in order to show trends since implementation of the domestic assistance programs of the Great Society legislation of the 1960s and 1970s.

---

[1]The older or aged population is defined as persons aged 65 and over, unless otherwise noted.
[2]See Manuel (5) for a discussion of an alternative, more precise conceptualization for identifying minority and majority groups.

THE SIZE, GROWTH, AND DISTRIBUTION OF THE OLDER BLACK POPULATION

The population aged 65 and over has grown constantly throughout the history of the United States. The increase from 50,000 persons in 1790—the time of the first U.S. census—to somewhat over 28 million persons in 1985 has coincided, especially since the 1920s, with constant and relatively substantial decennial increases in the proportion of the population aged 65 and over. The data in Table 3.1, for example, show that while the total population grew by 11.7% between 1970 and 1980, the older population grew by roughly 28%.

What is demographically significant—and thus significant for societal planning in order to present a complete picture of the status of the aged—is that the black older population, at least since 1930, has been increasing at a substantially faster rate than the white older population.[3] While the elderly black and white populations increased between 1920 and 1930 by about 12% and 36%, respectively, the corresponding rates of increase between

TABLE 3.1 Decennial Percentage Increases for the U.S. Population Aged 65 and Over, by Race: 1900 to 1980

| Decade | U.S. all ages | Persons aged 65 years and over | | |
		Total	Black	White
1900	—	—	—	—
1910	21.0	28.2	12.7	29.7
1920	14.9	24.9	13.3	25.9
1930	16.1	35.5	12.0	36.2
1940	7.3	36.0	65.2	33.0
1950	14.9	36.1	40.8	37.1
1960	18.5	35.0	34.7	34.6
1970	13.3	20.6	35.9	19.8
1980	11.7	28.7	32.7	27.1

Source: Based on data from the United States Bureau of the Census (7, 16).

[3]The deficiencies of census data are well known. One of the frequently mentioned problems is that of the census undercount—especially for the black population—and its implication for conclusions about population growth or level of poverty. The point is often made, for example, that the level of poverty is actually underrepresented among older blacks because the black undercount leaves unanalyzed the supposed substantial level of poverty in the population not counted.

For the 1980 census, it has been shown that black Americans were undercounted at the rate of 5.6% (1.5 million persons); the U.S. overall population undercount was about 1% (2.2 million persons). Yet among older persons aged 65 and over, there was a net overcount among blacks (38,000 persons) as well as among whites (6). It is also noteworthy that whether a net over- or undercount is observed among the black older age cohort, the relative magnitude of the count to the total population count (2.1 million older black persons) has essentially no implications in percentaging for, say, the proportion of the total older black population having incomes below the poverty threshold.

TABLE 3.2 Size and Percentage Increase of the U.S. Population, by Age, by Race, by Gender, by Time Period

	Percentage increase					
	1960–80 % Increase			1980–85 % Increase		
Race by age	Total	Male	Female	Total	Male	Female
White						
All ages	22.7	21.9	23.5	3.9	4.0	3.8
60 +	51.9	39.5	62.3	9.6	10.0	9.4
65 +	56.9	40.2	70.5	10.5	10.9	10.2
75 +	86.1	55.1	108.7	14.2	13.1	14.8
85 +	168.3	121.2	195.2	18.6	11.0	21.8
Black						
All ages	42.0	40.3	43.5	7.8	8.0	7.7
60 +	80.5	65.7	92.9	11.4	10.9	11.7
65 +	83.4	63.6	100.0	11.3	10.1	12.1
75 +	116.3	83.2	143.3	16.6	13.0	18.4
85 +	118.9	86.2	140.0	26.5	20.4	29.6

Size[a,b] (in thousands)

	1960			1980			1985		
	Total	Male	Female	Total	Male	Female	Total	Male	Female
White									
All ages	159,372	78,372	81,000	195,571	95,525	100,046	203,159	99,361	103,798
60 +	21,353	9,762	11,591	32,425	13,617	18,809	35,547	14,975	20,572
65 +	14,851	6,685	8,166	23,297	9,370	13,926	25,743	10,390	15,353
75 +	4,939	2,091	2,848	9,190	3,245	5,945	10,495	3,670	6,824
85 +	778	283	495	2,087	626	1,461	2,475	695	1,779
Black									
All ages	18,948	9,099	9,849	26,903	12,769	14,135	29,012	13,790	15,222
60 +	1,653	750	903	2,984	1,243	1,742	3,325	1,379	1,946
65 +	1,148	522	626	2,106	854	1,252	2,343	940	1,403
75 +	349	155	194	755	284	472	880	321	559
85 +	74	29	45	162	54	108	205	65	140

[a]Includes armed forces overseas.

[b]Counts reflect modifications to the 1980 census results, whereby frequencies for the white and black races have now been increased to include frequencies initially coded as "other" races. The majority of these redistributed frequencies refer to persons who identified themselves as of Spanish origin and were coded "other" in the 1980 census reports (7).

Source: United States Bureau of the Census and tabulations based on the One-in-a-Thousand-Public-Use Sample of the 1960 census (U.S. Bureau of the Census) (7).

1930 and 1940 were roughly 65% and 33% (see Table 3.1). The greater relative growth rate among older blacks has continued since the 1930s and 1940s. As shown in Table 3.2, the 83% increase in the black older population from 1960 to 1980 eclipsed the corresponding 57% increase in the white older population. Both figures highlight the growth of the aged population when compared to the 25% increase in the total U.S. population during the same time period.

With the exception of the racial contrasts for males between 1980 and 2000, the data on projections in Table 3.3 show that the trend of faster relative older black growth is expected to continue throughout this century and into the next one. Thus, while the total U.S. population is only expected to grow by 18% between 1980 and 2000, the increase of black older females is projected at 68%. The population of white older females is projected to increase by 38% between 1980 and 2000. A similar pattern in the data prevails during each of the successive projected 20-year periods studied in Table 3.3.

One result of the faster rate of growth in the older black relative to older white population is that older blacks comprised slightly over 8% of the 28.5 million persons aged 65 and over in 1985, whereas older blacks comprised about 7% of the roughly 16 million persons aged 65 and over in 1960. In short, older blacks are constituting a greater and greater proportion of the total aged population.[4]

The 2,343,000 elderly blacks in 1985 also represented slightly over 8% of the total black population; about 12.5% of the white population was aged 65 and over in 1985 (see Table 3.4). When compared to the fact that in 1900, 4.2% of the total white population was aged, relative to about 2.9% of the black population, it is clear that both populations are aging.[5] Yet the white population is distinctly older than its black counterpart, despite the current generally faster rate of increase in the latter population.

Projections for the future show that these two populations will continue to age (see Table 3.3). A narrowing of the gap of the relative age status of the two groups, however, will not become evident until after the post–World War II baby-boom cohort has fully entered the ranks of the elderly, after 2020. Between 1980 and 2000, for example, the percentage of white female society that will be old will increase from 13.9% to 16.5%; the corresponding increase for black older females will be from 8.9 to 10.2%. In 2040, the percentages of these respective populations that will be old are 26.2 (white) and 19.5 (black); the respective percentages will be 27.4 and 25.1 in 2080. It is not clear, however, that this convergence will necessarily represent or reflect the homogenizing effect of similar lifestyles or circumstances at work in the two populations.

[4]Conclusions are based on tabulations of: (1) data in the public use file (One-in-a-Thousand sample) of the 1960 census and (2) data from the U.S. Bureau of the Census (1986) (7).
[5]An aging population is one whose total population count, over time, is characterized by increasingly greater proportions of persons aged 65 and over.

TABLE 3.3 Projections of the U.S. Population and Percentage Increases: Persons Aged 65 and over and Aged 85 and over, by Race, by Sex, by Year[a,b]

Year	Number (in thousands)				% of respective total populations				% increase: preceding 20 years			
	White		Black		White		Black		White		Black	
	Male	Female	Male	Female	Male	Female	Male	Female	Male	Female	Male	Female
65 years and over												
1990	11,439	17,156	975	1,604	11.1	15.9	6.5	9.7				
2000	12,382	18,744	1,059	1,917	11.4	16.5	6.2	10.2	32.1	34.6	24.0	53.1
2020	18,548	25,797	1,878	3,226	15.9	21.2	8.9	14.0	49.8	37.6	77.3	68.3
2040	22,930	32,506	3,259	5,111	19.6	26.2	13.5	19.5	23.6	26.0	73.5	58.4
2060	23,120	32,500	4,181	6,229	20.2	26.8	16.2	22.3	.8	-0.0	28.3	21.9
2080	23,192	32,711	4,980	7,276	20.7	27.4	18.7	25.1	.3	.6	19.1	16.8
85 years and over												
1990	828	2,190	77	180	.8	2.0	.5	1.1				
2000	1,217	3,227	110	302	1.1	2.8	.6	1.6	94.4	120.9	103.7	179.6
2020	1,734	4,496	154	491	1.5	3.7	.7	2.1	42.5	39.3	40.0	62.6
2040	3,303	7,643	354	1,002	2.8	6.2	1.5	3.8	90.5	70.0	130.0	104.1
2060	3,750	8,757	578	1,485	3.3	7.2	2.2	5.3	13.5	14.6	63.3	48.2
2080	4,433	9,858	842	1,993	4.0	8.3	3.2	6.9	18.2	12.6	45.7	34.2

[a] U.S. Census Middle Series projections: Assumes a completed cohort fertility of 1.9 births per woman, yearly net migration at 450,000, and a life expectancy at birth in 2080 of 81.
[b] Includes armed forces overseas.
Source: U.S. Bureau of the Census (17).

TABLE 3.4 Age Structure of the U.S. Population, by Race, by Gender, by Year (Numbers in Thousands)[a]

Age	1960			White 1980			1985		
	Total	Male	Female	Total	Male	Female	Total	Male	Female
All ages	159,372	78,372	81,000	195,571	95,525	100,046	203,159	99,361	103,798
	100%[b]	100%	100%	100%	100%	100%	100%	100%	100%
Under 60	86.6	87.5	85.7	83.4	85.8	81.1	82.6	84.9	80.2
60–64	4.1	3.9	4.2	4.7	4.4	4.9	4.8	4.6	5.0
65–74	6.2	5.9	6.6	7.2	6.4	8.0	7.5	6.8	8.2
75–84	2.6	2.3	2.9	3.6	2.7	4.5	3.9	3.0	4.9
85 +	.5	.4	.6	1.1	.7	1.5	1.2	.7	1.7
75 +	3.1	2.7	3.5	4.7	3.4	5.9	5.2	3.7	6.6
65 +	9.3	8.5	10.1	11.9	9.8	13.9	12.5	10.5	14.8
60 +	13.4	12.5	14.3	16.6	14.3	18.8	17.4	15.1	19.8

Black

	18,948	9,099	9,849	26,903	12,769	14,135	29,012	13,790	15,222
	100%	100%	100%	100%	100%	100%	100%	100%	100%
Under 60	91.3	91.8	90.8	88.9	90.3	87.6	88.6	89.9	87.1
60–64	2.7	2.5	2.8	3.3	3.0	3.5	3.4	3.2	3.6
65–74	4.2	4.0	4.4	5.0	4.5	5.5	5.0	4.5	5.6
75–84	1.5	1.4	1.5	2.2	1.8	2.6	2.3	1.9	2.8
85 +	.4	.3	.5	.6	.4	.8	.7	.5	.9
75 +	1.8	1.7	2.0	2.9	2.2	3.3	3.0	2.3	3.7
65 +	6.1	5.7	6.4	7.8	6.7	8.9	8.1	6.8	9.2
60 +	8.7	8.2	9.2	11.1	9.7	12.5	11.5	10.0	12.8

[a]Includes armed forces overseas.
[b]Percentages may not sum exactly to 100.00% because of rounding error.
Source: Based on tabulations from the United States Bureau of the Census and the One-in-a-Thousand-Public-Use Sample of the 1960 census (U.S. Bureau of Census) (7).

It is clear from the projections in Table 3.3 that older blacks, whether having more or less similar lifestyles to whites, will become a much more visible component of the aged population. While constituting about 8% of the total older population in 1980, by 2000, older blacks are projected to constitute 8.5% of the older population, and by 2040, they will constitute 12.5% of the older population.

Size and Growth: Population Aged 85 and Over

When considering population growth, the most significant percentage increases in Tables 3.2 and 3.3 are among the old-old, taken by Neugarten (8) to be those aged 75 and over. Rosenwaike's more recent designation of the oldest-old as those 85 and over (9) is consistent with the use of the term applied here. As a population at relatively high risk for dependence, it is this population that one most clearly has in mind today when speaking of the need for planning for increased potential dependence.

Between 1960 and 1980, the number of white Americans aged 85 and over increased from 778,000 to slightly over 2 million, a 168% increase. The 162,000 blacks aged 85 and over in 1980 represented a 119% increase from the 1960 total of 74,000 (see Table 3.4). In both groups, the growth was most prevalent among females. The fact that between 1980 and 1985 there was almost a 27% increase in the oldest-old among blacks, relative to a 19% increase among whites, suggests that the faster 1960-to-1980 growth rate in the older white population may be on the verge of reversing to a faster black growth rate. Certainly, the 20-year projections displayed in Table 3.3 show rather consistent higher black-to-white growth rates among those aged 85 and over. The need for special, minority-sensitive planning— for policy, research, or services—would surely seem warranted given the dramatically distinctive projected growth rates of both the white and black, particularly female, oldest-old. Increasing numbers of minority persons, who are often impoverished, entering the ranks of the oldest-old mean corresponding increases in the number of persons who will be potentially dependent on their families and the society.

The Distribution of the Black Older Population

In 1980, 56% of all black older Americans were concentrated in 10 states (see Table 3.5). New York, Texas, Georgia, North Carolina, and California accounted for almost one-third of the total population of older blacks in 1980.

Most older blacks in 1980 lived in urban locations (about 81%), and of that group who lived in urbanized areas, 69% were in central cities. In contrast, while older whites were also located primarily in urban locations, of those in urbanized areas, only 39% lived in central cities. Older whites more frequently live in the urban fringe (about 40% of all whites in

TABLE 3.5 U.S. Population Aged 65 and Over: Number and Percentage of Total in 1980, by Race, for Rural Urban Location, Along with the 10 Most Populated States with Blacks Aged 65 and Over

Geographical location	White		Black	
	No.	%	No.	%
Rural–urban distribution				
U.S. (Aged 65+)	22,942		2,067	
Urban				
Total urbanized areas:	16,927	73.8[a]	1,666	80.6[a]
Central city	6,602	39.0[b]	1,151	69.1[b]
Urban fringe	6,801	40.2[b]	256	15.4[b]
Rural	6,015	26.2[a]	401	19.4[a]
Total farm	691	11.5[b]	17	4.2[b]

	State distribution			
State	Rank	No. (in thousands)	Cumulative percent[c]	
New York	1	165	8.1	
Texas	2	137	14.8	
Georgia	3	123	20.9	
North Carolina	4	112	26.4	
California	5	110	31.8	
Florida	6	107	37.1	
Louisiana	7	102	42.1	
Michigan	8	98	46.9	
Mississippi	9	94	51.5	
Pennsylvania	10	92	56.0	

[a]Percent of U.S. total population aged 65 and over.
[b]Percent of total urban or total rural population aged 65 and over.
[c]Cumulation of the percentage of each state's population that is aged 65 and over and black.
Source: United States Bureau of the Census and tabulations from the One-in-a-Thousand-Public-Use Sample (Sample A) of the 1980 census (U.S. Bureau of the Census) (18).

urbanized areas) than their black counterparts, of whom about 15% are similarly situated. Clearly, older blacks are disproportionately concentrated in central cities and thus at greater risk for various urban problems, including criminal victimization, congestion, housing shortages, living costs, and general problems with health and well-being.

THE COMPOSITION AND CHARACTERISTICS OF THE OLDER BLACK POPULATION

Demography is the study of the size, composition, and distribution of populations. Until now, substantial effort has been given to describing the size, changes in size, and distribution of the older population and the position of blacks in that population. In this section, attention is given to the composition of the older population. Selected characteristics of the older population will be studied, with an emphasis on highlighting the position of blacks within this population.

Composition by Gender

The 1985, like the 1960, sex ratios (the number of males per 100 females) show a consistent female advantage (more females than males) throughout the age-by-race analyses in Table 3.6. In 1985, for example, there were about 67 black males for every 100 black females aged 65 and over. There were only 46 black males per 100 black females aged 85 and over.

TABLE 3.6 Sex Ratios and Projected Sex Ratios for the United States, by Race, by Age, by Year

Sex ratio,[a] by age, by year	White	Black
1960		
Under 60	98.8	93.3
60 +	84.2	83.1
65 +	81.9	83.4
75 +	73.4	79.9
85 +	57.1	64.4
1985		
Under 60	101.4	93.5
60 +	72.8	70.9
65 +	67.7	67.0
75 +	53.8	57.4
85 +	39.1	46.4
2000[b]		
65 +	66.1	55.2
85 +	37.7	36.4
2020[b]		
65 +	71.9	58.2
85 +	38.6	31.4
2040[b]		
65 +	70.5	63.8
85 +	43.2	35.3

[a]Males per 100 females.
[b]Projected. Assumes a completed cohort fertility of 1.9 births per woman, yearly net migration at 450,000, and a life expectancy at birth in 2080 of 81.
Source: Based on data from the United States Bureau of the Census and tabulations of data from the public-use file (One-in-a-Thousand Sample) of the 1960 Census (7, 17).

This male disadvantage has become much more accentuated since 1960. In 1960, the ratio was 83 among those aged 65 and over and 64 among those 85 and over. In 2000 the sex ratio among blacks aged 85 and over is projected to be 36 (see Table 3.6; see Table 3.2 for the data on which these ratios are based).

While the male disadvantage is evident in both the older black and white populations for 1985, there are varying racial differences by time and age cohort. In 1985, for example, the male disadvantage among blacks, inclusive of the young-old (aged 60 or aged 65 to 84), is only slightly more extreme than among whites of similar age. Among the oldest-old, the male disadvantage is clearly more extreme within the white population. Projections to the year 2000, however, show a less distinct racial gap among the oldest-old but a substantially increased gap when the total population aged 65 and over is studied. After 2020 the male disadvantage is consistently more extreme for blacks than whites, regardless of time or the age group studied. The important practical point to be made is that following some initial fluctuations, the pattern of sex ratios for the future suggests an eventual, consistent black disadvantage with both the young-old and the old-old black populations more densely comprised of females. The relatively frequent lament by older black women about the shortage of available black men will likely become a more prevalent one—with attendant psychological and socioeconomic problems represented by widowhood and singlehood. It is in this context that research on widowhood takes on special significance for the older black population.

Health and Survival Characteristics

In the preceding section it was established that the population of the United States is becoming demographically older. Moreover, it was concluded that the rate of increase in the aging of the population is and is projected to be greater for black Americans than for their white counterparts. The increase in the number and proportion of the more often impoverished older black population has prompted concern about the nature and circumstances of this population by, for example, Jackson (10), Manuel (5), and McNeely and Colen (11). One of the most important of these concerns is the health of the population. Tables 3.7 through 3.10 show several dimensions for documenting some of the questions and points that need to be raised about the health of older blacks: (1) What are the health needs? (2) What can persons do, or be provided incentive to do, to enhance their own health? (3) What components of the health care system can be additionally studied for the purpose of expanding knowledge about factors influencing the accessibility of health care to aging and aged blacks?

In addressing the question of the health needs of the older black population, a definition is required of normative health in the United States.

TABLE 3.7 Life Expectancy, by Age, by Year, by Race, by Gender for the United States

Age by year	Black male	White male	Black female	White female	All other male[a]	All other female[a]
At birth						
1900[b]	32.5	48.2	35.0	51.0		
1960[c]	61.5	67.6	66.5	74.2		
1982	64.9	71.5	73.5	78.8	66.8	75.0
At age 65						
1900[b]	10.4	11.5	11.4	12.2		
1960[c]	12.8	13.0	15.1	15.9		
1982	13.3	14.5	17.2	18.9	14.1	18.2
At age 85						
1900[b]	4.0	3.8	5.1	4.1		
1960[c]	5.1	4.3	5.4	4.7		
1982	4.8	5.3	6.5	6.7	5.8	7.5

[a]Includes data for blacks.
[b]Data are for death registration states for the period 1900–1902.
[c]Data are for "all other races" (other than white). Blacks, however, accounted for over 90% of all racial groups other than whites.
Source: National Center on Health Statistics (19).

TABLE 3.8 Ratio of Black-to-White Death Rates (Deaths per 100,000 Resident Population in the United States) for All Causes, by Age, by Gender, by Year

	1960[a]		1983	
	Males	Females	Males	Females
All ages[b]	1.36	1.65	1.46	1.50
Under 1	1.97	2.07	2.13	2.17
15–24	1.48	1.96	1.20	1.36
25–34	2.47	3.21	2.17	2.17
35–44	2.29	2.97	2.52	2.24
45–54	1.74	2.57	2.02	1.95
55–64	1.49	2.33	1.65	1.76
65–74	1.20	1.46	1.30	1.45
75–84	.84	.87	1.06	1.17
85 +	.68	.67	.77	.79

[a]Based on data that includes deaths of nonresidents of the United States.
[b]Age adjusted.
Source: Based on tabulations from the National Center for Health Statistics (20).

TABLE 3.9 Ratio of Black-to-White Death Rates (Deaths per 100,000 Resident Population in the United States) for the Five Leading Causes of Death Among Black Males, by Age, by Gender: 1983

Gender by age	Cause of death				
	Heart disease	Malignant neoplasm	Accidents[a]	Cerebrovascular diseases	Homicides/legal intervention
Males					
All ages[b]	1.20	1.46	.95	1.82	6.40
Under 1	2.26	1.11	.63	1.87	4.24
15–24	2.44	.83	.50	1.75	5.81
25–34	2.86	1.17	.97	3.10	6.85
35–44	2.10	1.86	1.38	4.42	6.56
45–54	1.64	1.89	1.54	3.88	6.35
55–64	1.38	1.64	1.57	2.90	7.30
65–74	1.13	1.37	1.32	1.97	6.11
75–84	.94	1.22	1.05	1.18	7.04
85+	.69	.92	.52	.79	4.82
Female					
All Ages[b]	1.51	1.20	.73	1.82	4.00
Under 1	2.36	.94	1.06	2.92	4.13
15–24	2.75	1.09	.46	2.29	4.24
25–34	3.58	1.41	.69	3.19	4.85
35–44	3.66	1.44	.82	3.59	4.23
45–54	2.71	1.36	1.02	3.30	3.27
55–64	2.18	1.23	.87	2.96	2.86
65–74	1.56	1.11	.76	2.13	3.50
75–84	1.14	1.06	.84	1.31	3.65
85+	.74	.89	.56	.81	2.24

[a]Only ratios for motor vehicle accidents are shown.
[b]Age adjusted.
Source: Based on tabulations from the National Center for Health Statistics (20).

TABLE 3.10 Persons Aged 65 and Over in the United States: Selected Indicators on Health Needs, Personal Health Practices (by Year), and Health Care System Accessibility, by Race: 1980[a]

	Race	
Health indicators	White	Black

Health need or status

A. Health conditions		
1. At least one health condition that limits activity	43.8%	56.6%
2. Persons with a second activity limiting health condition	9.4	12.8
3. Persons with a third activity limiting health condition	2.3	2.1
B. Poor self-perceived health	11.6	23.5
C. Two or more illnesses unattended by medical care system	.7	2.2
D. More than 20 bed-disability days in last year	12.8	20.0
E. Most severe functional limitations score	4.7	8.5

Health care system accessibility

A. Insurance Coverage		
1. Without Medicare	7.6	13.1
2. Without private insurance	26.7	57.7
3. Without Medicare and private insurance	3.0	8.4

Personal health practices

	White		Black	
	1977	1983	1977	1983
A. Average more/less than 7–8 hrs. sleep per day	44.4	32.4	47.0	32.8
B. Never/only sometimes eat breakfast	53.4	40.2	54.0	44.9
C. Perceived physical activity: Less than age-similar persons	16.4	11.5	18.3	13.2
D. Drink 5+ alcoholic drinks per setting (or day)	26.4	30.3	29.6	38.4
E. Smokes	42.0	35.2	37.1	32.0
F. Overweight by 20% or more[b]	38.0	24.1	37.3	25.8

[a]Data for health practices are for 1977 and 1983 for person aged 20 or more.
[b]Based on 1960 Metropolitan Life Insurance Company standards.
Source: Based on data from the Public-Use Data File of the National Medical Care Utilization and Expenditure Survey, 1980 (National Center for Health Statistics), and National Center for Health Statistics (21, 22).

Because no group in a democracy should deviate consistently in a substantial way from the health patterns generally present in the community, one useful indicator for establishing the health characteristics of older blacks, as a minority, is through a comparison of their health characteristics with the majority—that is, aged white—health patterns.

Life Expectancy

The average white newborn female in 1982 had a life expectancy of about 79 years.[6] Her black counterpart could expect to live about 74 years (see Table 3.7). Males had life expectancies of roughly 72 years (white males) and 65 years (black males). These life expectancies represent a roughly five (females) to seven (males) year white advantage. While the white advantage has been reduced by roughly two years among females since 1960, among males during the same time, the white advantage increased by half of one year.

The reader will note that while the preceding racial contrasts for 1982 are between whites and blacks, the 1960 contrasts are between whites and nonwhites. It has been typically assumed that life expectancy for nonwhites mirrors that of the black population, since prior to the 1970s well over 90% of nonwhites were black. Yet because blacks are currently less likely to account for nearly all of the nonwhite population, it is important to restrict the analysis of blacks and whites. The importance of this approach is highlighted when studying differential white/black versus white/nonwhite life expectancies between 1960 and 1982. For example, if it is assumed that the nonwhite population mirrors the black condition in 1960 only, and not in 1982, then indeed there is an increase of .5 year in the white male advantage from 1960 to 1982, as reported above. On the other hand, there is a reduction between 1960 and 1982 of somewhat over 1 year in the white male advantage when assuming the equivalence of nonwhite and black populations in 1960 and also in 1982. There are important differential sociological processes operating among different groups within the nonwhite population. One question for further research is whether, and to what extent, such intraminority differences exist and are changing within the nonwhite population. These potential differences will have major implications for conclusions about other developing concepts in the study of the minority aged. One such concept is that of the mortality crossover effect.

Evidence for a Crossover Effect

When comparing the race by gender life expectancies at birth to those at age 85 (Table 3.7), the racial crossover effect (12) is observed only in the 1982

---

[6]Life expectancy is a measure of the average number of years of life remaining at a given age as determined from death rates observed at a specific time.

data.[7] That is, when the data on race is simply operationalized as white versus nonwhite, the crossover effect, often taken as the black/white crossover, is clearly evident. In 1982, for example, white females at birth could expect to outlive their nonwhite (i.e., all races other than white; see Table 3.7) counterparts by 3.8 years. At age 85, white females could expect to live four-fifths of a year less than their nonwhite counterparts. On the other hand, when the nonwhite category is disaggregated such that blacks may be precisely studied, one sees in Table 3.7 that the crossover effect is not as evident by age 85. Thus white females at birth could expect to outlive their black counterparts by 5.3 years, and, although the difference is significantly lessened, they remained likely to outlive black females at age 85 by one-fifth of a year. The prevalent assumption that nonwhite patterns in mortality closely mirror the experiences of blacks must be questioned. The observation of variations in the applicability of the concept of the racial crossover of life expectancies by population, time, and the age at which it occurs for various population groups makes it a central target for new research initiatives.

Differential Mortality

Declines in mortality in earlier years contribute to the number of persons who survive or expect to survive to old age. The data in Table 3.8 show the black, relative to white, mortality trends since 1960. The black-to-white mortality ratio of 2.17 during the first year of life among females, for example, indicates that for every white female infant death per 100,000, there were 2.17 black female infant deaths; at ages 85 and over, there were .79 black female deaths per 100,000 for each white female death. Generally parallel to the patterning of life expectancies by race, one sees a corresponding patterning in black-to-white death rates in 1960 to 1983.

The racial crossover in death rates occurred near age 75 in 1960 but not until about age 85 in 1983. A related area for the formulation of hypotheses on the mortality crossover effect is that of the influence of characteristics of specific age cohorts.

Table 3.9 shows more detail on the 1983 racial mortality differentials. Differentials are shown for the five leading causes of death among black males. Male mortality ratios by race, such as those shown for homicide— the fifth leading cause of death among black males in 1983—or young victims of heart disease, or middle-aged victims of the cerebrovascular diseases are only a small part of why black life expectancy is less than that of whites. Research into the sociological and psychocultural factors that underlie these mortality patterns is the first step in untangling this puzzle.

---

[7]The black/white crossover effect refers to the phenomenon whereby white life expectancy is greater than black life expectancy from ages zero to about age 75, but after age 75, white life expectancy is less than that of blacks.

Health Needs, Practices, and Health Care Accessibility

Table 3.10 provides a brief descriptive approach to identifying the initial personal and sociological variables that might influence the survival of blacks. One observes that blacks are relatively disadvantaged on each of the indicators of health need. Older blacks, more often than their white counterparts, report (1) health conditions that limit their activity; (2) bed-disability days; and (3) illnesses that are unattended by medical personnel. The result is that older blacks are much more likely to be functionally limited and more likely to see themselves in poor health (see Table 3.10).

Health problems and risks do not begin in old age, however. Often it is what one does throughout life that eventually emerges as determining factors of health and survival. Table 3.10 shows data on the 1977 and 1983 personal health practices of the general population. To the extent that health practices influence health and mortality (13), then differential racial health practices may contribute to racial differentials in health status (14). The data in Table 3.10 (panel 3) are suggestive of the complexity of the hypotheses that need to be formulated. Examining the data for 1983, it is seen that black Americans, more often than white Americans, drink heavily, skip breakfast, and are possibly less active. Blacks are slightly more likely than whites to have weights that exceed 20% of their ideal weight, and they are as likely as whites to get more or less than the ideal 7 to 8 hours of sleep per night. Black Americans are less likely than their white counterparts to smoke.

It is not merely a matter of planning for and researching ways of promoting better health practices in reducing the relative health and survival risks of blacks. Findings that show older blacks are less frequently covered by Medicare or private insurance (see Table 3.10) indicate the importance of ensuring that the health care system in this country is more accessible to blacks throughout their lives. One general question derived from the current literature concerns the interactive and indirect effects, in addition to the direct effects, of minority status and accessibility on health care services utilization. Are there subtle relations of minority status with other variables influencing health care use?

ECONOMIC CIRCUMSTANCES IN THE BLACK OLDER POPULATION

Relative Income Status

Style of life, chances in life, and life expectancy are limited by one's income and economic resources. As a result, one dimension for understanding the preceding differences in the demography of the black and white aged is that of the differential income resources available to purchase, for example, health care.

By any indicator of income and economic well-being, the black aged are a particularly disadvantaged group. In 1984, the median income of black males aged 65 and over was $6,163, about 57% of the median income ($10,890) of white males in the same age group. The median income of black older females ($4,345) was 69% of the median income of their white counterparts ($6,309) (15).

The 1984 median income of families headed by a black older person was $11,983, about two-thirds (64%) of the median family income of white families headed by an older person ($18,775) (see Table 3.11).

The 1984 data illustrating the relative income disadvantage of older blacks is not unique. Whether prior or subsequent to the 1964 Civil Rights Act and other Great Society legislation, the ratio of income of older blacks to older whites has had a very narrow bound. The data in Table 3.11 show that the median income of older black families has consistently ranged between 54% and 64% of the comparable incomes of older whites. In 1984, almost 20 years after the 1965 initiation of several of the major federal domestic assistance programs, the ratio of median family income among older blacks and whites remains nearly at the level it was in 1970: 64% (1984) versus 62% (1970).

The Adequacy of Income

By virtue of their minority status, blacks in the United States have not had the opportunities to engage in those life-course employment and investment

TABLE 3.11 Median Income of Families Headed by a Person Aged 65 Years and over, by Race, by Year[a]

Year	Median income ($)		Ratio of black to white income
	White	Black	
1959	3311	1791	.54
1970	5263	3282	.62
1980	13382	8383	.63
1982	16809	9618	.57
1983	17442	10438	.60
1984	18775	11983	.64

[a]Incomes are reported in current, rather than 1984 constant dollar, amounts. The emphasis is not on income trends per se but rather the systematic relative income position of older black and white families.

Source: Based on tabulations of data from the United States Bureau of the Census (23) and various publications from the series *Current Population Reports* (United States Bureau of the Census).

activities that generate a more balanced income distribution relative to that of their white counterparts in old age. It could be argued, however, that the simple comparison of income distributions and statistics between older blacks and whites overstates the level of disadvantage in the older black population. To control for this possibility it is important to consider several additional factors.

Differences between the incomes of older blacks and whites might, for example, be erased if differences in the level of education of the two groups were taken into account. Of course, access to education itself, as many investigators have shown, is differentially affected by minority status. Nevertheless, a useful additional statement of the extent of the dis-advantaged resources of older blacks can be made by observing relative income in the light of educational attainment. Another desirable feature of a more precise study would include a control for differences in family size and type and would conceptualize income sufficiency.

The typically used measure for this purpose is the poverty ratio. Table 3.12 presents a display of these ratios for older blacks and whites over time. The racial contrasts are additionally summarized by a ratio of the percent-age of the black older population having incomes below the poverty cutoff to the comparable percentage of older whites. Generally, the data show that the black poverty rate has been consistently higher than the white rate. Moreover, relative to the 1959 ratio, which is reflective of the era before the Great Society domestic assistance programs, the most recent black/white ratios are, in fact, larger. That is, the gap between the proportion of the black aged having incomes below the poverty threshold and the proportion of the white aged with incomes below the poverty threshold has widened. In general, in 1959 the poverty rate for older blacks was approximately double the rate for older whites. Relative poverty for older blacks then increased, even before the Reagan era of federal retrenchment, and has been approx-imately triple the rate for older whites since 1981. Lower rates of poverty, over time, for both older whites and blacks, but a widening black-to-white ratio, reflect the fact that the decline in poverty for older whites has proceeded at a faster rate than that of their black counterparts.

Table 3.12 also extends the application of the poverty measure to include a control for educational attainment for the 1982 data. While controlling for education reduces the magnitude of the racial contrasts, it is obvious that, even with education controlled, the incidence of poverty among older blacks is more than twice that of older whites.

In short, the data on the relative incomes of older blacks and whites suggest one inescapable conclusion: the elderly blacks' income position, while improved over time, is as deprived, or more deprived, today—relative to their white counterparts—as it was in 1960. Moreover, it is not simply a matter of reducing the differences in the educational attainment of blacks and whites that will generate more equitable distribution of incomes. Even

TABLE 3.12 Persons 65 Years of Age and over in the United States with Incomes Below the Poverty Level, by Race, by Year, by Educational Attainment[a]

Year	Poverty rates		Ratio of black to white rate
	White	Black	
1959	33.1	62.5	1.89
1969	23.3	50.2	2.15
1979	13.3	36.2	2.72
1980	13.6	38.1	2.80
1981	13.1	39.0	2.98
1982	12.4	38.2	3.08
1983	12.1	36.2	2.99
1984	10.7	31.7	2.96
After controlling for educational attainment			
1982 Elementary or less	19.7	45.6	2.31
College: 5 or more years	4.9	10.1	2.06

[a]The data for the study of poverty and educational attainment are for 1982 only.
Source: Based on data from various publications from the United States Bureau of the Census's *Current Population Reports* and tabulations of data from the Public-Use File of the March 1983 Current Population Survey (United States Bureau of the Census).

with similar educational backgrounds, the prevalence of poverty in the older black population remains twice as high as in the older white population. In addition to emphasizing education as a means for improving the situation of older blacks, research is needed on what factors mediate the relationship of educational preparedness and income in old age. Educational preparedness is only one part of a network of other influential life course factors having an impact on income in later life. Much more effort is needed in identifying these other factors. In addition to the need for research on how to effectively promote good personal health practices, discussed in the last section, there is a need for basic research on how to effectively promote sound financial planning for the retirement years. This research is especially needed on persons who have few economic resources and, perhaps, believe that they have no control over their lives.

SUMMARY

The discussion in this chapter demonstrates the relative plight, demographically, of older blacks in the United States. Using the situation of older whites as a normative standard of the lifestyle and chances in life potentially available in the United States for older persons, older blacks were shown systematically to have disadvantaged and inadequate incomes. The poorer health of older blacks, their inaccessibility to the health care system, and the fact that black Americans of all ages seemingly do not consistently observe good health habits to the extent of their white counterparts translates into generally higher relative death rates or lower life expectancies.

A revealing conclusion from the examination, over time, of several of these demographic indicators is that circumstances for older blacks are not necessarily improving. The life situations of older blacks relative to older whites is not substantially different today, and in some cases is worse, than 25 years ago, before the advent of special federal assistance programs.

It is not necessary to belabor the debate about whether the social legislation of the 1960s and 1970s has worked or not. Clearly the data distributed throughout the tables of this chapter confirm that both the white and the black populations have benefited from such legislation as the Older Americans Act, Medicare, and extensions of the Social Security Act. The point that needs emphasis is that not enough has been done to ensure that the special circumstances of minorities in this country are considered in the design of legislation. Color-blind legislation is certainly the goal for this country, but today's older black population represents the legacy of a past, color-sensitive society. As a special older population their unique needs call for legislation that responds to these needs. Unfortunately, the knowledge available about the unique circumstances of older blacks and minorities remains too descriptive and general to inform minority-sensitive direction in aging policy. The discussion in this chapter (and the remaining chapters of this book) is intended, in part, to contribute to the derivation of explanatory research directions. The eventual answers will help fill in the void of what is now known about an obviously heterogeneous, but too frequently assumed homogeneous, population.

REFERENCES

1. *New York Times*. Old doesn't mean poor anymore. November 9, 1982: A31.
2. *New York Times*. More gold in the golden years. March 12, 1985: A30.
3. Seaberry J. CEA says aged have achieved economic parity. *Washington Post;* February 6, 1985: A1.
4. Stern M. Tarnished golden years: many city elderly live in poverty and isolation. *Washington Post;* May 18, 1983: D.C.1.
5. Manuel RC, ed. *Minority Aging: Sociological and Social Psychological Issues.* Westport, CT: Greenwood Press; 1982.

6. Passel JS, Robinson JG. Revised estimates of the coverage of the population in the 1980 census based on demographic analysis: a report on work in progress. Paper presented at the annual meeting of the American Statistical Association; August 1984.

7. United States Bureau of the Census. *Estimates of the population of the United States by Age, Sex, and Race: 1980 to 1985 (Current Population Reports, Series P–25, No. 985).* Washington, DC: U.S. Government Printing Office; 1986.

8. Neugarten BL. Age groups in American society and the rise of the young old. *Annuals of the American Academy of Political and Social Science* 1974; 415: 187–198.

9. Rosenwaike I. A demographic portrait of the oldest old. *Milbank Memorial Fund Quarterly/Health and Society* 1985; 63: 187–205.

10. Jackson JJ. *Minorities and Aging.* Belmont, CA: Wadsworth; 1980.

11. McNeely RL, Colen JN. *Aging in Minority Groups.* Beverly Hills, CA: Sage Publications; 1983.

12. Manton KG. Differential life expectancy: possible explanations during later ages. In: Manuel R, ed. *Minority Aging: Sociological and Social Psychological Issues.* Westport, CT: Greenwood Press; 1982: 63–68.

13. Berkman LF, Breslow L. *Health and Ways of Living: The Alameda County Study.* New York: Oxford University Press; 1983.

14. Manuel RC. Minority and nonminority differential health practices as determinants of minority and nonminority differentials in concurrent health status. Paper presented at the annual meeting of the Gerontological Society of America; November 1983.

15. United States Bureau of the Census. *Money Income: Households, Families and Persons in the United States, 1984* (Current Population Reports Series P–60, No. 151). Washington, DC: U.S. Government Printing Office; 1986.

16. United States Bureau of the Census. *Historical Statistics of the United States, Colonial Times to 1970: Bicentennial Edition, Part 1.* Washington, DC: U.S. Government Printing Office; 1975.

17. United States Bureau of the Census. *Projections of the United States Population by Age, Sex and Race, 1983 to 2080* (Current Population Reports, Series P–25, No. 952). Washington, DC: U.S. Government Printing Office; 1984.

18. United States Bureau of the Census. *Census of the Population, 1980: Characteristics of the Population, United States Summary.* Washington, DC: U.S. Government Printing Office; 1984.

19. National Center for Health Statistics. *Vital Statistics of the United States, 1982, Vol. 11, Sec. 6: Life Tables.* Washington, DC: U.S. Government Printing Office; 1985.

20. National Center for Health Statistics. *Health, United States: 1985.* Washington, DC: U.S. Government Printing Office; 1985.

21. National Center for Health Statistics. *Health Practices Among Adults, United States: 1977 Advance Data from Vital Health Statistics, No. 64.* Washington, DC: U.S. Government Printing Office; 1980.

22. National Center for Health Statistics. *Trends in Smoking, Alcohol Consumption and Other Health Practices among U.S. Adults: 1977 and 1983. Advanced Data from Vital and Health Statistics No. 118.* Washington, DC: U.S. Government Printing Office; 1986.

23. United States Bureau of the Census. *United States Census of the Population: 1960, Subject Reports: Families.* Washington, DC: U.S. Government Printing Office; 1963.

4

Cancer Prevention and Control in the Black Population: Epidemiology and Aging Implications

Claudia R. Baquet

Cancer is the second leading cause of death in the United States. This group of heterogenous illnesses has major public health significance, especially for black populations who incur a disproportionate burden of the disease. Although blacks experience excess morbidity and mortality for many diseases, cancer is becoming an increasingly significant burden in the overall illness spectrum in the black population (1, 2).

Excesses occur in cancer incidence and mortality in blacks compared to whites. Major differences affecting blacks adversely also exist for cancer patient survival (3, 4). Although the black population has a younger age structure than whites, older blacks until approximately the eighth decade of life have a particularly severe cancer experience for a number of cancer sites (5).

The purpose of this chapter is to present an overview of the epidemiology of cancer in black populations, with specific references to aging black populations, and to summarize the cancer prevention and control needs of the black aged.

METHODOLOGY

The descriptive, etiologic, and prevention and control information provided here has various sources. Cancer incidence and survival data are derived from the National Cancer Institute (NCI) SEER Program (Surveillance, Epidemiology, and End Results Program)—a population-based tumor registry reporting system in 11 areas of the United States (6). Cancer mortality data are derived from the National Center for Health Statistics (NCHS death registration) and the Bureau of the Census (population counts) (7). Data pertaining to factors that appear to contribute to the cancer experience of blacks are derived from selected scientific citations and are referenced. Selected citations on cancer control science and its application are also referenced.

Descriptive cancer statistics that will be referred to in this paper are generally defined as follows:

- *Incidence rate:* The cancer incidence rate is the number of cancer cases newly diagnosed during a calendar year divided by the midyear population and multiplied by 100,000.
- *Mortality rate:* The cancer mortality rate is the number of deaths from cancer that occur during a calendar year in a specified population. It is expressed as a number per 100,000 population and includes those deaths where cancer is the reported underlying cause of death. This can be calculated for each specific type of cancer as well as for all cancer sites combined.
- *Age-adjusted rate:* An age-adjusted cancer rate is a weighted average of the age-specific cancer mortality (or incidence) rates where the weights are the numbers of persons in age groups of a standard population. This has the effect of eliminating age distribution differences in the two populations as a factor when comparing their mortality (or incidence) for all ages combined. For this report, the 1970 U.S. population is used as the standard.
- *Age-specific rate:* Age-specific cancer rates are calculated because cancer incidence and mortality vary with age. By calculating separate incidence and mortality for each age group, diversities often hidden in overall rates are more evident.
  - *Incidence:* The age-specific cancer incidence rate is the number of new cases of cancer occurring to persons in a given age group during a calendar year divided by the midyear population of all persons in that same group. This is then multiplied by 100,000.
  - *Mortality:* The age-specific cancer mortality rate is the number of cancer deaths occurring to persons in a given age group during a

calendar year divided by the midyear population of all persons in that
same age group. This is then multiplied by 100,000.

- *Relative survival rate:* The ratio of the observed survival rate for the patient
  group to the expected survival rate for persons in the general population
  similar to the patient group with respect to age, sex, race, and calendar
  year of observation. Since almost half the cancers occur in persons 65 year
  of age or older, many of these individuals die of other causes, with no
  evidence of recurrence of the cancer. Thus, because it is obtained by
  adjusting observed survival for the normal life expectancy of the general
  population of the same age, the relative survival rate is an estimate of the
  chance of surviving the effects of cancer. The 5-year relative survival rate
  then can be considered the proportion potentially curable.

EPIDEMIOLOGY AND SURVIVAL EXPERIENCE

Incidence and Mortality (1978–1981)

Blacks have the highest age-adjusted incidence rate for all cancers combined
of any of eight racial/ethnic groups for which SEER data are available (see
Table 4.1). Compared to whites, blacks have higher age-adjusted incidence
rates for several cancers, including breast (females under 40), cervix uteri,
esophagus, lung (males), multiple myeloma, prostate, and stomach. Overall
age-adjusted mortality is also highest in blacks (see Table 4.2). Notable
cancer sites with higher mortality include breast (females under 40), cervix
uteri, corpus uteri, esophagus, larynx, multiple myeloma, prostate, and
stomach.

The following overview refers to age-specific rates in blacks compared to
whites for the years 1978 to 1981:

- *Age-specific incidence:* For all cancers combined, black males have a
  higher rate than whites until age 75. Black females have higher age-
  specific incidence of breast cancer up to around age 40; then the reverse
  occurs. Black females have higher age-specific rates for invasive cervical
  cancer at all age groups, and the differences between blacks and whites
  are much greater in over-60 age categories. Esophageal cancer rates
  for black males and females are greater at all ages. For laryngeal
  cancer, black males have greater rates at all age groups. Lung cancer
  rates in black males are higher up to the 70–74 group. For multiple
  myeloma and pancreatic cancer, blacks of both gender have higher rates
  at all age groups. Prostate cancer rates for black males are higher at all
  age groups. Stomach cancer rates are higher in blacks at all age groups
  for both sexes.

TABLE 4.1 Average Annual Age-Adjusted Cancer Incidence Rates per 100,000 by Primary Site and Racial/Ethnic Group, SEER Program, 1978–1981

Primary site	Whites	Blacks	Hispanics*	Japanese	Chinese	Filipinos	Native Hawaiians	Native Americans
All sites	335.0	372.5	246.2	247.8	252.9	222.4	357.9	164.2
Bladder	15.4	8.6	8.2	7.7	7.7	5.1	8.2	1.1
Breast, female	86.5	71.9	54.1	53.1	54.0	43.4	111.1	28.5
Ages <40	8.2	10.7	7.9	8.6	7.4	7.1	7.1	4.0
Ages 40+	221.1	179.3	134.9	146.5	141.0	117.0	300.0	71.4
Cervix uteri	8.8	20.2	17.7	7.6	11.2	8.8	14.1	22.6
Colon & rectum	49.6	48.9	25.2	50.4	40.8	30.1	32.7	9.9
Colon	34.6	37.9	15.8	34.0	27.7	17.7	18.4	8.0
Rectum	15.0	11.7	9.4	16.4	13.1	12.4	14.3	1.9
Corpus uteri	25.1	13.4	11.1	18.6	17.6	11.7	27.1	2.6
Esophagus	3.0	11.5	1.6	2.4	3.4	3.6	6.4	2.4
Larynx	4.6	6.6	2.6	2.6	1.9	1.8	5.2	0.9
Lung, male	81.0	119.0	34.3	45.1	62.6	38.1	100.9	14.6
Lung, female	28.2	30.5	13.0	14.1	31.2	18.4	38.6	3.1
Multiple myeloma	3.4	7.9	2.5	1.2	1.6	4.1	5.5	2.8
Ovary	13.6	9.5	10.4	8.7	9.1	9.4	13.5	3.2
Pancreas	8.9	13.6	10.8	7.4	9.3	6.7	10.0	6.0
Prostate	75.1	120.3	76.5	44.2	26.1	48.9	57.9	45.4
Stomach	8.0	13.8	15.7	27.9	9.0	7.0	32.4	19.3

*Cancer incidence data for Hispanics come from New Mexico only.
Source: Cancer Among Blacks and Other Minorities: Statistical Profiles (NIH Publication No. 86-2785). National Cancer Institute, March 1986.

TABLE 4.2 Average Annual Age-Adjusted Cancer Mortality Rates per 100,000 by Primary Site and Racial/Ethnic Group, Total United States, 1978–1981

Primary site	Whites*	Blacks	Japanese	Chinese	Filipinos	Native Hawaiians	Native Americans
All Sites	163.6	208.5	104.2	131.5	69.7	200.5	87.4
Bladder	3.9	3.8	1.8	1.7	1.5	1.6	1.0
Breast, female	26.6	26.3	9.9	13.0	8.0	33.0	8.2
Ages <40	1.6	2.5	1.1	0.8	0.9	1.2	1.1
Ages 40+	70.2	68.1	25.2	34.6	20.6	88.7	20.6
Cervix uteri	3.2	8.8	2.7	2.9	1.6	4.2	5.8
Colon & rectum	21.6	22.3	17.2	19.3	8.1	15.0	8.6
Colon	18.1	18.8	13.6	15.5	5.8	11.4	6.8
Rectum	3.5	3.5	3.6	3.8	2.3	3.6	1.8
Corpus uteri	3.9	6.6	3.9	4.3	2.0	3.0	1.8
Esophagus	2.6	9.2	1.9	3.3	1.9	6.5	2.1
Larynx	1.3	2.5	0.2	0.7	0.4	1.4	0.9
Lung, male	69.3	91.4	32.7	48.2	20.0	88.0	28.0
Lung, female	20.2	20.1	8.6	21.2	6.8	31.5	8.6
Multiple myeloma	2.4	5.0	1.2	1.2	1.2	2.8	1.9
Ovary	8.1	6.4	4.3	4.2	2.8	7.0	3.3
Pancreas	8.4	11.0	7.0	7.4	3.3	10.9	4.5
Prostate	21.0	43.9	8.8	7.5	8.2	11.6	15.5
Stomach	5.3	10.0	17.5	7.8	3.3	25.3	6.2

*The National Center for Health Statistics, from which these data are derived, does not code ethnicity for Hispanics.
Source: Cancer Among Blacks and Other Minorities: Statistical Profiles (NIH Publication No. 86-2785). National Cancer Institute, March 1986.

- *Age-specific mortality:* Overall blacks have higher rates up to the 70–74 age group. Disaggregated by sex, black males have higher rates for all cancer sites combined up to age 70–74 and black females have higher rates up to around age 65. Bladder cancer in black females is higher up to age 70–75. As with incidence, cervical cancer mortality is greater at all age groups. For corpus uteri cancer, black females have higher rates than white females after age 44, and the differences are much greater after age 60. Esophageal cancer rates for blacks of both sexes are higher than for whites at all age groups, and this is also true for larynx cancer in black males. Lung cancer rates are higher in black men up to age 60–64. Multiple myeloma mortality in both sexes is higher at all ages for blacks. For pancreatic cancer, mortality is higher at all ages up to age 75 in blacks in both sexes, and prostate cancer mortality is higher at all ages, as is stomach cancer mortality.

Survival (1973–1981)

Five-year relative survival rates from the SEER program for cancers diagnosed during 1973–1981 are presented in Table 4.3. Overall, 5-year relative survival was 12 percentage points less in blacks, and site-specific differentials were marked for cancers of the bladder, breast (female), corpus uteri, prostate, and rectum.

Age-specific survival rates (from SEER registries) for black and white cancer patients diagnosed between 1973 and 1979 and followed through 1980 were presented by Ries, Pollack, and Young in 1983 (8). The data on black age-specific survival are based on 15,671 cancers in black males and 13,280 cases in black females. When disaggregated by age and cancer site, the numbers in many cells become very small. Therefore information on selected cancers where the standard error of the 5-year relative survival rate is greater than 10% is generally not presented. A number of age-specific differences by sex and race exist:

- *Black males:* For all cancers generally, the older age groups have poorer survival than younger groups. Survival for persons under age 15 was 49%, whereas it was 28% in the group 75 years of age or older. Although survival is generally better for whites than for blacks, for prostate cancer survival is similar at various age groups up to age 65, after which black survival decreases more than does white survival.
- *Black females:* Survival in black females compared to black males is higher at every age for all sites combined. For black females, survival in the under-15 age group was 54%, while it was only 33% for black females over age 75. For breast cancer in black women under age 35, the relative survival rate was 54%, whereas in the over-75 age group

TABLE 4.3 Five-Year Relative Survival Rates by Primary Site and Racial/Ethnic Group, SEER Program, 1973–1981 (percent)

Primary site	Anglos[3]	Blacks	Hispanics	Japanese	Chinese	Filipinos	Native Hawaiians	Native Americans
All sites	50	38	47	51	44	45	44	34
Bladder	74	50	70	72	74[1]	49[1]	48[2]	37[2]
Breast, female	75	63	72	85	78	72	76	53[1]
Cervix uteri	68	63	69	72	72[1]	72[1]	73	67[1]
Colon & rectum	51	44	46	59	50	41	51[1]	37[1]
Colon	52	46	48	61	53	38	59[1]	44[1]
Rectum	49	37	44	55	44	45	42[1]	24[1]
Corpus uteri	88	57	86	86	87	78[1]	80[1]	66[2]
Esophagus	5	3	—	—	11[1]	—	—	—
Larynx	67	59	60[1]	75[1]	67[2]	57[2]	79[2]	—
Lung & bronchus	12	11	11	14	15	12	16	5
Male	11	10	9	13	15	12	13	2
Female	16	14	15	17	15	11	24	—
Mutiple Myeloma	24	27	21	30[1]	24[1]	29[1]	26[1]	—
Ovary	37	39	41	41	42[1]	52[1]	36[1]	43[1]
Pancreas	3	3	2	3	3	2	—	—
Prostate	69	59	71	76	76[1]	73	85[1]	47[1]
Stomach	14	15	16	28	16	16	14	9

[1] Standard error between 5 and 10%.
[2] Standard error 10%.
[3] Caucasians not of Hispanic origin or surname.

Source: *Cancer Among Blacks and Other Minorities: Statistical Profiles* (NIH Publication No. 86-2785). National Cancer Institute, March 1986.

survival was 68%. Survival for cervix uteri cancer decreased with age; survival in the under-35 age group was 83%, while in the over-75 group it was 56%. Similarly, survival for corpus uteri cancer decreased with age from 72% in the under-45 age group to 47% in the over-75 age group. Survival in general was proportionately lower for black females than for white females, and the difference increases with advancing age for black females.

It should be noted that information on extent of disease (stage) and histologic pattern was not analyzed. Differences in stage and histology within age groups may partially account for some survival differences.

CONTRIBUTING FACTORS

Many factors that contribute to the excessive cancer rates in blacks are suggested in analytic epidemiological (case-control and prospective) studies, survey research, and health-services research. Unfortunately, many of these studies have small samples of blacks. In many cases, research results from studies of white populations have been assumed to be applicable to blacks, even though these research results all too often have not been validated for black populations. Recognizing these limitations, possible factors have been placed into the following categories in accordance with the prevailing priorities identified in recent key studies on cancer prevention and control potential (9, 10): major risk factors/exposures; health and medical resources; knowledge, attitudes, practices; and "other."

Major Risk Factors/Exposures

Risk factors typically refer to those environmental, lifestyle, or host factors that can be identified as being linked to incidence rates of any particular cancer. The greater the frequency, dose, and duration of exposure to these factors, the higher the incidence rates are likely to be. The following major factors have priority in cancer prevention:

- *Tobacco:* Smoking is believed to account for roughly 30% of cancer deaths (10). Blacks have higher prevalence rates for smoking than whites [41% of black males, 32% of white males; 32% of black females, 28% of white females (11)]; blacks are reported to be lighter smokers, but to smoke cigarettes higher in tar than whites (12, 13). Many of the cancers with higher incidence in blacks (Table 4.1) are tobacco related.

- *Occupation:* For many historical reasons, blacks are believed to have higher occupational exposures compared to whites, due to placement in less skilled and more hazardous jobs (14–18).
- *Tobacco and alcohol:* Combined exposure to alcohol and smoking is a risk for cancers of the head, neck, and esophagus and is thought to be especially significant in black men (19–23).
- *Diet/nutritional factors:* Diet is increasingly being recognized as being significantly associated with cancer incidence rates (24–27). However, characterization of the diet of blacks is highly inadequate at this time (28, 29). Anecdotal data suggest that blacks have high levels of fat consumption—a potentially significant risk factor for cancers of many sites. Additionally, roughly 60% of black females over the age of 45 have been estimated to be obese, that is, at least 20% overweight (30)—another significant risk factor for various cancer sites, including colon and breast. Obesity is almost twice as prevalent for black women as it is for white women.

Health and Medical Resources

The provision and use of medical services impact on cancer survival rates. In terms of the traditional health-services research models (31), the following factors are believed to be especially important:

- *Access to care:* Because of the greater proportion of blacks in lower socioeconomic groups, reliance on public providers of medical care, including emergency rooms and outpatient clinics, is greater than in the general population (32–34). Reduced mobility in the aged segments of the population may further aggravate this problem, and of special concern to blacks may be the increased problems of mobility associated with living in rural areas (35).
- *Availability of care:* Although still largely unsubstantiated in terms of research, it is now widely suggested that the impact of DRG-imposed limitations on hospital length of stay may especially affect disease outcome in low-income and elderly populations because of greater disease morbidity (36).
- *Quality of care:* Little is known about differences in the specific quality of care affecting cancer. In terms of two major indications that are thought to affect quality of care and outcome, blacks have been underrepresented: (1) blacks are underrepresented in clinical trials of cancer therapies, and (2) cancer therapies have not been validated in trials specifically aimed at black cancer patients.
- *Continuity of care:* Relating to the "access-to-care" issues noted above, it is likely that the continuity of care is a more pronounced problem for

blacks than for the general population. For instance, one study has found high rates of failure to follow up a positive or suspicious Pap test result in emergency rooms and outpatient clinics (37). This discontinuity is thought to affect minorities and the aged in particular. Another example, which is of special significance to the aged female, also involves the delivery of Pap smears and pelvic examinations. Pap smears are a routine part of service in family-planning clinics. As a woman ages, the delivery of Pap smears and pelvic examinations becomes irregular or even ceases. Studies of cervical cancer screening patterns revealed that older females were more likely to report long intervals since the last Pap smear. Older females also were more likely to report never having had a Pap smear (38, 39). Another continuity problem relates to the categorical nature of health-services delivery. One study of invasive cervical cancer patients revealed that they tended to be older, minority, and low-income women but did have routine encounters with the health care system for monitoring of other problems, such as hypertension or diabetes mellitus. Unfortunately, Pap smears were not offered at the hypertension or diabetes clinic. These women, therefore, had their hypertension and diabetes controlled while remaining at risk for dying from cervical cancer (40, 41). Cancers of the uterus and ovary are also important in this regard, as is breast cancer. And this problem is not limited to women. A current study in Boston of head and neck cancers, which are closely tied to advancing age and low socioeconomic status, suggests that individuals at risk have frequent encounters with the health care system but do not receive a simple examination of the oral cavity (42).

Compliance, Knowledge, Attitudes, Practices

In general, data on the cancer-related knowledge, attitudes, and practices of blacks (including the aged) are limited. It appears that blacks tend to be less knowledgeable about cancer than whites (43). Blacks tend to underestimate the prevalence of cancer and the significance of its common warning signs (44). Blacks also tend to be less aware of the benefits of specific cancer tests (45, 46). Blacks are reported to be more fatalistic about cancer and less likely to believe that early detection will make a difference in terms of outcome or that treatment can be effective (43, 44).

Other Factors

Variations in the distribution of histology for certain cancer sites suggest that host vulnerability may affect cancer rates. For instance, blacks have a greater distribution of histologically aggressive tumors for cancers of the corpus uteri and bladder—cancers with significant black/white survival differentials (3, 4).

CANCER CONTROL

The national cancer control effort as reconstituted in the 1980s is comprised of two major components: cancer control science and the cancer control objectives for the year 2000.

Cancer control is defined as the reduction of cancer incidence, mortality, and morbidity through an orderly sequence of research on interventions designed to ultimately improve cancer rates. Cancer control encompasses both primary prevention (prevention of disease onset) and secondary prevention (prevention of disease sequelae) that will improve survival and mortality rates (47).

The cancer control research process is viewed as a continuum from etiological research to establish associations, to prospective intervention experiments to determine causality through prevention, to broad demonstration and application of research results (47). The scientific method is as important throughout this continuum as it is in basic research.

In 1983 a "reasonable target" for cancer control was announced. This target suggested the reduction of cancer mortality rates by 50% by the year 2000, and subsequently national objectives were published relating to the achievement of the target (9). The focus of the effort was on applying state-of-the-art knowledge with vigor in the following areas:

- *Prevention:* reduced exposure to risks from smoking, diet, and occupation.
- *Screening:* for cervical cancer and breast cancer.
- *Treatment:* improved patterns of delivery and use.

Implementation of strategies directed at these areas would be both broad and aimed at the general population, and targeted at special population segments who either have disproportionately severe cancer rates or are underserved in terms of cancer prevention and control research and services. Blacks in particular are considered such a special population (9).

Related to this cancer control orientation, research is vital to reducing the differentials in cancer rates that affect blacks adversely compared to whites. Intervention methods need testing and validation in black populations. Approaches to improving the delivery of efficacious methods also need to be studied. Research that results in the development, application, and evaluation of specific cancer control interventions is a critically important approach to reducing the burden of cancer in black populations; the NCI has initiated a major program of research to this end (4).

DISCUSSION

Cancer is a group of diseases that are highly age dependent in terms of clinical manifestations. In general, a lengthy latency period averaging approximately 20 years separates exposures and clinical manifestations (48). Therefore, in the continuum from exposure to risk factors to disease outcome, the older the population, the more significant becomes the emphasis on the prevention of disease outcome and mortality. Consequently, secondary prevention is of prime concern to the aged. Early detection, vigorous and effective treatment, and continuity in terms of follow-up are thus critical goals for both research and policy formulation. Because the main concern in secondary prevention is ensuring access to and delivery of state-of-the-art medical care, the disciplines most central to cancer control science in relation to the cancer needs of the aged are those involved in health-services research and the quality of medical care delivery.

The emphasis on secondary prevention does not mean exclusion of primary prevention efforts in the elderly. Indeed, it is probable that the lack of prior research clouds our perspective on the significance of primary prevention in the aging population. For instance, research on cigarette smoking (49) suggests that the later in life exposure commences or ceases, the shorter is the time interval within which the effect on disease incidence rates can be measured. This is consistent with some of the data on the incidence of heart disease attributed to smoking. The area of diet and nutrition also warrants attention. However, in the aging population this area appears to relate particularly to treatment outcome, to the extent that a well-nourished patient is likely to experience better survival than the patient with a poor nutrition profile (50).

The differentials in cancer rates between blacks and whites have been presented in the scientific literature for two decades (3, 51–55). Blacks experience cancer patterns that are quite different from patterns in the majority population. Cancer is more significant in magnitude to blacks for both incidence and mortality. Survival rates for blacks are also disproportionately severe. The differentials in rates between blacks and the majority population have not been reduced significantly over time (56, 57). Recently, however, specific proposals for the design of approaches to reducing these differences have been proposed (58, 59), and a major, national program of cancer prevention and control research in black populations has been initiated (4).

In relation to aging, fundamental definitional issues need resolution. Given the excess in mortality and significantly reduced life expectancy for blacks, these definitional issues are particularly important in the context of this chapter. What is aging, and when does it begin? Should there be specific lower age cutoffs, and if so, should these limits be the same for all segments of the population?

The epidemiology of cancer in blacks and the available scientific literature suggest the following areas of research needs in relation to aging in the black population:

1. *Data development (needs assessment).* A paramount epidemiological need is to develop age-specific data on survival by stage category, and histology where possible. Such data would provide much more reliable and predictive information about cancer control needs for secondary prevention.
2. *Awareness and screening practices.* Data on knowledge, attitudes, and practices (KAP) are limited for blacks in general, and the data on the aging segment of the black population are extremely sketchy. More cross-sectional surveys are needed, and longitudinal studies that relate reported KAP to outcome should be conducted as validation of survey results.
3. *Health-services patterns.* Patterns-of-care studies have begun to appear in the cancer control literature (e.g., 38, 41, 58) and might shed light on many aspects of cancer control relating to aging. Fundamental questions have as yet to be addressed, such as why black women tend to have favorable survival rates compared to black men and what factors might help explain the differences in survival between blacks and whites, in particular for the following sites: corpus uteri, bladder, breast (female), rectum, prostate.
4. *Primary prevention and aging.* Studies are needed to identify more clearly areas where primary prevention might apply in the aging populations and "ceilings," if any, after which the effects of risk factor reduction cease to result in rate changes. Primary prevention, such as smoking cessation, may reduce cancer incidence rates, even when initiated after midlife (49).
5. *Co-morbidity and competing risks.* Co-morbidity also should be analyzed as a risk factor for poor cancer survival. Blacks experience higher prevalence and mortality rates for a number of major diseases (1) in addition to cancer. Additionally, another interesting observation, which should be interpreted with caution due to small numbers, is the suggestion that blacks in some cases experience better survival that whites in the 80-and-older age category. Does co-morbid selection affect the residual population's survivability? A particular area

that might shed light on both of these research problems is the effect of the rapidly declining incidence of and mortality from stroke on cancer rates in the aging segment of the black population.

6. *Intervention research and health-services delivery.* Targeted intervention research for the aged black population is needed, especially relating to improving health services delivery. The following areas are of special concern.

Improving state-of-the-art care: It has been estimated that mortality rates in the United States could be reduced by at least 10% if state-of-the-art care were provided to all cancer patients (9). Research is needed to determine whether the delivery of cancer therapy in the aged population is optimal in terms of dosage, frequency, and duration of therapy. This problem is probably of special urgency to blacks, as reflected in the poor survival rates that blacks experience. For instance, efforts are urgently needed to increase the representation of blacks in clinical therapy trials, as are efforts to involve more black clinicians in clinical trials research.

Improving access to care: Research suggests that basic cancer control services, such as Pap smears, are not being received by aging blacks (38, 40). Research into improving access should focus on services aimed at improving survival for the following target (or sentinel) sites: corpus uteri, cervix, bladder, breast (females), rectum, prostate.

Improving continuity of care: Continuity of care may be as important as access and has been overlooked as an area of research. For instance, access to screening and detection services alone is of limited value if follow-up diagnosis and treatment services are not accessible. One study in Los Angeles has found that abnormal Pap smears taken in emergency rooms or outpatient clinics are routinely not followed up (37). Perhaps the most significant discontinuity of medical care takes place for women in midlife. This discontinuity may have a profound effect on the delivery and use of Pap smears, pelvic examinations, and breast examinations.

CONCLUSIONS

Research on the cancer experience of the elderly black population is limited. Available registries cover only a small portion of the population, and this limits the degree to which disaggregation of data is feasible by cancer site and within site by stage and histology. It would be particularly useful to analyze age-specific survival rates by stage and histology in order to better understand the discrepancies that exist between black men and women and between blacks and the majority population. Studies of mortality data to define co-morbidity patterns would be useful both in relation to increased incidence and reduced survival.

Analytical epidemiology that relates to the aging black population also is limited. In particular, analysis of knowledge, attitudes, and practices needs to be conducted and validated against disease outcome. Research also is needed to determine the value of primary prevention, such as smoking cessation and dietary change, in relation to cancer incidence and mortality at different age levels in the population.

Intervention research should be conducted to test methods and approaches for improving the quality of state-of-the-art care (both diagnostic and therapeutic) and ensuring access and continuity in the delivery of care.

Blacks have special cancer needs, as is evident from the disproportionate incidence, survival, and mortality rates they experience. Systematic research into the distribution and causes of these severe rates can help define better the risk factors that exist for both incidence and survival in relation to age. As risk factors become defined more clearly and validated against outcome, intervention research should be extended without delay toward the most significant risk factors. It is scientifically documented that intervention research could be conducted to address basic secondary prevention needs, including access, continuity, and quality in medical care use and delivery. Such research would be initially directed at the following target cancer sites: bladder, breast, corpus uteri, prostate, rectum, and uterine cervix.

SUMMARY

Cancer is a group of diseases with increasing public health significance. In addition to the fear that cancer strikes in the population, its prevalence is rising significantly. The significance of this disease is much greater in the black population: blacks experience much higher incidence and mortality rates and much lower survival rates than the majority population. Cancer also is significantly related to aging because it is among the most age-dependent diseases in terms of clinical manifestation. The data on risk factors that may explain the disadvantage that blacks face in terms of cancer rates are scarce, and this is especially true for the aged black population. However, in general it can be expected that those risk factors that the majority population faces are aggravated by the overrepresentation of blacks in the lower socioeconomic strata.

In terms of cancer prevention and control strategies, as a general rule, the older the population is the more important secondary prevention becomes. This is especially true for the aging black population in relation to cancer, because of the great discrepancies that exist in survival rates between blacks and whites following diagnosis. Consequently, in addition to analytic epidemiological studies to better clarify why blacks are disproportionately affected by cancer, applied epidemiology studies are needed to develop interventions that will reduce these discrepancies.

REFERENCES

1. Secretary's Task Force on Black and Minority Health. *Report of the Secretary's Task Force on Black and Minority Health, Vol. I: Executive Summary.* Washington, DC: U.S. Government Printing Office; 1986.
2. Secretary's Task Force on Black and Minority Health. *Report of the Secretary's Task Force on Black and Minority Health, Vol. III: Cancer.* Washington, DC: U.S. Government Printing Office; 1986.
3. Baquet C, Ringen K, Pollack E, Young J, Horm J, Ries L., Simpson N. *Cancer Among Blacks and Other Minorities: Statistical Profiles* (NIH Publication No. 86-2785). Bethesda, MD: National Cancer Institute; 1986.
4. Baquet C, Ringen K. Cancer control in blacks: epidemiology and NCI program plans. In: Mortenson LE, Engstrom PF, & Anderson PN, eds., *Advances in Cancer Control: Health Care Financing and Research.* New York: Alan R. Liss; 1986: 215–227.
5. Bureau of the Census. *America's Black Population, 1970 to 1982: A Statistical View.* Washington, DC: U.S. Department of Commerce, Bureau of the Census; 1985.
6. National Cancer Institute. *Cancer Incidence and Mortality in the United States: SEER, 1973–81.* (NIH Publication No. 85-1837). Bethesda, MD: National Cancer Institute; 1985.
7. National Center for Health Statistics. *Vital Statistics of the United States.* (NIH Publication No. 79-114). Washington, DC: Department of Health and Human Services; 1979.
8. Ries LG, Pollack ES, Young, J. Cancer patient survival: Surveillance, Epidemiology, and End Results Program 1973–79. *J Natl Cancer Inst* 1983; 70: 693–707.
9. Greenwald P, Sondik E (eds.) *Cancer control objectives for the nation: 1985–2000.* NCI Monographs 1986; 2.
10. Doll R, Peto, R. The causes of cancer: quantitative estimates of avoidable cancer risk in the United States today. *J Natl Cancer Inst* 1981; 66: 1191–1308
11. National Center for Health Statistics *Health, United States, 1986.* [DHHS Pub. No. (PHS) 87-1232]. Washington, DC: U.S. Government Printing Office; Dec. 1986.
12. Robinson R. Strategies for black communities. In: *Proceedings, The Pennsylvania Consensus Conference on Tobacco and Health Priorities.* Harrisburg: Commonwealth of Pennsylvania, Department of Health; Oct 1985: 80–95.
13. Glynn TJ. Smoking-related cancers and the U.S. black population. Paper presented at the Conference on Cancer in Black Americans, Florida A&M University, College of Pharmacy, Tallahassee; Nov 1984.

14. Mancuso TF, Sterling TD. Lung cancer among black and white migrants in the U.S.: etiological considerations. *J Natl Med Assoc* 1975; 67(2): 102, 106–111.
15. Michaels D. Occupation and cancer in the black population: the health effects of job discrimination. *J Natl Med Assoc* 1983; 75: 1014–1018.
16. Miller W, Cooper R. Rising lung cancer death rates among black men: the importance of occupation and social class. *J Natl Med Assoc* 1982; 74(3):253–258.
17. Lloyd JW. Long-term mortality study of steel workers. V. Respiratory cancer in coke plant workers. *J Occ Med* 1971; 13: 53–68.
18. Schulte P, Ringen K, Hemstreet G, Altekruse EB, Gullen WH, Patton MG, Allsbrook WC Jr., Crosby JH, West SS, Witherington, R. Risk assessment of a cohort exposed to aromatic amines: initial results. *J Occ Med* 1985; 27: 115–121
19. Rothman K. The proportion of cancer attributable to alcohol consumption. *Prev Med* 1980; 9: 174–179.
20. Schottenfeld D. Alcohol as a co-factor in the etiology of cancer. *Cancer* 1980; 43(5): 1962–1966.
21. Pottern LM, Morris LE, Blot WJ, Ziegler RG, Fraumeni JF. Esophageal cancer among black men in Washington, DC. I. Alcohol, tobacco, and other risk factors. *J Natl Cancer Inst* 1981; (67(4): 777–783.
22. Keller, A. Liver cirrhosis, tobacco, alcohol, and cancer among blacks. *J Natl Med Assoc* 1978; 70(8): 575–580.
23. Williams RR, Horn JW. Association of cancer sites with tobacco and alcohol consumption and socioeconomic status of patients: interview study from the Third National Cancer Survey. *J Natl Cancer Inst* 1977; 58(3):525–547.
24. Committee on Diet, Nutrition and Cancer, National Research Council. *Diet, Nutrition and Cancer*. Washington, DC: National Academy Press; 1983.
25. Wynder E. Dietary habits and cancer epidemiology. *Cancer* 1979; 43: 1955–1961.
26. Miller A. Nutrition and cancer. *Prev Med* 1980; 9: 189–196.
27. Gori G. Dietary and nutritional implications in the multifactorial etiology of certain prevalent human cancers. *Cancer* 1979; 43: 2151–2161.
28. Mettlin C. Nutritional habits of blacks and whites. *Prev Med* 1980; 9(5): 601–606.
29. Hargreaves MK, Baquet C. Diet, nutritional status and cancer risk in American blacks. (In preparation).
30. Roland M. Data from the Nutrition and Health Examination Survey II. Hyattsville, MD: National Center for Health Statistics, Personal Communication; Jan 1987.
31. Myers BZ. *A Guide to Medical Care Administration, Vol. I: Concepts and Principles*. Washington, DC: American Public Health Association; 1965.
32. Latourette HB. Economic status and survival of cancer patients. *Cancer* 1977; 39: 467–477.
33. Linden G. The influence of social class in the survival of cancer patients. *Am J Public Health* 1969; 59: 267–274.
34. Lipworth L, Abelin T, Connelly RR. Socioeconomic factors in the prognosis of cancer patients. *J Chronic Dis* 1970; 23: 105–116.

35. Navarro V. The political and economic determinants of health and health care in rural America. *Inquiry* 1976; 13: 111–121.
36. Prospective Payment Assessment Association. *Report and Recommendations to the Secretary, U.S. Department of Health and Human Services, Technical Appendixes A and C.* Washington, DC: U.S. Government Printing Office; April 1986.
37. Marcus A. Evaluating continuity problems in health care. Presentation at workshop on Approaches to Reducing Avoidable Cancer Mortality. Bethesda, MD: National Cancer Institute (Special Populations Studies Branch, Division of Cancer Prevention and Control); Nov 1986.
38. Celentano D, Shapiro S, Weisman C. Cancer preventive screening behavior among elderly women. *Prev Med* 1982; 11:454–463.
39. Warnecke R, Graham S. Characteristics of blacks obtaining Papanicolaou smears. *Cancer* 1976; 37: 2015–2025.
40. Fruchter RG, Boyce J, Hunt M. Missed opportunities for early diagnosis of cancer of the cervix. *Am J Pub Health* 1980; 70: 418–420.
41. Fruchter RG, Boyce J, Hunt M. Invasive cancer of the cervix: failures in prevention. I. Previous Pap smear tests and opportunities for screening. *NY State J Med* 1980; 80(5): 740–745.
42. Prout MA. The applied epidemiology of oral cancer in Boston. Presentation at workshop on Approaches to Reducing Avoidable Cancer Mortality. Bethesda, MD: National Cancer Institute (Special Populations Studies Branch, Division of Cancer Prevention and Control), Nov 1986.
43. Cardwell J, Collier W. Racial differences in cancer awareness—what black Americans need to know about cancer. *Urban Health* Oct 1983: 29–32.
44. Butler L, King G, White J. Communications strategies, cancer information, and black populations: an analysis of longitudinal data. In: Mettlin C, Murphy G, eds., Progress in Cancer Control IV: Research in the Cancer Center. New York: Alan R. Liss; 1983: 171–182.
45. Warnecke R, Havlicek P, Manfredi, C. Awareness and use of screenings by older-aged persons. In: *Perspectives on Prevention and Treatment of Cancer in the Elderly.* New York: Raven Press, 1980: 275–287.
46. Manfredi C, Warnecke R, Graham S, Rosenthal S. Social psychological correlates of health behavior: knowledge of breast self-examination techniques among black women. *Soc Sci Med* 1977; 11:433–440.
47. Greenwald P, Cullen J. The new emphasis in cancer control. *J Natl Cancer Inst* 1985; 74(3): 543–551.
48. Armenien J, Lilienfeld, A. The distribution of incubation periods for neoplastic diseases. *Am J Epid* 1974; 99: 92–101.
49. Doll R, Peto R. Mortality in relation to smoking: 20 years' observation on male British doctors. *Br Med J* 1976; 2: 1525–1536.
50. Heber D, Byerley L, Chi J, Gosvenor M, Bergman RN, Coleman M, Chlebowski RT. Pathophysiology of malnutrition in the adult cancer patient. *Cancer* 1986; 58(8): 1867–1873
51. Cornely PB. Health status of the Negro today and in the future. *Am J Pub Health* 1968; 58(4): 647–654.
52. Henschke UK, Leffall LD Jr., Mason CH, Reinhold AW, Schneider RL, White

JE. Alarming increase of the cancer mortality in the U.S. black population (1950–1967). *Cancer* 1973; 31(4): 763–768.

53. Silverberg E, Poindexter C. Cancer facts and figures for black Americans. New York: American Cancer Society; 1979.

54. White J, Enterline J, Alan Z, Moore R. Cancer among blacks in the U.S.: recognizing the problem. In: Mettlin C, Murphy G, eds., Cancer among Black Populations. New York: Alan R. Liss; 1981: 35–53.

55. Myers MH, Hankey BF. *Cancer Patient Survival Experience. Trends in Survival 1960–3 to 1970–3. Comparison of Survival for Black and White Patients. Long-Term Effects of Cancer* (NIH Publication no. 80-2148). Washington, DC: U.S. Department of Health and Human Services; 1980.

56. Axtell LM, Myers MH. Contrasts in survival of black and white cancer patients 1960–73. *J Natl Cancer Inst* 1978; 60(6): 1209–1215.

57. Young JL Jr., Ries LG, Pollack ES. Cancer patient survival among ethnic groups in the United States. *J Natl Cancer Inst* 1984; 73(2): 341–352.

58. Shapiro S, Venet W, Strax P, Yenet L, Roeser R. Prospects for eliminating racial differences in breast cancer survival rates. *Am J Public Health* 1982; 72: 1142–1145.

59. Warnecke R. Interventions in black populations. In: Mettlin C, Murphy G, eds., Cancer Among Black Populations. New York: Alan R. Liss; 1981: 167–183.

5

Social Determinants of the Health of Aging Black Populations in the United States

Jacquelyne Johnson Jackson

A very critical gap in the development of further research about the social determinants of the health of aging or biologically mature black populations in the United States (hereafter, *blacks*) is the absence of any comprehensive and recent review of the applicable literature. Although many researchers may believe that they know well the nature and effects of those social determinants, the literature appears to be relatively scant, fragmented, and inconclusive.

The scantness, fragmentation, and inconclusiveness of the literature effect, *inter alia*, the scientific merit of ethnogerontologic and related debates about black health, including especially the labyrinthine debates about the causes of racial differences in morbidity and mortality. These debates generally need to be elucidated by more bountiful, integrated, and conclusive research. Periodic reviews of the resulting research findings and theories could then illuminate more fully public debates about health policies and programs for blacks.

Unfortunately, a comprehensive review of the literature about the social determinants of the health of blacks is beyond the scope of this chapter. But the first of its three major sections stresses the need for such a review as well as the need for periodic reviews of the applicable literature. Also included are some suggestions for the scope of an initial review.

The second section contains some of my tentative conclusions about the applicable literature. This discussion is based largely on my analysis of the *Report of the Secretary's Task Force on Black and Minority Health,* Volume 1: Executive Summary (1); my own limited reviews of demographic, epidemiological, and gerontological works about urban black health (2); ethnogerontologic publications about minorities (3); and comparative health statuses of older blacks and whites (4).

The implementation or further implementation of the suggestions presented in the third section could improve both the theoretical and empirical quality and quantity of our knowledge and understanding of the social determinants of black health and of the changes in the effects of those determinants with successive cohorts of blacks. The primary focus of these suggestions is on issues of conceptualization, methodology, funding, affirmative action, and the dissemination and use of valid and reliable research findings.

THE NEED FOR A COMPREHENSIVE REVIEW

Apologia

Predicated on my strong belief that the availability of a comprehensive and recent review of the relevant literature would foster better research about the social determinants of black health, the initial stage of the preparation of this discourse involved a bibliographic search for such a review. The search that was conducted was futile.

After much deliberation, the scope of the topic was narrowed to "Statistical Associations Between the Socioeconomic Statuses and Health Conditions and Resources of Aging Black Women and Men, United States, 1969–1985." But the absence of financial support for preparing a discourse precluded the inclusion of a comprehensive review of the applicable literature and limited severely my recommendations for further research. Given the absence of any financial support, refocusing the topic on the social determinants—as opposed to the socioeconomic determinants—of black health fits the speculative nature of this chapter and permits the important consideration of race as a social determinant of black health.

Need for Periodic Reviews

Within the context of the Workshop on Research on Aging Black Populations, one of the stated goals in the official program was to "promote the development of improved grant proposals from minorities." Perhaps the most obvious reason for needing periodic and systematic reviews of the literature about the social determinants of black health, which must be linked to or combined with systematic reviews of the literature about the biological and behavioral determinants of black health, is to help black researchers who seek federal funding for investigations of particular phenomena related to aging or to age changes (e.g., multifactorial investigations of the relationships between social network support and health, between poverty and health, or between stress and hypertension).

A major drawback of research grant applications submitted by many blacks to federal agencies such as the National Institute on Aging (NIA), and especially so from the predominantly black colleges and universities, is their failure to demonstrate convincingly a sufficient awareness of the relevant literature. Quite often, the insufficient awareness of the relevant literature adversely affects their formulations of testable hypotheses and the means of testing those hypotheses. This, in turn, has a decidedly negative effect on the competitive quality of their applications.

This observation does not imply that research applications submitted by nonblacks are always better than those submitted by blacks. In fact, many are not. It does mean, however, that, for a variety of objective and subjective reasons, many white applicants have better support services for preparing and receiving funding for their applications, including especially the time-consuming and costly process of reviewing adequately the applicable literature. An apt analogy may be drawn from rubber bridge: partners who have more usually bid more, thereby accumulating more points above and below the scoring line. In general, black research applicants have less, bid less, and win less.

The much earlier and substantially greater funding by NIA and its predecessor (housed in the National Institute on Child Health and Human Development) of aging research and training programs at such institutions as Duke University, the University of Michigan, and the University of Southern California abets their employment of personnel whose duties, in terms of grant applications, often include thoroughly reviewing the applicable literature and providing procedural expertise about sampling, statistics, and computer analyses. The ready availability of these personnel clearly gives their institutions a head start over many other institutional applicants. In terms of NIA funding, where there is no consideration of affirmative action, these more favored institutional applicants usually fare much better than their more disadvantaged competitors.

Consequently, most of the funded research about the aging of black populations is not overseen by investigators whose knowledge and understanding of aging blacks may, in some respect, be superior to that of the typical employees who control federal funding for research on aging black populations and the typical recipients of that funding. This consequence may account for the fact that, to the best of my limited knowledge, NIA has never funded and may never fund any research designed to investigate fully, clearly, and precisely the direct and indirect effects of institutional and personal racism on the aging of blacks, such as the effects of the institutional and personal racism experienced by some older blacks in white-controlled hospitals.

There are, of course, many other justificatory reasons for developing and disseminating periodic reviews based on the meticulous mining of the relevant literature about the determinants of black health and changes in the influence of those determinants over time. In light of the growing numbers of aging blacks and their increasing demands for medical services, there is an urgent need for cogent assessments of the dominant theories and research and the identification and resolution of the various problems that presently impede the acquisition of valid and reliable findings about the determinants of black health.

Periodic and systematic reviews of the determinants of black health might reveal a need for substantially greater consensus among researchers of the conceptual and operational definitions of certain concepts, such as that of *excess deaths*. This concept has been used as a measure of health disparities between blacks and whites (e.g., 1, p. 3). Given the inescapable links between theory and research, is this a useful concept? What does it reveal about the determinants of black health? Does it perhaps imply that being black is adversely related to good health? What is its prevailing ideology?

Aside from my own doubts about its theoretical and methodological usefulness, many critical theorists (e.g., 5, pp. 27–46) might oppose, as I do, any attempt to legitimate a belief that the lack of mortality differences between blacks and whites in the United States is an appropriate measure of racial equality by health status. Should racial equality of health status be measured by the extent to which blacks emulate whites? Should more blacks commit suicide to equalize the black and white suicide rates? I think not. The scientific and political advantages and disadvantages of using a *ratio-standards* model, where the characteristics of blacks should approximate those of whites (6), should be given serious consideration.

The sociocultural and authoritative implications of language used in any research involving blacks cannot be overlooked. As an additional example to that of *excess deaths*, consider Sadowsky's (7, pp. 3–4) characterization of blacks as "black nonhispanics [sic]," where black is employed as an adjective. There is, I submit, a critical difference between the concepts of *black non-Hispanics* and *non-Hispanic blacks*. Critical theory "tries to make our use of language as transparent and as clear as possible, so that it becomes fully understandable to us . . . [and] it works to undermine the legitimacy of those social institutions that help to organize the means of exploitation or injustice" (5, p. 43).

The availability of periodic reviews about the determinants of black health could also reduce the considerable and unnecessary repetition in the literature. The ethnogerontologic literature about black health tends to be dominated by similar comparisons of blacks and whites, such as comparisons of their mortality rates, without sufficient updating of those comparisons.

During the past several decades, when I have attended conferences related to black aging or black health or read the reports of such conferences, I have often been surprised by the lack of awareness of the existing literature exhibited by some of the scholarly participants. For example, at a 1984 conference on Blacks in an Aging Society sponsored by the Aging Society Project of Carnegie Corporation of New York, Charles V. Willie, a black sociologist, indicated, in effect, that the racial crossover in mortality had not been studied "because we do not think blacks are worthy of studying. We only study how badly off they have been. This should be an area of extensive study" (cited in 8, p. 30). Some years ago, among others, Nathaniel O. Calloway, a black physician and gerontologist, emphasized the need to search for valid explanations of the then higher life expectancy of older blacks than of older whites. He suspected "that the answers do not lie in genetic patterns but in social and cultural adjustment patterns" (cited in 6, p. 175). Contrary to Willie's assertion, a few investigators have examined the black/white crossover in mortality (see, e.g., 9). Willie's unfounded observation may have been due to his apparent unfamiliarity with the applicable literature, a situation that might have been ameliorated by the availability of periodic reviews of that literature.

Suggested Scope of an Initial Review

The preparation of a comprehensive review of the literature about the biological, behavioral, and social determinants of black health should include systematic library research of epidemiological, gerontological, and related journals. One major problem in using topical catalogue searches and searches of journal abstracts, however, is that they do not identify many of the relevant works. Some research articles containing data about black subjects are not so identified in topical indexes and journal abstracts. Their titles do not refer to the inclusion of black subjects. Therefore, to the extent possible, an exhaustive search of applicable journals should involve, where necessary, the direct scanning of their articles.

A comprehensive review could also identify the major sources of unpublished data related to the determinants of black health and provide general descriptions of these data. The availability of this information could, for instance, encourage more black researchers to seek funding for meta-analyses of race-, sex-, and age-specific data collected by such federal agencies as the National Center for Health Statistics, the National Institute for Mental Health, and the Social Security Administration.

The task of a comprehensive and thorough review of the literature might best be approached through a team effort, with the finished product including a critique and annotated bibliography. Annual periodic reviews would then be helpful. An additional outcome of the initial review might be the increased development of ways to identify relevant works about blacks in topical indexes and journal abstracts, as well as the comprehensive inclusion of those works on computerized compilations of health references. The accrued benefits of this proposal could flow to black and nonblack applicants for research grants about black health or racially comparative health studies.

LIMITED REVIEW OF THE LITERATURE

This section contains (1) a brief description and evaluation of the four reviews I primarily relied on to reach my tentative conclusions about the current status of our knowledge and understanding of the social determinants of the health of aging black populations in the United States, (2) a discussion of conceptual definitions of health and its social determinants, and (3) my tentative conclusions.

Brief Description and Evaluation

In addition to the executive summary of the *Report of the Secretary's Task Force on Black and Minority Health* (1), my discussion of the current status of the literature about the social determinants of black health is based largely on three of my related reviews of that literature.

According to the chairman of the Task Force on Black and Minority Health, the "report is a landmark effort in analyzing and synthesizing the present state of knowledge of the major factors that contribute to the health status of" blacks and other minorities (10, p. vii). The claim is ill founded because, despite the availability of financial support, the report provides no comprehensive and systematic analysis and synthesis of the major factors that have affected or continue to affect black health.

Following editorial directives, my work on urban black health (2) was organized around the illness episode to stress "practical implications of the available research data for the delivery of health care" (11, p. 16) and structured around the nine topics of identification of blacks, evaluation of the existing medical data, epidemiological characteristics, concepts of disease and illness, becoming ill, coping with illness outside the mainstream medical system, encounters with mainstream medical practitioners, adherence to biomedical treatment, and recovery, rehabiliation, and death.

In preparing that manuscript, I located and read over 1,000 journal articles that focused fully or partially on various aspects of black health in a wide variety of professional journals. While this task alone consumed at least 4 full months of my time as a single investigator without any support services, the time required for a comprehensive and systematic analysis and synthesis of the literature about the social determinants of black health would have been much longer and, despite NIA's contrary judgment, would have required some financial support.

My focus on the current and prospective status of ethnogerontology (3) did not contain an analysis of the social determinants of black health. But I did, albeit briefly, note the inconclusive findings about the relative health statuses of older blacks and whites.

My manuscript on the comparative health statuses of older blacks and whites (4) concentrated largely on a review of gerontological journals and selected medical and epidemiological articles containing empirical data about various health conditions of blacks and whites in the United States. My major focus was on four major theoretical or methodological problems in the ethnogerontologic and related literature about black health, specifically the problems of (1) genetic misclassification of blacks, (2) ethnic misclassification of blacks, (3) insufficient collection and use of descriptive data, and (4) inadequate explanations of racial disparities. I also called attention to some empirically or logically flawed suggestions for improving black health in that literature (see e.g., 12, 13, 14) and decried the sophistry with which those authors handled racial matters.

Conceptual Definitions of Health

Liang (15) emphasized correctly the need to distinguish between theoretical conceptions and operational definitions of physical health. Noting that the three primary approaches to measuring physical health were the *medical model* (a physiological definition), the *functional model* (a social definition), and the *psychological model* (a subjective definition), Liang (15, p. 249) indicated that, "In almost all survey research. . . . the respondents are questioned about their health problems or illnesses."

My limited review of the applicable literature showed clearly that, when not based on mortality rates, the bulk of that literature was based on cross-sectional and survey data of racial comparisons of a psychological model of health using self-report data. Much of the reported data about the incidence and prevalence rates of illnesses, diseases, and disabilities also relied heavily on a psychological model of health.

A reasonable conclusion may be that the typical construct of the physical health of blacks in the ethnogerontologic literature is measured psychologically, thereby raising questions about the correlations among their physiological, social, and psychological constructs and measures of health. The usual finding of a significantly positive correlation between medical assessments and self-reports of health (see e.g., 16) probably applies to older blacks as well, but we definitely need more evidentiary data about this matter. We also do not yet know the extent to which this finding can be generalized to younger black adults or to black adults who do not receive or rarely receive medical feedback about their health conditions.

Given the overriding issue of the comparative health statuses of older blacks and whites in the ethnogerontologic literature (4), an important area of concern is that the use of different measures of physical health leads to different conclusions about that issue. More specifically, when controlled at least by age, sex, and socioeconomic status, the use of a physiological model of health rarely reveals any significant differences by race in overall or disease-specific health status.

Conversely, the use of social and psychological models of health, frequently inappropriately controlled by socioeconomic variables, often leads to the conclusion that the health of blacks is quite inferior to that of whites, resulting thereby in a concentration on racial disparities in health, as evidenced especially by the report of the Task Force on Black and Minority Health.

Thus, in addition to the heavy reliance in the literature measuring black health on a psychological model of health, we might add a fourth model of health disparities. This model of health disparities, which invokes the previously mentioned *ratio-standards* model, simplistically assumes that there should be no significant differences between blacks and whites in their mortality and morbidity rates for various illnesses, diseases, and disabilities. This comparative health model usually depends on raw data generated by physiological, social, and psychological measures of physical health.

One assumption of the health-disparities model seems to be that environmental factors account for the observed differences in black and white mortality and morbidity rates. This assumption is supported by Cooper's (17) argument that black and white disparities in disease, including hypertension, are not due to genetic race but to such environmental factors as racism.

The global application of the health-disparities model only on the basis of race or race and sex may exaggerate racial differences. For example, in contrast to most findings of significantly higher rates of hypertension among black than among white females, when Langford (18) analyzed data controlled by education and obesity, the black and white female blood pressures were similar. As will be discussed in more detail later, this kind of finding raises anew questions about the effects of race on black health.

Conceptual Definitions of Social Determinants

The concept of *social determinant* is variously defined in the literature about black health, but it most often refers to a demographic or social structure variable (e.g., age or marital status) that is causally associated with an effect and is, therefore, regarded as a necessary part of the cause.

There is some overlapping use between social and cultural variables, due in large measure to differing classifications of these variables. But this is not a serious problem inasmuch as the social determinants used most often in the literature about black health are race, sex, and age. However, for example, when diet is causally associated with gout, under what conditions should diet be treated as a social, cultural, sociocultural, or even behavioral determinant?

TENTATIVE CONCLUSIONS

This section presents and discusses four tentative conclusions about the current status of research and knowledge about the social determinants of the health of aging black populations in the United States. These four conclusions deal with the (1) availability and use of relevant data, (2) analytical analyses, (3) time analyses, and (4) the shifting emphasis from social to behavioral determinants. The overriding concern is whether or not there are existing gaps in what is known and what should be known about those social determinants and, if so, how aging research can help reduce them. The conclusions are tentative because they are *not* based on a comprehensive and systematic review of the applicable literature, but only on a sample of that literature.

Availability and Use of Data

Aside from the continuing accumulation of mortality and morbidity data by the National Center for Health Statistics (NCHS), there has been a substantial increase during the past decade in the collection of useful or potentially useful data by or sponsored by other agencies of the U.S. Department of Health and Human Services.

For example, the Health Care Financing Administration has some non-white and white data about coverage by and use of Medicare and Medicaid. The National Institute of Mental Health's (NIMH) collaborative Epidemiological Catchment Area Program (ECAP), designed as "a multisite epidemiological and health services research study that addresses mental disorder prevalence, incidence, and service use rates in about 20,000 community and institutional residents" (19, p. 1), may also be useful, but its theoretical and methodological flaws (see, e.g., 20) may weaken considerably the usefulness of its findings. The Surveillance, Epidemiology, and End Results (SEER) program of the National Cancer Institute (NCI) now collects incidence and survival data from selected population areas in the United States. Both ECAP and SEER have black subjects.

The growing availability of data related to aging black populations, however, is still hampered by a number of longstanding, but resolvable, problems. These problems include (1) the generally persisting use of small samples or, less often, oversampling, of blacks, (2) the insufficient inclusion of all of the variables that are known to affect or thought to affect black health, and (3) the frequent lack of black specific data (see, e.g., 1, 2, 21).

When blacks are involved, a major dilemma of the federal agencies that collect health data falls between their conceptual and operational definitions of blacks as a population and their willingness to allocate funds to treat blacks as a population. More specifically, contrary to the usual sample design, the descriptions and analyses of the collected data are treated as if blacks in the United States constitute a separate population, but the usual sample design treats the total population of all races as the universe, which leads to the insufficient sampling of blacks.

The mere fact that some investigators, in their terminology, *oversample* blacks, is an explicit recognition of their conception of blacks as a separate population. If the literature suggests, as it does, quantitative and qualitative differences between black health and the health of nonblacks, then the most reasonable theoretical and methodological solution is to treat blacks as a separate population until the need to do so no longer exists. In short, my argument is that federal agencies that collect health data must allocate appropriate funds to the systematic collection of valid and reliable data about the black population of the United States.

Another major dilemma of federal agencies that collect or report on health data about blacks lies between their recognition of the vast differences in the health conditions of various minority groups and their decided unwillingness to allocate sufficient funds to collect appropriate data about each minority-specific group in the United States, such as Cubans, Dominican Republicans, Mexicans, and Puerto Ricans.

However, except for NCHS, these agencies are increasingly unwilling to collect, present, and analyze black-specific data unless they also provide data about other minority groups, to whom they usually apologize profusely for the greater abundance of black-specific data. This dilemma usually leads to a muddy discussion of the health of minorities and a set of findings and public policy recommendations quite inappropriate for each and every minority group, as many be seen clearly in the muddled organization and recommendations of the various volumes of the report of the Task Force on Black and Minority Health.

An additional problem with the growing availability of data related to aging black populations is that the data are usually cross-sectional, which, by and large, prohibits investigations of age changes causally associated with the social determinants of the aging of black populations; too few studies, to date, have analyzed the available data by age cohorts.

The analysis of incidence data by age in a cross-sectional sample is rarely, if ever, supplemented by an analysis of incidence data for an age cohort over time. For example, aside from the fact that the prevalence of cancer of all sites tends to increase with age, what is the relationship between the incidence of breast cancer and age over time in black females born between 1920 and 1924?

The available data sets about blacks rarely contain information about all of the variables that are believed to affect black health, including the likely social determinants. While it is true that "[a]lthough people may be characterized with respect to an almost infinite number of variables, in practice the number must be limited according to the purposes and resources of the specific study" (22, p. 43), the point is that the purposes of most epidemiological studies using black subjects concentrate more heavily on broad racial comparisons than on careful investigations of the social and other determinants of black health.

For example, even when data are presumably collected about socioeconomic status, the proxy for socioeconomic status is usually that of education, income, or occupation, as if they were congruent. Given the incongruence of education, income, and occupation of many blacks, the collected data should at least include measures of education, income, *and* occupation. Education affects health knowledge, but income and occupation affect the use of that knowledge.

Some theoretical consideration might even be given to modifying the traditional concepts and measures of education, income, and occupation. Inasmuch as, for example, many high school graduates are functionally illiterate, the measure of education by the number of years of formal schooling of individuals no longer permits the traditional assumptions about their level of knowledge, including their knowledge about health. Income data would be much more useful if they were presented not only by the amount of income from earnings or from all sources for individuals, families, or households, but also by major sources of income, amount of disposable or discretionary income after the basic costs of shelter and food, and the like. When occupation is used in health analyses, additional data are often needed about the extent of health insurance provided by employment.

Aside from race, sex, and age, almost none of the data sets contain simultaneous information about education, income, occupation, employment, marital status, living arrangements, accessibility of medical facilities, and the like, all of which are or may be social determinants of black health.

The problem of the frequent lack of black-specific data is lessening, and

NCHS now provides black mortality rates for all causes and specific causes of death by age and sex. However, investigators who earlier substituted nonwhite mortality rates for black mortality rates could have computed the latter by using the number of deaths from NCHS data and population estimates from the U.S. Bureau of the Census.

Analytical Analyses

An important distinction between descriptive and analytic epidemiology is that the former studies "the *amount* and *distribution* of disease within a population by person, place, and time," and the latter focuses on "the *determinants* of disease or *reasons* for relatively high or low frequency in specific groups," such as blacks (22, p. 43) (italics in original). The fulfillment of "the ultimate goal of epidemiology [of] the search for causes (determinants) of disease as the key to identifying effective preventive measures" often necessitates reliance on the establishment of causal associations from observational studies, where the five criteria to evaluate the evidence for causal association are the "strength of the association, consistency, temporal relations, specificity, and coherence with existing knowledge" (22, p. 109).

The above distinction and criteria may be used to evaluate the epidemiologic and related studies about the social determinants of black health. Due partially to the paucity of morbidity data (especially incidence rates), results dealing with the social determinants of black health are generally sparse, fragmented, and inconclusive (see, e.g., 23). Most of the analytical analyses concentrate heavily on race and use a social definition of race. Many of these analyses also attempt to control their data by sex, age, or socioeconomic status (usually measured by income or education) or by any combination of these variables. The NCHS incidence and prevalence rates for blacks are usually reported only by race and age. When there is a disease-specific focus, as opposed to self-reports of disabilities or limitations of activities, the focus is most often placed on cardiovascular and cerebrovascular disorders (especially on hypertension and stroke) and on malignant neoplasms.

Perhaps the most important conclusion to be reached is that we now know little about the current effects of race on black mortality and morbidity, owing in large measure, no doubt, to the changing effects of race over time. We also do not know when race should and should not be equated with minority-group membership. For example, a considerable diminution of the differences between blacks and whites by access to health resources, including physician visits, has occurred during the past several decades. Some persons contend that the greater white than black use of office visits to physicians is an indicator of inferior health care for blacks. However, this assumption is not based on an evaluation of the quality of care available at different medical sites. In some instances, blacks who use clinics attached to medical schools may fare better than blacks and whites using office-based physicians.

Caplan, Robinson, French, Caldwell, and Shinn (24, p. 48), who reviewed the literature on determinants of adherence by hypertensive patients, concluded that "demographic variables [i.e., age, race, sex, education, income, and socioeconomic status] are global surrogate variables, that is, each represents a host of confounding variables." If race is a global surrogate variable, as it appears to be, what confounding variables does it mask and how should it be treated in epidemiologic investigations? Cooper (17) contended that race should be treated as an antecedent variable. In light of a finding of insignificant differences between black and white homicide rates adjusted by occupants per household room and similar findings that diminish or eliminate differences when adjusted by certain relevant variables (4, 17), more research is needed to determine the host of confounding variables represented by race, so as to shed more light on the social determinants of black health.

As suggested earlier, but reemphasized here, new measures of social class and of socioeconomic status are also desirable. Pointing out that an "occupation is not the same as a job," Campbell and Parker (25, p. 464) recommended against using the Duncan Socioeconomic Index (SEI) as a standard measure of socioeconomic status. Cooper (17) argued—and rightly so—that black and white socioeconomic statuses are not directly comparable.

More investigators have recently expanded their black and white comparisons to include comparisons of whites, blacks, and other minority groups, usually without distinguishing between their native and foreign-born subjects. These comparisons, which most often use very small samples of each racial or ethnic group, rarely produce comparatively useful findings of an analytical nature. Also apparent in the recent literature is a slight increase in epidemiologic comparisons of various groups of blacks (e.g., by age, sex, income, and education).

My limited examination of the studies that actually or presumably established causal associations between social determinants and various measures of black health, including measures restricted to cause-specific diseases, showed that they usually do not adequately meet each of the five criteria for causal associations set forth by Mausner and Bahn (22).

By way of illustration, consider the frequently reported statistically strong associations by race for prevalance rates of hypertension. The finding that the black rates are significantly higher than the white rates is generally consistent, even when controlled by sex. That is, there seems to be a consistency of the association. But most of the studies use similar, as opposed to diverse, circumstances for determining hypertensive rates, without considering the possibility of a systematic error that could lead to a spurious consistency. Also, while stress and high sodium intake are often flagged as contributing factors to hypertension among blacks, the studies usually do not provide sufficient data to show that those factors are antecedent to hypertension among blacks. Those studies also rarely deal with the specificity of the association in terms, for example, of how racial stress predicts elevated blood pressure rates. A very serious problem is the lack of coherence with existing data of many of these studies, due partially to insufficient data currently available about the etiology of essential and secondary hypertension. One remaining critical question is whether or not the incidence rates of hypertension by race and sex are significantly different when controlled by the physiological, psychological, and social determinants of hypertension.

We can, then, characterize the current analyses of the social determinants of black health as being in a quandary. This is due in part to the lack of conclusive findings about the additive and interactional effects of social determinants on black health, including the variations in those effects for specific diseases, disabilities, and the like, and the changes that occur over time in the nature and weight of those effects.

Time Analyses

The usual associations found between age and morbidity (e.g., acute and chronic diseases) and between age and mortality are also found among blacks. The incidence and prevalence of acute diseases tend to be inversely associated with age, and the incidence and prevalence of chronic diseases increases with age. Mortality rates also rise with age. The usual associations found between sex and morbidity and sex and mortality are also generally found among blacks. For example, the mortality gap by sex favors females. Prevalence rates for the adult onset of diabetes mellitus, higher for females than for males among both blacks and whites, also tend to increase with age.

The morbidity and mortality patterns of different cohorts of black adults vary by age, sex, and time, as may be seen in Table 5.1, which contains 4-year annual averages of the crude death rates per 100,000 of all causes of death of blacks, 65 years of age or more, by sex, in the United States between 1967 and 1982. Table 5.1 also contains male/female ratios of the 1967–1970 and 1979–1982 death rates for each age group of 65–69, 70–74, 75–79, 80–84, and 85 or more years of age.

With the exception of persons who were 85 years of age or more, the mortality improvement evident for both sexes over time was greater among females than among males. Thus the mortality gap by sex favoring females

TABLE 5.1 Four-year Annual Averages of the Crude Death Rates per 100,000 of All Causes of Deaths of Blacks, 65 Years of Age or More, by Sex, United States, 1967–1982, and Male/Female Ratios for 1967–1970/1979–1982[a]

Sex and years	Age group (in years)				
	65–69	70–74	75–79	80–84	85+
1967–1970					
Black women	3,466.9	4,525.6	6,043.9	7,807.5	12,164.6
Black men	5,151.5	6,886.6	7,314.3	9.945.5	14,465.4
1971–1974					
Black women	2,896.6	5,170.4	5,915.8	7,077.8	11,311.9
Black men	4,704.6	7,241.6	8,953.4	9,936.0	13,886.0
1975–1978					
Black women	2,275.6	4,665.8	7,010.3	6,654.4	9,235.3
Black men	4,056.2	6,780.0	9,618.6	9,922.0	12,058.2
1979–1982					
Black women	2,461.0	3,574.5	4,902.7	7,540.2	11,735.7
Black men	4,390.8	5,920.3	7,552.4	10,776.0	15,269.6
Male/female ratios for 1967–1970 and 1979–1982					
1967–1970	1.49	1.52	1.21	1.27	1.19
1979–1982	1.78	1.66	1.54	1.43	1.30

[a]This table was adapted from Jackson (4). The raw data used to compute the rates for 1967–1975 were obtained from the *Vital Statistics of the United States, Volume II-Mortality, Part A* and from then-unpublished numbers of death by cause, race, sex, and age of the National Center on Health Statistics for 1976–78, based on estimated population data from the U.S. Bureau of the Census. The 1979–1982 data are averages of the crude death rates for each year from "Trend B, Table 291. Death rates for 72 selected causes, by 5-year age groups, color, and sex: United States, 1979–82 (rates per 100,000 population)," unpublished data dated 84/07/25 received by personal request from the National Center for Health Statistics, Hyattsville, Maryland.

increased. The consistent decrease in the male/female ratios with increasing age between 1979 and 1982 was not present between 1967 and 1970. The greatest male/female gap by age group occurred among persons who were 70 to 74 years of age in 1967–1970, in contrast to the age group of persons who were 65 to 69 years of age in 1979–1982.

What are the social determinants or the changing social determinants that help to explain these variations over time? What social determinants are useful in helping to explain the decreasing mortality rates between 1967 and 1978 for persons who were 85 years of age or more, and their increased mortality rates in 1979–1982?

Among blacks who were 85 years of age or more between 1975 and 1978 and between 1979 and 1982, mortality rates increased by 27.1% for women and 26.6% for men. In contrast, the rise among their white counter-parts was only 0.2% for women and 0.6% for men. Why?

Perhaps one social determinant of the increased mortality of very old blacks may be found by investigating the effects of their increased use of medical resources on the phenomenon of the "survival of the fittest." That is, there may well be an inverse relationship between their use of medical resources (including the growing medical technology available to prolong life) and their overall health status.

The changing mortality patterns of older blacks also raise descriptive and analytical questions about the stability of the *racial crossover in mortality* (i.e., the age point where the mortality rates previously higher for blacks become higher for whites). The age point of the crossover has increased considerably during the past few decades, thereby giving further support to social, as opposed to genetic, explanations of this phenomenon.

The male crossover for all causes of death occurred in the group aged 75 to 79 between 1967 and 1970, and thereafter shifted upward to the group aged 80 to 84. The differences between the black and white male mortality rates of the group aged 80 to 84 also narrowed over time. The white rate was 25.0% higher than the black rate in 1971 to 1974, but only 1.9% higher in 1979 to 1982 (4).

The female crossover for all causes of death took place in the group aged 80 to 84 between 1967 and 1978, shifting thereafter to the group aged 85 and older. Unlike the male pattern, the female gaps widened over time. The white female mortality rates were 17.2 and 22.6% higher than the black female mortality rates in 1967 to 1970 and 1979 to 1982, respectively (4).

The variations in mortality rates also obviously affect life expectancy values. Table 5.2 shows the life expectancy values of blacks and whites by sex at 0–1 year, 65–70 years, and 85 years of age or more in 1979 and 1982, and at 0–1 year, 65 years, and 85 years of age in 1983. Although the data are not directly comparable for the two older ages, Table 5.2 also shows percentage changes between 1979 and 1983, as well as gaps by years between the races by sex and between the sexes by race.

The life expectancy values for any year and population are, of course, based on the mortality rates of that population in the given year. Thus fluctuations in life expectancy values are a function of fluctuating mortality rates. Table 5.2 shows that at 0–1 years of age, black males had the shortest life expectancy, followed, in descending order, by white males, black females, and white females. At 85 years of age or more, white males had the shortest life expectancy, followed by black males, and, except for 1982, by white females and then by black females.

The life expectancy values at 0–1 year and 65–70 years generally increased between 1979 and 1983, with the greatest increase in years for

TABLE 5.2 Life Expectancy (in Years) of Blacks and Whites at 0–1, 65–70, and 85 Years of Age or More, by Sex, United States, 1979, 1982, and 1983, and Percentage Changes, 1983/1979

| Age and year | Race and sex | | | |
	Black males	White males	Black females	White females
At 0–1 years				
1979	64.0	70.6	72.7	78.2
1982	64.9	71.5	73.5	78.8
1983[a]	65.9	71.5	73.9	78.4
Percentage change	3.0	1.3	1.6	0.3
At 65–70 years				
1979	13.3	14.2	17.2	18.7
1982	13.3	14.5	17.2	18.9
1983[a]	13.4	14.5	17.3	18.7
Percentage change	0.8	2.1	0.6	0.0
At 85+ years				
1979	6.8	5.5	9.2	7.0
1982	4.8	5.3	6.5	6.7
1983[a]	6.0	5.2	7.5	6.5
Percentage change	−11.8	−5.4	−18.5	−7.1

[a]The life expectancies for 1983 are at 0–1, at 65, and at 85 years of age.
With the exception of the 1983 data, this table was adapted from Jackson (4). The data for 1979 and 1983 were obtained by telephone from the National Center for Health Statistics, Hyattsville, Maryland, in October 1985 and November 1986, respectively. The source for the 1982 data is National Center for Health Statistics: Advance report, final mortality statistics, 1982. *Monthly Vital Statistics Report.* Vol. 33, No. 9, Supp. DHHS Pub. No. (PHS) 85-1120. Public Health Service, Hyattsville, Md., Dec. 20, 1984.

black males at 0–1 year. These values decreased at 85 years of age or more, however, for each race–sex group, with the greatest decrease occurring among black females, followed by black males. These data reflect the increased mortality rates of persons who were 85 years of age or more between 1979 and 1983.

The gaps by race within each sex group were generally lower than the gaps by sex within each racial group. The gaps between blacks and whites by sex were higher for males than females at 0–1 year and, thereafter, almost always lower for males. The gaps by sex within each racial group were higher for blacks than for whites at 0–1 years in the youngest and oldest age category, but higher for whites in the middle-aged category.

While the above discussion about race–sex differences emphasizes anew the importance of employing the variables of race, sex, and age in any descriptions and analyses of mortality, life expectancy, and related data, it does not rule out the additional need for the coterminous use of other variables that are likely social determinants of the resulting patterns.

For example, the mortality data published by NCHS do not reveal the social class of the deceased. They also do not provide data about their use of health resources and the like prior to their deaths. Recognizing clearly that financial resources and other factors prevent NCHS from providing all of the kinds of data that may be useful in furthering our knowledge and understanding of the social determinants of mortality, as well as morbidity, among aging black populations, some investigators may wish to examine retrospectively the social determinants of black deaths caused by diseases. After drawing a randomly stratified sample of such deaths in a localized area, for instance, they could then rely on various medical and other applicable records and try to obtain relevant information from the family and friends of the deceased.

Although the trend in the literature is toward a growing number of studies that provide time-series analyses of mortality and morbidity data for aging black populations, too many of these studies still do not use the latest data (even when they are available in unpublished form), do not analyze their data by highly refined categories of at least race, sex, and age, do not specify clearly the strengths and weaknesses of their data, and, based on the available data, do not examine as clearly and precisely as possible the similarities and differences among successive cohorts of blacks.

Longitudinal studies of aging black populations are also quite rare. The first longitudinal study of aging conducted by Duke University's Center for Aging and Human Development contained very little data about its non-representative sample of blacks. Its second longitudinal study deliberately excluded blacks. Both of these studies included medical examinations that provided clinically determined diagnoses of diseases.

Epidemiological follow-up studies with black subjects are less rare than gerontological studies using longitudinal samples, but they also are still too rare to provide much-needed data about age changes associated with the social determinants of black health. Perhaps the best such study to date is the study of heart and related diseases in Evans County, Georgia (see, e.g., 26). Data from this study were also used to examine the racial crossover in mortality (27).

SHIFTING EMPHASIS FROM SOCIAL
TO BEHAVIORAL DETERMINANTS

A growing trend in the literature seems to be a shifting emphasis from the social to the behavioral determinants of black health, perhaps owing to the increasing stress placed by the medical and other health communities on preventive health measures. Much of this emphasis is being placed on not using tobacco, alcohol, and illegal drugs, on changing dietary patterns and reducing overweight, on exercising, and on complying adequately with medically prescribed regimes.

My concern about this apparent shift is not that behavioral factors do not affect black health, sometimes adversely, but that the links between social and behavioral determinants of health are too often overlooked (4). Many public and private sponsors of health educational programs and advertisements that attempt to induce behavioral changes among blacks (e.g., the efforts of the American Cancer Society and the U.S. Office of the Surgeon General to reduce or eliminate smoking) are not also directly involved in efforts to improve the overall socioeconomic status of blacks.

Ross and Mirowsky (28, p. 288), who used representative samples of Anglos in Texas and Mexicans in Texas and Mexico in their investigation of the relationships among social class, ethnicity, and overweight, lamented the fact that "few studies have examined the social and cultural determinants of relative weight in representative community samples." Finding that social "class and cultural positions are associated with weight and that their effects differ for men and women," they stressed that "social and cultural factors should not be overlooked in the investigation of overweight" (28, pp. 296–297). Among the women in their sample, the prevalence of overweight and social class were inversely associated, while the opposite pattern was more characteristic of men.

Based on data collected more than a decade ago, the relationship among obesity, sex, and social class may be somewhat different among blacks. Self-reported and clinically determined obesity, higher among black women than black men (2, 29), does not seem to be consistently associated with income when controlled somewhat by age, but the consistency is much greater for men than for women (see 2, Table 1.11, p. 72). There may be, however, a consistently positive relationship between clinically determined obesity and income (i.e., above or below the poverty level) for men. Specifically, obesity has been less pronounced among poor men.

To the extent, however, that obesity and social class are positively correlated among black women, then efforts to reduce black female obesity should not be restricted to behavioral modifications, but should also—and simultaneously—include upgrading their social class. This observation brings us full circle to my belief that health educational programs designed to modify black behavioral patterns to favor preventive health measures must not ignore, where appropriate, the social determinants or mediators of their behavioral determinants of health.

SUGGESTIONS

Aside from my first suggestion, the primary focus of my suggestions about furthering our knowledge and understanding of the social determinants of black health is on the five issues of *conceptualization, methodology, funding, affirmative action,* and the *dissemination and use of valid and reliable research findings for theory, research, and public policy.* If implemented, these suggestions could, in general, benefit ethnogerontology and, in particular, benefit black researchers who need to keep abreast of the current status of the literature.

Literature Reviews

As previously indicated, there is an urgent need for a comprehensive, systematic, and integrated review of all of the literature about the genetic, physiological, behavioral, cultural, and social determinants of black health conditions and resources, including the use of resources that are related to black aging. Periodic updates of that literature, perhaps every 2 or 3 years, may also be useful.

The funding for the first review, which would probably be the most costly, could be a line item in a forthcoming budget of NIA or another relevant agency of the U.S. Department of Health and Human Services. The volumes released by the Secretary's Task Force on Black and Minority Health (1, 30–36) do not contain a comprehensive, systematic, and integrated review of the available literature.

NIA could also make available periodic listings of its funded research projects using black subjects. The most recent listing I found on blacks and other minorities (36, pp. 329–331) listed only five programs that were so related. These five programs referred to a standing program announcement for proposals about social and behavioral research, a study of anti-hypertensive treatment in aged patients with isolated systolic hypertension, participation in the Smithsonian Folklore Festival, a market-research study of aging and health promotion, two epidemiologic and demographic studies (one funded to Duke University in 1984, and one, a 5-year prospective study initiated in 1980, to Yale University), and one study involving secondary analyses of the NHANES data for 1971–1974.

After obtaining the above information, I polled by telephone a small, nonrepresentative sample of black researchers who had some gerontological background or interests. Almost all of them were familiar with the standing program announcement, but almost none of them were aware of the NIA-funded projects at Duke and Yale.

The availability of such a review could also help quell misinformed statements that compare blacks and other minorities, as well as reduce the growing tension between blacks and other minorities, especially between blacks and Hispanics. For example, Trevino (37, p. 46) erroneously concluded that NCHS's National Health Interview Survey (NHIS) collected valuable data for blacks, but not for Hispanics, because its "sample design samples Hispanics in proportion to their representation in the population... [a method that] yields too few Hispanics in the sample to allow precise estimates for the Hispanic national origin groups." Until 1985, blacks were also sampled by proportional representation within the total population, which also yielded insufficient data. Further, no data are available about the black national origin groups, such as Haitians, Jamaicans, and Nigerians. Data are also not presented for black Puerto Ricans living on the mainland. Torres-Gill (38, p. 145) believes that, when compared to other minorities, Hispanics are "disproportionately disadvantaged," in part because the "civil rights protections and advances have not been as useful for Hispanics as they have been for blacks." He does not, however, provide any black and Hispanic comparisons or other evidence to support his sweeping generalization.

The organization of the volumes issued by the Secretary's Task Force on Black and Minority Health (1, 30–36) reflects, on the one hand, a recognition of the differences among minority groups, but, on the other hand, a considered and tenacious reluctance to separate them. Almost every volume jumps within its covers from minority group to minority group, which is highly disconcerting to readers who are only interested in a specific minority group, such as blacks. If black researchers with little or no discretionary income wished to add the materials on blacks to their personal libraries, they would have to purchase *all* of the volumes. A better organizational scheme, which could have aided the dissemination of information to black researchers interested in blacks, would have been the publication of an overall executive summary and separate volumes for each minority group.

Conceptualization

The considerable lack of conceptual agreement among ethnogerontologists, epidemiologists, and related scientists about the key concepts in studies of the social determinants of black health is one barrier to the greater acquisition of knowledge and understanding about them and their weighted effects, largely because the results of many studies are not directly comparable. Among the key concepts in need of consensual agreement are those of *excess deaths* (discussed previously), *race, social class,* and *socioeconomic status*.

Race is almost never treated as a genetic or biologic concept. Instead, it is used in a social context where it is rarely clear if it is operationalized as race or as minority status (see 39). Most often, it is employed in the latter context. Conceptual agreements about race as a genetic, physiologic, behavioral, cultural, and social factor are needed. Race can be used in each of the aforementioned ways. At the very least, studies should define explicitly their conceptual and operational definitions of race and analyze their data accordingly.

The distinction between race as a social factor and race as a cultural factor must be made in any relevant descriptions and analyses of social race and cultural race as determinants of black health. Such statements as, "another consequence of the relatively small number of Black physicians is that the likelihood that a Black patient would be seen by a Black cardiologist with whom there would be some cultural affinity, is very low" (32, p. 55), represent an example of the confusion between race as a social and cultural factor. What, for example, is the critical relationship between the race of a cardiologist and the diagnosis and treatment of a black patient with hypertension or coronary heart disease? The author of the above quotation demonstrated no such relationship.

There is also some confusion in the literature between the concepts of social class and socioeconomic status of blacks, as well as between the conceptual and operational definitions of those concepts. What is most clear is that, in my judgment, social class should always include the variable of race and that the socioeconomic statuses of blacks cannot be measured merely by one or two variables, such as by education or occupation.

In discussing the pathogenesis of coronary heart disease, Myers (40, pp. 312–313) proposed the multidimensional subsuming of socioeconomic and sociocultural factors "under the generic heading of social status," which would also include sociostructural (e.g., race) and sociopsychological (e.g., personality traits and life stresses) characteristics, so as to separate eventually "the influence of social status on the presence or absence of risk factors for coronary heart disease for blacks, as well as factors of coronary heart disease that influence their risk management, morbidity, and mortality.

Myers's (40) generic definition of social status is probably too broad to capture the essence of social status, but it does indicate clearly that social status in the traditional sense can and does influence cultural and psychological patterns that, in turn, may have various effects on physical health. A drawback to his broad definition of social status may be his failure to recognize clearly the highly differential effects of social status on black psychological traits.

My major suggestion here is that concerted attention should be given to the reconceptualization and operationalization of the various concepts of excess deaths, race, social class, and socioeconomic status for blacks, and, by extension, of the comparative use of those concepts for blacks and other racial, ethnic, or minority groups. A careful review of the literature on the conceptualized and operationalized measures of these concepts would also be useful in this endeavor.

My final concern about conceptualization within the present context is that of *aging*. My review of the literature, as well as my careful attention to the workshop presentations, suggests that almost no emphasis has been placed on the relationships between the social determinants of black health and the age changes of blacks. In fact, to be quite candid, the workshop presentations did not really have a gerontological orientation. That is, due, no doubt, to the dearth of information, there was no specific focus on *age changes* among aging black populations. The limited focus on *age differences* of a few presentations should not be confused with *age changes*.

If we are interested in the study of aging, then we, as ethnogerontologists or gerontologists, are necessarily interested in the genetic, physiological, behavioral, cultural, and social factors that accompany aging or that are causally related to aging, and we must be concerned about age changes. Almost all of the data that were presented at the workshop were cross-sectional data, although some of the data could have been formulated in a longitudinal fashion for population aging, and cross-sectional data simply do not provide data about age changes.

Some conceptual discord about the age of the onset of aging also arose, but was not clarified, at the workshop. This discord, I suspect, was due to disciplinary differences about conceptual and operational definitions of aging. Individuals who seemed to be more oriented toward the natural sciences or the direct-care health professions seemed to be more likely to regard the onset of aging as beginning at conception or birth, while those more oriented to the behavioral or social sciences tended to define aging as occurring with the onset of biological, psychological, and social maturity.

I dare not offer here a precise definition of aging that would suffice for each of the various disciples, but I do suggest strongly that research on aging black populations could be fostered by some conceptual and operational definitions of the concept of aging. At the very least, the social definition of aging should be restricted to biologically mature blacks or biologically mature black populations. This definition, however, is not as precise or clear as it might be, because it does not combine the biological and social qualifications of maturity. More information about the associations between the biological, psychological, and social maturity of blacks might speed the conceptual and operational definitions of aging blacks or of aging black populations. I would argue, however, that, under normal circumstances, the definition of aging should be restricted at least to biologically mature blacks.

Methodology

The methodologies of studies of the social determinants of the health of aging black populations could be improved in a number of ways. Foremost among these ways would be the development and implementation of a massive longitudinal study that meets the ideal research conditions, including a nationwide representative sample stratified by the social variables that affect health or that are believed to affect health. If the initial sample contained persons between the ages of 20 and 49, the survivors of the group could be followed for a period of 30 to 40 years. Such a study should not, however, be confined only to the social determinants of health, but should be expanded to include the genetic, physiological, psychological, and cultural determinants.

The significant information that could be obtained from such a study could serve as a benchmark in helping to further our knowledge and understanding of the relationships between aging and health among blacks and of the factors that influence those relationships.

Many contemporary researchers could also improve the methodologies of their studies, where appropriate, by revising the operational definitions of their key concepts, such as socioeconomic status, by using representative samples of blacks in cross-sectional, longitudinal, or follow-up studies, by carefully controlling their comparisons of blacks with other groups, by not using sophistry in their recommendations for public policies for aging blacks, and the like.

In addition to greater agreement among researchers about the conceptual and operational definitions of key concepts, such as excess deaths and socioeconomic status, attempts to reach agreement should be considered from the standpoint of critical theory, and the resulting concepts should be realistic and reflect changing social, technological, and other conditions. These kinds of changes have led to the modification or expansion of some sociological concepts, such as the *modified extended family* (see, e.g., 41), and the revision of questionnaire or interview items, such as measuring the distance between adult children and parents in terms of travel time as opposed to miles.

I would explore the feasibility of modifying the concept of socioeconomic status to include the variables of education, occupation, employment, income, major source of income, area of residence, housing tenure, marital status, familial or household size, and household composition, and treating the variable of race as an antecedent to socioeconomic status. At the very least, per capita income within a household or family is a better indicator of income status than are individual, household, or familial income. The amount of income remaining after the necessary expenses for shelter, utilities, food, transportation, and the like may also be a better indicator of income than the traditional measures.

Funding

My major suggestion for funding research on aging black populations is that it should be ample enough to (1) conduct a comprehensive, systematic, and integrated review of the applicable literature, which would include the determinants of black health for specific diseases, (2) launch a major longitudinal study of the health of aging blacks, and (3) provide appropriate seed monies to black researchers to enhance their chances in bidding for competitive NIA research grants. As I indicated earlier, those who have more can bid more.

Affirmative Action

The topic of affirmative action is extremely sensitive, in part because it has never been clearly and precisely defined in federal circles. Two of the major issues of affirmative action are whether or not racial quotas are involved and, if so, whether or not quality should be sacrificed. These are important issues, partially because much of the federally mandated research funds during the past few years to traditionally black colleges and universities have not usually yielded significant research findings or innovations. That is, to put it bluntly, they have not generally paid off.

A more careful examination of the distribution of federal research funds to traditionally black institutions will probably reveal that the vast majority of them are not research institutions. Instead, they are institutions largely devoted to teaching undergraduates, and few of them have graduate or professional programs that attract the kinds of students who can assist their professors in major research activities, including the study of aging.

My final comment about affirmative action is that NIA and other federal agencies that sponsor workshops on blacks should provide the resources needed to make them successful and productive.

Disseminating and Using Research Findings

Many of the journal articles I reviewed about black aging and black health did not display a sufficient familiarity with the available literature (4), a problem that may be attributed to unfamiliarity with the literature on the part of both the authors and the journal reviewers and editors. Considering how difficult it is to locate and thoroughly review the applicable literature, however, this problem could be reduced by better dissemination and use of research studies about black aging and black health.

An important step in that direction could be, as earlier suggested, the provision of a comprehensive, systematic, and integrated review, periodically updated and made available at reasonable costs through the U.S. Government Printing Office. Other steps might include the comprehensive listing of all pertinent works in the computerized bibliographic search materials, the periodic holding of workshops that provide comprehensive reviews and unstifled discussions of the applicable works, and the greater use of knowledgeable reviewers by editors of refereed journals.

SUMMARY

This presentation about the social determinants of the health of aging black populations in the United States, severely limited by both the lack of any comprehensive and recent review of the applicable literature and the absence of funds to conduct such a review, focused largely on an apologia for the omission of such a review, stressed the need for such reviews, presented some tentative conclusions drawn from a limited review of the literature, and provided some suggestions that might reduce some of the problems now encountered in determining the current status of that literature.

Premised on the workshop's objective to "promote the development of improved grant proposals from minorities," my most important conclusion is that this objective could best be promoted through the provision and periodic updating of a comprehensive, systematic, and integrated review of the genetic, physiological, psychological, social, and cultural determinants of black health that are associated with or causally related to *aging*. The emphasis on aging is especially important because, as I look back on the three NIH conferences on black aging, including the workshop on which this volume is based, none of them have dealt clearly and precisely with aging patterns and processes or provided comprehensive reviews of the current literature (see, e.g., 42). The promotion of improved grant applications from black researchers also requires the necessary monetary support, including, where appropriate, access to computer, sampling, and statistical experts.

Set forth below are the remainder of my major conclusions, some of which are tentative because they are based on a limited review of the applicable literature.

1. Conceptual and operational agreement about key concepts (e.g., aging, aging populations, excess deaths, race, social class, and socioeconomic status) is sorely needed. The rejection of some concepts (e.g., excess deaths) should also be pondered carefully.
2. The considerable repetition in the ethnogerontologic literature about blacks should be reduced, but further efforts should be made not only to replicate good studies, but also to launch major longitudinal studies of aging blacks.
3. Much of the gerontological and related literature about black health relies on mortality rates and on cross-sectional survey data of the psychological model of health of self-reported health measures, where racial comparisons are quite common. A growing number of recent studies suggest that many of the findings of causal associations between race per se and health are spurious. These studies and related data also point to the changing trends in and the complexity of the mix

of social determinants of black health. They also support the supposition that we now know relatively little about the mortality and morbidity (including especially incidence rates) of aging black populations in the United States, and even less about the social determinants of specific diseases. We also need to know much more about the relationships between the various determinants of black health.

4. However, the number of studies about social and psychological determinants of health, which also use black subjects, is growing. Many of them contain promising findings (see, e.g., 43–47) that point to considerable similarities between blacks and whites and considerable variations among blacks.

5. The changing mortality patterns of older blacks raise descriptive and analytical questions about the stability of the racial crossover in mortality, including the rising age of that crossover. If all other things remain equal (e.g., proportion of natives in the black population and black access to Medicaid and Medicare), it is quite likely that the racial crossover in mortality will disappear over the next several decades.

6. Finally, public efforts to modify black behavioral patterns that are or are presumed to be negatively related to good health will undoubtedly be more successful if they are accompanied by public efforts to modify drastically the social determinants that are causally associated with bad health.

REFERENCES

1. U.S. Department of Health and Human Services. *Report of the Secretary's Task Force on Black and Minority Health, Volume I: Executive Summary.* Washington, DC: Author; 1985.

2. Jackson JJ. Urban blacks. In: Harwood, A, ed. *Ethnicity and Health Care.* Cambridge, MA: Harvard University Press; 1981: 37–129.

3. Jackson JJ. Race, national origin, ethnicity, and aging. In: Binstock RH, Shanas E, eds. *Handbook of Aging and Social Sciences,* (2nd ed.), New York: Van Nostrand Reinhold; 1985: 264–303.

4. Jackson JJ. Ethnogerontologic comparisons of black and white health in the United States: problems and prospects. In: Weiss DM, ed. *Gerontological Problems and Prospects* (monograph series). Brookville, NY: Long Island University Center on Aging; in press.

5. Ashley D, Orenstein DM. *Sociological Theory, Classical Statements.* Boston, MA: Allyn and Bacon; 1985.

6. Jackson JJ. Social gerontology and the Negro: a review. *The Gerontologist* 1967; 7:168–178.

7. Sadowsky J. Women fifty-five and over in New York City and New York State: A demographic profile. Unpublished manuscript prepared for the Housing Committee, Governor's Task Force on Older Women; 1986.

8. Gibson RC. *Blacks in an Aging Society*. New York: Carnegie Corporation; 1986.

9. Manton K, Poss SS, Wing S. The black/white mortality crossover: investigation from the perspective of the components of aging. *The Gerontologist* 1979; 19:291–300.

10. Malone E. Letter of transmittal. In: U.S. Department of Health and Human Services, *Report of the Secretary's Task Force on Black & Minority Health, Volume I: Executive Summary*. Washington, DC: U.S. Department of Health and Human Services; vii–viii.

11. Harwood A. Introduction. In: Harwood A, ed. *Ethnicity and Medical Care*. Cambridge, MA: Harvard University Press; 1981: 1–36.

12. Myers JE, Wass H, Murphey M. Ethnic differences in death anxiety among the elderly. *Death Education* 1980; 4:237–244.

13. Satariano WA, Albert S, Belle SH. Race, age and cancer incidence: a test of double jeopardy. *Journal of Gerontology* 1982; 37:642–647.

14. Palmore EB, Nowlin JB, Wang HS. Predictors of function among the old-old: a 10-year follow-up. *Journal of Gerontology* 1985; 40:244–250.

15. Liang J. Self-reported physical health among aged adults. *Journal of Gerontology* 1986; 41:248–260.

16. Shanas E, Maddox G. Health, health resources, and the utilization of care. In: Binstock RH, Shanas E, eds. *Handbook of Aging and the Social Sciences* (2nd ed.). New York: Van Nostrand Reinhold; 1985: 697–726.

17. Cooper R. A note on the biologic concept of race and its application in epidemiologic research. *American Heart Journal* 1984; 108:715–723.

18. Langford HG. Is blood pressure different in black people? *Postgraduate Medical Journal* 1981; 57:749–754.

19. Locke BZ, Regier DA. Prevalence of selected mental disorders. In: Taube CA, Barrett SA, eds. *Mental Health, United States 1985*, (DHHS Publication No. (ADM) 85-1378). Washington, DC: U.S. Government Printing Office; 1985: 1–2.

20. Kermis MD. The epidemiology of mental disorder in the elderly: a response to the Senate/AARP report. *Journal of Gerontology* 1986; 26:482–487.

21. Jackson JJ. The blacklands of gerontology. *Aging and Human Development* 1971; 2:156–171.

22. Mausner JS, Bahn AK. *Epidemiology: An Introductory Text*. Philadelphia: W. B. Saunders; 1974.

23. Markides KS. Minority status, aging, and mental health. *International Journal of Aging and Human Development* 1986; 23:285–300.

24. Caplan RD., Robinson EAR, French, JRP Jr, Caldwell JR, Shinn, M. *Adhering to Medical Regimens: Pilot Experiments in Patient Education and Social Support*. Ann Arbor: Institute for Social Research, The University of Michigan; 1976.

25. Campbell RT, Parker RN. Substantive and statistical considerations in the interpretation of multiple measures of SES. *Social Forces* 1983; 62:450–466.

26. Tyroler H, Knowles MG, Wing SB, Logue EE, Davis CE, Heiss G, Heyden S, Hames CG. Ischemic heart disease risk factors and twenty-year mortality in middle-age Evans County black males. *American Heart Journal* 1984; 108:738–746.

27. Wing S, Manton KG, Stallard E, Hames CG, Tryoler HA. The black/white mortality crossover: investigation in a community-based study. *Journal of Gerontology* 1985; 40:78–84.
28. Ross CE, Mirowsky J. Social epidemiology of overweight: a substantive and methodological investigation. *Journal of Health and Social Behavior* 1983; 24:288–298.
29. Ostfeld AM, Shekelle RB, Tufo HM, Wieland AM, Kilbridge JA, Drori J, Klawans H. Cerebrovascular disease in an elderly poor urban population. *American Journal of Public Health,* 1971; 61:19–29.
30. U.S. Department of Health and Human Services. *Report of the Secretary's Task Force on Black & Minority Health, Volume II: Crosscutting Issues in Minority Health.* Washington, DC: Author; 1985.
31. U.S. Department of Health and Human Services. *Report of the Secretary's Task Force on Black & Minority Health, Volume III: Cancer.* Washington, DC: Author; 1986.
32. U.S. Department of Health and Human Services. *Report of the Secretary's Task Force on Black & Minority Health, Volume IV: Cardiovascular and Cerebrovascular Disease, Parts 1 and 2.* Washington, DC: Author; 1986.
33. U.S. Department of Health and Human Services. *Report of the Secretary's Task Force on Black & Minority Health, Volume V: Homicide, Suicide, and Unintentional Injuries.* Washington, DC: Author; 1986.
34. U.S. Department of Health and Human Services. *Report of the Secretary's Task Force on Black & Minority Health, Volume VI: Infant Mortality and Low Birthweight.* Washington, DC: Author; 1986.
35. U.S. Department of Health and Human Services. *Report of the Secretary's Task Force on Black & Minority Health, Volume VII: Chemical Dependency and Diabetes.* Washington, DC: Author; 1986.
36. U.S. Department of Health and Human Services. *Report of the Secretary's Task Force on Black & Minority Health, Volume VIII: Hispanic Health Issues, Inventory of DHHS Programs, and Survey of Non-Federal Community.* Washington, DC: Author; 1986.
37. Trevino F. National statistical data systems and the Hispanic collection. In: U.S. Department of Health and Human Services. *Report of the Secretary's Task Force on Black & Minority Health, Volume VIII: Hispanic Health Issues, Inventory of DHHS Programs, and Survey of Non-Federal Community.* Washington, DC: U.S. Department of Health and Human Services; 1986: 45–52.
38. Torres-Gil F. An examination of factors affecting future cohorts of elderly Hispanics. *The Gerontologist* 1986; 26:140–146.
39. Van Den Berghe L. Review of Jonathan Udell's *Toward Conceptual Codification in Race and Ethnic Relations. Social Forces* 1983; 62:564–565
40. Myers, HF. Coronary heart disease in black populations: Current research, treatment, and prevention needs. In: U.S. Department of Health and Human Services. *Report of the Secretary's Task Force on Black & Minority Health, Volume IV: Cardiovascular and Cerebrovascular Disease, Part 2.* Washington, DC: U.S. Department of Health and Human Services: 1986: 303–344.
41. Sussman MB. The family life of old people. In: Binstock H, Shanas E, eds. *Handbook of Aging and the Social Sciences* (2nd ed.). New York: Van Nostrand Reinhold; 1985: 415–449.

42. Jackson JJ, ed. *Proceedings of the Research Conference on Minority Group Aged in the South.* Durham, NC: Duke University; 1972 (mimeographed). [These are the proceedings of the first federally funded conference on black and other minority aged.]
43. Cohen CI, Teresi J, Himes D. Social networks, stress, and physical health: a longitudinal study of an inner-city elderly population. *Journal of Gerontology* 1985; 40:478–486.
44. Haug MR. Age and medical care utilization patterns. *Journal of Gerontology* 1981; 36:103–111.
45. Homan SM, Haddock CC, Winner CA, Coe RM, Wolinsky FD. Widowhood, sex, labor force participation, and the use of physician services by elderly adults. *Journal of Gerontology* 1986; 41:793–796.
46. Kushman JE, Freeman BK. Service consciousness and service knowledge among older Americans. *International Journal of Aging and Human Development* 1986; 23:217–237
47. Sharp K, Ross CE, Cockerham WC. Symptoms, beliefs, and the use of physician services among the disadvantaged. *Journal of Health and Social Behavior* 1983; 24:255–263.

6

Social Participation in Later Life: Black–White Differences

Linda K. George

Social scientists have long viewed social participation as an important and rewarding component of social life. Social participation refers to meaningful involvement in formal and informal groups—and its significance for personal well-being is considerably more complex and pervasive than this simple definition suggests. Social participation serves several important functions for the individual, including the provision of (1) sources of social and personal identity, (2) networks within which services are both given (thus generating feelings of usefulness) and received, and (3) sources of meaning for life experiences (1–3). Social participation also benefits the society by (1) ensuring that members perform important social roles and tasks and (2) providing a form of social control that reduces the risks of asocial or antisocial behaviors (3).

This chapter examines black–white differences in social participation among older adults and is divided into five sections. First, a detailed discussion of the nature, antecedents, and consequences of social participation in later life is presented. This is followed by a brief review of methodological obstacles that limit our understanding of black–white differences in social participation among older adults. The two major sections examine available evidence concerning black–white differences in social participation during later life. One section focuses on participation in formal groups; the other addresses involvement in informal groups. The final section pro-

Preparation of this paper was supported by grant AG00371 and contract AG4-2110 from the National Institute on Aging.

poses an agenda for future research and briefly describes surveys currently in progress that offer methodologically superior data bases for examining black–white differences in social participation during later life and linking levels of social participation to relevant outcomes.

THE SIGNIFICANCE OF SOCIAL PARTICIPATION

Traditionally, social participation has been viewed as a social resource, yielding social rewards. Participation in social groups has been linked, for example, to more stable identities and increased feelings of self-worth, to perceptions of usefulness and social cohesion, to the availability of social support during times of crisis or need, and to perceptions that life is meaningful (1–3).

In gerontological research, the primary consequence to which social participation has been causally linked also is a social resource: subjective well-being (or, as this overarching perception of life quality is variously termed, life satisfaction or morale). These studies have been characterized by considerable diversity in the specific dimensions of social participation examined and in the ways that even conceptually similar dimensions of social participation are operationalized. And, indeed, results are not uniformly consistent across studies. Nonetheless, taken as a whole, the research base suggests that social participation is an efficacious determinant of subjective well-being.

The benefits of social participation, however, may extend beyond the social arena. Some authors suggest that social participation may contribute to life quality via positive effects upon physical and mental health (4) and even the quantity of life via direct effects upon longevity (5). Given the methodological difficulties of available studies, however, the premise that social participation contributes directly to health and longevity should be viewed as a promising hypothesis rather than documented fact. Nonetheless, the likelihood that social participation has far-reaching implications for life quality highlights its importance as a topic for systematic review and further empirical study.

Informal and Formal Groups

The definition of social participation used here includes involvement in both formal and informal groups. Formal groups are socially recognized units that (1) exist independently of the individuals who participate in them, (2) actively recruit and/or select members (who may be required to meet formal eligibility criteria), (3) have an explicit purpose or mandate, and (4) have formal structures governing their operation. Examples of formal groups include voluntary organizations, political parties, and religious organizations. Informal groups, in contrast, have much less social recognition, rely more heavily upon the desires and personalities of members, and often have diffuse mandates and fluid structures. Friendship networks and recreational groups are examples of informal groups. The major differences between formal and informal groups, then, are in the areas of social visibility, rigidity of structure, and independence of the unit from the personal idiosyncracies of members.

Traditionally, sociologists focused upon the importance of participation in formal groups because of their superiority in providing individuals with links to the social structure. In addition, formal groups are viewed as providing more direct benefits to society itself because of their greater potential for social control (3). More recently, sociologists recognized that informal groups provide greater benefits to members than had previously been acknowledged. This is especially obvious in the burgeoning research base documenting the importance of social support for avoiding and/or ameliorating stress, facilitating effective coping, and linking individuals to appropriate bureaucratic structures (6, 7). Efforts to determine the relative importance of participation in formal versus informal groups are ultimately misguided. Rather, each type of group offers benefits to participants and each is best suited to serving different functions. The ideal situation is to be actively involved in both types of groups, and increased participation in one type is unlikely to compensate for decrements in the other.

Although the distinction between formal and informal groups is conceptually useful, it is less than precise in reality. The boundaries between formal and informal groups are fuzzy and permeable. Informal networks often develop as spinoffs of formal group participation—as, for example, when one's friends are one's co-workers or members of a church form a bowling league. The reverse (i.e., informal participation leading to affiliation with a formal group) also is very common. Members of an organization, for example, often recruit new members from friends, neighbors, and kin. In addition, many formal groups began as informal groups of individuals with similar interests or concerns. The family poses a special challenge to those interested in distinguishing between formal and informal groups. More than any other social unit, the family straddles the formal–informal line. The family is a formal group in the sense that it is socially recognized and, to some extent, socially controlled. But the family also is an informal group in terms of its salience for personal identity and its preferential status as a source of intimacy and mutual support.

Age and Social Participation

Much, probably most, of the gerontological literature assumes that aging is accompanied by decreased levels of social participation (3, 8). And, clearly, a number of highly visible events (e.g., retirement, widowhood) suggesting decrements in social participation are common during later life. Though this assumption is widely accepted, however, it is not correct—at minimum, it is oversimplistic.

One of the uncertainties about this assumption concerns its basic premise about change over time. Most gerontologists clearly imply that the transition to old age involves an intraindividual decrease in levels of social participation. And yet, most of the evidence concerning the relationship between age and social participation is based on cross-sectional rather than longitudinal data.

A second complicating issue is the distinction between participation in formal and informal groups. To the extent that older people exhibit less social involvement than their younger peers, this pattern appears to be specific to participation in *formal* groups (9, 10). And, indeed, loss of roles in formal groups may increase the time available for participation in informal groups (e.g., Palmore, Fillenbaum, and George found that retirement leads to increased time spent with friends) (11). Moreover, *within* the categories of formal and informal groups, there is undoubtedly great variation in levels and patterns of participation during later life. For example, although levels of labor-force participation decline dramatically during later life, available evidence suggests that older adults are as likely as their younger peers to be politically active (12). Thus, any overall generalization about the relationship between age and social participation is likely to be misleading. A variety of patterns is likely, with some types of participation exhibiting declines during later life, others displaying stability, and still others exhibiting increases.

A final relevant issue is that of thresholds or how much social participation is enough (13). Does every hour spent in social participation add to life quality? Or is there a threshold level or optimal range of social participation—below which life quality is compromised, but above which further increments lead to diminishing returns? This is an important and largely unexplored question. The relevant research question may not be whether aging leads to decreases in social participation—but rather whether and under what conditions older people are at risk of falling below the threshold level of social participation necessary to reap the benefits of group membership.

Race and Social Participation

The same arguments posited concerning the relationship between age and social participation have been made regarding the relationship between race and social participation—perhaps because both older adults and blacks have been viewed as minority groups (14). Thus it is generally assumed that, compared to whites, blacks are disadvantaged in terms of social participation. The major factors believed to account for black–white differences in social participation are restricted access to social groups as a result of racial discrimination, cultural differences in preferred levels of social participation, and socioeconomic obstacles that discourage social participation. Again, however, the accuracy of the conclusion that blacks exhibit lower levels of social participation merits qualification and refinement.

Two of the criticisms raised with regard to the assumed relationship between age and social participation are equally applicable to racial differences in social participation. First, conclusions about racial differences in social participation depend on the specific form of social participation under consideration. Not all types of social participation are unevenly distributed across racial subgroups. Indeed, blacks may exhibit higher rates of participation than whites in some types of social groups. Second, the threshold issue also may be relevant to racial differences in social participation. Thus aggregate differences in levels of social participation may be less important than whether blacks and whites differ in the likelihood of falling below the minimum threshold associated with beneficial outcomes.

METHODOLOGICAL OBSTACLES

The quality of the literature examining black–white differences in social participation during later life is, unfortunately, less than adequate. A significant proportion of the problem is simply the scarcity of relevant information. Beyond the issue of data scarcity, two methodological issues render existing research highly inadequate for reaching conclusions about black–white differences in social participation: quality of the samples and, especially, neglect of multivariate models.

Quality of Samples

Sample quality is determined largely by two criteria: size and representativeness. Sample size must be sufficient to (1) provide stable estimates of population parameters, (2) permit the multivariate analyses required to untangle causality, and (3) capture the underlying heterogeneity in the population. If possible, samples should be selected using probability procedures to maximize representativeness. In practical terms, random samples of defined populations often are unfeasible. In such cases, investigators nonetheless can and should attempt to maximize sample heterogeneity and caution readers about threats to generalizability.

Criticisms of sample quality could be leveled at most social science research. This problem is particularly acute, however, in aging research in

general and studies of minority elderly in particular. There are some understandable (if not excusable) reasons for these patterns. First, with regard
to both the aged and members of racial or ethnic minorities, it is especially
expensive (in terms of both time and money) to implement a probability-
based sampling strategy. Second, most researchers neglect the strategy of
oversampling certain demographic subgroups to ensure adequate size and
representativeness. The simple fact of the matter is that in most areas of the
United States a random sample of 1,000 adults will not generate sufficient
older adults—and certainly not a sufficient number of older blacks—to
permit stable estimates of age and race differences. Oversampling can be
used to ensure adequate representation of important demographic subgroups. Unfortunately, practice lags considerably behind capabilities.

Some investigators have sampled only older blacks in order to examine
that group in greater depth. Unfortunately, those samples are, on average,
of even poorer quality than those in the gerontological literature as a whole.
In some cases such samples are very small, precluding multivariate analyses
and precluding population estimates. It also appears that a greater proportion of black than white samples are based on convenience rather than
probability sampling. Of particular concern, given the sizable correlations
between race and socioeconomic status, is the fact that most convenience
samples of older blacks exclude or underrepresent middle-class blacks.

There are a few high-quality samples of older black adults. Examples
include the Harris Survey of the Myth and Reality of Aging (15) and the
University of Michigan's National Survey of Black Americans (16).
Nonetheless, most research examining black–white differences in later life,
as well as variation within the older black population, is compromised
because of poor-quality samples.

The Need for Multivariate Models

The need for accurate estimates of the relationships between social
participation and demographic variables such as race and age has already
been noted. Even such estimates, however, would not be sufficient for
understanding the role of social participation in promoting quality of life. In
particular, effort is needed to explicate the antecedents and consequences of
social participation in later life. Multivariate models are required to achieve
those goals.

Let us assume that there are significant black–white differences in levels
of some important types of social participation during later life. What are
the reasons for those differences? Race itself cannot explain the causal
processes that operate to produce those differences. Ultimately, the mechanisms generating racial differences in levels of social participation must be

identified. Two probable explanations for racial differences in social resources are typically offered. First, and most obvious, racial differences are
viewed as the products of socioeconomic differences between blacks and
whites. There is no question that blacks are, on average, socioeconomically
disadvantaged compared to whites in this society. Consequently, many
aggregate differences between blacks and whites are due to socioeconomic
factors and disappear (or are substantially reduced) when income, assets,
occupational status, and educational attainment are controlled. The second
major explanation for racial differences rests on the rather elusive notion of
culture. According to this perspective, blacks retain certain beliefs and social
preferences that are distinctive from those held by the larger society—beliefs
that have emerged from their unique collective history and are transmitted
relatively intact because of intragroup commitment and separation (17, 18).
Obviously these two theories are not mutually exclusive; a racial difference
may be generated by both socioeconomic factors and cultural preferences.

There is an important qualitative difference between these two explanatory schemes. When racial differences reflect the impact of socioeconomic factors, blacks are viewed as experiencing involuntary deprivation
relative to whites. In contrast, racial difference due to cultural factors may
reflect subgroup preferences that are voluntarily generated.

In theory, if relevant variables are measured and statistical modeling is
rigorously performed, it is possible to identify the social factors and processes generating racial differences in social resources. Socioeconomic factors, however, are much easier to measure than cultural factors. Consequently, we are better informed about the effects of socioeconomic factors
than about the effects of culture.

The search for explanatory factors is not the only reason that multivariate
examinations of social participation are needed. The black and white populations also are compositionally different. Gender, age, and other demographic variables are differentially distributed across racial groups (14,
19). Consequently, what appear to be racial differences in social participation may in fact be due to compositional differences in the black and white
populations.

Multivariate analyses also are needed to identify the consequences of
social participation. If social participation is a determinant of life quality, it
must be shown to exert a unique impact upon life quality once other
determinants are taken into account. Current evidence suggests that the
relationships between some kinds of social participation and positive outcomes in later life are spurious. Typically such studies indicate that health
and income lead to both higher levels of social participation and higher
quality of life. Other forms of social participation, however, appear to exert
independent and meaningful influences upon life quality.

A final methodological issue of concern is measurement. Social participation is typically measured in one of two ways: a count of the groups in which a person participates (e.g., number of organizational memberships) or the frequency of/time spent in social participation. Both measurement strategies seek relatively objective information about social participation and index social participation in terms of volume of involvement. These measurement strategies have generated important evidence concerning the distribution and correlates of social participation. Nonetheless, our understanding of social participation might be extended by a more comprehensive assessment strategy. Examination of subjective dimensions of social participation might be profitable. In particular, perceptions of satisfaction with or the adequacy of levels of social participation merit increased attention. There are two rationales for including subjective evaluations of the quality of social participation in future studies. First, it may be the perceived quality of social participation rather than its absolute value that impacts upon life quality. Second, patterns of satisfaction with social participation may help to specify the thresholds of social participation required for positive impact on outcomes of interest.

PARTICIPATION IN FORMAL GROUPS

In this section, black–white differences in participation in formal groups among older adults are examined. Six types of participation are considered: (1) labor-force participation (2) political participation, (3) voluntary organizations, (4) religious participation, (5) marital status, and (6) living arrangements. The latter two could be viewed as participation in informal rather than formal groups, but are included in this section because (1) they are relatively objective indicators of social participation and (2) public programs that are relatively insensitive to patterns of informal affiliation nonetheless recognize and take into account marital status and household composition. This section also examines black–white differences in the relationship between formal participation and quality of life.

This review will focus on relative differences across racial subgroups rather than absolute levels of participation. For example, discussion of voting patterns will focus on whether blacks or whites are more likely to vote, rather than reporting percentages of blacks and whites who voted in recent elections. The rationale for this approach is straightforward; in many studies, the quality of the data is so suspect that I would be uncomfortable reporting population estimates. Poor-quality samples obviously can affect relative as well as absolute differences across racial subgroups. Nonetheless, relative differences are less sensitive than population estimates to unreliability.

Labor-Force Participation

Because of normative beliefs concerning the appropriateness of retirement and economic incentives to retire, the majority of Americans aged 65 and older are not employed and are not seeking work (14, 20, 21). Thus, although there are black–white differences in levels of labor-force participation during later life, they are modest in relation to the similarities created by societal consensus concerning the appropriateness and desirability of retirement. Indeed, in light of substantial black–white differences, on average, in work history, lifetime earnings, and occupational attainment, the similarities in levels of labor-force participation between older blacks and whites are perhaps more surprising than the few differences.

Available data suggest two major black–white differences in levels of labor-force participation during later life. First, there is an interesting race by sex interaction in levels of labor-force participation among persons aged 65 and older. Older black men are slightly less likely to be employed than are older white men. In contrast, older black women are substantially more likely to be employed than their white counterparts (14, 20, 21). There are several possible reasons for this interactions; among the possibilities are that (1) older black men are singled out for the greatest amount of discrimination in the labor market, (2) the patterns reflect lifelong differences in labor-force participation that simply carry over to late life, (3) older black women are at greatest risk of poverty and thus cannot afford to relinquish the economic benefits of employment, and (4) differences in marital status, especially between older black and white women. Any or all of these factors may be part of the observed race/sex differences in labor-force participation in later life. Systematic investigation is needed in order to better explain the reason for this pattern.

A second and better understood black–white difference in labor-force participation concerns the probability of and reasons for early retirement among men. Early retirement refers to departure from the labor force before age 65. Available evidence suggests that there are two distinct subgroups of early retirees: those who retire early because of health problems and those who can afford to retire early and desire a leisure-oriented lifestyle (20). Not surprisingly, given aggregate differences in socioeconomic attainment, black men are overrepresented among the group that retires early in poor health and underrepresented among leisure-oriented early retirees. Available evidence suggests that socioeconomic factors account for this race difference (20, 22).

Political Participation

A thorough understanding of political participation requires examination of its multiple dimensions, including party affiliation, voting behavior, participation in political organizations, and involvement in politics via running for office and leadership roles in political parties. Unfortunately, the gerontological literature reveals little attention to any dimension of political participation, other than voting behavior.

In terms of political affiliation, older blacks are more likely than older whites, by a wide margin, to be registered Democrats. This racial difference in party affiliation is unrelated to age; at all ages, blacks are more likely than whites to affiliate with the Democratic party. This pattern has been stable for 20 to 25 years, since the civil rights movement and the concomitant increased voter registration among blacks (23).

Data concerning voting behavior are plentiful and reveal relatively stable patterns of voting among demographic subgroups during the past 20 to 25 years. There are black–white differences in levels of voting during later life, but it is necessary to consider age, sex, and race differences simultaneously. There is substantial evidence that rates of voting are high and remain stable from middle age until well into old age. Though levels of voting decline somewhat after age 75 (thought to reflect primarily health and mobility problems), older persons are more likely to vote than young adults (12, 14, 24, 25). In terms of gender, at all ages and for both blacks and whites, men are more likely to vote than women (14, 24). Also at all ages and for both sexes, blacks are less likely to vote than whites (12, 14, 25). It should be noted, however, that both the sex and race differences are relatively small, averaging about 5 to 7%.

Although blacks are less likely to vote than whites throughout adulthood, the surprising fact is the small magnitude of the difference. There are three reasons that the small size of the black–white difference in voting is surprising. First, this difference does not take socioeconomic status into account. Education, in particular, is a significant predictor of voting, with higher levels of education predicting higher levels of voting (24). This issue has received almost no attention in the literature. At least one study suggests, however, that blacks may be *more* likely to vote than whites after education is taken into account (2). Second, compared to other racial/ethnic minorities, blacks exhibit substantially *higher* levels of voting—especially compared to Hispanics (14). Thus the relatively high levels of voting among blacks appear to be unique among racial/ethnic groups. Third, the history of black Americans has been characterized by unprecedented political disenfranchisement. At first glance, this historical deprivation might be expected to decrease levels of political participation among blacks. Other authors suggest the opposite, however—that precisely because voting rights have been so hard-earned, black Americans exercise them at high levels (14). Available data largely support the latter interpretation.

There are virtually no data about black–white differences during later life in the remaining dimensions of political participation: involvement in political organizations, leadership in political parties, and running for political office. It seems certain, however, that very small proportions of older blacks and whites are party leaders or political candidates. Nonetheless, information about these dimensions would flesh out our portrait of black–white differences in political participation.

Voluntary Organizations

General literature concerning the determinants of participation in voluntary organizations emphasizes the role of socioeconomic status in predicting both level of participation (with higher socioeconomic status associated with increased participation) and the types of voluntary organizations joined (with higher-status persons more likely to join civic and charitable groups and lower-status individuals more likely to join social or recreational organizations) (26). If these patterns transfer to later life, we would expect that older blacks would be less likely than older whites to belong to voluntary organizations and would affiliate with different kinds of groups. Available research findings are inconsistent with regard to both of these hypotheses.

In terms of sheer numbers of memberships in voluntary organizations, research findings are mixed. In bivariate examinations, some studies report increased participation among older whites, some report increased participation among older blacks, and others report no black–white differences (2, 14, 27, 28). The few multivariate studies available do not clarify this situation. As expected, the major control variable examined has been socioeconomic status. In some cases, controlling on socioeconomic variables reduces or eliminates significant race differences in levels of participation. In other cases, black–white differences remain robust in spite of socioeconomic controls (27, 28). Confident conclusions thus await more definitive research.

There are very few studies of black–white differences in the types of organizations in which older adults participate, and the results of these studies are inconclusive. Most studies suggest that older blacks are more likely than older whites to participate in senior citizen centers and similar age-homogeneous, socially oriented clubs (15, 29–31). Few of these studies take socioeconomic status into account, although some authors suggest (in the absence of multivariate analyses) that this race difference is partly or entirely due to social class (31). There also is limited evidence that older blacks are less likely to join organizations that emphasize educational and informational activities (26). This pattern also may reflect socioeconomic factors.

At this point, confident conclusions about black–white differences in participation in voluntary organizations during later life are not possible.

There are at least two reasons for this beyond the usual problems of poor data quality and neglect of multivariate causal models. First, there are wide variations across studies in the types of organizations included in measures of organizational participation. Of particular importance, some measures include religious organizations and others do not—a topic examined separately below. If there are relationships between race (or socioeconomic status) and the types of organizations with which older adults affiliate, the specific types of clubs included in the measure will affect conclusions about racial differences in levels of participation.

Second, existent literature is insensitive to the fact that participation in voluntary organizations reflects not only personal preferences and the effects of socioeconomic factors, but also access to opportunity structures. For example, many organizations recruit only individuals viewed as desirable members and/or establish eligibility criteria for membership. Thus participation in voluntary organizations reflects, in part, access to recruiters or the ability to meet eligibility criteria. As another illustration of opportunity structures, consider senior citizen centers. A large proportion of government-subsidized senior citizen centers are purposely established in low-income neighborhoods in order to serve populations that have limited access to other social outlets. If black and/or low-income older persons disproportionately belong to senior citizen centers, this may reflect simply their increased access to those kinds of organizations.

Religious Organizations

There is general consensus that the church has been a historically important institution for American blacks. Though a review of the black church is beyond the scope of this chapter, it is important to note briefly that the church has served important functions for blacks, including the provision of a belief system for giving coherent meaning to life and a philosophical system that permitted blacks to cope with social, economic, and political inequities (32). Traditionally, the church served as the major vehicle for organizational participation by American blacks. More recently, the church played a vital role in promoting racial equality, simultaneously helping to keep civil rights efforts within socially acceptable limits and linking those efforts to Judeo-Christian values (32). Religious participation has been important to U.S. whites also, of course. Nonetheless, many social scientists hypothesize that the church plays a more central role in the lives of American blacks than whites.

In terms of black–white differences in religious participation, the common assumption of increased participation by older blacks is based more on stereotype than empirical data. Most studies suggest that there are not significant differences between older blacks and whites in religious affiliation or in frequency of church attendance (14, 15, 33). Findings contrary to this pattern, however, consistently report increased religious involvement among older blacks (34, 35). Overall, firm conclusions about black–white differences in religious participation during later life must await better-quality data and multivariate analyses.

No studies examine black–white differences in religious participation in the context of multivariate statistical controls. The need to examine the relationship between race and religious participation controlling on socio-economic variables is obvious. Beyond that, however, two factors appear to be potentially important control variables. First, there are substantial regional differences in both the geographical distribution of racial subgroups and aggregate levels of religious participation. Compared to whites, blacks tend to be more concentrated in the southeastern United States. In addition, levels of religious participation are significantly higher in the "Bible Belt" of the Southeast. Thus, there may indeed be black–white differences in levels of religious involvement—but they may represent the effects of place of residence rather than race.

Second, it may be important to take type of religion or, among Protestants in particular, specific religious denomination into account. Compared to whites, blacks are more highly concentrated in Protestant churches and, within Protestantism, in specific denominations, especially Baptist churches. If religious denominations provide members with opportunities for varying levels of involvement, racial differences in religious participation may reflect the effects of church affiliation rather than different orientations toward religious involvement.

Marital Status

In this society, the marital bond is viewed as the pivotal link in family formation. This view remains strongly held by both social scientists and the general public in spite of the fact that rates of separation, divorce, and never marrying have increased substantially in the past 20 years. Considerable evidence documents that being married is an especially important social resource during later life. Being married, for example, is positively related to health, income and income adequacy, and the availability of social support (9, 36, 37). And these relationships are significant for both older whites and older blacks (36).

Unlike most dimensions of formal participation, there is plentiful, high-quality data about black–white differences in marital status during later life—and those differences are substantial. Prior to reviewing those differences, however, it must be noted that sex is a far more powerful predictor of marital status in later life than race (38). Overall, older men (both black and white) are nearly twice as likely to be married as their female peers—primarily reflecting the increased longevity of women and the higher remarriage rates of men.

Turning to racial differences, older whites (both men and women) are much more likely to be married than older blacks (38). In addition, there are considerable differences between the distributions of unmarried older blacks and whites. Greater proportions of older blacks than whites are widowed, separated, and divorced. It is only among the never married that older blacks and whites are found in similar proportions (38).

When sex and race differences are jointly considered, an interesting pattern emerges. Older black women are least likely to be married, followed by older white women, older black men, and older white men. The reverse order is observed for widowhood. The pattern for separation and divorce is somewhat different. Older black women are most likely to be divorced or separated. But they are followed, in descending order, by older black men, older white women, and older white men. Thus older white men are consistently most advantaged in terms of marital status and older black women are consistently most disadvantaged (38).

Black–white differences in marital status during later life reflect, in part, the effects of socioeconomic status. Even with such controls, however, the general pattern of black–white differences remains substantial (38). The race differences observed among older adults also are exhibited by middle-aged adults (38). This pattern suggests that black–white differences in marital status emerge relatively early in life and are carried over to old age. It will be interesting to observe racial differences in marital status during later life among future cohorts. Given increasing rates of divorce and never marrying, especially among whites, racial differences in marital status may be reduced in future cohorts of older adults.

Living Arrangements

One reason that marriage is a social resource during later life is because spouses share living quarters, thus benefiting from the economies of shared living and a proximate source of social support. And because most older couples live as independent nuclear dyads, living arrangements of older adults are highly correlated with marital status. Nonetheless, living arrangements are more complex than marital status and merit separate examination. Unmarried blacks and whites, for example, may differ in the likelihood of living alone. Moreover, some authors suggest that older blacks may be more likely than their white peers to live in intergenerational households.

As was true for marital status, there is considerable data of good quality concerning the living arrangements of older adults. These data reveal both similarities and differences between older blacks and whites (39). There are five major similarities in the living arrangements of older blacks and whites. First, in both races, a majority of older adults living in families are in households headed by an older adult (as either household head or spouse of head). Second, for both races, a majority of adults aged 65 to 74 live in family-based households. In contrast, a majority of adults aged 75 and older do not live in family-based households (i.e., they live alone or with unrelated individuals). Third, for both races, widowed and divorced older adults are more likely to live alone than the never married (and, of course, all un-married older adults are more likely to live alone than their married peers). Fourth, older women (both blacks and whites) are more likely than older men to live alone or with unrelated individuals. Finally, most aged blacks and whites do not live with their children (39).

In spite of these similarities, there also are significant black–white differences in living arrangements among older adults. Overall, older blacks are less likely than older whites to live in family-based households consisting of only the marital dyad. Thus, because older blacks and whites are equally likely to live in family-based households, larger proportions of blacks live in households with relatives other than or in addition to their spouses. In particular, older blacks are more likely to live with their children (i.e., children of any age) and to live in households in which at least one member is less than 18 years old (39). Thus the proportion of intergenerational households is significantly larger among aged blacks.

Again, socioeconomic factors appear to explain most, but not all, of the black–white differences in living arrangements during later life (19, 40). The usual explanation for this finding is that financial deprivations promote intergenerational households among older blacks. Differences not due to socioeconomic factors have not been well explained but may represent cultural preferences or conditions that are not directly linked to financial resources, such as poorer health of older blacks or decreased marital stability among middle-aged and younger blacks. Moreover, most of these studies control only on the financial status of the household head. It may be, however, that intergenerational households reflect the socioeconomic status of other adult members as well as that of the household head. Thus previous studies may underestimate the total effects of socioeconomic factors on black–white differences in living arrangements during later life.

In contrast to other indicators of formal participation (where more can generally be assumed to be better), it is difficult to identify optimal living arrangements for older adults. On the one hand, living alone appears to be less advantageous, on average, than having at least one other household member available as a source of social support. On the other hand, it is not clear that multiple household members are preferable to a single co-resident. It is particularly unclear whether intergenerational households, especially those including minor children, are advantageous living arrangements for older household members. As long as (1) most Americans (both black and white) express an attitudinal preference for family generations maintaining separate households (15, 41) and (2) intergenerational households are largely explained by financial exigencies, we cannot know whether the disproportionate number of older blacks living in intergenerational households are advantaged or disadvantaged.

Formal Participation and Quality of Life

For the purposes of this chapter, quality of life is defined as including feelings of satisfaction with life, health, and mental health. As noted earlier, it is commonly assumed that formal social participation is conducive to quality of life. In terms of older adults, however, this assumption has not yet been convincingly supported—though it certainly has not been refuted either. The majority of evidence bearing on this assumption concerns the impact of formal participation on life satisfaction—and even it is inconclusive.

Labor-force participation has been repeatedly documented to have non-signficant effects on life satisfaction, which is not surprising given the normative nature of the retirement transition (42–44). The effects of political participation on life satisfaction have not been examined. Results concerning the effects of participation in voluntary organizations and religious participation are inconsistent. Some studies report these forms of formal participation are significantly related to life satisfaction (with other predictors statistically controlled) (35, 45); other studies fail to detect significant relationships (46, 47). Results concerning the impact of marital status are substantial, significant, and consistent: married older adults are more satisfied, on average, than the unmarried (42, 48, 49). Living arrangements also appear to be related to life satisfaction in most studies, with the crucial distinction being between those who live alone versus those who do not. As expected, those who live alone report lower levels of life satisfaction (9, 42). Some studies that fail to detect significant direct effects suggest that formal participation nonetheless influences life satisfaction indirectly through effects on more proximate predictors. These findings should not be overlooked, because they, too, document the importance of social participation for quality of life.

Very few studies of the determinants of life satisfaction include examination of black–white differences in the impact of formal participation. Overall, these studies suggest that there are few black–white differences (50, 51). There are dissenting opinions, however. Ortega, Crutchfield, and Rushing, for example, found that older blacks reported higher levels of life satisfaction than older whites—and that the higher levels of religious participation among blacks in the sample fully explained the difference (34). Black–white differences in the role of formal participation in promoting life satisfaction clearly merit more systematic inquiry.

The impact of formal participation on health and mental health is unknown—and there also is no information about race differences in the effects of formal participation on health and mental health outcomes. This lack of knowledge is largely due to the fact that these issues have not been empirically examined. But that is not totally the case. A number of previous studies report significant, positive relationships between health or mental health and dimensions of formal participation, such as labor-force participation and membership in voluntary organizations. Unfortunately, these relationships are based on cross-sectional data and causal order remains unclear.

INFORMAL PARTICIPATION

In this section, black–white differences in participation in informal groups during later life are examined. Two types of informal participation are examined: (1) involvement in friendship networks and (2) involvement in family-based social support networks. Although there is a substantial amount of research on family-based social support networks, that literature will be only briefly summarized because Chapter 12 of this volume focuses specifically on those issues. This section also reviews evidence concerning black–white differences in the role of informal social participation in promoting quality of life in old age.

Friendship Networks

Information about friendship networks during later life is limited in volume and methodological rigor. Some investigators report that friendships increase in later life—that size of the friendship network and time spent with friends increase as employment roles and other responsibilities are relinquished (11). Other authors, however, report decreases in the number of friends and time spent with friends in later life (35, 52–56). From this perspective, the conditions of later life—including role loss, health problems, transportation difficulties, and decreased financial resources—are obstacles to friendship involvement (57). Both perspectives may be accurate—older persons with high levels of social resources may increase their friendship involvement; those without adequate resources may find friendship an unaffordable luxury.

The literature reveals almost no systematic comparisons of the friendship involvement of older blacks and whites. Data from two surveys of older adults suggest that older blacks have fewer friends and spend less time with friends, on average, than older whites (35, 56). Nonetheless, these differences are small, and there are no apparent racial differences in satisfaction with either number of friends or frequency of friend interactions (15, 35). In addition, for both races and at all ages, women report more friends than men—and the size of the sex difference is much larger than race or age differences (53). Data from this same study suggest that the observed racial differences are almost totally explained by socioeconomic status. Moreover, black–white differences in friendship networks among older adults appear to be a carryover of patterns observed among young and middle-aged adults.

Research findings are inconsistent, however. Ortega, Crutchfield, and Rushing, using data from a sample of older residents of a southern community, reported that blacks had more friends and spent more time with friends than whites—and that those differences increased when socioeconomic variables were controlled (34). Moreover, both black and white respondents reported more friendship involvement than is typically reported in other studies. The authors recognize the discrepancies between their results and those of other investigators and suggest that social structure in the South may be especially supportive of the friendship networks of older adults.

A relatively broad body of research suggests the importance of age density for friendship in later life—and this issue may help account for social-class differences in friendship involvement. In the classic study of this type, Rosow found that the higher the proportion of older adults in the immediate environment (i.e., the neighborhood), the larger the friendship networks of older residents, the more time they spent with friends, and the more satisfied they were with life (58). Age density also was more important for lower-class than middle-class older persons. Rosow suggested that middle-class older adults have the financial resources to engage in active friendship networks at a distance, whereas lower-class persons are more dependent upon opportunities in the immediate environment. A number of studies support the relationship between age density and friendship involvement among older adults (8, 59). Although a number of these studies, including Rosow's pioneering work, included racially mixed samples, no investigators have reported black–white differences in the effects of age density on friendship networks.

Other studies of a more qualitative nature suggest that the nature of friendship varies substantially along class lines (53). Compared to middle-class persons, working- and lower-class individuals are more likely to (1) maintain sex-segregated friendship networks (60), (2) prefer to spend leisure time with family rather than friends (53, 60), and (3) engage in less self-disclosure with friends (60). Overall, these differences suggest that friendship may be less central to the identities and, perhaps, well-being of working- and lower-class individuals. There are no data concerning either black–white or age differences in these qualitative dimensions of friendship involvement. One possible exception to this conclusion is the phenomenon of "para-kin," noted in several studies of lower-class blacks (61, 62). Para-kin are unrelated individuals with whom interpersonal relationships are so close that they are viewed as family members.

Family-Based Social Support Systems

The previous description of black–white differences in marital status and living arrangements provided information relevant to the availability of family- or household-based social support. The availability of social support is distinct, however, from actual participation in supportive exchanges. Moreover, older adults are providers as well as recipients of social support. In order to understand older adults' participation in family-based support systems, the flow of supportive services must be examined both to and from the older adult.

There is general consensus that older adults typically maintain active relationships with offspring and other relatives (9, 36, 63). Any fears that older Americans are deserted by or isolated from their families have been laid to rest by a large body of empirical research. There also is general consensus that receipt of supportive services—including companionship, household tasks, nursing care, and direct financial transfers—increases during later life (9, 36, 63).

There are black–white differences in family interaction and levels of social support during later life. Nonetheless, those differences are modest in relation to the similarities across races. Both older blacks and whites are in frequent contact with relatives, especially children (15, 19, 40, 64); both groups are typically active participants in family-based support systems (15, 19, 64). Two specific patterns also have been replicated in multiple studies for both older blacks and whites. First, older women are both in more frequent contact with their families and more frequently receive supportive services from family members (36, 65, 66). There are several possible reasons for this gender difference, though previous research does not identify which are operative. Women may initiate more contact with family members or, alternately, family members may seek more contact with older female relatives. In terms of social support, women may have a greater need for such services (e.g., they may be financially worse off, in poorer health, or less likely to be married). Or their increased interaction (and perhaps closeness) to other family members may increase the likelihood of social support.

The second similarity between blacks and whites is what Marjorie Cantor refers to as the principle of compensatory substitution in the allocation of family members to the role of major helper or caregiver for impaired older relatives (65). This principle posits that there is a hierarchy by which persons take on responsibility for providing supportive services to impaired older family members. This hierarchy is based on both kinship and sex. Spouses, if available, are the first source of social support. If the older person is widowed, children become the major providers of social support—especially daughters or daughters-in-law. If neither spouse nor children are available, more distant relatives, including siblings and grandchildren, are turned to for social support. This hierarchical scheme is applicable to both blacks and whites (64, 65, 67–69).

Although patterns of family interaction and support are similar among older blacks and whites, there also are differences across the two groups. First, most (but not all) comparisons of older blacks and whites suggest that, in absolute terms, older blacks interact more frequently with and receive higher levels of social support from family members (19, 34, 40, 64, 70, 71). Second, there is general consensus that older blacks are more likely than their white peers to provide social support services to other family members (19, 40).

Multivariate analyses have been used to examine both of these black–white differences, controlling on the effects of other demographic variables, especially socioeconomic variables. The results of those analyses are inconclusive. Some studies suggest that older blacks retain their advantage in frequency of family interaction and support after socioeconomic factors are controlled (19, 64, 70); other suggest that the race difference disappears in the face of statistical controls (40, 71). Only a few investigators have applied multivariate controls to measures of social support provided to other family members by older adults. Results of these studies indicate that the difference remains significant, net of socioeconomic variables (19, 40).

Informal Participation and Quality of Life

As was true for formal participation, it is commonly assumed that informal participation is conducive to quality of life—that frequent and supportive interactions with friends and relatives impact favorably on life satisfaction, health, and mental health. Considerable evidence suggests that this conclusion is reasonable for satisfaction during later life. A broad body of research has examined the relationships between family and friend interaction and life satisfaction. A majority of relevant studies indicate that interaction with significant others is a powerful predictor of life satisfaction, net of relevant controls (19, 31, 35, 45, 72, 73). Two caveats must be appended to this conclusion, however. First, family interaction is a more powerful predictor of life satisfaction than interaction with friends—indeed, some studies do not find the latter to be a significant predictor net of other controls (34, 35,

74). Second, studies of life satisfaction typically do not include measures of the assistance received from others. The few studies that include such measures are based on specialized samples (typically caregivers), but they suggest that social support is a significant predictor of life satisfaction (75, 76).

Only a few studies have examined whether the effects of family and friend interactions upon life satisfaction differ for older blacks and whites. The results of those studies are inconsistent. Some find informal participation to be important for both racial groups (34, 45, 72). Two studies, however, report frequency of family interaction to be a significant predictor of life satisfaction only for older whites (50, 77).

No conclusions can be made about the effects of informal participation on health and mental health. Similar to evidence for formal participation, the overarching problems are scarcity of studies examining these topics among older adults and problems of causal order. Claims that informal participation has health and/or mental health benefits during later life await empirical substantiation—as does examination of black–white differences in those relationships.

FUTURE DIRECTIONS

Throughout this review, areas in which data are lacking, methodological problems, and threats to the validity of available findings have been highlighted. There is no need to repeat those issues here. In this final section, two issues will be addressed: (1) an assessment of what is most needed by researchers examining black–white differences in social participation and quality of life during old age and (2) a brief description of data collection efforts in progress that may be suitable candidates for future analyses in this area.

Perhaps the greatest obstacle to advancing our understanding of black–white differences in social participation in later life is the scarcity of suitable data bases. In order to add to the current knowledge base, future data sources will have to meet three criteria: samples must (1) be of high quality, including adequate numbers of older blacks and whites; (2) include adequate measures of social participation, outcome measures, and relevant control variables; and (3) be longitudinal to permit clarification of causal order. Though these criteria are straightforward, development of a data base that meets them would be a major undertaking.

To my knowledge, no existing data base meets these criteria. There are a few surveys that meet the first criteria—having adequate numbers of older blacks and whites selected on the basis of probability techniques. Those surveys, however, are deficient in terms of the scope and adequacy of measures of social participation and health/mental health outcomes. Perhaps most importantly, they are not longitudinal. Measurement issues require considerable effort. One of the reasons that the effects of social participation on health and mental health are unknown is that most social surveys include, at best, only rudimentary measures of physical and mental health. A single-item measure of self-rated health, for example, is simply not an adequate assessment of physical health. Multidisciplinary teams may be needed to design an interview schedule capable of measuring social participation and its hypothesized consequences with sufficient precision to permit valid conclusions. And, of course, longitudinal data—preferably collected on multiple occasions over a period of years—will be required before temporal order can be unraveled.

I would like to end this chapter on an optimistic note. That can be accomplished by briefly describing two federally initiated multisite research efforts that will be superior to those currently available and offer important opportunities for learning about black–white differences during later life. One of these efforts is the Epidemiologic Catchment Area Program, supported by NIMH; the other is the Established Populations for Epidemiologic Studies of the Elderly, initiated by NIA.

Epidemiologic Catchment Area (ECA) Program

The major goals of the ECA Program are to (1) estimate the prevalence and 1-year incidence of specific psychiatric disorders among American adults; (2) identify the social and environmental risk factors of psychiatric disorder; and (3) estimate the treated and untreated prevalences of mental illness, as well as identify barriers to health service use. Five geographically dispersed universities participated in the ECA effort: Yale University, surveying greater New Haven; Johns Hopkins University, surveying East Baltimore; Washington University, surveying greater St. Louis; Duke University, surveying one urban and four rural counties in north-central North Carolina; and UCLA, surveying East Los Angeles.

Several identical design features were implemented across the five ECA sites. At each site, multistage probability sampling was used to generate samples of at least 3,000 community and 500 institutional residents aged 18 and older. Institutional respondents were selected from three strata: nursing and rest homes, prisons, and long-term psychiatric facilities. Three of the sites—Yale, Johns Hopkins, and Duke—also surveyed oversamples of community-dwelling older adults (in addition to the 3,000 respondents comprising the "core" community samples). Data were collected on three occasions: two personal interviews, a year apart, and a brief telephone interview, 6 months after the first personal interview (78).

A rich body of data was collected during the personal interviews. (The telephone survey focused on health-service use and changes in basic social circumstances and will not be discussed further.) Topics covered in the interview schedule included: mental health, physical health, demographic characteristics, socioeconomic status, use of health and mental health services, use of psychotropic drugs and other medications, formal and informal social participation, and stressful life events. Of particular interest is the detailed and sophisticated measurement of mental illness. The Diagnostic Interview Schedule (DIS) was administered to all ECA participants. The DIS is a recent development in psychiatric epidemiology. It measures the presence or absence of specific psychiatric disorders (rather than symptom counts or level of impairment) and operationalizes the diagnostic criteria of DSM-III (i.e., the diagnostic criteria of standard psychiatric practice) (79).

The ECA data will provide a unique opportunity to examine black–white differences in later life. The three ECA sites that included oversamples of the elderly include sufficient numbers of older blacks and whites to permit reliable racial comparisons. The Duke ECA site, in particular, was chosen in part because the population permits simultaneous consideration of black–white and urban–rural differences. From the perspective of social participation, the ECA data are particularly exciting because of the opportunity to examine black–white differences in social participation during later life and to link social participation to mental health outcomes. The ECA data base is not ideal—it is longitudinal, but only covers a 1-year interval, and some of the measures outside the mental health domain are less detailed than is optimal. Nonetheless, careful analysis of the ECA data promises to generate important knowledge about social participation in later life.

Established Populations for Epidemiologic Studies of the Elderly (EPESE)

The major goals of the EPESE are to (1) estimate the prevalence and incidence of physical illnesses, conditions, and types of disability in later life; (2) monitor significant health-related events (i.e., hospitalizations, mortality, and institutionalization) and identify the antecedents of those events, and (3) through the activities of related clinical studies, obtain new information about the mechanisms underlying illness and disability in later life. Four universities are participating in the EPESE Program: Harvard University, surveying East Boston; Yale University, surveying greater New Haven; the University of Iowa, surveying two rural Iowa counties; and Duke University, surveying one urban and four rural countries in north-central North Carolina.

Several common design features were implemented at the four EPESE sites. Large and representative samples of community-dwelling adults aged

65 and older were surveyed at each site. The Harvard, Yale, and Iowa samples include approximately 3,000 older adults; the Duke sample is targeted at 4,200 older adults. Data are being collected on five occasions, on an annual basis. On the first and fourth test dates, detailed personal interviews are administered. On the other occasions, brief telephone interviews focus on changes in physical health and health-service use. The personal interviews generate a broad body of data about EPESE participants. Interview topics include detailed questions about physical illness, disability, and activities of daily living; screening instruments for cognitive impairment and depression; demographic and socioeconomic characteristics; a detailed inventory of medications; and questions about formal and informal social participation.

The EPESE program also will generate an important data base for examining black–white differences in later life. Only the Duke EPESE data will permit systematic racial comparisons. The size and representativeness of that sample are clearly adequate, the scope of data collected offers opportunities for multivariate modeling, and longitudinal data covering a relatively lengthy interval will be available. The EPESE data will be especially useful for relating social participation to specific health outcomes. Again, the data base is not ideal. Many social variables are measured in rather simplistic ways because of limitations in the length of the interview. Nonetheless, the EPESE data will generate important information about black–white differences in later life.

Interest in social participation and its possible benefits is a longstanding interest of social scientists. In spite of its central role in social science theory, empirical data about the nature, distribution, and consequences of social participation remain fragmented and methodologically compromised. Hence our conclusions must be speculative. Late life in general, and racial differences during later life in particular, offer strategic arenas for exploring the nature and consequence of social participation. In addition, variability in social participation among older blacks clearly merits increased attention.

REFERENCES

1. Theodorson GA, Theodorson AG. *Modern Dictionary of Sociology.* New York: Thomas Y. Crowell; 1969.
2. Rubenstein DI. An examination of social participation found among a national sample of black and white elderly. *International Journal of Aging and Human Development* 1971; 2:172–188.
3. Rosow I. *Socialization to Old Age.* Berkeley: University of California Press; 1974.

4. Scheidt RJ, Windley PG. The mental health of small-town rural elderly residents: an expanded ecological model. *Journal of Gerontology* 1983; 38:465–471.

5. Palmore E. The relative importance of social factors in predicting longevity. In: Palmore E, Jeffers FC, eds. *Prediction of Life Span*. Lexington, MA: D.C. Heath, 1971:237–248.

6. Gottlieb BH. Social networks and social support in community mental health. In: Gottlieb BH, ed. *Social Networks and Social Support*. Beverly Hills: Sage, 1981:11–42.

7. House JS. *Work Stress and Social Support*. Reading, MA: Addison-Wesley; 1981.

8. Hochschild AR. *The Unexpected Community*. Berkeley: University of California Press, 1973.

9. George LK. *Role Transitions in Later Life*. Monterey, CA: Brooks/Cole; 1980.

10. George LK. Socialization, roles and identity in later life. In: Kerckhoff AC, ed. *Research in the Sociology of Education and Socialization, Volume IV: Personal Change Over the Life Course*. Greenwich, CT: JAI Press; 1983: 235–263.

11. Palmore EB, Fillenbaum GG, George LK. Consequences of retirement. *Journal of Gerontology* 1984; 39:109–116.

12. Hudson RB, Binstock RH. Political systems and aging. In: Binstock RH, Shanas E, eds. *Handbook of Aging and the Social Sciences*. New York: Van Nostrand Reinhold; 1976:369–400.

13. Lowenthal MF, Haven C. Interaction and adaptation: intimacy as a critical variable. *American Sociological Review* 1968; 33:20–30.

14. Jackson JJ. *Minorities and Aging*. Belmont, CA: Wadsworth; 1980.

15. Harris L. *The Myth and Reality of Aging in America*. Washington DC: National Council on Aging; 1975.

16. National Survey of the Black Aged. *Social Security Bulletin* 1978; 41:33–35.

17. Holzberg CS. Ethnicity and aging: anthropological perspectives on more than just the minority elderly. *Gerontologist* 1982; 22:249–257.

18. Rosenthal CJ. Family supports in later life: does ethnicity make a difference? *Gerontologist* 1986; 26:19–24.

19. Mutran E. Intergenerational family support among blacks and whites: response to culture or to socioeconomic differences? *Journal of Gerontology* 1985; 40:382–389.

20. Palmore E, Burchett B, Fillenbaum GG, George LK, Wallman L. *Retirement: Causes and Consequences*. New York: Springer; 1985.

21. Jackson JJ. Race, national origin ethnicity, and aging. In: Binstock R, Shanas E, eds. *Handbook of Aging and the Social Sciences (2nd ed.)*. New York: Van Nostrand Reinhold; 1985:264–303.

22. Fillenbaum GG, George LK, Palmore EB. Determinants and consequences of retirement among men of different races and economic levels. *Journal of Gerontology* 1985; 40:85–94.

23. Davis JA. *General Social Surveys, 1972–1984: Cumulative Data*. Chicago: National Opinion Research Center; 1984.

24. Nie N, Verba S, Kim J. Political participation and the life-cycle. *Comparative Politics* 1974; 6:319–340.
25. Brotman HB. Voter participation in November, 1976. *Gerontologist* 1977; 17:157–159.
26. Smith DH. The importance of formal voluntary organizations for society. *Sociology and Social Research* 1966; 50:483–494.
27. Clemente F, Rexroad PH, Hirsch C. The participation of the black aged in voluntary associations. *Journal of Gerontology* 1975; 30:469–472.
28. Hyman H, Wright C. Trends in voluntary association memberships of American adults: replication based on secondary analyses of national sample surveys. *American Sociological Review* 1971; 36:191–206.
29. Ralston PA. Senior center utilization by black elderly adults: social attitudinal and knowledge correlates. *Journal of Gerontology* 1984; 39:224–229.
30. Hanssen AM, Meima HJ, Buckspan LM, Henderson BE, Helbig TL, Fair SH. Correlates to senior center participation. *Gerontologist* 1978: 18:193–199.
31. Tissue T. Social class and the senior citizen center. *Gerontologist* 1971; 11:196–200.
32. Carter A. Religion and the black elderly: the historical basis of social and psychological concerns. In: Manuel R, ed. *Minority Aging: Sociological and Social Psychological Issues.* Westport, CT: Greenwood Press; 1982:191–226.
33. Gray RM, Moberg DO. *The Church and the Older Person.* Grand Rapids, MI: Eerdmans; 1977.
34. Ortega ST, Crutchfield RD, Rushing WA. Race differences in elderly personal well-being. *Research on Aging* 1983; 5:101–118.
35. Palmore E. *Social Patterns in Normal Aging.* Durham, NC: Duke University Press; 1981.
36. Shanas E. The family as a social support system in old age. *Gerontologist* 1979; 19:169–174.
37. Johnson CL. Dyadic family relations and social support. *Gerontologist* 1983; 23:337–343.
38. U.S. Bureau of the Census. *Marital Status and Living Arrangements: March 1981* (Current Population Reports, Series P-20, No. 372). Washington DC: U.S. Government Printing Office; 1982.
39. U.S. Bureau of the Census. *Household and Family Characteristics: March 1982* (Current Population Reports, Series P-20, No. 381). Washington DC: U.S Government Printing Office; 1983.
40. Mitchell J, Register JC. An exploration of family interaction with the elderly by race, socioeconomic status, and residence. *Gerontologist* 1984; 24:48–54.
41. Hanson SL, Sauer WJ, Seelbach WC. Racial and cohort variations in filial responsibility norms. *Gerontologist* 1983; 23:626–631.
42. Larson R. Thirty years of research on the subjective well-being of older Americans. *Journal of Gerontology* 1978; 33:109–129.
43. Streib GF, Schneider CH. *Retirement in American Society.* Ithaca, NY: Cornell University Press; 1971.
44. George LK, Maddox GL. Subjective adaptation to loss of the work role: a longitudinal study. *Journal of Gerontology* 1977; 32:456–462.

45. George LK, Landerman LR. Health and subjective well-being: a replicated secondary data analysis. *International Journal of Aging and Human Development* 1984; 19:133–156.
46. Bull CN, Aucoin JB. Voluntary association participation and life satisfaction: a replicated note. *Journal of Gerontology* 1975; 30:73–76.
47. Cutler SJ. Voluntary association participation and life satisfaction: a cautionary research note. *Journal of Gerontology* 1973; 28:96–100.
48. Hutchinson IW III. The significance of marital status for morale and life satisfaction among lower-income elderly. *Journal of Marriage and the Family* 1975; 37:287–293.
49. Lee GR. Marriage and morale in later life. *Journal of Marriage and the Family* 1978; 40:131–139.
50. Sauer W. Morale of the urban aged: a regression analysis by race. *Journal of Gerontology* 1977; 32:600–608.
51. Jackson JS, Bacon JD, Peterson J. Life satisfaction among the black urban elderly. *Aging and Human Development* 1977; 8:169–179.
52. Walster E, Walster G, Berscheid E. *Equity: Theory and Research*. Boston: Allyn and Bacon; 1978.
53. Bell RR. *Worlds of Friendship*. Beverly Hills: Sage; 1981.
54. Usui WM. Homogeneity of friendship networks of elderly blacks and whites. *Journal of Gerontology* 1984; 39:350–356.
55. Verbrugge LM. The structure of adult friendship choices. *Social Forces* 1977; 56:576–597.
56. Shanas E, Townsend P, Wedderbum D, Friis H, Milhot P, Stehovwer J. *Older People in Three Industrial Societies*. New York: Atherton; 1968.
57. George LK. Non-familial support for older persons: who is out there and how can they be reached? In: Lesnoff-Caravaglia G, ed. *Handbook of Applied Gerontology*. New York: Human Sciences Press; 1987.
58. Rosow I. *Social Integration of the Aged*. New York: Free Press; 1967.
59. Teaff JD, Lawton MP, Nahemow L, Carlson D. Impact of age integration on the well-being of elderly tenants in public housing. *Journal of Gerontology* 1978; 33:130–133.
60. Komarovsky M. *Blue Collar Marriage*. New York: Vintage; 1967.
61. Liebow E. *Tally's Corner: A Study of Negro Streetcorner Men*. Boston: Little, Brown; 1967.
62. Stack CB. *All Our Kin*. New York: Harper & Row; 1974.
63. Lee GR. Kinship in the seventies: a decade review of research and theory. *Journal of Marriage and the Family* 1980; 42:923–934.
64. Cantor MH. The informal support system of New York's inner city elderly: is ethnicity a factor? In: Gelfand DE, Kutzik AJ, eds. *Ethnicity and Aging: Theory, Research and Policy*. New York: Springer; 1979:153–174.
65. Cantor MH. Strain among caregivers: a study of experience in the United States. *Gerontologist* 1983; 23:597–604.
66. Wolf JH, Breslau N, Ford AB, Ziegler HD, Ward A. Distance and contacts: interactions of black urban elderly adults with family and friends. *Journal of Gerontology* 1983; 38:465–471.

67. Chatters LM, Taylor RJ, Jackson JS. Size and composition of the informal helper networks of elderly blacks. *Journal of Gerontology* 1985; 40:605–614.
68. Chatters LM, Taylor RJ, Jackson JS. Aged blacks choices for an informal helper network. *Journal of Gerontology* 1986; 41:94–100.
69. Taylor RJ. The extended family as a source of support to elderly blacks. *Gerontologist* 1985; 25:488–495.
70. Dowd JJ, Bengtson VL. Aging in minority populations: an examination of the double jeopardy hypothesis. *Journal of Gerontology* 1978; 33:427–436.
71. Krishef CH, Yaelin ML. Differential use of informal and formal helping networks among rural elderly black and white Floridians. *Journal of Gerontological Social Work* 1981; 3:45–59.
72. George LK, Okun MA, Landerman R. Age as a moderator of the determinants of life satisfaction. *Research on Aging* 1985; 7:209–233.
73. Creecy RF, Wright R. Morale and informal activity with friends among black and white elderly. *Gerontologist* 1979; 19:544–554.
74. Woods V, Robertson JF. Friendship and kinship interaction: differential effect on the morale of the elderly. *Journal of Marriage and the Family* 1978: 40:367–375.
75. George LK. *Caregiver Well-Being: Correlates and Relationships with Participation in Community Self-Help Groups.* Durham, NC: Duke University Center for the Study of Aging and Human Development; 1983.
76. Mindel CH, Wright R Jr. Satisfaction in multigenerational households. *Journal of Gerontology* 1982; 37:483–489.
77. Usui WM, Keil TJ, Phillips DC. Determinants of life satisfaction: a note on a race-interaction hypothesis. *Journal of Gerontology* 1983; 38:107–110.
78. Eaton WW, Kessler LG, eds. *Epidemiologic Methods in Psychiatry: The NIMH Epidemiologic Catchment Area Program.* New York: Academic Press; 1985.
79. Robins LN, Helzer JE, Croughan J, Ratcliff KF. National Institute of Mental Health Diagnostic Interview Schedule: its history, characteristics and validity. *Archives of General Psychiatry* 1981; 38:381–389.

PART III
Biological and Health Status of Older Black Adults

7

Dietary Intake and Nutritional Status of Older U.S. Blacks: An Overview

Norge W. Jerome

The literature on nutrition and diet pertaining to U.S. blacks over the age of 60 suffers from many of the deficiencies and limitations affecting research on older Americans in general. However, the limitations and deficiencies in the data base are significantly more serious for blacks and other U.S. minority groups than for whites.

Examples of the deficiencies are numerous. We have, for example, no good data on the patterns of food consumption of older blacks residing in the different geographic regions and demographic sites in the United States, particularly for those older than 74 years of age. Also, the literature does not depict, as it does for whites, the dietary patterns and nutritional status of healthy older blacks studied systematically in a prospective research design. The literature is particularly deficient in portraying objective biological differences between blacks and whites that could make a difference in nutritional assessments, for example, iron status, vitamin status, and anthropometric and bone measurements. Moreover, we have no knowledge of the food intake patterns and nutritional status of blacks living in diverse domestic and institutional arrangements throughout the country. In fact, we know practically nothing about how food preparation methods and consumption patterns of blacks change as they age, the physiological and social conditions accompanying or catalyzing dietary change, or the impact of these changes on nutritional status, functional health, and disease onset.

All tables and figures in this chapter are from C. M. Dresser, Division of Health Examination Statistics, National Center for Health Statistics; NHANES I, 1971–1974; NHANES II, 1976–1980.

129

Information of this type is needed at several levels—for policy development, program planning and design, health and nutritional services, and effective nutritional self-care.

AVAILABLE INFORMATION ON NUTRITION AND DIET OF OLDER BLACK AMERICANS

Basically, the available information on the nutrition and diet of older black Americans can be organized into four major categories: (1) cross-sectional national nutrition surveys in which blacks constituted a proportion of the large probability sample of the U.S. civilian noninstitutionalized population, (2) small-scale comparison studies of U.S. blacks and other U.S. subgroups, (3) localized clinic-based or community-based descriptive studies of inner-city residents, and (4) one localized community-based prospective study on dietary change in aging blacks. Information on each of these categories will be addressed in this chapter. This will be followed by a critical evaluation of the data needed to provide quality nutrition services to the aging black population.

Cross-Sectional National Nutrition Surveys

The National Center for Health Statistics (NCHS) has conducted two National Health and Nutrition Examination Surveys (NHANES) to date. NHANES I, conducted from April 1971 through June 1974, was designed to assess overall health status and the nutrition status of the population 1 to 74 years of age. The sample consisted of 28,043 persons; 74% or 20,749 persons were examined (1).

The NHANES II study was conducted from February 1976 through February 1980. It was also designed to assess overall health status and the nutritional status of the population aged 6 months to 74 years. The sample consisted of 27,801 persons; of these, 19,996 (73%) were examined (2). Older adults, aged 55 to 74, constituted 40% of the sample examined in NHANES II, that is, 8,080 persons (2).

Dietary information was obtained by two methods—the 24-hour recall and the food-frequency technique. The 24-hour recall method provided data on the types and amounts of foods and beverages consumed by the respondent during a weekday—the 24 hours prior to the interview. The frequency method provided data on the usual pattern of consumption over the 3 months prior to the interview, with special emphasis on customary daily and weekly consumption habits and on food groups that were rarely or never consumed. Additional dietary information included vitamin and mineral supplements used routinely and the use of table salt.

Data from the 24-hour recalls analyzed by sex and race for adults 55–64 and 65–74 years of age are presented in Tables 7.1 and 7.2 and Figures 7.1 through 7.10. In general, the dietary patterns and nutritional quality of the diets of blacks and whites are similar, particularly for those between the ages of 65 and 74 years. Some differences in dietary-item selection are noted, particularly by those in the 55–64 age group. Data obtained from approximately 15,000 households in the Nationwide Food Consumption Survey (NFCS) conducted by the United States Department of Agriculture (USDA) in 1977–1978 also showed this general phenomenon of consuming from a "common table," regardless of socioeconomic standing (3, 4).

Table 7.1 presents, in descending order, the food groups most prominent in the intake of older Americans. The consumption patterns of blacks and whites 65–74 years of age are more similar than for those 55–64 years of age. Sugar products have an important place in the dietary patterns of blacks in both age categories, but particularly for those 55–64 years of age.

TABLE 7.1 Major Contributing Food Groups[a] to the Intakes of Older Americans

55–64 years		65–74 years	
White	Black	White	Black
SFB[b]	SFB[b]	SFB[b]	SFB[b]
Dairy	Sugar products	Dairy	Dairy
Fruits	Fruits	Fruits	Fruits
Vegetables	Dairy	Vegetables	Sugar products
Sugar products	Grains	Grains	Grains
Grains	Vegetables	Sugar products	Vegetables
Meats	Meats	Meats	Meats

[a]Based on grams of food consumed.
[b]Sugar free beverages.

TABLE 7.2 Median Intakes of Dietary Components That Approached but Did Not Meet Dietary Recommendations in NHANES I or NHANES II

Component	Group
Kilocalories	All those aged 55–74
Carbohydrates	Males aged 55–74
Protein	Most black females
Calcium	All those aged 55–74
Phosphorous	Most black females
Iron	All females and black males aged 65–74
Potassium	All black females and black males aged 65–74
Vitamin A	Majority of those aged 55–74
B-complex vitamins	Majority of those aged 55–74

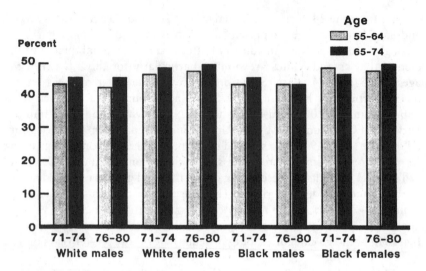

FIGURE 7.1 Percent of kilocalories from carbohydrates, United States, 1971–1974 and 1976–1980.

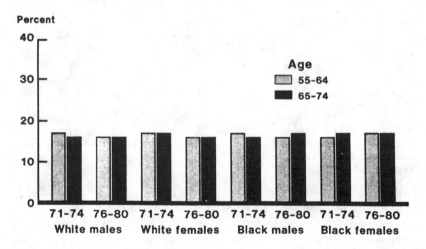

FIGURE 7.2 Percent of kilocalories from proteins, United States, 1971–1974 and 1976–1980.

As shown in Table 7.1, the pattern of consuming vegetables differed between the racial groups. The specific vegetable item selected also differed between blacks and whites. Blacks frequently reported cabbage, collard, mustard, and turnip greens, and sweet potatoes, whereas whites frequently reported green salads. Both blacks and whites frequently reported potatoes and tomatoes. Grains held similar positions in the diets of blacks and whites. Grain products most often reported by both blacks and whites were

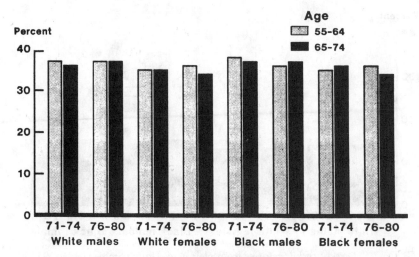

FIGURE 7.3 Percent of kilocalories from fats, United States, 1971–1974 and 1976–1980.

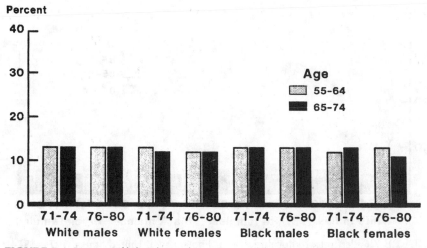

FIGURE 7.4 Percent of kilocalories from saturated fatty acids, United States, 1971–1974 and 1976–1980.

white bread, biscuits, muffins, and rolls. In addition, blacks often reported grits, cornbread, and rice, whereas whites reported pasta and whole-wheat and rye breads. For both blacks and whites, meat ranked seventh among the seven major food groups contributing to their intakes. Ground beef was reported most often by both blacks and whites. In addition, blacks reported luncheon meats and sausages, whereas whites reported lean steak, roast beef, or luncheon ham.

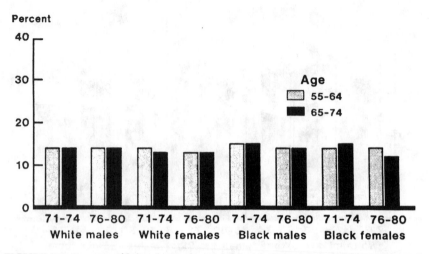

FIGURE 7.5 Percent of kilocalories from oleic acid, United States, 1971–1974 and 1976–1980.

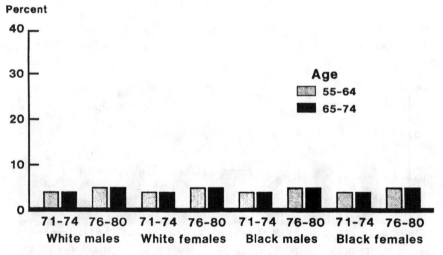

FIGURE 7.6 Percent of kilocalories from linoleic acid, United States, 1971–1974 and 1976–1980.

Figures 7.1–7.3 present the dietary pattern based on kilocalorie distribution of carbohydrates, proteins, and fats in the diet; similarly, Figures 7.4–7.6 provide data on the distribution of calories from saturated and unsaturated fatty acids. Once more, similarities between blacks and whites are striking, particularly for calories obtained from protein by the 55–64 year age group (Figure 7.2), for calories obtained from saturated fatty acids

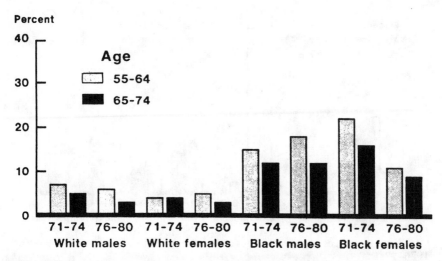

FIGURE 7.7 Percent of persons who skipped breakfast, United States, 1971–1974 and 1976–1980.

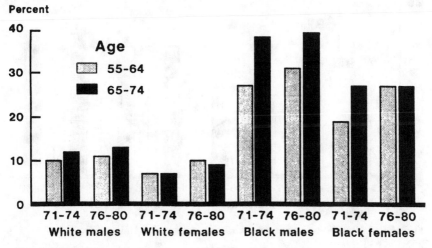

FIGURE 7.8 Percent of persons who skipped lunch, United States, 1971–1974 and 1976–1980.

and oleic acid in black and white males (Figures 7.4 and 7.5), and for calories obtained from linoleic acid (Figure 7.6).

Caloric distribution from the energy-producing nutrients—carbohydrates, proteins, and fats—have been addressed by the American Heart Association, the National Cancer Institute, the U.S. Dietary Goals, the Recommended Dietary Allowances, and the Dietary Guidelines for

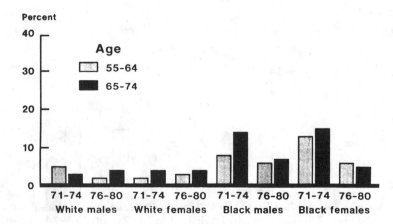

FIGURE 7.9 Percent of persons who skipped dinner, United States, 1971–1974 and 1976–1980

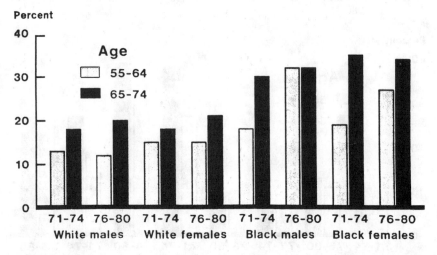

FIGURE 7.10 Percent of persons who skipped snacks, United States, 1971–1974 and 1976–1980.

Americans developed by the Departments of Agriculture and Health and Human Services. Their dietary recommendations to promote health and to reduce risks of chronic disease among older adults include (1) consuming approximately 55% of calories derived primarily from complex carbohydrates; (2) reducing total fat from 40% to 25–35% of the caloric intake; (3) reducing protein intake to 12–15% of the caloric intake; (4) using fats with a lower saturated fatty acid content and increasing the polyunsaturated fatty acids; and (5) limiting table salt intake to approximately 5 grams daily.

Blacks and whites were similar with respect to the recommendations cited above. All exceeded the recommendations for proteins and fats and none met the recommendation for carbohydrates.

Median intakes of dietary components that approached but did not meet dietary recommendations are presented in Table 7.2. In general, black females, followed by black males, showed the greatest nutritional inadequacies. Calories, calcium, Vitamin A, and B-complex vitamins were inadequate in the diets of all groups. Most black females had diets limited in protein and phosphorous, and all black females had diets limited in potassium. All black males 65–74 years of age had diets low in iron and potassium. All males 55–74 years of age showed inadequacies in carbohydrates. As a group, blacks consumed 300 fewer calories per day than did whites (5).

Nutritional inadequacies are probably linked to the specific items selected and to meal skipping. Patterns of meal and snack skipping are presented in Figures 7.7–7.10. The figures show that a higher percentage of black males and females in both age categories consistently skipped breakfast, lunch, dinner, and snacks than did whites. Lunch, in particular, was skipped by 40% of black males in the 65–74 age group.

In summary, the largest body of data on food consumption patterns of Americans between the ages of 55 and 74 for the periods 1971–1974 and 1976–1980 show that similarities and differences occur in the food consumption and selection patterns of older blacks and whites. Nutritional inadequacies were more often present in the diets of black females, followed by black males, than in the diets of whites as a group. Calories were inadequate in the diets of all groups, yet blacks consumed fewer calories than did whites (5).

By itself, dietary information gives an incomplete picture of a group's nutritional status. A complete nutritional profile should also include data derived from clinical assessments, laboratory assessments of biological fluids and other materials (e.g., blood, urine, hair, saliva), anthropometric assessments of body size and composition, and lifestyle assessments. Although each assesses a different state of nutrition and does not necessarily correlate with the others, all should be included when presenting a comprehensive picture of nutritional status. NHANES I data are available for some of these components and are presented below.

Lowenstein's report (6) on the nutritional status of the elderly in NHANES I was limited to the 3,479 persons aged 65–74. However, it is fairly comprehensive and focuses on selected findings from dietary intake assessments (based on the 24-hour recall), biochemical and hematological assessments, clinical signs associated with the deficiencies identified, and anthropometric measurements. As presented in Table 7.2 and discussed above, mean caloric intakes were low.

Biochemically, serum protein, albumin, and Vitamin A were essentially within standard for blacks and whites of both sexes and income categories. The picture was different for urinary thiamin and riboflavin and serum magnesium. The percentages below the cutoff points were always greater in blacks than in whites, particularly in black males. Mean serum cholesterol values were highest in black women.

Clinically, men showed greater prevalences of signs associated with nutritional deficiencies, except for iodine deficiency (goiter), than did women. Yet almost all prevalences were greater in black women than in white women, except for protein and riboflavin. White men had greater prevalences of signs associated with protein, riboflavin, and niacin deficiencies than black men, but prevalences of signs associated with the other six nutrients—thiamin, ascorbic acid, Vitamin A, Vitamin D, iodine, and calcium—were higher in black men. This was most pronounced in the case of Vitamin C (ascorbic acid), in which the prevalence rate of nutrition deficiency was double that found in white men.

Anthropometrically, obesity was determined from triceps skinfold measurements. White men had greater percentages of obesity than black men, regardless of income. In contrast, black women in the poverty income ratio (PIR) group above unity showed significantly greater percentages of obesity than white women in the same income group. The situation was reversed in the PIR group below unity.

As noted by Brown (7, p. 171), "the problem of obesity in black women is confusing." As she states, "if black women indeed consume less food than white women, one would expect the incidence of obesity to be less." She strongly believes that "the paradox of a greater prevalence of obesity among black women in conjunction with lower energy intakes deserves study, including careful evaluation of the validity of dietary data."

Frisancho, Leonard, and Bolletino (8) analyzed data sets from NHANES I containing information on blood pressure and 24-hour dietary intakes of sodium and potassium for blacks and whites between the ages of 20 and 74. The age groups for analysis were 20–24, 25–34, 35–44, 45–54, 55–64, and 65–74 years of age. The results showed that except among males aged 25–34 and females aged 20–24, the dietary intake of sodium and potassium was lower in blacks than in whites. However, the sodium/potassium ratios were systematically lower among whites than among blacks, indicating that the intake of potassium, relative to sodium, was less in blacks than in whites. In contrast, the systolic and diastolic blood pressures among whites after the age of 35 years were significantly lower than among blacks. These findings that blacks have a lower, not higher, sodium intake than whites of the same age group were unexpected; earlier reports depicted higher sodium intakes in blacks. However, Frisancho and colleagues are in agreement with others who had indicated that blacks ingest less potassium than whites (9). Frisancho and colleagues speculate that the low potassium intake, along with an increased susceptibility to salt, may be important in the development of hypertension in both blacks and whites. Curiously, assessments of the same data sets led Harlan, Hall, Schmouder, Landis, Thompson, and Larkin (10, 11) to conclude that alcohol consumption and low dietary calcium and phosphorous were associated with high blood pressure in the elderly, but not dietary sodium and salt.

These controversial aspects of the diet and nutritional status of blacks cry out for immediate attention and should be addressed in combined field and laboratory research in well-controlled studies. We need to understand the various functions of dietary sodium, potassium, calcium, phosphorous, and magnesium, as well as their interactive roles in the diet and in the body in essential hypertension—a major health risk for black adults of all ages.

Similarly, the iron status of the black population, particularly of aging blacks, is not well understood. Evaluations of national data on iron status in elderly Americans were recently reported by Lynch, Finch, Monsen, and Cook (12). They noted a consistent increase in iron consumption for both males and females of all age groups in NHANES II as compared with NHANES I. In general, NHANES II data indicated that the mean dietary iron intake for older Americans (both men and women) met the 1980 Recommended Dietary Allowances (RDA) of 10 mg per day. However, the mean intakes of certain subgroups of women failed to do so. Citing earlier studies, the authors indicated that the lowest values had been found for low-income black women over 59 years of age. Using hematological criteria, the NHANES I survey recorded a high prevalence (29.6%) of low hemoglobin values in blacks over the age of 60 in the low-income group and 22.8% in the income group above poverty. Comparable values for whites were less than 10%. Lynch and colleagues, as have others before them, questioned the use of hemoglobin as a suitable screening test for iron deficiency in the elderly, particularly the black elderly, who consistently present hemoglobin values well below those of whites.

The practice of using common criteria for comparing physical and biological values in blacks and whites should be evaluated. In the United States, comparison of blacks with whites is appropriate and essential when using social and economic criteria. However, physical and biological differences between the races make such comparisons untenable in some circumstances. There is an urgent need to determine physical and biological norms for blacks in order to appropriately assess nutritional deficits and excesses in the black population, particularly in the black elderly. The goal is to objectively define optimal nutrition and functional health for both racial groups.

Small-Scale Comparison Studies

Small-scale studies conducted in various parts of the United States often clarify questions raised in larger national studies. This has not been the case with research on diet and nutrition among elderly blacks and whites. Results from small-scale comparison studies are not very different from those obtained in large-scale national studies. For many important indices of quality nutrition, blacks trail whites, despite some parallels in food consumption patterns.

Learner and Kivett's rural respondents (N = 402) in North Carolina rated the adequacy of their customary diets (13). Blacks constituted 37% of the sample, with an age range from 65 to 99 years. Based on discriminant analysis procedures, the authors concluded that "being black was a risk factor for perceived dietary inadequacy" (13, p. 335). Race was fourth in importance for discriminating between persons who perceived their diets as inadequate and those who did not. Todhunter (14) arrived at similar results for her elderly sample in Tennessee, and Templeton (15) for her geriatric population in Michigan. These authors stated that elderly blacks were more likely to have inadequate intakes of specific nutrients than elderly whites, especially if they were women. Undoubtedly, in these dietary assessments, inadequate diets were inextricably bound with inadequate economic resources.

Other studies aimed at environmental determinants of dietary patterns among elderly Americans clearly demonstrated that ethnicity and social class were important determinants of diet quality. Hunter and Linn (16) evaluated the dietary patterns of 94 black and 88 white men and women 65 years of age or older in a Miami study. The majority of blacks met Hollingshead's criteria (17) for placement in the lowest socioeconomic group; by contrast, most whites were of middle- to lower-middle-class standing. Although black males were found to eat a full morning meal more often than any other group, they were at highest nutritional risk. Eggs formed the core of the breakfasts. Blacks of both sexes were more apt to rely on eggs and fatty meats and to have negative overall meal ratings than were whites. The authors concluded that social class and education were highly related to quality of meals; lower social class and less education were good predictors of poor nutrition.

Food/beverage selection patterns are important determinants of diet quality; selection patterns often vary with income, social class, and ethnicity. Marrs's study tested this principle (18). Her study of milk-drinking patterns of older Americans participating in congregate meal programs in south Texas included members of three ethnic groups—blacks, Mexican-Americans, and Anglos. She reported that each group showed definite preferences for certain types of milk, with blacks selecting buttermilk more often than Mexican-Americans and Anglos. However, blacks and whites made more choices that were similar than did any other two groups. The similarities shown by blacks and whites when selecting core foods and beverages have been demonstrated in national studies and discussed in the previous section of this paper.

One study on aging blacks presented an entirely different nutritional picture. Reporting on her Indianapolis sample obtained from representative congregate meal sites serving older Americans, Greger (19) listed other similarities. She found no difference in the zinc levels of elderly blacks and whites. Their dietary zinc intake and taste acuity were also similar. However, blacks consumed significantly more calories, fats, phosphorous, iron, Vitamin A, thiamin, and riboflavin than the white subjects. In many respects, these findings differ substantially from others reported in the literature. The author linked the favorable nutrition of blacks to their greater food intake, but no explanation was offered for the greater caloric intake by that group of elderly blacks.

Localized Clinic-Based or Community-Based Descriptive Studies of Older Inner-City Blacks

Only a handful of such studies were found in the literature. Two important surveys of this genre were conducted in Dade County, Florida. Bailey, Wagner, and Christakis at the Universities of Florida and Miami (20) conducted a clinic-based study of an inner-city elderly population (aged 60–90) in Dade County, Florida in the late 1970s. Of the 193 respondents, 170 were black and the remainder were Spanish-speaking Americans. Folacin, iron status, and other hematological assessments were performed in this clinic-based study in order to characterize the anemia and evaluate the status of a number of hematopoietic factors.

The results indicated that the iron status of the population appeared to be normal. The incidence of anemia (hemoglobin 12g/dl) was approximately 14%. Low hematocrits (37%) were found in 16% of the population.

Red blood cell folacin concentration, however, indicated that 60% of the population could be classified as "high risk" and 11% as "medium risk." Evidence of widespread folacin deficiency per se can produce a malabsorption involving changes in the intestinal epithelium, in addition to the other physiological changes associated with aging. No differences were found between the blacks and Spanish-speaking members of the population.

The authors emphasized the necessity of characterizing the anemia and evaluating the status of other hematopoietic factors, rather than assuming that anemia always reflects dietary iron deficiency. Further, they commented on the food consumption and preparation practices of the respondents. They estimated that approximately 17% of the people were consuming fresh vegetables and only 30% were consuming citrus fruit. Food preparation practices included boiling vegetables for several hours, a technique leading to significant folacin loss. The authors believe that the true incidence of iron deficiency should be reassessed worldwide in view of mounting evidence of the extent of folacin deficiency.

Additional data on serum and hair levels of zinc were obtained on 135 of the 170 blacks in this population. Wagner, Krista, Bailey, and colleagues conducted this study in order to develop a better definition of zinc status, particularly in the elderly population (20). The absence of reference data presents difficulties in evaluating the results. However, of the 83 respondents for whom both hair and serum zinc data were obtained, only five (6%) had low values. This is not surprising since, compared with serum, hair values reflect zinc nutriture of very long standing and would vary with hair type and rate of hair growth in blacks.

Socioeconomic data provided by Wagner and colleagues (21) indicate that the respondents lived in a densely populated poverty area and had minimal social interaction outside of the domestic environment. The average food-shopping frequency was less than twice per month. Only 28% of the sample participated in the community's congregate meal program for the elderly, although 51% reported using food stamps. One-third of the household income was spent for food. It would have been useful to have had the analysis show how the socioeconomic variables were linked to folacin and zinc status. Through their participation in these landmark studies, this group of low-income black elderly men and women in Miami have made a significant contribution to the folacin and zinc assessment data bases and to the nutritional assessment literature in general.

Exton-Smith (22) has offered a useful classification of factors that can increase the risk of malnutrition among the elderly. These factors are of particular relevance to the U.S. black elderly, who are often economically disadvantaged and also at high nutritional risk. Primary factors that increase the risk include: (1) lack of understanding of the need for a balanced diet; (2) restriction, because of poverty, of the variety of foods purchased; (3) physical disabilities that prevent the elderly from shopping around; (4) social isolation due to being restricted to the house, resulting in the loss of interest in food; and (5) mental confusion and depression. Secondary factors listed by Exton-Smith are largely diseases and malfunctions, including malabsorption, impaired appetite, alcoholism, masticatory inefficiency, and interference with nutrient function by some therapeutic drugs.

A Localized Community-Based Prospective Study on Dietary Change in Aging Blacks

Prospective community-based nutrition studies grounded in the anthropological technique of participant observation are invaluable for identifying community problems and strengths. The study reported below is of this genre.

Jerome (23) conducted a nutri-ethnographic study in 1980–1981 to measure changes in diet, nutrition, and lifestyle for 30 black residents of Kansas City, Kansas, age 60 or over, who had participated in a similar study in 1970–1971. Eighty percent of the respondent group was under 69 years of age in 1970–1971 when baseline data for the study were obtained. The remaining 20% were between 60 and 75 years of age in 1970–1971. Data on changing conditions and adaptation to change largely reflect that 80% which was not classified as "old" in 1970–1971. (The respondents were the "aging subsample" of the larger sample of 150 households—a 5% random sample of households in an urban community of three census tracts).

The respondents were intimately involved in the research by participating in repeated interviews over a period of time for a total of four to six hours. They also maintained dietary records during one week for three weekdays, Saturday, and Sunday. The data obtained in 1970–1971 were not revealed to them.

The economic situation of these older Kansans changed significantly during the intervening 10-year period. Personal incomes were severely reduced. In 1970–1971, the annual income range of half of the group was between $9,000 and $10,999. By contrast, half reported incomes between $3,000 and $4,999 in 1980–1981. This severe income reduction was not offset by any significant change in household structure or size. Living arrangements remained the same, except in a few instances of death of a spouse or children moving away. The number of married couples did not change. However, the number of individuals living alone increased, as did the number living in extended households; households with dependent children decreased.

Changes in personal, family, and social life occurred frequently. There were 33 episodes of deaths of either spouse or kin and 22 episodes of death of very close friends. Marriage of children and births of grandchildren occurred frequently. Forced retirement also occurred frequently, as did major personal injury or illness.

Changes in food selection, preparation, and consumption accompanied changes in health and in socioeconomic situation. Other major changes occurred in sleeping and activity patterns, including travel and recreation. In 1970–1971, there were 10 incidents of illness, injury, or disability and 25 incidents in 1980–1981. The increases were due to diabetes, coronary heart disease, stroke, ulcer, and cataracts. Hypertension increased only slightly.

Despite the many changes in the respondents' health and personal situations, an overwhelming majority rated their current health status as "good." In 1970–1971, half of the respondents rated their health as "fair" and the other half as "good." In 1980–1981, 74% rated their health as "good."

Dietary Changes

Dietary change was widespread and was associated with illness and disease. A majority of the respondents eliminated or decreased the amount of pork, wild game, and alcoholic beverages in their diets. Significantly decreased were total food intake, as well as intakes of salt, sugar, fat, and citrus beverages. In addition, many respondents reported that they now substituted "diet products," such as low-sodium and low-calorie foods, for traditional dietary items. Some respondents also reported that they had changed food preparation methods. For example, many had substituted boiling and baking for frying and stewing. Herbs and lemon juice as seasonings had replaced salt, and corn oil had been substituted for animal fats.

Few of these changes were accompanied by self-administered nutritional supplements. Only five respondents supplemented their diets with multivitamin or mineral preparations.

Despite the changes, many items remained stable in the dietary pattern, that is, they were consumed as frequently in 1980–1981 as they were in 1970–1971. These were "core" items customarily consumed at least once per week by a majority of the sample. The core items were whole milk, eggs, tomatoes, bacon, carbonated beverages, coffee, orange juice, white bread, lettuce, potatoes, chicken, cheese, tea, ground beef, oatmeal, jelly, and Kool-aid. Some new items were introduced into the dietary pattern during the 10-year period under consideration. These included imitation bacon, egg substitutes, rye bread, diet soda, decaffeinated coffee, and instant puddings.

It is worth noting that none of the respondents participated in any of the community-based senior adult programs, although these programs were designed to ease the multiple problems associated with growing old, such as changing one's diet for health reasons. Some respondents admitted to some vague knowledge of programs for the elderly but showed no interest in them. The notion that programs existed—but "not for me"—should be addressed directly and practically, with reference to dietary change for therapeutic purposes.

Nutritional Quality of the Diet

Dietary records maintained for 5 days—3 weekdays and the 2 weekend days—were analyzed to determine the nutritional composition of both the weekday and weekend diet. Nutrient values obtained by these analyses (using a reliable nutrient data base) were compared with the National Research Council's 1980 Recommended Dietary Allowances and the Council's other recommendations for energy, sodium, and potassium. The results showed that the weekday diet was of higher nutritional quality and of higher nutrient density than the weekend diet. Mean intakes of iron, vitamin A, thiamine, riboflavin, niacin, and ascorbic acid in the weekend diet varied sufficiently from those of the weekday to warrant separate analysis.

For both weekday and weekend diets, the mean energy and calcium intakes for both males and females were far below recommended levels but were similar to the data obtained in the 1977–1978 USDA's Nationwide Food Consumption Survey from a representative sample of 4,991 respondents over the age of 64 and in NHANES I and II. The mean intake of phosphorous by females was below recommended levels, while that of males was above the recommended levels. By contrast, the mean intake of ascorbic acid was significantly lower in males than in females. Females surpassed the RDA for ascorbic acid, while the mean intake of males was approximately 50% below recommended levels. Both males and females surpassed the recommended levels for protein. The mean iron intake of females was at the recommended level, while males greatly surpassed the recommendations for iron. All of these findings were consistent with those reported for large national samples. The interrelationships of dietary calcium, phosphorous, and protein are of concern here, as they are nationally, because of possible links to osteoporosis in old age. Mean intakes of sodium and potassium were within the recommended range, but the ratio of sodium to potassium was approximately 1:2 in males and 1:1.5 in females.

In summary, for this group of aging urban blacks, the dietary pattern of 1970–1971 had undergone many changes by 1980–1981; however, there were many areas of stability and continuity in the dietary pattern, particularly among the core dietary items. Dietary change was largely associated with changes in personal life and living conditions, particularly health status. Many of the items entering or leaving the dietary pattern were associated with the therapeutic uses of food. The nutritional quality of the diet varied with time of week. The weekday diet was of better nutritional quality and of higher nutrient density than that of the weekend. Individuals appeared to have adjusted remarkably well to changes in personal and social conditions.

Strategies of Food Acquisition

The data show a very high degree of continuity in the production and acquisition of food. Half of the respondents raised some of their food, the overwhelming majority shopped for groceries once per week, and all owned or had access to cars to conduct their major shopping in the few large supermarkets that are still just outside of the community.

Communication

Local and national news, friends, and relatives were the main sources of information for the group. One-half of the respondent group subscribed to the larger metropolitan and community newspapers. Health-related information was discussed with friends and relatives rather than specialists and professionals. It appeared, however, that each individual had his or her own information exchange network locally, which could be tapped and utilized to transmit nutrition- and health-related information.

RESEARCH NEEDS ON DIET AND NUTRITION IN AGING BLACKS

The paucity of comprehensive data on the diet and nutritional status of aging U.S. blacks should concern us all, particularly policy makers, program designers, health practitioners, and nutrition-service providers. The consequences of formulating policy and designing programs without an appropriate or adequate data base are well known. Program plans become flawed; designs miss their targets; program participants respond negatively or drop out completely; and tensions develop among providers, evaluators, and program participants.

A great deal of information is needed to close the information chasm. Immediate needs include a well-designed longitudinal study to determine the effects of true age changes on nutritional status, as well as the effects of past and current lifestyles, dietary patterns and cooking methods, and social and economic conditions. To determine reasons for poor participation by elderly blacks in congregate meal programs, we also need to know the influence of past socialization on the current public behavior of older blacks and, in turn, types of policy adjustments for accommodating these behaviors. There is also an immediate need for quantitative and qualitative data on current and past food selection strategies, preparation methods, and food presentation styles of older blacks. Many of the black–white differentials in calories could be accounted for with good data on selection patterns, cooking methods, and food presentation prior to eating. In addition, there is the need to better understand the customary patterns of daily food intake by older blacks in order to clarify the "meal-skipping" issue raised in the NHANES findings.

The following questions are among those needing answers in the near future:

1. What are the functional nutritional consequences of changes in stature and in body composition (e.g., decrease in lean body mass and increase in adipose tissues) in blacks as they grow older?
2. What are the best methods of determining excess adiposity in aging blacks?
3. What are the functional long-term health and nutritional consequences in older blacks whose nutritional intake and nutritional status had been either marginal or poor?

4. Is the rate of aging in blacks (e.g., rate of bone loss) adversely affected by nutritional deficiencies or excesses in midlife?
5. What are the most effective methods of characterizing nutritional subgroups in the black adult population?
6. What are the social and demographic characteristics of the groups at greatest nutritional risk? Of those in functional health? Of those in optimal nutritional status?
7. Are current reference data and measurement criteria appropriate for assessing the nutritional status of aging blacks? How can they be improved?
8. What are the patterns of energy expenditure and intake in blacks from mid-adulthood through late adulthood?
9. What are the early warning signs of nutritional risk for subgroups among the black elderly?
10. What are the roles of sodium, potassium, calcium, and magnesium in the etiology of hypertension?
11. How do patterns and levels of physical activity vary for black and white adult females and males from midlife onwards? And why?
12. What are effective strategies for presenting nutrition information to the various subgroups in the older black population?

SUMMARY

An overview of diet and nutrition in aging U.S. blacks has been presented. Literature on the subject is sparse; only a handful of studies have been specifically designed to investigate the dietary patterns and nutritional status of aging blacks, and most of these lack two or three components of well-designed nutritional assessment studies.

The available information on diet and nutrition of older black Americans was presented in four study categories to differentiate research strategies and size of the data base. The largest body of data shows that similarities and differences obtain in the food consumption and selection patterns of older blacks and whites. Nutritional inadequacies are more often present in the diets of black females, followed by black males, than in the diets of whites as a group. Other studies, smaller in scale, support these findings, although differences between black males and females are not as clearcut. These discrepancies should be resolved as soon as possible. Moreover, there is an urgent need to understand the sources and meaning of these differences. Not a single study assessed the diet and nutritional status of healthy older blacks with diverse lifestyles in a prospective research design.

The problem of obesity in black women is troublesome, particularly since most studies show an energy deficit in the dietary intakes of older blacks. Other nutritional issues needing further study include dietary intakes of sodium, potassium, calcium, phosphorous, and magnesium, particularly in relation to protein intake. It would be particularly helpful to have reliable data on cooking methods, as well as food presentation and consumption styles, of aging blacks in a prospective research design.

There is a serious need for age- and race-specific indices for assessing such aspects of nutrition status as iron, folacin, and adiposity. There is also a serious need for data on activity patterns in black women as they age.

If anything, this review of the available information points to the serious need for well-designed studies of healthy blacks as they age in order to better understand how their diverse social and economic conditions influence nutritional status and health.

REFERENCES

1. Dresser CMV, Carroll MD, Abraham S. *Food Consumption Profiles of White and Black Persons Aged 1–74 Years: United States, 1971–74.* (DHEW Publication No. PHS 79-1658). U.S. Government Printing Office; 1979.
2. Dresser CM. Dietary status of community-based older persons. Paper presented at the annual meeting of the American Dietetic Association; 1984.
3. Windham CT, Wyse BW, Hansen RG, Hurst RL. Nutrient density of diets in the U.S.D.A. Nationwide Foods Consumption Survey, 1977–1978. I. Impact of socioeconomic status on dietary density. *J. Am. Diet. Assoc.* 1983;82:28–34.
4. Windham CT, Wyse BW, Hansen RG. Nutrient density of diets in the U.S.D.A. Nationwide Food Consumption Survey, 1977–1978. II. Adequacy of nutrient density consumption practices. *J. Am. Diet. Assoc.* 1983;82:34–43.
5. Dresser CM, Carroll MM. NHANES nutrition monitoring. (In preparation).
6. Lowenstein FW. Nutritional status of the elderly in the United States of America, 1971–74. *J. Am. Coll. Nutr.* 1982;1:165–177.
7. Brown ML. black women's nutritional problems. In: Berman PW, Ramey EW, eds. *Women: A Developmental Perspective,* (NIH Publication No. 82-2298. Washington, DC: U.S. Government Printing Office; 1982:167–176.
8. Frisancho AR, Leonard WR, Bolletino LA. Blood pressure in blacks and whites and its relationship to dietary sodium and potassium intake. *J. Chron Dis.* 1984;37:515–519.
9. Grim CE, Luft FC, Miller JZ, Meneely GR, Battarbee HD, Hames CF, Dahl LK. Racial differences in blood pressure in Evans County, Georgia: Relationship to sodium and potassium intake and plasma renin activity. *J. Chron. Dis.* 1980;33:87–94.
10. Harlan WR, Hull AL, Schmouder RL, Landis JR, Larkin FA, Thompson FE. High blood pressure in older Americans: the First National Health and Nutrition Examination Survey. *Hypertension* 1984;6:802–809.
11. Harlan WR, Hull AL, Schmouder RL, Landis JR, Thompson FE, Larkin FA. Blood pressure and nutrition in adults. *Am. J. Epi.* 1984;120:17–28.
12. Lynch SR, Finch CA, Monsen ER, Cook JD. Iron status of elderly Americans. *Am. J. Clin. Nutr.* (Supplement) 1982;36:1032–1035.

13. Learner RM, Kivett UR. Discriminators of perceived dietary adequacy among the rural elderly. *J. Am. Diet. Assoc.* 1981;78:330–337.
14. Todhunter EN. Lifestyle and nutrient intake in the elderly. In: Winick M, ed. *Nutrition and Aging,* Vol. 4. New York: Wiley; 1976:pp 119–127.
15. Templeton CL. Nutrition counseling needs in a geriatric population. *Geriatrics.* 1978;33:59–66.
16. Hunter KI, Linn MW. Cultural and sex differences in dietary patterns of the urban elderly. *J. Am. Ger. Soc.* 1970;27:359–363.
17. Hollingshead AB. Two-factor index of social position. Manuscript, New Haven, CT; 1957.
18. Marrs DC. Milk drinking by the elderly of three races. *J. Am. Diet. Assoc.* 1978;72:495–498.
19. Greger JL. Zinc nutriture of elderly participants in an urban feeding program. *J. Am. Diet. Assoc.* 1977;70:37–41.
20. Bailey LB, Wagner PA, Christakis GT. Folacin and iron status and hematological findings in predominantly black elderly persons from urban low-income households. *Am. J. Clin. Nutr.* 1979;32:2346–2353.
21. Wagner PA, Krista ML, Bailey LB, et al. Zinc status of elderly black Americans from urban low-income households. *Am. J. Clin. Nutr.* 1980;33:1771–1777.
22. Exton-Smith AN, Caird FI, eds. *Metabolic and Nutritional Disorders in the Elderly.* Bristol, England: John Wright & Sons; 1980.
23. Jerome NW. Stability and Change in Diet, Nutrition and Lifestyles of Some Older Kansans in Wyandotte County 1970–1971 and 1980–1981. Final research report submitted to the Kansas Dept. on Aging, 1982.

8

Diabetes and Obesity in Elderly Black Americans

Leslie Sue Lieberman

Both diabetes and obesity represent enormous health problems for elderly black Americans. The morbidity, mortality, and social and economic costs associated with these disorders of energy use and storage are described in this chapter. Research areas and strategies are suggested to aid in redirection of the prevalence and incidence of these disorders and their deleterious complications.

DIABETES MELLITUS

Classification and Diagnosis

Diabetes mellitus is a heterogeneous group of disorders characterized by hyperglycemia. Descriptions of diabetes mellitus date back at least two millennia, but only within the last decade has there been a consensus on classification (1, 2). The work of the National Diabetes Data Group (3) led to the classification described in Table 8.1 (4). Type I diabetics are insulin-dependent or insulin-requiring (IDDM). Type I diabetes may occur at any age but commonly occurs in youth. Of approximately 5.8 million people in the United States diagnosed as diabetic, 5 to 10% of all cases may be classified as Type I.

Type II diabetes mellitus is noninsulin-dependent (NIDDM), although individuals may be on insulin therapy. Type II occurs primarily in adults and shows an increase in prevalence with increasing age. The majority of

TABLE 8.1 Diagnosis and Classification of Diabetes Mellitus

I. Diagnoses associated with glucose intolerance
  A. Diabetes mellitus (DM)
    1. Type I. Insulin-dependent-type (IDDM). Ketosis prone. Insulin deficient due to islet cell loss. Often associated with specific HLA types, with predisposition to viral insulitis or autoimmune (islet cell antibody) phenomena. Occurs at any age, common in youth.
    2. Type II. Noninsulin-dependent-type (NIDDM). Ketosis resistant. More frequent in adults but occurs at any age. Majority are overweight. May be seen in family aggregates as an autosomal dominant genetic trait. May require insulin for hyperglycemia during stress.
    3. Diabetes associated with certain conditions or syndromes. Hyperglycemia occurring in relation to other disease states. Pancreatic diseases, drug- or chemical-induced diabetes, endocrinopathies, insulin receptor disorders, certain genetic syndromes.
  B. Impaired glucose tolerance (IGT). Abnormality in glucose levels intermediate between normal and overt diabetes. May "worsen to diabetes," improve toward normal, or remain unchanged on serial testing.
  C. Gestational diabetes (GDM). Glucose intolerance with recognition of onset during pregnancy.
II. Criteria for diagnosis
  A. Diabetes mellitus—adult
    1. Unequivocal elevation of plasma glucose (≥ 200 mg/dl) and classic symptoms of diabetes including polydipsia, polyuria, polyphagia, and weight loss.
    2. Fasting plasma glucose ≥140 mg/dl on two occasions.
    3. Fasting plasma glucose <140 mg/dl and 2-h plasma glucose ≥200 mg/dl with one intervening value ≥200 mg/dl following a 75-g glucose load (OGTT).

Source: Shuman, C. R., Spratt, I. L. Office guide to diagnosis and classification of diabetes mellitus and other categories of glucose intolerance. *Diabetes Care 335*, 1981: 4(2). Reproduced with permission from the American Diabetes Association, Inc.

individuals presenting with Type II diabetes are overweight. Approximately 90 to 95% of all diabetics may be classified as Type II.

Diabetes mellitus may be secondary to certain conditions or syndromes resulting in pancreatic dysfunction: diseases, genetic syndromes, drugs, and chemicals. Approximately 2% of diabetics are this type (5).

Impaired glucose tolerance is a state of elevated levels of plasma glucose that do not reach the criteria for overt diabetes. Individuals with impaired glucose tolerance may improve, remain unchanged, or move to overt diabetes.

The final classification for diabetes is a transient condition that occurs during pregnancy. Gestational diabetes occurs in about 2 to 5% of pregnancies (5).

Three other disorders have been described as infrequently occurring but distinct subtypes of diabetes mellitus. In the 1970s Tattersall and Fajans (6, 7) described maturity onset diabetes of youth (MODY) as a subtype of noninsulin-dependent diabetes. MODY accounts for approximately 5% of the youth-onset diabetes in whites. Its prevalence is unknown among blacks. MODY patients frequently have no symptoms and are diagnosed primarily through glucose-tolerance testing. They are not ketosis prone and complications are rare.

Two other syndromes affect primarily blacks. Both have an age of onset in late adolescence or young adulthood. In 1955 Hugh-Jones (8) described a form of diabetes that developed in young Jamaicans (J-Type). Subsequent studies have demonstrated that J-Type diabetes is most frequent in tropical areas and is related to low protein intake and possibly cassava consumption (1, 8, 9). Recently a new syndrome affecting black American youth has been described by Maclaren, Winter, and colleagues (10, 11). Like J-Type diabetes, the new syndrome is biphasic. At times individuals require insulin, at other times they do not (10, 11).

This review will focus on Type II diabetes (NIDDM). More than 95% of black Americans who have diabetes have NIDDM (12).

The diagnosis of diabetes mellitus in adults may be made by three sets of criteria (1, 2, 3, 4) (see Table 8.1). In each set the basis for diagnosis is an elevation in blood glucose levels during fasting or with glucose challenge. The classic symptoms of diabetes—polydipsia, polyuria, polyphasia, and weight loss—may or may not be present.

These criteria are clearly defined, but they do not always serve as the basis for prevalence studies. Physician diagnosis, for example, may be based on glycosuria, and national surveys may be based on self-report with no designation of criteria (13).

Prevalence and Incidence

Noninsulin dependent diabetes mellitus is one of the most common diseases in the United States. Nearly 2.5% of the population (5.8 million people) have been diagnosed by physicians as having diabetes. An additional 4 to 5 million persons aged 20 to 74 years of age may have undiagnosed diabetes. Black diabetics make up 15% of the total population of known diabetics (3, 12, 13, 14). The prevalence of diabetes has steadily increased in all groups since the first systematic health survey of the United States was conducted in the mid-1930s (13). Over the past 25 years diabetes mellitus has been one of the diseases included in the National Health Interview Surveys (NHIS) and the Health Examination Surveys (13). In addition, the Second National Health and Nutrition Examination Survey (NHANES II) conducted in 1976–1980 employed an oral glucose-tolerance test to diagnose diabetes (13).

Overview

Diabetes mellitus is more common among older individuals, increasing with age. It is more common among black Americans and other minority groups, and more common among females (1, 5, 12, 13, 14, 15). In all adult age/sex categories diabetes is 33% higher among black Americans than among white Americans (12, 15, 16) (see Tables 8.2 and 8.3). Among black diabetics, diabetes is eight times more frequent in the oldest age group, 65–74 years (25.9%), than in the youngest age group, 20–44 years (3.1%) (16) (see Table 8.2). Sixty-eight percent of known diabetics are in the group aged 50–79 years. This age group comprises only 30.4% of the more than 15 million black Americans (14) (see Table 8.4).

The data from the 1979–1981 National Health Interview Survey (NHIS) show a rate of diabetes mellitus in black males 16% greater than the rate in white males and a rate in black females 50% greater than the rate in white females (12) (see Table 8.3). Based on these interview data there are approximately 262,000 black Americans over the age of 65 years who are known to have diabetes (15). However, estimates of individuals with Type II diabetes are generally *twice* the diagnosed number (13). Therefore, approximately half a million black elderly probably have diabetes mellitus (13) (see Table 8.5).

Age

Diabetes predominates in the older age group among black Americans. Approximately 40% of all known U.S. diabetics are 65 years of age or

TABLE 8.2 Percent of the U.S. Population with Diabetes, 1976–80[a]

Population group	Age (years)				
	20–74	20–44	45–54	55–64	65–74
White	6.2	1.7	8.2	11.9	16.9
Male	5.3	1.0	7.7	9.1	18.1
Female	7.0	2.2	8.5	14.5	16.1
Black	9.6	3.1	12.9	20.8	25.9
Male	8.5	2.8	11.1	14.4	29.4[b]
Female	10.5	3.5	14.5	25.4	23.1[b]

[a]Sum of percent of persons with a physician-diagnosed medical history of diabetes and of undiagnosed diabetes using National Diabetes Data Group criteria.
[b]In this table the oldest males have a higher percentage of diabetes than the oldest females (65–74 years). This reversed trend is, in part, due to the small sample sizes and the large standard errors for this group.
Source: Everhart J., Knowler W. C., Bennett P. H. Incidence and risk factors for non-insulin dependent diabetes. In: National Diabetes Data Group, eds. *Diabetes in America* [HHS (PHS) NIH Publication No. 85-1468]. Washington, DC: U.S. Government Printing Office; 1985: IV–12.

TABLE 8.3 Number and Rate of Diagnosed Diabetes in Blacks and Whites, United States, 1979–1981

Age (years)	Black diabetic population (thousands of persons)			Rate of diabetes per 1,000 black persons			Rate of diabetes per 1,000 white persons		
	Both sexes	Male	Female	Both sexes	Male	Female	Both sexes	Male	Female
All ages	834	305	529	32.2	25.4	38.2	23.8	21.9	25.6
0–24	20	6	14	1.5	.9	2.1	2.0	1.7	2.2
25–44	144	59	85	21.6	20.0	22.8	11.0	9.1	12.8
45–54	194	92	102	85.3	87.9	83.1	37.4	36.0	38.9
55–64	215	73	142	118.1	89.2	141.5	62.8	67.3	58.7
65–74	172	57	115	129.3	102.1	149.5	83.4	86.8	80.7
75+	90	19	71	130.9	72.6	168.1	86.0	79.5	89.8

Source: Roseman J. M. Diabetes in black Americans. In: National Diabetes Data Group eds. *Diabetes in America* [HHS (PHS) NIH Publication No. 85-1468]. Washington, DC: U.S. Government Printing Office; 1985: VIII–5.

TABLE 8.4 Number and Percent Distribution of U.S. Blacks in the General Population and with Diabetes by Age and Sex

Number (thousands)	U.S. black population			Black diabetics		
	Both sexes 15,286	Men 6,747	Women 8,538	Both sexes 825	Men 305	Women 520
Age (years)						
20–34	42.5	42.8	42.2	6.9	8.4	6.0
35–49	25.1	25.3	25.0	21.1	23.9	19.5
50–64	19.2	19.7	18.9	40.3	42.7	38.9
65–79	11.2	10.5	11.8	27.7	23.6	30.1
80+	2.0	1.7	2.2	4.1	1.5	5.6

Source: Drury TF, Danchik KM, Harris MI. Sociodemographic characteristics of adult diabetics. In: National Diabetes Data Group, eds. *Diabetes in America* [HHS (PHS) NIH Publication No. 85-1468]. Washington, DC: U.S. Government Printing Office; 1985:VII–5.

older, and 53% are 60 years of age or older (14). The older age of diabetics contrasts sharply with the age composition of the general U.S. adult population. The median age of adult diabetics was about 61 years in the 1979–1981 NHIS survey, while the median age of all persons over 20 was about 42 years (14). The difference in the median ages of diabetics and the general population occurred in all race/sex groups.

Sex

Another striking feature of the demographic structure of the diabetic population is the predominance of women. The majority of adults aged 10 years and over in the United States are women (52.9%), but the percentage is higher among diabetics (56.7%). In 1979–1981 there were only about 77 men to every 100 women with diabetes, while in the general population the sex ratio was 89 : 100.

The National Diabetes Data Group (14) estimates that there are 305,000 black male and 520,000 black female diabetics in the United States (Table 8.4). Among black diabetics the ratios are about 59 males per 100 females, in contrast to 79 per 100 for the general black population. The sex ratio is 1 male to 1.5 females for the group aged 20–64 years. However, the percentage of black male diabetics is higher than female diabetics for this age group (Table 8.4).

Race

Four out of five adult diabetics are white (83.1%), and about one out of seven are black (15.4%). While the majority of diabetics are white, the

proportion of blacks and minorities is much greater in the diabetic population than in the general population. For every 100 white diabetics there are
18.6 black diabetics, while in the general population the ratio is 100 to 11.7.
Among men this black/white ratio for diabetic men is 15.5 and for diabetic
women, 21.1. The black/white ratio in the diabetic population begins to
decline after the age of 50. Among diabetics 80 years of age or over there are
as few as 13 blacks for every 100 whites (14).

Secular Trend

Roseman (12) has reviewed 26 studies done between 1924 and 1981 on the
prevalence of diabetes among black Americans. He notes that there is a
secular trend of increasing prevalence. From 1963 to 1979–1981 the prevalence of diabetes increased 175% in blacks and 106% in whites (12). In
the population-based surveys black/white ratios have tended to remain
around 1.0 : 1.3 (12). Eleven studies indicate a secular trend in the declining

TABLE 8.5 Average Annual Number of Persons with Known Diabetes per 1,000
Population by Age and Selected Sociodemographic Characteristics: United States,
1979–1981

Characteristic	65 years and over		
	All persons 65 years and over	65–74 years	75 years and over
Total[a]	88.4	87.7	89.4
Sex			
Male	85.1	87.9	79.3
Female	90.7	87.7	95.3
Race			
White	84.3	83.4	86.0
All other	127.7	128.4	126.5
Black	129.8	129.3	130.9
Education of individual			
Less than 12 years	104.0	104.7	102.9
12 years	65.6	69.6	56.0
More than 12 years	68.9	64.6	78.6
Marital status			
Married	90.9	91.4	89.5
Formerly married	89.4	87.6	91.1
Never married	56.8	47.3	72.9
Education of head of family			
Less than 12 years	99.2	100.7	96.8
12 years	72.9	71.5	75.9
More than 12 years	72.6	68.1	81.5

Family income[b]

Less than $7,000	108.1	98.9	119.7
$7,000–$9,999	72.1	80.7	54.7
$10,000–$14,999	90.3	93.1	83.7
$15,000–$24,999	96.7	89.1	115.2
$25,000 or more	73.1	62.5	97.2
Location of residence			
SMSA[c]	86.2	85.4	87.6
Central city	86.9	88.2	84.9
Outside central city	85.6	83.1	90.1
Outside SMSA	92.2	92.0	92.7
Nonfarm	92.5	90.2	96.5
Farm	89.7	109.5	52.5
Geographic region			
Northeast	85.6	86.0	84.9
North-central	86.8	78.8	100.1
South	95.6	100.9	86.1
West	80.7	77.9	85.6

[a]Includes unknown Hispanic origin, education of individual, marital status, education of head of family, and family income.
[b]Data are for 1981 only because information on annual family income is only available for broad income categories and is technically difficult to adjust for inflation over the three-year time period.
[c]SMSA = standard metropolitan statistical area.
Source: Drury TF, Powell AL. Prevalence, impact, and demography of known diabetes in the United States. NCHS Advance Data No. 114; 1986:7.

female/male sex ratio among black diabetics. The sex ratio trend may be an artifact, because early samples from the 1930s, 1940s, and 1950s were ascertained in clinics, where a higher proportion of patients were women (12). Later samples were population-based.

Incidence

Approximately half a million people are diagnosed as diabetic each year. The annual incidence of noninsulin-dependent diabetes mellitus is about 320 per 100,000 persons aged 20 years and older. The incidence of Type II diabetes appears not to have increased in the United States during the period in which it has been studied (1965–1980). However, during the 1960s there was a rise in the incidence of total diabetics, possibly due to active screening. From a peak incidence of 300 per 100,000 population in 1973, the rate has declined to 230 per 100,000 in 1979–1981. Prevalence has continued to rise because of the decline in mortality of diabetics (5) (see Table 8.6). Incidence rates are approximately the same for black and white males and are significantly less than for black and white females. Incidence rates are highest for males aged 45 to 64 years and highest for females 65 years of age or older (13, 17) (see Table 8.6).

TABLE 8.6 Estimated Diabetes Incidence, United States, 1980

Age		U.S. rate 1973 (per 1,000)[a]	Estimated incidence U.S., 1980[b]
<45		1.0	66,886
45–64	White males	5.4	104,434
>65+		4.9	45,405
<45		1.8	117,854
45–64	White females	6.1	129,922
>65+		11.3	154,394
<45		1.0	11,547
45–64	Nonwhite males	5.4	12,332
>65+		4.9	4,996
<45		1.8	21,943
45–64	Nonwhite females	6.1	16,211
>65+		11.1	15,479
		Total	698,403

Sources:
[a]National Commission on Diabetes, Reports of Committees, Subcommittees, and Workgroups, Volume III, Part 1, DHEW Publication No. (NIH) 76-1021.
[b]Calculated from rates in column 1 and 1980 population figures from "Age, Race, Sex, and Spanish Origin of the Regions, Divisions, and States: 1980," U.S. Bureau of the Census, PC 80-31-1.

In summary, there has been an overall increase in the prevalence of diabetes among black Americans. This increase is due to the increase in incidence of *diagnosed* Type II diabetes; an increase in the size of the elderly population at risk for the disease; and an increase in longevity of individuals with diabetes (13).

Sociodemographic Characteristics of Type II Diabetics

The adult diabetic population is similar to the general adult population with respect to geographical distribution, marital status, and living arrangements. It is different with respect to age structure, sex and race composition, educational attainment, labor-force status, and annual family income distribution. Many of these differences are related to the biological variables of age, sex, and race.

Age

Demographic factors, particularly the gradual aging of the U.S. population (13), have contributed to the increase in the rate of diabetes. Furthermore, as described above, adult diabetics as a group are much older than the general population. Data based on the 1979–1981 National Health Interview Survey indicate that 53% of diabetics were 60 years of age or older and 40% were over the age of 65.

Sex

The differences in the sex composition of diabetics compared to the general population primarily reflect the higher percentage of diabetic women (14) (see Table 8.4). Within the black population 59 men per 100 women are diabetics. Other sex ratios presented by Roseman (based on population and clinic samples) show a range of female to male ratios of 0.6 to 5.0 (12).

Race

The diabetic population has a higher proportion of blacks and other minorities and a lower proportion of whites than does the general population. Among diabetics 80 years of age or older there are as few as 13 blacks for every 100 whites. The greater rate of diabetes among blacks is particularly clear in the age range from 50 to 79 years.

Geographic Distribution

The adult diabetic population is similar to the general population with respect to its geographic distribution. The largest segment (36.2%) lives in the South, followed by the north-central area (26.1%) and the Northeast (22.4%) (14). The geographic concentrations of elderly blacks and whites differ. White persons aged 65 or over are evenly distributed among the four major regions. In contrast, three-fifths of blacks aged 65 or older were living in the southern states in 1977 (15, 18) (see Table 8.5).

The vast majority of adult diabetics reside in metropolitan areas. More than 1.3 million known diabetics over the age of 65 reside in standard metropolitan statistical areas (SMSAs). An additional 790,000 known elderly diabetics reside in rural nonfarm and farming environments (15) (see Table 8.5).

Marital Status and Living Arrangements

Two-thirds of adult diabetics are married, with marital status higher among younger diabetics. As many as two-fifths of elderly diabetics are formally married. For known diabetics over the age of 65, 1.2 million (90.9/1000) are married, while an additional .9 million are widowed, divorced, or never married (15) (see Table 8.5).

In March 1978 the most common marital status among elderly black men was to be married. This contrasts with older black women, whose most common marital status was that of widowhood, reaching a proportion of 78% for those over 75. About three-fifths of the black men and one-third of the women aged 60 or older were married and living with their spouses, compared with four-fifths of white men and about one-half of white women (18).

Patterns of living arrangements among diabetics closely follow those in the general population. Two-thirds of adult diabetics are married and living with their spouses. As the proportion of widows rises with increasing age, the proportion of elderly diabetic women living alone also increases, to 35.5% in the group aged 65 and older (14). A significant proportion of adult diabetics regardless of race who are not currently married reside with relatives (16.6%), but very few live with nonrelatives (1.7%) (14).

About 29% of elderly black family heads are women, compared to only 11% of white family heads (18). Elderly blacks of both sexes who are heads of families tend to have a greater proportion of younger family members living with them than their white counterparts (18). The average size of all families headed by elderly blacks is 3.1 members, compared to 2.4 for white families headed by persons aged 60 and over (18).

Education

Adult diabetics regardless of race have less formal education than the general population of persons aged 20 and over. In 1979–1981 54% of adult diabetics compared to 29.4% of the general population had fewer than 12 years of schooling (14). In 1978 the median number of school years completed by blacks over the age of 60 was 7.6 years, compared to 10.8 years for white elderly (18). Only one-sixth of elderly blacks have completed 12 or more years of school, while 28% had no schooling or less than 5 years of schooling (18). I know of no specific statistics on education for the black elderly diabetic population.

Occupation

Compared to the general population, diabetic men and women are less likely to be working or in the labor force (14). In 1979–1981 about half of the diabetic men and one-fourth of the diabetic women were in the work-force on a regular basis. Black diabetics have lower rates of participation than do white diabetics, and those with fewer years of educational attainment have lower rates of labor-force participation than those with more years (14). About one-fourth of elderly blacks and whites were in the civilian labor force in 1978.

The occupations of employed diabetics are different from those of the general population. Elderly diabetic men are proportionally more likely to be in white-collar and service jobs than elderly men in general.

Most diabetics are diagnosed in later adulthood and have already assumed an occupational role. Therefore, it is assumed that the forces shaping the occupational distribution of diabetic men and women are largely independent of those that reflect the diabetic state and dependent instead on education, geography, and other social factors.

Family Income

Family income data reveal a better picture of the economic position of older persons than do personal income data. In 1981 15.9% of the general population aged 20 and older, in contrast with 29.4% of adult diabetics, were living in families with annual incomes of less than $7,000 (14) (Table 8.5). Only 23.4% of diabetics had family incomes over $25,000. This is approximately 12.5% less than the general population. Diabetic women were more likely (37.4%) than men (19.5%) to live in families with incomes below $7,000. The low incomes of elderly adult diabetics may be partially due to age-related patterns in family income.

Family income comes from a variety of sources. In black families with heads aged 65 or older a significant part of income came from Supplemental Security Income (SSI) and public assistance. Income from earnings was reported by about three-fifths of black families compared to about one-half of white families. The proportion of black families receiving SSI was four times greater than corresponding white families (29% vs 7%) (18). In addition to wages, salary, and federal support programs, approximately one-third of black families headed by persons over 65 years of age received income from assets, pensions, annuities, and other sources. Yet in 1977 33% of elderly blacks and 11% of elderly whites were below the poverty level (18).

Summary

In summary, a number of sociodemographic risk factors are associated with diabetes among elderly black Americans. Older black females and males are at greater risk for diabetes than are their white counterparts. Diabetes also has a higher prevalence rate among individuals who live in standard metropolitan statistical areas, live in the southern part of the United States, are involved in service occupations, have lower than average educational attainment, and have annual family incomes below the poverty level.

Biomedical Risk Factors

A large number of biomedical factors have been implicated in the etiology of diabetes (1, 16). This review will concentrate on genetic and nutritional factors. Two other factors that have been implicated but will not be discussed are parity and mental stress. The former has less relevance to the elderly population, and the latter is difficult to evaluate based on the available literature.

Genetic Risk Factors: Population and Race

Prevalence studies suggest that there are important differences in the likelihood of developing diabetes among various populations, particularly those of certain ethnic groups and races (Tables 8.2, 8.3, 8.4) (1, 19, 20, 21). One of the problems in interpreting ethnicity and race as risk factors is the genetic heterogeneity of populations that are socially labeled as ethnic and racial groups. Cooper (22) is one of the few investigators to note the epidemiologic importance of the fact that the percentage of white admixture in the American black population varies geographically. It is highest in the South.

One possible explanation for population differences, particularly among ethnic and racial minorities, is the natural history of these groups. Using a microevolutionary model, including Darwinian natural selection and genetic drift, Neel (23) and Lieberman (24, 25) hypothesized that diabetogenic genotypes and phenotypes may have had an adaptive advantage in populations living a relative feast-and-famine lifestyle, such as those in slavery. Cahill (26) speculated that a "touch" of diabetes might have saved a gram or two of nitrogen on each feeding–fasting cycle and, therefore, had a selective advantage. Other investigators have felt that hyperinsulinemia would have allowed an increase in the storage of available nutrients during the feasting stage of the cycle. This stored energy could then be called on during periods of relative fasting, when energy expenditure exceeds energy intake. The diabetogenic phenotype becomes disadvantageous under conditions of rapid acculturation—particularly Westernization, when there is a substantial reduction in activity levels and energy expenditure coupled with ample energy intake (23).

Although some genetic markers (e.g., HLA haplotypes) have been found in populations for Type I diabetes, no widely distributed population markers have been found for Type II diabetes.

Genetic Risk Factors: Family Studies

Familial patterns of Type II, or noninsulin-dependent diabetes mellitus (NIDDM), have been noted in all groups. In 1976 the National Health Interview Survey found that 29% of people with a medical history of diabetes reported having a diabetic sibling, compared to 4% of nondiabetic persons. In the 1976–1980 NHANES II survey, 35% of people aged 35 to 74 with a medical history of diabetes reported that the mother, father, or both were diabetic (16). The evidence suggests that there is both a male and female contribution as a risk for diabetes and that the parental contributions may be additive (16). Since there are no adequate genetic markers, it becomes difficult to disassociate the risk of family resemblances by virtue of living together versus family resemblances by virtue of genetic inheritance.

The twin study data indicate high concordance rates for NIDDM among both dizygotic and monozygotic twin pairs. The concordance rates among monozygotic twins have been reported to be as high as 90% (16).

Metabolic Risk Factors

An elevated blood or plasma glucose concentration resulting in impaired glucose tolerance (see Table 8.1) has consistently been a strong predictor for the development of noninsulin-dependent diabetes mellitus. The mean plasma glucose values for blacks and whites show no significant differences (12). Impaired glucose tolerance rates for blacks do not increase with age, and these rates are lowest for black females (12).

In other studies diminished insulin response following an oral glucose challenge was an independent predictor for the development of diabetes. These results have been shown in populations of Japanese, Pima Indians, and British (16). This reviewer knows of no comparable studies on insulin concentrations in black Americans.

Nutritional Risk Factors: Obesity

Obesity is the most powerful risk factor for diabetes. The prevalence of obesity is far more important in determining the frequency of NIDDM than any other factor (1, 20). Many studies have shown that two-thirds to nine-tenths of individuals may be classified as obese at the time of diagnosis of diabetes mellitus (1, 20, 28). For those over 25% of ideal body weight, obesity correlates with an increasing incidence of diabetes mellitus (20). Although there was little consistent difference among the various age groups between the mean weights of black and white men, black women at each age group between 18 and 74 years of age had larger mean weights than white women. The differences averaged about 20 pounds for the groups aged 35 to 64 (29). These data are based on the first NHANES survey from 1971–1974.

More recent work by Bonham and Block (30) shows that the prevalence of obesity among black females is striking when compared with the white population. Using the body mass index (weight in kg/height in square meters) with a cutoff of 28.49+ for males and 35.29+ for females, these authors found that 50% of black females compared to 22% of white females in the group aged 55 to 64 were classified as obese. These percentages diminished in the group aged 65 and older to 38.5% for black females and 18.8% for white females. Racial differences were less marked for males. In the 55–64 age range 23.7% of black males and 16.2% of white males were classified as obese. For the group aged 65 and older 18.6% of black males and 10.9% of white males were classified as obese (29, 30, 31). Kelly West's work (1) clearly demonstrates that the relationship between obesity and NIDDM occurs for many ethnic groups and in all three major racial groups. Studies of siblings of diabetics also show a relationship of obesity to diabetes. The frequency of diabetes was 2.5 times higher in obese than lean siblings of a diabetic (32).

The duration of obesity as well as the amount of adiposity is significantly correlated with NIDDM. A number of longitudinal studies (28) confirmed this relationship. A comparison of the 1960–1962 Health Examination Survey data with the 1971–1974 NHANES data showed increases in weight for black and white males and females aged 18 to 74. Greatest increases took place for females in the group aged 55 to 64.

The distribution of body fat may be an additional risk factor associated with adiposity (16). Feldman and his colleagues (33) had noted that a central distribution of body fat created a body type positively associated with diabetes among black and white females. Later work has confirmed that a greater waist to hip ratio is found among diabetics compared to age/sex-matched controls.

Clearly, the problem of obesity is a problem of energy balance (32). However, the balance between caloric intake and expenditure is not clearly related to the degree of obesity. There is little information about exercise and the risk for NIDDM. Exercise does diminish insulin resistance and, of course, uses calories (16). Recent studies on Polynesians (2) undergoing different rates of modernization indicate that there are ethnic-specific interactions betwen activity levels and obesity as concomitant risk factors for NIDDM. Zimmet and others (34) have suggested that exercise may indeed be a precursor to both obesity and diabetes. However, data from HANES II did not show a significant correlation between various physical activity categories and glucose tolerance (16).

A number of authors have addressed the issue of whether obesity and diabetes are the outcome of common metabolic problems (16, 28, 31, 32). One unanswered question is what comes first—obesity, resistance to insulin action, or hyperinsulinemia? Initial research indicated that cellular resistance developed as adiposity increased. More recent evidence seems to indicate that hyperinsulinemia may be primary and that this leads to a down regulation or a decrease in sensitivity of cells to the transport of insulin (27, 28, 32). Mesbin, O'Leary, and Pulkkinen (35) have suggested that there is no decrease in insulin binding in obese individuals and that the problem is a postreceptor one. Mesbin has also presented data that indicate that hyperinsulinism may be due to two mechanisms: increased pancreatic production of insulin and decreased hepatic clearance of insulin (36).

There is, apparently, an interaction of obesity with unknown genetic factors. The diabetogenic effect of obesity is most striking in families with a history of diabetes. In one study (27) 27% of obese siblings of nonobese diabetics became diabetic, compared to 11% of obese siblings of obese diabetics. Diabetes was five times more likely to occur in obese siblings of nonobese diabetics than in nonobese siblings of obese diabetics (27, 37). On a population level, obesity may have a greater diabetogenic effect in those populations with a history conducive to the adaptive thriftiness of hyperinsulinemia and enhanced fat storage (23–26).

Many reviews of the available data (1, 27, 28) fail to confirm a relationship between specific dietary items and obesity or diabetes. Furthermore, with the exception of obesity, most other prospective studies have failed to confirm an association of diabetes with other nutritional variables (16). Although glucose levels are associated with adiposity, they may not be associated with histories of total food energy intake (16, 38).

Dietary Risk Factor

Many dietary components have been investigated as potential risk factors for noninsulin-dependent diabetes mellitus. Most researchers agree that at this point there is no convincing evidence that dietary composition influences the incidence of diabetes (16). For example, in 1978 West (1) reported that 21 studies indicated sucrose consumption as a risk factor for diabetes and 22 studies reported that it was not.

The distinction between simple and complex carbohydrates has been called into question in recent years. A number of researchers using isocaloric quantities of previously designated simple and complex carbohydrate foods have demonstrated no consistent increases in insulin or glucose levels in nondiabetics and diabetics in these two categories of carbohydrates (39). In fact, the ingestion of previously designated complex carbohydrates, such as potatoes, led to increases in plasma glucose concentrations that were similar to sugars (39). The implications of these studies are far-reaching for both nondiabetics and diabetics. Currently test meals combining a number of carbohydrates, proteins, and fats are being tested for their glycemic indices (the area under the 2-hour glucose response curve for a particular food item/the area under a 2-hour glucose response curve for glucose).

The results of experiments measuring the glycemic indices of foods also argue against a simple fiber hypothesis as proposed by Trowell and Burkitt (40). These researchers propose that the reduction in dietary fiber and increase in sugars and highly processed carbohydrates have led to a number of diseases of Westernization. They suggest that dietary fiber favorably alters absorption patterns and speeds the transit of food through the gastrointestinal tract. Some studies have demonstrated an inverse correlation between crude dietary fiber intake and death from diabetes (20, 40). Current studies are examining the many forms of dietary fiber to determine how individual types may affect carbohydrate absorption and produce an alteration in glycemic response. American slave diets, in particular, were based on low-glycemic-index and high-fiber foods (24, 25).

Dietary fats and proteins have also been implicated as dietary risk factors. The studies investigating fat intake are often confounded because of the higher caloric density of fat compared to carbohydrates and proteins. Furthermore, high fat intake is generally associated with low fiber intake (20, 40).

Deficiencies in micronutrients, in particular chromium, have been postulated as possible risk factors for diabetes. There is little epidemiologic data to support these conclusions, which are based primarily on laboratory work (20).

NHANES I food consumption patterns for black elderly revealed few significant differences in the frequency of intake of specific food items compared to the general population (41). In the group aged 65 to 74, black Americans consumed the following foods in greater frequency than their white age counterparts: fish and shellfish, eggs, fruits, and vegetables rich in Vitamin A, fruits and vegetables rich in Vitamin C, bread, and sweetened beverages. Elderly black Americans have lower frequencies of intake of dairy products, fats and oils, desserts, cereals, meat, and poultry. These data, based on 24-hour recalls and food-frequency questionnaires, do not reveal any significant patterns linked to diabetes.

In summary, the relative risks are greater for older females of ethnic or minority groups who have a family history of diabetes and who themselves are obese.

Complications of Diabetes

The mortality and morbidity associated with diabetes are due to vascular complications rather than elevated glucose levels per se. The Airlie House Conference in June 1980 (42) defined five complications of diabetes for which proper treatment could reduce the frequency of their occurrence. These complications include blindness, renal disease, amputations, diabetic ketoacidosis, and poor perinatal outcomes. Other complications include cardiovascular disease, hypertension, and neuropathy, as well as reductions in activity level, changes in lifestyle, and the economic burden associated with treatment.

Retinopathy

Diabetic retinopathy is the leading cause of new cases of blindness in people aged 20 to 74 in the United States. Approximately 5,800 diabetics become blind each year. Cataracts and glaucoma are also associated with diabetes, and these rates are two to three times those reported in the general population (5). Prevalence data indicate that retinopathy occurs with higher frequency among black than white diabetics. Age-standardized prevalence of blindness secondary to diabetic retinopathy was more than twice as great for nonwhites (13.6 per 100,000) than whites (5.9 per 100,000). Rates are consistently higher in older individuals, with longer duration of the disease. Females had almost three times the rate of males (12).

Effective treatment is possible. Photocoagulation using lasers can reduce the incidence of blindness by about 50% in persons with severe proliferative retinopathy (5).

Nephropathy

Approximately 10% of diabetics have diabetic nephropathy, as marked by the presence of constant proteinuria. Prevalence increases with duration of diabetes, and after 15 years of diabetes about one-third of persons with insulin-dependent diabetes and one-fifth of those with noninsulin-dependent diabetes have developed nephropathy (5). The annual incidence of diabetic endstage renal disease is about 18 per million population. Hypertension as well as hyperglycemia are associated with higher prevalences of nephropathy. Kidney disease is three times more common in black (40 per 1,000,000) than in white (14 per 1,000,000) diabetics (5).

Control of both hypertension and hyperglycemia may reduce nephrotic complications. One-year survival of diabetic patients treated with dialysis is about 75%, and of those treated with transplantation, 82% (5, 12).

Peripheral Vascular Disease

Peripheral vascular disease (PVD) of the extremities is due to the diminished arterial perfusion in the legs and feet. This condition is present in 8% of adult diabetics at diagnosis and in 45% with diabetes duration less than 20 years. The incidence of PVD in diabetic men and women is four to seven times greater than in nondiabetics. About 15% of diabetics have experienced ulcers on the feet or ankles. Diabetes accounts for 40 to 45% of all nontraumatic amputations, and an amputation occurs annually in about 60 per 10,000 diabetics (5). Survival for 3 years after amputation is only about 50%.

There is a paucity of published information on the incidence and prevalence of PVD among U.S. blacks. One study in South Carolina indicated that about 95 per 10,000 black diabetics aged 45–64 experienced a lower-extremity amputation. For individuals over the age of 65, the rate was 150 per 10,000. The amputation rate in black diabetics was 2.3 times that of white diabetics. Peripheral neuropathy, foot injury, and infection contribute to the high rates of amputation (12). Periodic foot examinations, early treatment, and the use of prosthetic shoes could reduce foot complications.

Diabetic Ketoacidosis

Approximately three to eight episodes of diabetic ketoacidosis occur annually per 1,000 diabetics. Infections and noncompliance with diet and medication appear to precipitate at least 50% of these episodes. Two to fourteen percent of all hospitalizations for diabetes involve acidosis or coma. The age-adjusted death rate (1970–1978) from diabetes with acidosis or coma was three times higher for nonwhites (3.4) compared to whites (1.1). Rates were particularly high in the South (12). A secular trend in acidosis- or coma-associated deaths since 1970 has shown a significant reduction for all diabetics, but it is greater for nonwhites (12).

Cerebral Vascular Disease

The occurrence of stroke in diabetics is about two to six times greater than in nondiabetics, and it is higher in black than white diabetics. In the group aged 65 to 84, stroke occurs annually in 100–175 per 10,000 diabetics (12).

Hypertension

About half of diabetics have a medical history of hypertension. The rate of hypertension in elderly diabetics is 1.5 times greater than in nondiabetics. Rates are higher in females than in males and in blacks than in whites. Hypertension rates increase with age but not with duration of diabetes or degree of glucose control (5). Increased blood pressure is a major risk factor for the development of retinopathy, nephropathy, cerebrovascular disease, and heart disease. In one recent survey the rate of hypertension in blacks with diabetes was 53.8% versus 29.2% among nondiabetic blacks. The hypertension rate among black diabetics was only slightly greater than the white diabetic hypertension rate of 51.3% (5). The control of blood pressure would also have a significant impact on the other complications of diabetes.

Heart Diseases

Approximately twice as many diabetics as nondiabetics have a medical history of a heart condition. Coronary heart disease is present in about 13% of adult diabetics and congestive heart failure in about 7%. Rates increase with age. Ischemic heart disease is involved in about 50 to 60% of recorded deaths of adult diabetics.

There is evidence that blacks with diabetes relative to blacks without the disease have an increased risk for heart disease. However, myocardial infarction appears to be less frequent among blacks than among whites. In one study, after adjusting for blood pressure, cholesterol, and cigarette smoking, the rate of cardiovascular disease was lower for blacks with diabetes than blacks without diabetes (12).

The National Diabetes Advisory Board (42) has widely disseminated its book on *The Prevention and Treatment of Five Complications of Diabetes*. A number of state and federal health units have implemented these suggestions. Preliminary evidence from Florida indicates that low-cost diagnostic and educational procedures can be introduced in the public health setting and that their potential contribution to the reduction of retinopathy, nephropathy, and amputations may be substantial (43).

Disabilities

Table 8.7 (15) outlines the impact of diabetes in terms of limited activity, days of restricted activity, bed days, work-loss days, physician visits, hospitalization, medication, and the perceived impact of the disease. Based on the National Health Survey data, 20.8% of known diabetics over the age of 65 indicate that they are bothered all the time by diabetes. An additional 12.8% state that they are bothered a great deal of the time.

Blacks aged 65 and older compared to whites suffer more disability days. During 1975 noninstitutionalized blacks averaged over 60 days of restricted activity per person versus 38 days for whites. Blacks experienced twice as many bed-disability days as whites (25 days vs. 12 days) (18). The black/white ratio for individuals aged 65 or older for limitation of activities was 1:3; limitation of mobility, 1:4; the number of restricted days, 1:6, and number of days of bed-disability, 2:1 (18).

For individuals with known diabetes, nearly 90% have seen a physician one or more times in the past year for their diabetes (15) (see Table 8.7). About half of adult diabetics have seen a physician for their diabetes in an ambulatory setting within the past two to six months, but about 10% report that they have not seen a physician for over a year (5). For diabetics aged 65 and older, the annual hospitalization rate is about 50 per 10,000. A large portion of these hospitalizations are for diabetes control (5).

Approximately 190,000 diabetics are in nursing homes, comprising 15% of nursing home residents. About 75% are aged 75 and older, and 75% are female (5).

The economic disabilities and financial risks associated with diabetes are profound for elderly minorities. Recent congressional reports have investigated the severity of the financial burden of health care and have suggested that out-of-pocket costs for the elderly should not be allowed to rise beyond the current level of 15% of their income (44, 45).

About 90% of adult diabetics and almost all of those over the age of 65

TABLE 8.7 Impact of Known Diabetes by Age and Selected Health Status Indicators, United States, 1979–1981

	Persons with known diabetes 65 years and over		
	All persons 65 years and over	65–74 years	75 years and over
Disability status	Percent		
Persons with limitation of activity due to one or more chronic conditions or impairments	65.7	62.4	70.9
Persons for whom diabetes is a cause of limitation of activity	32.0	33.2	30.0
Persons with one bed day or more in the past year for diabetes	10.8	11.9	9.0
Disability days	Number		
Restricted activity days due to diabetes per person per year	24.2	28.0	17.7
Bed days due to diabetes per person per year	7.4	5.7	10.3
Bed days due to diabetes per person having one bed day or more in the past year for diabetes	62.7	39.8	114.0
Work-loss days due to diabetes per currently employed person with diabetes per year	0.6	0.7	—
Medical care	Percent		
Persons who have ever seen a physician for diabetes	99.7	99.8	99.5
Persons with one or more physician visits in the past year for diabetes	87.8	87.7	88.1
Persons ever hospitalized for diabetes	29.4	30.0	28.5
Persons taking medicine or treatment recommended by their physician for diabetes	81.5	83.1	79.0
Perceived impact			
Persons bothered all the time by diabetes	20.8	21.4	19.7
Persons bothered a great deal by diabetes	12.8	13.3	11.9
Persons bothered a great deal by diabetes all the time	7.2	7.9	6.0
Persons reported to be in fair or poor health	50.7	52.9	46.9

Source: Drury TF, Powell AL. Prevalence, impact, and demography of known diabetes in the United States. NCHS Advance Data No. 114; 1986:9

have some form of health insurance. However, these insurance programs do not pay for the total amount of health care.

The lowest estimate of cost directly attributable to diabetes is $13.8 billion annually (3.6% of the total U.S. health cost): $7.4 billion is for medical care expenses, including hospitalization and nursing home care, and $6.3 billion is due to indirect cost attributed to disability and premature death (5).

Mortality

In 1982 over 34,500 deaths were attributed to diabetes as the underlying cause. This resulted in diabetes being ranked as the seventh leading cause of death; 95,000 additional deaths listed diabetes as a contributing cause. Table 8.8 lists the number of deaths and the death rate per 100,000 living persons in each for black males and females. For the group aged 65 and older, black males had death rates higher than those of white male diabetics. The rate was nearly one-third higher in the group aged 65 to 84. Death rates from diabetes as an underlying cause for older black females aged 60 to 74 were nearly 2.5 times greater than for whites. Death rates were nearly twofold greater in the group aged 75 to 85 and older. Overall the death rate for black females in these later years was higher than that of black males (12) (see Table 8.8). Survival of 25 years after diagnosis of NIDDM may be about 70 to 80% of expected survival in the general adult population (5).

TABLE 8.8 Number of Deaths and Death Rate from Diabetes as the Underlying Cause of Death for U.S. Blacks by Age and Sex, United States, 1980

Age at death (years)	Number of deaths	Death rate*	Number of deaths	Death rate*
	Black males		Black females	
All ages	2,010	16.05	3,534	25.30
Under 25	26	0.39	20	0.29
25–34	55	2.81	58	2.58
35–44	120	9.75	107	7.23
45–54	216	21.18	328	26.24
55–64	489	57.45	739	70.0
65–74	577	102.1	1,143	147.7
75–84	415	182.8	806	224.5
85+	112	211.3	333	314.2

*Death rate: Number of underlying cause deaths in each age/sex group divided by the number of 100,000 living persons in the group.
Source: Roseman J. Diabetes in black Americans. In: National Diabetes Data Group, eds. *Diabetes in America* [HHS (PHS) NIH Publ. No. 85-1468]. Washington, DC: U.S. Government Printing Office; 1985:VIII–16.

Roseman (12) cautions that mortality rates may have questionable validity in estimating the scope and impact of diabetes in the black population because they may depend on access to and adequacy of medical care. There is also underreporting of diabetes as an underlying or contributing cause of death.

One new approach to looking at the mortality data is to assess "excess deaths." This is the difference between the number of deaths observed in minority populations and the number of deaths that would have been expected if the minority population had the same age- and sex-specific death rates as the nonminority population (31). Diabetes accounts for 3.1% of the excess deaths among blacks under age 70. Excess mortality is 2% for males and 5% for females. Diabetes ranks sixth in the excess causes of death among blacks. The Task Force on Black Minority Health also looked at relative risk by dividing minority death rates by the white death rate. Using this criterion, diabetes ranked fourth in males as a cause of death and second in females. Relative risk due to diabetes is 17.7 for black males versus 9.5 for white males, with a ratio of 1:9. For black females the relative risk is 22.1 versus 8.7 for white females, with a ratio of 2:5 (31).

In summary, the complications of diabetes take a tremendous toll on the black elderly. The prevalence of macrovascular disease causing heart disease and stroke and of microvascular disease leading to kidney failure and blindness appears to be more frequent among black diabetics than white ones. All these diseases increase with increasing age, and many of them show an increase with the duration of diabetes. The additional social and economic consequences of lost work time and income and the cost of treatment for diabetes are overwhelming in this already low-income segment of the U.S. population.

OBESITY

Obesity is one of the major health problems in the United States. An estimated 20 to 60 million Americans are substantially above ideal body weight (38, 46). Most perceptions of obesity are based on visual assessment or measurements of body weight. Obesity, however, is more properly defined as excessive accumulation of body fat: in excess of 20% in males and 28% in females (46).

Obesity has been associated with an increased risk for diabetes (as previously discussed), hypertension, cardiovascular problems, and, in general, a reduced life expectancy (38). In addition, there is the psychosocial stigma placed upon individuals who are corpulent. A quadruple set of prejudices faces black elderly females who are also obese.

Definitions and Diagnosis of Obesity

Overweight and obesity are not the same, although they have often been used synonymously. Abraham, Carroll, Najjar, and Fulwood (47) have clearly made the distinction in analyzing the NHANES I data. Overweight is defined as an excess in body weight relative to standards for height. In this report individuals over the 85th percentile are considered overweight. Obesity is defined as an excess of body fat based on the sum of the triceps skinfold and subscapular skin fold. Recent studies have used a weight/height index of weight divided/height squared. This is the Quetelet Index or the Body Mass Index (48).

Body weight is the most widely used anthropometric indicator of nutritional reserves, and weight relative to height has been shown to be an acceptable measure of body mass for most epidemiological surveys (48). Many studies have suggested that the Body Mass Index and the Metropolitan Life Standards Weights are the most appropriate for epidemiologic work focusing on obesity as a risk factor (48).

Other anthropometric measurements have been used as alternatives to body weight. Body-girth measurements or circumferences measured at specific locations have a high correlation with body mass. The most commonly used measure of girth is the circumference of the upper arm. This measurement in conjunction with the triceps skinfold has been used to compare the fat and lean components of the arm and thus provide a measurement of energy and protein stores.

More sophisticated, expensive, and time-consuming techniques have been used to assess the fat component of the body. These techniques have included underwater weighing or densitometry, x-rays, ultrasound, electrical impedence, and measurement of the lean body mass by total body water and body potassium levels (48).

Prevalence of Obesity

The prevalence rates calculated from the NHANES I data indicate that 11 million adult men (19%) and 18 million adult women (28%) were overweight based on the 85th percentile weight/height criterion. The proportion of adult males and females who are overweight was significantly higher than the proportion who are obese (47). For each age group the proportion of women who are obese based on skinfold thicknesses is greater than that of males.

Among those aged 65 and older, 16.6% of males were classified as obese and 22% as overweight, while 26.1% of females were classified as obese and 40% as overweight (47). Using the Body Mass Index, Boham and Brock

(30) found that 23.7% of black males and 50% of black females aged 55 to 64 were obese. Among those aged 65 and older, 18.6% of black males and 38.5% of black females were classified as obese.

Data on the percentile of weight distribution for elderly black and white males are presented on Table 8.9. Black/white differences at the 90th and 95th percentiles were similar for the groups aged 55 to 64 (29 lbs) and 65 to 74 (7–8 lbs). The black/white differences at the 90th percentile for women aged 55 to 64 were 28 pounds and for the group over age 65, 22 pounds. At the 95th percentile female black/white differences were 96 pounds for the group aged 55 to 64 and 27 pounds for the group over 65 years of age. Therefore, for both age/sex groups there is a reduction in weight in the decade over 65 compared to earlier decades. The highest mean weights for black males occur in the decade from 35 to 44 years and for females in the decades from 45 to 64 years (29).

In summary, obesity occurs in higher prevalence among middle-aged and older black males and females. It decreases in the oldest age groups. A significantly higher proportion of older black females are obese compared to any other age/sex/race groups (29, 46, 47).

Risk Factors for Obesity

A multitude of studies have implicated a number of environmental and genetic risk factors for the development of obesity. This review will focus on factors important in describing obesity among older individuals. Many other reviews have shown the importance of childhood obesity in predicting weight levels in adulthood (49).

TABLE 8.9 Weight Centiles in Pounds for Black and White Males and Females over the age of 55 Years

	Age			
	55–64 years		65–74 years	
	90th%	95th%	90th%	95th%
Males				
White	208	220	198	210
Black	237	249	205	218
Females				
White	187	201	180	192
Black	215	297	202	219

Sociodemographic Risk Factors

Economic Associations

Many studies have demonstrated a striking association between socioeconomic status and the prevalence of obesity, particularly among women (49). This relationship is true regardless of whether socioeconomic status is based on family income, education, occupational status of the subjects, or socioeconomic status of the family of origin. Fully 30% of women of lower socioeconomic status are obese, compared with less than 5% of the upper-status groups. The prevalence of obesity for men of lower socioeconomic status was 32%, compared to 16% among upper-class men. Recent data (45) indicate that among the poor, 49% of black and 26% of white women aged 45 to 64 are obese. In groups above the poverty level, 40% of black women and 28% of white women are classified as obese. Four percent of older black men and 5% of white men below the poverty level are obese, compared to 12% of black and 13% of white men above the poverty level. Some studies (50) have demonstrated that groups that are upwardly mobile tend to have a reduction in the percentage of women who are obese.

Ethnicity

Ethnicity may also be a predictor of obesity. Groups of Eastern European and Hispanic origins have been shown to be particularly obese.

Religion

Religious affiliation is another social factor that has been linked to obesity. The greatest prevalence of obesity has been found among Jews, followed by Roman Catholics and Protestants (50).

Education

Educational levels have been related to the prevalence of obesity. Among males with more than 12 years of school, the average thickness of four fat folds was 10% greater than among individuals with 8 years or less of education. In females the opposite trend was observed. The higher educational group averaged 20% smaller fat folds compared to females in the lower educational group (51).

Dietary Factors

Although obesity is due to an excess of energy stored as fat, there is a surprising relationship between reported caloric intake and the prevalence of obesity in older Americans. Black and white males and females 55 years of age or older report caloric intakes that range from 57 to 81% of standards. Highest intakes are reported by white males and females above the poverty level in the age range of 55 to 64 (81.2% and 81.1%, respectively). Lowest caloric intakes (57%) are reported by black males aged 55 to 64 who have incomes below the poverty level. The lowest caloric intakes reported by black females aged 55 to 64 are 66.2% to 74.1% of standard intake (52, 53). Therefore, the lowest reported caloric intake for females was found in the group with the highest prevalence of obesity. Caloric intakes for older black males above the poverty level were highest (2,018 kcal) and lowest for the same age group below the poverty level (1,479 kcal). Daily caloric intake for black females above the poverty level was 1,261 kcal and below the poverty level 1,059 kcal. For all race/sex groups caloric intake decreased with increasing age.

Excess caloric intake will in most instances lead to increases in fat stores (46, 48). However, experimental evidence indicates that there are great individual differences in the "costs" of a pound of fat. Experiments using overfeeding in individuals of normal weight found that observed weight gains were low compared to expected weight gains. Weight gains have been reported to be as low as one-third of the expected amount (49). However, obese rats and humans who lose weight and are then refed regain weight on fewer calories and in shorter periods of time with each weight loss/regain cycle (38, 49).

The sources of calories, whether from proteins, fats, or carbohydrates, have not shown a consistent relationship to the prevalence of obesity (41, 52, 53). Food frequency profiles as identified in the NHANES surveys indicate few significant differences between black and white intakes. These data were discussed above (41).

Since energy input has had relatively low explanatory value for obesity for older Americans, other factors should be investigated.

Metabolic Risk Factors

Recent evidence (38) suggests an important role of energy utilization in the determination of body weight. Experiments indicate that animals and humans who are overfed will increase basal metabolic rates and physical activity to increase the number of calories dissipated as heat (38). Conversely, with caloric restriction, heat production and basal metabolic rate are reduced. This is a set-point mechanism of weight regulation. The importance of diet-induced thermogenesis and the possible mediation of heat production via brown adipose tissue has not been investigated on a population level.

In older individuals thermoregulation may be disturbed, so the outcome is a reduction in the caloric cost of basal metabolism. Thermoregulatory abilities may have a genetic component (38), since obese women who gain weight readily have a family history of obesity and exhibit a reduced thermogenic response.

Involvement of the metabolic sodium-potassium pump in obesity has been explored only recently. This pump is involved in cellular energy expenditure. The sodium-potassium pump accounts for up to 50% of basal metabolic caloric expenditures. Evidence summarized by Kanarek (38) indicates that obese persons have a reduction in sodium pump units.

Other metabolic changes, such as hyperinsulinism as discussed above, also enhance fat deposition. Since these metabolic alterations are the result of genotype–environmental interactions, a number of researchers have suggested population differences in fat deposition ability related to genetic selective pressures (23, 24, 25, 54). A metabolic genotype allowing for the "thriftiness" of fat storage during times of abundance would be advantageous in populations that had absolute or relative cycles in caloric intake ranging from abundance to deprivation. A number of researchers have suggested that these selective pressures operated within the black American population during the period of slavery (23–26). With an increased stability in the food supply and the reduction of caloric expenditure, a "hyperefficient" metabolic system can lead to a state of corpulence.

Psychological Risk Factors

Kanarek, Orthen-Gambill, Barks-Kaufman, and Mayer (38) have reviewed a number of possible psychological and behavioral determinants of obesity. However, most of these studies have been with college-aged individuals. They review the evidence for "obese eating styles," including the rate of food intake and meal size, in terms of restrained and unrestrained eating behavior, set-point theory, and the theory that eating behavior of obese individuals is triggered mainly by salient external food-related cues. Their comprehensive review highlights the fact that there is a paucity of data on psychological factors on the eating behavior of elderly and minority populations.

Activity Levels as Risk Factors

As noted in the section on caloric intake and dietary risk factors, adults differ substantially in energy expenditure. Even when matched for age, sex, and weight, individuals may differ in basal metabolic rates by 30% (55). In addition, physical activity levels vary greatly within and between populations. Many studies have shown that both obese youngsters and adults are less physically active than their lean counterparts. However, evidence indicates that physical exercise is not the main factor in determining energy expenditure or energy intake because energy expenditure due to exercise may be countered by increases in food consumption. The result may be that greater food intake outweighs the calories expended.

Many studies have demonstrated a negative effect of obesity on the maximum amount of oxygen that can be utilized by muscles. Because body fat acts as an excess load, obese individuals undergo greater physiological strain than lean individuals during exercise (48). These factors may lead to reduced activity for obese individuals.

Genetic Risk Factors

There may be population differences in terms of propensity for obesity. These have been discussed above in light of a metabolic thriftiness hypothesis (23).

There is clearly a familial tendency to become obese. Early work has shown that nearly 70% of obese subjects had at least one obese parent (49). The results of many studies indicate that although there is a genetic component, environmental factors play a significant role in the etiology of obesity. The exact nature of the inherited component is not known. It may involve the amount or activity level of brown fat (38) or the regulation of energy metabolism in other ways (55).

Garn and his colleagues (51, 56) have conducted a number of analyses in an attempt to disaggregate the genetic effects from the other familial effects of cohabitation. They observed the fatness correlations of skinfold measurements of related and unrelated individuals who reside in the same household. They found no significant difference in correlations between biological parent–child correlations (0.21) and singly adopted parent–child correlations (0.23) and the amount of body fatness. However for doubly adopted parent–child correlations (i.e., no genetic relationship between parent and child) the correlation was only 0.11 for the triceps skinfold (51, 56). Family-line resemblances were also investigated longitudinally. Husband and wife fatness changes were highly correlated. Greatest gains occurred in the greater than 85th percentile weight group (51, 56).

Changes in weight followed a similar trend. The correlation between biological parents and children was approximately 0.25; between adoptive parent and child, .17; between siblings, approximately 0.33; and between husband and wife, 0.11 to 0.14 (56). These findings clearly indicate that family-line resemblances have both a genetic and environmental component.

Complications Associated with Obesity

Excess adiposity is a risk factor for a number of noninfectious diseases and deleterious metabolic states. The relationship of obesity to these diseases is not a simple one. Most studies have looked at the amount of fatness. Other studies have looked at the correlations between duration of obesity, maximum weight in the lifetime, and the distribution of adiposity. These relationships have been discussed in the section on diabetes.

Obesity has been related to high blood pressure, gout, diabetes, gall bladder disease, arthritis, cancer, and cardiovascular disease. However, many of these relationships are weak and do not suggest any specific causal mechanisms (57). Furthermore, few studies focus on the black elderly population.

Hypertension

A review of 39 studies indicates a linear relationship between hypertension and increases in weight (57). Data also indicate that a high waist-to-hip circumference ratio, indicating a central distribution of fat, is an additional relative risk factor for hypertension. The correlations between relative weight and systolic and diastolic blood pressure actually decline with age from 0.29 in the age range from 35 to 44 to 0.19 in the age range from 75 to 79. Females follow a similar trend. Highest correlations (0.37) occur in the decade from 35 to 44, with lowest values (0.08) in the age range from 75 to 79 for systolic pressures. Correlations with diastolic pressure fluctuate more widely (57).

Diabetes

The relationship between diabetes and obesity has been discussed above. It is apparent from a number of studies that the amount of obesity, the duration of obesity, and the central distribution of fat are risk factors for the development of NIDDM. The risk associated with obesity is enhanced by a family history of diabetes.

Gout and Arthritis

Gout and arthritis have also been related to body weight. In women the occurrence of arthritis was 55% greater in the obese group than the lean group, and gout was six times more frequent in the obese group. The Framingham study indicated that gout is related to obesity in men (57).

Heart Disease

Increases in body weight have also been associated with artherosclerosis and cardiovascular disease. In the Framingham study, which controlled for such confounding factors as blood pressure, cholesterol, smoking, age, and diabetes, the association for relative weight and cardiovascular disease was maintained.

Mortality

There is ample evidence that obesity, or at least overweight, is associated with increasing mortality. However, for elderly black individuals the relationship between mortality and obesity is clearly confounded by factors involved in the provision of medical care.

The risk for death increases proportionately with the percentage of overweight in both men and women. For example, men 20% above average weight showed about a 25% increase in mortality, while those 40% and 60% above average showed an increase in mortality of 67% and 150%, respectively. The rise in mortality in overweight women was distinctly lower. The mortality rate among overweight persons was significantly increased by the presence of other medical conditions. Earlier mortality may explain, in part, the lower weights seen in the higher age groups of elderly blacks and whites.

In summary, obesity is implicated in a number of metabolic diseases that result in increased mortality. The precise role of obesity in other disease states has not been well described.

RESEARCH NEEDS

The following research agenda addresses the problems in the prevention and treatment of diabetes and obesity and their complications. Because of the close association of diabetes with obesity, it has been estimated that control of obesity could prevent nearly 300,000 cases of diabetes per year (31). The following research agenda is based primarily on the *Report of the Secretary's Task Force on Black and Minority Health* (31), *The Prevention and Treatment of Five Complications of Diabetes* (42), *Obesity In America* (46), *Health: United States 1981. Prevalence and Management of Diabetes* (58), and the *Review and Response to the Final Report of the National Black Health Providers Task Force on High Blood Pressure Education and Control* (59).

One area of research underlying all others is the nature and content of data bases. At present national data bases underestimate the disease frequency in blacks and particularly among black elderly. Oversampling of these groups would help this problem. Furthermore, many data bases use a variety of ethnic/racial identifiers that are not comparable. The development of appropriate racial/ethnic identifiers and a test of their accuracy would be a useful and necessary first step in linking data bases.

The remainder of this review is divided into research questions involved broadly with the areas of prevention and treatment.

Prevention Research Agenda

Prevention involves both basic research on the causes and pathogenesis of diabetes and obesity and their complications and applied research on the detection of disorders, and prevention through health promotion.

Basic Research on Risk Factors

Basic research is needed on both diabetes and obesity to identify risk factors and define risk status for elderly black Americans. Longitudinal, community-based studies are needed to establish risk profiles and risk patterns. Lifestyle patterns in middle age may be precursors to the risks detected in older individuals through cross-sectional studies. Community-based studies of black Americans would also allow for the designation of low-risk members of this group. Intragroup heterogeneity in risk status may be underrecognized because of problems of sampling minority elderly.

Specifically, research is needed to:

1. Develop new methods to assess obesity. The use of skinfold calipers and circumferences may not be adequate to measure adiposity in obese individuals. Skin and fat compressibility and the internal/external distribution of fat change with age. New methods suitable for epidemiological surveys are needed. For example, knee height is a useful proxy for stature among bed-ridden elderly.

2. Research protocols should include information on duration of obesity, the history of weight gain, and the relative fat patterning. These variables, in addition to amount of obesity, have been shown to be important and independent risk factors for diabetes, hypertension, and other metabolic diseases.

3. New techniques are needed to be able to accurately quantify activity levels and energy expenditure in activity. Information on activity patterns over time may be important in the etiology of both diabetes and obesity.

4. Activity levels and heat production should be related to food intake patterns and quantity. Little is known about these patterns among elderly individuals.

5. Social science research is needed to define the complex of sociocultural and psychosocial conditions that promote and maintain high levels of obesity among the elderly. Among those over 75 years of age, obesity is less of a problem than among the middle-aged and the young-old. Different biomedical as well as sociocultural factors may be operating in different age groups of elderly.

6. Basic research is needed on the control of food ingestion. Elderly individuals, particularly those with perceptual deficits in hearing, seeing,

smelling, and tasting, may attend to different internal and external cues than younger individuals. These cues may be physiological, environmental, or social. The roles psychological states play in food ingestion need elucidation.

7. Studies are needed to elucidate the relationships among specific foods, eating patterns, and normal and pathogenic metabolic processes.

8. Basic research is needed to explain the relationship of hypertension to obesity, diabetes, and the retinal, kidney, and macrovascular complications of diabetes mellitus.

Applied Research on Detection and Health Promotion

Applied research and recommendations for action are needed in the provision of health care to the black elderly.

1. Research is needed into the development of cost-effective and cost-beneficial large-scale screening programs among black elderly. Screening for hypertension and diabetes are particularly important, since it is estimated that 50% of Type II diabetics remain undetected.

2. Mechanisms should be developed to allow governmental and private agencies or institutions and members of the target population to develop screening programs for their workers, clients, or participants.

3. The development of mobile screening units for multiphasic screenings may be important in reaching the rural elderly. Research is needed to discover the best approaches to enhance accessibility to screening programs.

4. Public health efforts directed at black elderly must be culturally sensitive and appropriate (e.g., educational level, reading abilities, interests) to reach the target population.

5. Investigations are needed into the appropriate media and mass media approaches to promote healthful living that are specific for black elderly. Techniques may include the use of television and radio, mobile vans, or individual door-to-door health promotion campaigns. Additional research is needed to discover the sources of dietary and health information that the black elderly are using.

6. Disease prevention and health promotion campaigns must be tailored to the specific economic and social constraints in the target population. Barriers and promoters of healthful behaviors, particularly weight reduction, must be identified for the black elderly.

7. The identification of health-promoting behaviors practiced by some members of the community may serve as culturally appropriate models to be used for more extensive public health efforts.

8. Assessment should be made of the perceived costs and disabilities associated with diabetes and obesity among black elderly.

Treatment Research Agenda

Three areas of research are needed concerning the provision of treatment to the black elderly population. These include access to health care, patient education, and the prevention of complications.

Access to Health Care

1. Problems concerning minority access to health care are basic to many other problems encountered in public health efforts. Research is needed to establish easily accessible health services and programs. The type, placement, and number of such units would be specific to individual communities.

2. One frequently encountered barrier to access is transportation. New research solutions are needed to provide, at low or no cost, transportation to health care facilities.

3. New and cost-effective ways are needed to educate minority physicians and health care personnel. These individuals are not only health care providers but may serve as appropriate models.

4. Appropriate networks must be developed so that there is referral to and follow-up with easily accessible physicians, clinics, and hospitals.

5. The cost of health care must be contained. New approaches to financing health care, particularly for the elderly, must be investigated and implemented.

6. Research is needed to develop new ways to enhance accessibility to and delivery of drugs (e.g., insulin) and prosthetic devices.

7. Research is needed into the cost-effectiveness of home visits by health care workers.

Patient Education

1. Appropriate sites for patient education must be explored and developed. These might include clinics, the patients' homes, churches, worksites, social clubs, and congregate meal sites.

2. Appropriate materials for education must be developed and tested. Education should stress particular skills or behaviors necessary for home management. Perceptual deficits, reading levels, and educational ability must be assessed and considered in the development of these materials. The materials should be culturally sensitive to the diversity of dietary and health beliefs and behaviors practiced by black elderly.

3. Health educators should check the home environment to see if it is conducive to the implementation of home-management techniques (e.g., urine testing, blood glucose monitoring, blood pressure measurement,

weight measurement) and make appropriate adjustments in the environment or management protocols.

4. Programs must be developed to assure that low-income and limited-
mobility elderly have access to materials needed for treatment and home
management (e.g., insulin, tablets, syringes).

5. Health-related personnel should be trained to be sensitive to cultural
differences. This approach is necessary in order to integrate educational
material into the lifestyle of their patients in the most effective ways.

6. Research is needed to determine the best course of follow-up and
continued surveillance of black elderly patients. Periodic monitoring of their
compliance and success are necessary both for data collection and for the
continued promotion of appropriate health-related behaviors.

7. New guidelines for dieticians and patient educators prescribing weight
reduction and diabetic diets need to be developed for the target population
of black elderly. These diets must take into account present food items and
consumption patterns of the group as well as the individual. The health
educator should elicit information about the patient's perception of the
relationship between health and food.

8. Patient educators should develop new approaches and utilize the
group context, such as social groups and church groups, as a means of
reinforcing appropriate treatment and health-management behaviors.
Specific clubs such as Weight Watchers developed for the elderly may be a
useful adjunct to individual patient education.

9. Research is needed into the various roles of traditional health practitioners and medical practices concerning hypertension, diabetes, and their
complications.

10. New approaches to financing health education must be sought.
Third-party reimbursement for health education is most likely cost-
effective, yet only a few major providers will underwrite these costs.

Prevention of Complications

Prevention of complications relies on the knowledge and practice of physicians and health care providers, patients, and their families. New
approaches to both patient and professional education are needed to encourage the prevention, detection, and treatment of the complications of
diabetes and obesity.

1. Diabetic retinopathy accounts for approximately 5,000 new cases of
blindness each year, and 80% of individuals with diabetes of 15 years or
more have visual problems. New techniques must be employed to alert
physicians to the importance of annual ophthalmoscopic exams, tests of

visual acuity, evaluation of patient's reports of blurring and other visual changes, and blood pressure measurement. New materials should be developed that instruct patients at the appropriate level of their understanding about the relationship between diabetes control and retinopathy and the need to report any visual problems to their physicians. Individuals with visual problems need to have information on and access to treatment options.

2. Foot problems that lead to amputation could be reduced by an estimated 50 to 75% with appropriate detection. Physicians need to examine feet more frequently and refer patients for special podiatric services. Patients (or family members) need to be instructed on daily examination of their feet, on appropriate interventions when lesions or other problems are encountered, and on the availability of corrective shoes and prostheses. Injuries, ulcerations, gangrene, and infection commonly go undetected because individuals do not examine their feet, have a high pain threshold due to neuropathy, or may be visually and/or tactilely impaired.

3. Renal disease is a deadly complication of diabetes. Early detection of proteinuria is important. Educational materials relevant to the black elderly population are needed. The relationship between hypertension, sodium intake, and weight should be carefully explained to the diabetic patient and appropriate urine test skills taught.

4. Hyperosmotic nonketotic coma in diabetics over the age of 60 years is not uncommon. Complications of this condition include myocardial infarction and premature death. Frequent patient education is needed to reduce the causes of nonketotic coma, which include poor patient treatment and noncompliance. Elderly diabetic patients (or their family members) should be taught to assess urinary glucose and ketone levels.

5. Obesity is a social-psychological as well as a biomedical problem. Many studies have documented that physicians treat obese patients in a more punitive fashion than their nonobese patients. Physician education and attitude changes promoting more effective interactions with obese patients are desirable.

6. Research is needed to develop instruments to predict the most appropriate intervention techniques for successful weight reduction for particular patients. Specialized approaches should be developed for the black elderly.

In summary, an extensive number of research questions remain concerning the prevention and treatment of diabetes and obesity. Perhaps the most pressing problems are those involved in the access to health care, patient education, and the prevention of complications of diabetes and obesity.

REFERENCES

1. West KM. *Epidemiology of Diabetes and Its Vascular Lesions.* New York: Elsevier; 1978.
2. World Health Organization Expert Committee on Diabetes Mellitus. *Second Report* (Technical Report Series No. 646). Geneva: World Health Organization; 1980.
3. National Diabetes Data Group. Classification and diagnosis of diabetes mellitus and other categories of glucose intolerance. *Diabetes* 1979; 28:1039–1057.
4. Sherman CR, Spratt IL. Office guide to diagnosis and classification of diabetes mellitus and other categories of glucose intolerance. *Diabetes Care* 1981; 4:335.
5. National Diabetes Data Group. *Diabetes in America* [HHS (PHS) NIH Publication No. 85-1468]. Washington, DC: U.S. Government Printing Office; 1985.
6. Tattersall RB. Mild familial diabetes with dominant inheritance. *Quart. J. Med.* 1974; 43:339–357.
7. Tattersall RB, Fajans SS. A difference between the inheritance of classical juvenile-onset and maturity-onset diabetes of young people. *Diabetes* 1975; 24:44–53.
8. Hugh-Jones P. Diabetes in Jamaica. *Lancet* 1955; 2:891–897.
9. Rao PH. The role of undernutrition in the pathogenesis of diabetes mellitus. *Diabetes Care* 1984; 7:595–601.
10. Spillar RP, Winter WE, Kappy MS, Clarke DW. Biochemical characterization of a novel diabetes syndrome in American blacks. *Diabetes* 1985; 34:87–87A.
11. Winter WE, Riley WJ, Kappy MS, MacLaren NK, Clarke DW, Spillar RP. Maturity onset diabetes of youth in black Americans. *New England J. Med.* 1987; 316:285–291.
12. Roseman JM. Diabetes in black Americans. In: National Diabetes Data Group. *Diabetes in America* [HHS (PHS) NIH Publication No. 85-1468]. Washington, DC: U.S. Government Printing Office; 1985:VIII-1–24.
13. Harris MI. Prevalence of non-insulin-dependent diabetes and impaired glucose tolerance. In: National Diabetes Data Group. *Diabetes in America* [HHS (PHS) NIH Publication No. 85-1468]. Washington, DC: U.S. Government Printing Office; 1985: VI-1–31.
14. Drury, TF, Danchik KM, Harris MI. Sociodemographic characteristics of adult diabetes. In: National Diabetes Data Group. *Diabetes in America* [HHS (PHS) NIH Publication No. 85-1468]. Washington, DC: U.S. Government Printing Office; 1985; VII-1–37.
15. Drury TF, Powell AL. Prevalence, impact, and demography of known diabetes in the United States. *Advance Data* 1986; 114:1–16.
16. Everhart J, Knowler WC, Bennett PH. Incidence and risk factors for non-insulin dependent diabetes. In: National Diabetes Data Group. *Diabetes in America* [HHS (PHS) NIH Publication No. 85-1468]. Washington, DC: U.S. Government Printing Office; 1985: IV-1–35.
17. National Commission on Diabetes. *Reports of Committees, Sub-Committees and Workgroups* (Vol. III, Part 1). (DHEW NIH Publication No. 76-1021). Washington, DC: U.S. Government Printing Office; 1976.

18. Office of Human Development Services. *Characteristics of the Black Elderly: Non-Statistical Reports on Older Americans* (HHS, Administration on Aging, National Clearinghouse on Aging). Washington, DC: U.S. Government Printing Office; 1980:1–40.
19. Hamman RF. Diabetes in affluent socieites. In: Mann JI, Pyrola K, Teuscher A, eds. *Diabetes in Epidemiological Perspective.* Edinburgh: Churchill-Livingstone; 1983: 7–42.
20. Mann JI, Houston AC. The aetiology of non-insulin dependent diabetes mellitus. In: Mann JI, Pyrola K, Teuscher A, eds. *Diabetes in Epidemeological Perspective.* Edinburgh: Churchill-Livingstone; 1983: 122–157.
21. Kirk RL, Serjeantson SW, King H, Zimmet P. Genetic epidemeology of diabetes mellitus. In: Chakraborty R, Szathmary EJE, eds. *Progress in Clinical and Biological Research, Vol. 194: Disease of Complex Etiology in Small Populations, Ethnic Differences and Research Approaches.* New York: Alan R. Liss; 1985: 119–146.
22. Cooper R. A note on the biologic concept of race and its application in epidemiologic research. *Am Heart J.* 1984; 108: 715–723.
23. Neel JV. The thrifty gerotype revisited. In: Kibberling J, Tattersall RB, eds. *The Genetics of Diabetes Mellitus* (Serono Symposium No. 47). London: Academic Press; 1982: 283–293.
24. Lieberman LS. Genetics and life style aspects of diabetes in American blacks: a refined thrifty gene hypothesis. *Am J Epi.* 1984; 120: 502.
25. Lieberman LS. Dietary changes and disease consequence among Afro-Americans. *Am J Phy Anthro.* 1985; 66:196.
26. Cahill GF. Human evolution and insulin-dependent (IDD) and non-insulin dependent diabetes (NIDD). *Metabolism* 1979; 28:389–393.
27. Baird JD. Is obesity a factor in the aetiology of non-insulin-dependent diabetes? In: Kibberling J, Tattersall RB, eds. *The Genetics of Diabetes Mellitus* (Serono Symposium No. 47). London: Academic Press; 1982: 233–241.
28. Berger M, Mullen WA, Renold AE. Relationship of obesity to diabetes: some facts, many questions. In: Katzen HM, Mahler RJ, eds. *Advances in Modern Nutrition, Vol 2: Diabetes, Obesity and Vascular Disease.* New York: Wiley; 1978: 211–228.
29. Abraham S, Johnson CL, Najjar MF. *Weight and Height of Adults 18–74 Years of Age: United States 1971–74* [NCHS Series 11, No. 211, DHEW Publication No. (PHS) 79-1659]. Washington, DC: U.S. Government Printing Office; 1979.
30. Bonham GS, Brock DW. The relationship of diabetes with race, sex and obesity. *Am J Clin Nutri* 1985; 41: 776–783.
31. Heckler MM. *Report of the Secretary's Task Force on Black and Minority Health, Vol I: Executive Summary.* HHS, Washington, DC: U.S. Government Printing Office; 1985, August.
32. Atkinson RL, Bray GA. Energy balance in obesity and its relationship to diabetes mellitus. In: Katzen HM, Mahler RJ, eds. *Advances in Modern Nutrition, Vol. 2: Diabetes, Obesity and Vascular Disease.* New York: Wiley; 1978: 373–391.
33. Feldman R, Sender AJ, Sieglaub AB. Differences in diabetic and non-diabetic fat distribution patterns by skinfold measurement. *Diabetes* 1969; 18:478–486.

34. Zimmet PZ, Kirk RL, Serjeantson SW. Genetic and environmental interactions for non-insulin-dependent diabetes in high prevalence Pacific populations. In: Kobberling J., Tattersall R., eds. *The Genetics of Diabetes Mellitus.* Serono Symposium No. 47. New York: Academic Press; 1982: 211–224.
35. Mesbin RI, O'Leary JP, Pulkkinen A. Insulin receptor binding in obesity: a reassessment. *Science* 1979; 205: 1003–1004.
36. Mesbin RI. Hyperinsulinemia in obesity: overproduction of insulin or decreased insulin clearance? In: Bjoerntorp P, Vahouny GV, Kritchevsky D, eds. *Dietary Fiber and Obesity.* New York: Alan R. Liss; 1985: 19–31.
37. Keen H, Jarrett RJ. Environmental factors and genetic interactions. In: Creutz-feldt W, Kobberling J, Neel JV, eds. *The Genetics of Diabetes Mellitus.* Berlin: Springer-Verlag; 1976: 115–124.
38. Kanarek RB, Orthen-Gambill N, Barks-Kaufman R, Mayer J. Obesity: possible psychological and metabolic determinants. In: Geller JR, ed. *Human Nutrition: A Comprehensive Treatise No. 5. Nutrition and Behavior.* New York: Plenum; 1984: 339–396.
39. Jenkins DJA, Wolever TMS, Taylor RH, Barker H, Hashmein F, Baldwin JM, Bowling AC, Newman HC, Jenkins AL, Goff DV. Glycemic index of foods: a physiological basis for carbohydrate exchange. *Am J Clin Nutri* 1981; 34: 362–366.
40. Trowell HC, Burkitt DP *Western Diseases and their Emergence and Prevention.* London: Edward Arnold; 1981.
41. Dresser CV, Carroll MD, Abraham S. *Food Consumption Profiles of White and Black Persons Aged 1–74 Years: United States 1971–74* [Series 11, No. 210 DHEW Publication No. (PHS) 79-1658]. Washington, DC: U.S. Government Printing Office; 1979.
42. National Diabetes Advisory Board. *The Prevention and Treatment of Five Complications of Diabetes* (HHS 83-8392). Washington, DC: U.S. Government Printing Office; 1983.
43. Deeb LC, Shirah JK, Pettyjohn FP. Application of epidemiology to the design of complication specific interventions for the Florida Diabetes Control Program. Tallahassee, FL: State of Florida, Department of Health and Rehabilitative Services; 1986. (Unpublished manuscript).
44. Select Committee on Aging, House of Representatives. *America's Elderly at Risk* (Comm. Publication No. 99-508). Washington, DC: U.S. Government Printing Office; 1985.
45. Committee on Energy and Commerce, U.S. House of Representatives. *Health Problems Confronting Blacks and Minorities.* A Legislative Forum of the National Medical Association, Washington, DC: U.S. Government Printing Office; 1985.
46. Bray GA, ed. *Obesity in America* [HHS (PHS) NIH Pub. No. 79-359]. Washington, DC: U.S. Government Printing Office; 1979.
47. Abraham S, Carroll MD, Najjar MF, Fulwood R. *Obese and Overweight Adults in the United States* [NCHS Series 11 No. 230; DHHS Publication No. (PHS) 83-1680]. Washington, DC: U.S. Government Printing Office; 1983.
48. Haas JD, Greksa LP. Nutrition and biological fitness. In: Chakraborty R, Szathmary EJE eds. *Progress in Clinical and Biological Research, Vol. 194:*

Diseases of Complex Etiology in Small Populations: Ethnic Differences and Research Approaches. New York: Alan R. Liss; 1985: 255–281.

49. Beller AS. *Fat and Thin: A Natural History of Obesity.* New York: McGraw-Hill; 1977.
50. Stunkard AJ. Obesity and social environment: current status, future prospects. In: Bray GA, ed. *Obesity in America* [HEW (PHS) NIH Publication No. 79-359]. Washington, DC: U.S. Government Printing Office; 1979.
51. Garn SM, Bailey SM, Cole PE, Higgins ITT. Level of education, level of income and level of fatness in adults. *Am J Clin Nutri* 1978; 29:1067–1068.
52. Abraham S, Carroll MD, Dresser CM, Johnson CL. *Dietary Intake Source Data, United States, 1971–74.* [NCHS NEW (PHS) Publication No. 79-1221]. Washington, DC: U.S. Government Printing Office; 1979.
53. Carroll MD, Abraham S, Dresser CM. *Dietary Intake Source Data, United States 1976–80* [Series 11 No. 231; NCHS HHS (PHS) Publication No. 83-1681]. Washington, DC: U.S. Government Printing Office; 1983.
54. Gibbs T, Cargill K, Lieberman LS, Reitz E. Nutrition in a slave population: an anthropological examination. *Med. Anthro* 1980; 4:175–262.
55. Rodin J. Pathogenesis of obesity: energy intake and expenditure. In: Bray GA, ed. *Obesity in America* [HHS (PHS) NIH Publication No. 79-359]. Washington, DC: U.S. Government Printing Office; 1979.
56. Garn SM, Cole PE, Bailey SM. Living together as a factor in family-line resemblances. *Hum. Biol.* 1979; 51:565–587.
57. Rimm AA, White PL. Obesity: Its risks and hazards. In: Bray GA, ed. *Obesity in America* [HEW (PHS) NIH Publication No. 79-359]. Washington, DC: U.S. Government Printing Office; 1979.
58. Drury TF, Harris M, Lipsett L. *Health: United States 1981. Prevalence and Management of Diabetes* (HHS 1981) (PH582-1232). Washington, D.C.: U.S. Government Printing Office; 1981.
59. U.S. Department of Health and Human Services. *Review and Response to the Final Report of the National Black Health Providers Task Force on High Blood Pressure Education and Control* [HHS (PHS), NIH]. Washington, DC: U.S. Government Printing Office; 1986.

9

Aging and Hypertension among Blacks: A Multidimensional Perspective

Norman B. Anderson

According to recent data from the National Center for Health Statistics (1), the life expectancy at birth has risen consistently over the last 25 years, to a high of 74.7 years in 1983. These encouraging longevity statistics must be tempered, however, by the realization that the life expectancy for black Americans continues to lag behind that of their white counterparts. In 1983, the average life expectancy for white males was 72 years, compared to only 65 years for black males. White females had a life expectancy of 79 years, as compared to 74 years for black females. What accounts for these disparities in longevity? According to a Health and Human Services Task Force on Black and Minority Health commissioned in 1983, a number of factors exist that contribute to the excess death rate among black Americans. For individuals less than 45 years of age, over 50% of the excess in deaths among blacks can be attributed to factors such as homicides and accidents (over 30%), infant mortality (over 20%), and heart disease and stroke (over 10%). When older age groups are also considered, however, there is a shift in the relative importance of the various contributors to mortality. Among

Preparation of this chapter was supported in part by a Rockefeller Foundation Research Fellowship, and a New Investigator Research Award, HL-368630, from the National Heart, Lung and Blood Institute.

individuals up to age 70, over 30% of the excess deaths in blacks can be attributed to heart disease and stroke, while homicides and accidents and cancer contribute less than 20% each (2). Black females up to 70 years of age seem particularly susceptible to heart disease and stroke, since over 40% of the excess deaths in this group can be attributed to these disorders (2).

Unquestionably, a major contributor to the excess in heart disease and stroke among blacks is essential hypertension (2), defined as a systolic blood pressure of 160 mmHg or diastolic pressure of 95 mmHg or more. Although essential hypertension is a common problem in the general population, affecting 18% of adults between the ages of 25 and 74 (3), blacks are roughly twice as prone to develop hypertension as whites. The hypertension rate is approximately 18.1 per 100 for white males aged 25–74, as compared to a rate of 35.3 per 100 for black males of the same ages. Similarly, the rate for white females aged 25–74 is 14.8 per 100, compared to 29.7 per 100 for black females (3). Moreover, though the prevalence of hypertension increases with age in both races, blacks maintain their higher prevalence into the later years. The rate of definite hypertension among white adults increases from 4.8 per 100 for those aged 25–34 to 33.1 per 100 at ages 65–74. This is compared to an increase among black U.S. adults from 14.1 per 100 adults aged 25–34 years to approximately 44 per 100 at ages 65–74. The highest prevalence rate of hypertension among blacks occurs in the 55–64 age group, where the rate is 51.5 per 100 (3).

Given these extraordinarily high morbidity statistics, it is not surprising that blacks experience high rates of hypertension-related vascular diseases (4). In addition to the high rates of heart disease and cerebral vascular disease (i.e., stroke), blacks also exhibit a significantly higher prevalence of renal disease and renal failure compared to whites (5). Thus, hypertension is frequently considered the number-one health problem among blacks today (6).

Although a considerable body of literature has accumulated concerning the dimensions of hypertension among blacks as a whole (7–9), very little of this literature has focused on the black elderly in particular or has examined the disorder from the perspective of aging. It is possible that many of the dimensions of hypertension in the elderly black patient may be qualitatively or quantitatively different from those of other age or race groups. The purpose of this chapter, then, is to provide a discussion of hypertension in blacks from the perspective of aging, focusing on the dimensions and contributors to hypertension in elderly blacks that might be distinct from those of younger black or white hypertensives. Five components of the problem will be addressed: biological factors, behavioral and psychological factors, nutritional factors, social and environmental factors, and treatment considerations. Within each section, a review of the current state of knowledge will be presented, along with recommendations for future research to help clarify unresolved issues.

BIOLOGICAL ISSUES

Although essential hypertension is a disorder of unknown origin, it is generally agreed that its etiology involves any number of pathophysiological mechanisms (10). A number of studies have examined physiological differences between blacks and whites that might account for the high morbidity rates of hypertension in blacks. The majority of these studies can be placed into two broad categories: studies of the sympathetic nervous system functioning, and studies of sodium-regulatory mechanisms operating through the kidney. Additional factors include the role of obesity and stress reactivity.

Sympathetic Nervous System (SNS) Activity

Plasma Norepinephrine: Activity of the sympathetic nervous system has been frequently hypothesized to play a role in the etiology and maintenance of high blood pressure (11, 12). In assessing sympathetic nervous system function, most studies have relied on the measurement of plasma norepinephrine (NE). Stimulation of the sympathetic nervous system causes the release of NE from sympathetic nerve endings and from the adrenal medulla (13). It is currently believed that plasma NE plays an etiological role in the development of hypertension in some but not all patients (11, 14). In fact, recent studies have indicated that the contribution of circulating NE to the maintenance of elevated blood pressure may be dependent on patient age. For example, Goldstein (14), in an initial review of the literature, reported that 88% of the studies comparing plasma NE concentrations in hypertensive and normotensive groups reported higher levels in the hypertensive group. Yet in a subsequent review of 78 comparative studies Goldstein (15) reported that virtually all studies that found differences in NE between hypertensive and normotensive groups were conducted using relatively young patients. Patients below the age of 40 exhibited consistently higher NE levels compared to their normotensive counterparts. Patients over the age of 40 did not exhibit higher plasma NE levels than age-matched normotensives, though it was higher than in the younger patients. Thus Goldstein concluded that elevated plasma NE is a feature and possibly a contributor to the pathophysiology of essential hypertension in younger patients. This conclusion was subsequently corroborated by an experiment that indeed found that hypertensive–normotensive differences in NE were apparent only in subjects 40 years of age or younger but not among older age groups (16).

What, then, is the relationship between plasma NE and hypertension among blacks in general and black elderly in particular? In his review of the literature, Goldstein (15) reported that only 8 out of 78 comparative studies listed the racial makeup of the subject population. Of these, 5 used all white patients. Only one study was found that presented data separately by race. No significant differences in NE were observed when black and white hypertensives were compared, although black hypertensives showed an age-related increase in NE levels, while the white hypertensives did not (17). Generally, studies of NE levels in black hypertensives have focused on differences between black and white subjects, not on changes in NE levels as a function of age in blacks. Although the available research suggests that sympathetic nervous system overactivity, as measured by resting NE, does not seem to be a feature of hypertension in blacks as compared to whites, it is currently unclear whether elderly black hypertensives exhibit higher or lower NE levels compared to younger black patients.

Renal Functioning

The kidneys have been identified as major contributors to the long-term maintenance of elevated blood pressure (18). Two aspects of the renal system that have been studied extensively in reference to hypertension among blacks are the renin-angiotensin system and sodium regulation.

Plasma Renin: Renin is released by the kidneys in response to a number of physiologic stimuli, including sympathetic nervous system activity (19). Once released, renin aids in the production of angiotensin II, a powerful vasoconstrictor, which in turn increases arterial pressure. Renin has been implicated as a contributor to elevated blood pressure and hypertension (20). It is therefore surprising that studies have consistently shown that black hypertensives and normotensives have lower resting and stimulated plasma renin levels compared to whites (21–23).

Only a few studies have examined plasma renin levels as a function of age in black hypertensives. Bruner, Sealey, and Laragh (20) discovered that, for both black and white subjects, most hypertensives under age 30 exhibited low or normal renin values. In subjects over 50 years of age, however, there was a significantly greater preponderance of low renin hypertension among blacks. Similarly, it has been found that black hypertensives over the age of 40 have significantly lower plasma renin levels than black hypertensives under the age of 40 (24). Thus, while much more research is needed, the data collected so far are indicative of generally lower plasma renin levels in hypertensive and normotensive blacks compared to whites, with the lowest levels observed in older black hypertensives. The role of low renin levels in the pathogenesis of hypertension remains to be clarified.

Sodium Excretion: Another mechanism by which the kidneys affect blood pressure is through the regulation of sodium and water excretion. The body's balance of sodium and water is felt to be crucial to maintaining appropriate blood volume and blood pressure. Inhibited sodium excretion, however, results in volume expansion and augmented blood pressure (19). For a number of years, researchers have been interested in sodium homeostasis in blacks as a possible mechanism for the high rates of hypertension (23). Using protocols involving the administration of fixed amounts of sodium (sodium loading) to normotensive subjects, researchers at Indiana University have found several racial differences. Following sodium loading, black subjects have been shown to excrete less sodium in urine and exhibit greater blood pressure increases than their white counterparts (23, 25). It is conceivable, then, that inhibited sodium excretion in blacks may be one mechanism contributing to the high rate of hypertension in this group. Studies were not found that examined age changes in sodium retention and excretion in blacks or that examined sodium excretion rates in elderly black hypertensives and normotensives. There may exist an age-related increase in sodium retention among blacks, which might contribute to the steeper rise in hypertension prevalence in this group (26). Sodium retention may be most apparent in elderly black hypertensives.

Glomerular Filtration Rate: A process closely related to sodium excretion, glomerular filtration rate (GFR), has been examined in blacks and whites as a function of age (27). The GFR, as measured by creatinine clearance, is one index of the kidney's ability to clean ions from the blood stream. It represents an early stage in the natriuretic process. Luft, Fienberg, Miller, Rankin, Grim, and Weinberger (27) found that in normotensive subjects, there was an inverse relationship between GFR and age in both races. That is, as subject age increased, there was a decreased capacity of the kidney to remove creatinine from plasma (creatinine clearance). This decrease in creatinine clearance with age was more marked among the black subjects. The authors stated that it is unclear at this time whether the relatively exaggerated decrease in GFR among blacks was the result or cause of the observed racial differences in sodium excretion.

Kallikrein-Kinin System: One humoral system that has received comparatively little attention, but that nonetheless could be related to black–white differences in blood pressure, is the kallikrein-kinin system. Activity of this system, via secretion of renal kallikrein and ultimately kinin, produces both renal vasodilatation and natriuresis (28). A deficiency in this mechanism has been hypothesized to play a role in the excessive rates of hypertension in blacks (28). In support of this hypothesis, Levy, Lilley,

Frigon, and Stone (29) found that during unrestricted sodium ingestion, urinary kallikrein was greater in white normotensives than in black normotensives and hypertensives, or in white hypertensives. However, during restricted sodium intake, all groups showed increased urinary kallikrein excretion, but the increase was blunted in the black hypertensives. It has been suggested that a deficient kallikrein-kinin system could explain the inhibited sodium excretion in blacks, as well as generally lower renin levels in older black hypertensives (28).

Blood Volume: The relationship between ethnic group, hypertension, and blood volume has been the focus of several studies (for a review, see 30). Of the studies conducted on blood volume, two studies found ethnic group differences (22, 31), while two failed to detect differences (32, 33). Chrysant, Danisa, Kem, Dillard, Smith, and Frohlich (22), using a sample of 35 black (mean age, 50 years) and 95 white (mean age, 48 years) hypertensives, determined the proportion of each group with expanded versus contracted plasma volume. It was found that 43% of the black subjects but only 21% of the white subjects were volume expanded; conversely, 57% of blacks but 79% of whites were volume contracted. However, no relationship was found between blood pressure or renin as a function of volume expansion or contraction in blacks; among whites, subjects with contracted volume had significantly higher arterial pressures and plasma renin levels than those with expanded volume. In contrast, Messerli, Decarbalho, Christie, and Frohlich (32), in a study of normal, borderline hypertensive, and established hypertensive subjects (average age, 37.5), found no black–white differences in plasma volume, total blood volume, cardiac index, or total peripheral resistance.

The measurement of blood volume is relatively imprecise, and it has even proven difficult to demonstrate that diuretics cause a decrease. Thus it is possible that subtle racial differences in blood volume exist that are difficult to demonstrate.

Obesity

The prevalence of obesity among black females is significantly higher when compared with other aged-matched groups (see Lieberman, Chapter 8, this volume). Bonham and Brock (34) report that for individuals aged 20 to 24, the obesity rate for black males, white males, and white females was less than 15% for each group. This is compared to a rate of 23% for black females. This high rate of obesity among black females continues to increase with age, such that among women aged 55 to 64, there is a 50% prevalence of obesity (34). Among black women 65 years and above the rate drops to 38%, yet still remains roughly 20% higher than black and white males and white females. In 1978, data from the U.S. Department of Health, Education, and Welfare (35) indicated that the percentage of obesity among black females was roughly 25% among women aged 20 to 44, 45% among those aged 45 to 64, and roughly 30% among those aged 65 to 74 years. The percent of obesity among black males aged 20 to 44 was 12.8%, 8% among those aged 45 to 64, and 5.8% among those aged 65 to 74.

Although it is clear that black women experience overweight to a greater degree than black men, some interesting relationships were observed among black women as a function of income level. In the 20–44 and 45–64 age groups, obesity was more prevalent among women below the poverty level. In the 64–74 age group, however, those above the poverty level had the highest percentage of obesity. Among black males, those above the poverty level had the highest percentage of obesity for each age group, particularly those aged 45 to 64.

Overweight has been found to be positively associated with blood pressure in blacks as well as whites (36). Data from the Hypertension Detection and Follow-Up Program (HDFP) indicated that hypertensive black women were 28% above ideal weight, white men and women were 25% above ideal weight, and black men 20% above ideal weight (26). However, the obesity and high blood pressure picture in blacks is by no means complete. Two large epidemiologic studies, the Charleston Heart Study and the Evans County, Georgia, Study, found that the relation between weight and blood pressure was not as strong among blacks as with whites (36, 37). Thus while obesity is apparently a significant problem with advancing age among black females, the relationship between overweight and hypertension among blacks remains to be clarified.

Stress Reactivity

In recent years, biobehavioral researchers have begun exploring the role of physiologic responses to stress, specifically SNS responses, in hypertension development. The importance of transient increases in SNS activity in response to behavioral and environmental stressors grew out of animal research demonstrating that factors such as territorial conflict, crowding, or other psychosocial stressors produce sustained high blood pressure (38). This sustained high blood pressure has been shown to be preceded by activation of the "defense alarm" or "fight–flight" pattern of beta-adrenergically mediated SNS activity. It has been hypothesized that repeated elicitation of this response, when incongruent with metabolic needs, might ultimately lead to sustained high blood pressure (39, 40). Human studies have found that this response pattern of beta-adrenergic SNS activity to stress is greater among hypertensives compared to normotensives (41–43) and among those with a positive history of hypertension (44–46).

Research on racial differences in stress-induced cardiovascular reactivity is rapidly emerging as a prominent area of investigation designed to further our understanding of black–white differences in the prevalence of hypertension (47). Although findings to date are inconclusive, there is some preliminary indication that black subjects may have a tendency to exhibit greater peripheral vascular reactivity but less cardiac reactivity compared to their white counterparts. Fredrikson (48) examined SNS reactivity during an aversive reaction time task in three groups of black and white subjects: established hypertensives, borderline hypertensives, and normotensive controls. It was found that while resting cardiovascular activity was similar in black and white hypertensives and controls, heart rate and systolic pressure increased less in black patients and controls compared to whites. Muscle vascular resistance increased more in the black subjects, suggesting enhanced vasoconstriction. In a study of racial differences in vasoconstrictor responses in white and black males, Anderson, Lane, Muranaku, Williams, and Houseworth (49) measured blood pressure, heart rate, forearm blood flow, and forearm vascular resistance during the application of an ice pack to subjects' foreheads. This maneuver has been shown to elicit a profound peripheral vasoconstriction (50). In response to the cold stimulus, black subjects exhibited significantly greater systolic, diastolic, and forearm vascular resistance increases than white subjects. Finally, Light, Obirst, James, and Strogatz (51) found that black males with elevated blood pressure showed greater reactivity to competitive and noncompetitive tasks than blacks and whites with normal blood pressure and whites with elevated blood pressure. Since no heart rate differences were found, the high blood pressure responses in the blacks were suspected to be due to increases in vascular resistance rather than increases in cardiac output. To date, no published studies have been found that examined changes in cardiovascular reactivity to stress as a function of age in blacks. It is known that among whites, beta-adrenergic activity at rest, and in response to behavioral and physiological stress, decreases with age (52, 53). Research that clarifies the relation between age and cardiovascular reactivity in blacks would be helpful for understanding both normal aging processes and potential disease status in blacks.

NUTRITIONAL FACTORS

Nutritional factors have frequently been implicated in the etiology of hypertension in blacks and whites (54–56). The majority of research on the role of diet in hypertension has focused on three nutrients: sodium, potassium, and, most recently, calcium.

Sodium

Research has indicated that in most Westernized societies, excessive intake of sodium may predispose to the development of hypertension. Mechanisms underlying this sodium–blood pressure relationship have not been illuminated but could involve phenomena such as expansion of blood volume, edema of the walls of small arteries and arterioles, or increased sensitivity of the arterioles to sympathetic constrictor activity (21). Although some studies have reported greater dietary sodium intake among blacks (57, 58), most large-scale studies using probability samples have concluded that if racial differences in sodium intake exist, blacks exhibit lower rather than higher intake than whites (59–61). For example, Frisancho, Leonard, and Bollettins (59) examined 24-hour dietary intake and blood pressure of more than 1,900 black and more than 9,000 white adults from data sets of the United States National Health and Nutrition Examination Survey (NHANES I) of 1971–1974. Several age groups were studied: 20–24, 25–34, 35–44, 45–54, 55–64, and 65–74 years. Blacks were found to have lower dietary intake of sodium for all age groups with the exception of the males aged 25 to 34 and the females aged 20 to 24. Although blacks may not ingest more dietary sodium than whites, for a given amount of sodium intake blacks may excrete less than whites. Thus, even at low levels of sodium intake, the deleterious effects may be greater for blacks than for whites. Additionally, questions remain concerning the interaction among age, dietary sodium, and blood pressure in blacks. First of all, does dietary intake increase, decrease, or remain the same with advancing age among blacks? Are elderly blacks more susceptible to the health-damaging effects of sodium than are younger blacks? Finally, do elderly black hypertensives intake more sodium when compared to normotensive black elderly?

Potassium

Both low levels of potassium intake and a low sodium to potassium ratio (i.e., higher levels of sodium compared to potassium intake) have been linked to high blood pressure levels (59). Blacks have been found to ingest significantly less potassium and have a higher sodium/potassium ratio than whites (59, 60). Grim and colleagues (60) discovered that black men ingested significantly less sodium than white men, with the white men eating roughly 186 mEq per 24 hours and black men eating 136 mEq per 24 hours. On the other hand, the black men ingested 23 mEq per 24 hours of potassium versus 54 mEq per 24 hours for white men. Therefore, although black men had a lower intake of sodium, the lower potassium intake coupled with the high sodium to potassium ratio in this group may have contributed to their higher blood pressure levels. These findings closely parallel those of Frisancho and colleagues (59), who found that blacks, particularly males and females between 35 and 74 years of age, reported a lower sodium intake and a higher sodium/potassium ratio than their white cohorts as measured by 24-hour dietary recall. As with sodium, the studies on potassium and hypertension among blacks have focused primarily on racial differences to the exclusion of within-race, age, and gender comparisons.

Calcium

Dietary intake of calcium has only recently begun to be explored as a potential contributor to hypertension. Like potassium, low levels of calcium intake are thought to be associated with high blood pressure. The most frequently cited data on the role of calcium and hypertension are those of McCarron and associates (62, 63). Using data from the Health and Nutritional Survey, they found that among subjects aged 20 to 74, calcium intake was the best predictor of high blood pressure levels of 17 nutrients studied. Borderline hypertensive and normotensives reported similar calcium intakes, but individuals with definite hypertension (160/95 mmHg) consumed 18% less calcium. The higher intake of calcium among normotensives as compared to definite hypertensives was apparent in blacks and whites. Age differences in calcium intake were also observed. Among normotensive black males, subjects aged 55 to 74 ingested 624 mg per day of calcium, compared to 802 mg per day for those aged 35 to 54. Further, among black hypertensives, younger subjects reported eating significantly more calcium per day than the older subjects. Among black women, although the older age group reported eating slightly more calcium per day than the younger group (471 vs. 437 mg per day), younger hypertensives had a much higher calcium intake compared to the older hypertensives (462 vs. 688 mg per day).

In summary, current epidemiologic data suggest that high intake of sodium and low intake of potassium and calcium are related to essential hypertension. Though racial differences are not apparent in sodium intake, the sodium/potassium ratio is higher and calcium intake lower among middle-aged and older blacks compared to their white cohorts. Younger black normotensives and hypertensives tend to intake more calcium than older black normotensives and hypertensives. The reasons for these race and age differences in diet have not been specified but could be related to socioeconomic status.

BEHAVIORAL AND PSYCHOLOGICAL FACTORS

Theorizing and research on the role of behavioral and personality factors in hypertension have existed for over 40 years (64). Despite this long history, no single behavioral pattern or psychological characteristic has been consistently correlated with blood pressure levels (65). Nevertheless, researchers have in recent years attempted to draw links between personality, behavior, and hypertension by employing more thoughtful theoretical models.

Although most studies of personality factors have been conducted using white samples, studies conducted in the last 15 to 20 years have begun to focus on black hypertensives as well. The dominant theme across most of this research has been the role of suppressed hostility in the etiology of hypertension. This research owes its theoretical roots to Alexander (64), who hypothesized that hypertensive patients were characterized by an inability to express anger without conflict or guilt. More recently, theorizing by Leonard Syme (66) led Sherman James to hypothesize that an active-coping behavior pattern, which he labeled "John Henryism," may also be related to high blood pressure, particularly among blacks (72).

Suppressed Anger

Ernest Harburg and colleagues at the University of Michigan have conducted several epidemiologic studies on the association between suppressed hostility, blood pressure, and hypertension in blacks and whites (67, 68). These studies were based on community samples of black and white subjects who resided in either high or low socioecologic stress areas in Detroit (see below on the socioecological stress concept). In the initial study (63), suppressed hostility was determined by the subjects' responses to two hypothetical situations: being verbally attacked unjustifiably by a police officer and experiencing housing discrimination. For both black and white males between the ages of 25 and 60 who resided in high-stress residential areas, a tendency to hold anger in when provoked (anger-in) was associated with higher blood pressure and a greater prevalence of documented hypertension compared to those who reported an anger-out coping style. In a subsequent analysis of the Detroit data, Gentry, Chesney, Gary, Hall, and Harburg (69) determined that the anger-in or suppressed hostility hypothesis may also be relevant with black and white females.

Contrary to these positive findings, some studies have not found a simple anger-in/high blood pressure relationship. For example, Johnson and Broman (70) found in a national sample of black adults that anger expression was associated in a complex way with increased health problems. Blacks who were unemployed, single, and possessed less than a high school education were particularly at risk if anger was expressed outwardly and at higher levels during periods of emotional distress. In another study, Harburg, Blakelock, and Roeper (68) also found that blacks who reported a tendency to express anger outwardly to an angry boss had higher diastolic blood pressure compared to individuals who reported expressing anger inwardly or using a more reflective coping style. The authors reported that this anger-out effect held primarily for younger adults aged 25 to 39 and not for those 40 to 60 years of age.

John Henryism

Sherman James has hypothesized that an active, effortful stress coping style labeled "John Henryism" may be a key behavioral factor in the development of hypertension, particularly among blacks (71). This active coping style was named after the legendary black folk hero, John Henry, who epitomized hard work and determination against overwhelming odds. James speculated that blacks who exhibit this type of determination but also have few resources to help them cope successfully (e.g., low levels of formal education) might be at greatest risk for developing this disorder. This hypothesis was tested in an epidemiologic study in rural North Carolina using black males between 17 and 60 years of age (72). It was found that men who scored below the median on formal education (less than or equal to 11 years), but above the sample median on John Henryism, had the highest mean blood pressure levels. In a subsequent study, James, LaCroix, Kilenbaum, and Strogatz (73) discovered that not only does John Henryism interact with educational level; it also may interact with perceived job stress to influence blood pressure levels. It was found that among high John Henryism men who had achieved some measure of job success, those who felt that being black had hindered their chances to obtain success had significantly higher blood pressures than their counterparts who felt that being black had actually helped them.

In summary, the research on behavioral and psychological factors in hypertension among blacks has identified two potential contributors: suppressed hostility/anger-in and John Henryism. At this time, the relationship between these personality dimensions and aging among blacks has not been elucidated. Most of the reported studies have controlled for the effects of age statistically and thereby prevented an evaluation of the potential moderating effects of age on the personality/blood pressure relationship.

202 Biological and Health Status

SOCIAL FACTORS

The social variables that have been examined as potential contributors to hypertension among blacks may be grouped in three broad and overlapping categories: socioeconomic factors, socioecologic stress, and social disorganization. Research findings in each of these areas are summarized below.

Socioeconomic Status (SES)

Socioeconomic status is perhaps the social variable that has received the most research attention over the years. Although measured by a variety of indices (e.g., income, occupation, or educational level), socioeconomic status has provided a fairly consistent picture of the relationship between social status and blood pressure levels among both blacks and whites (74, 75). For example, the Hypertension Detection and Follow-up Program Cooperative Group (HDFP) (74) examined the relation between education and racial differences in hypertension prevalence among individuals aged 18 to 74 in 14 U.S. communities. Although the overall hypertension rate among blacks was almost twice that of whites, education was inversely related to hypertension in both race and gender groups; that is, the lower the education level achieved, the more likely a subject was to be diagnosed hypertensive. However, although controlling for education level reduced the discrepancy between blacks and whites in hypertension prevalence, blacks at the highest educational level (college graduates) were still twice as likely as whites to be diagnosed as hypertensive.

This education–hypertension correlation was not uniformly evident across all age groups. The HDFP report noted, for example, that blacks aged 30 to 39 with a college education had a hypertension rate 50% lower than those with less than 10 years of formal education (i.e., population prevalence rates of 13.7% vs. 26.6%). This education effect was reduced somewhat among blacks aged 40 to 49, where college graduates had almost a 40% lower morbidity rate than those with less than 10 years education (25.2% vs. 41.2%). Thus, as age increased, educational status became less predictive of blood pressure levels, such that in individuals 60–69 years of age there was no clear gradient of education level on hypertension prevalence (74). The authors note, however, that there was a relatively smaller number of blacks who had completed college in the older age category.

The reason for the high hypertension prevalence rates among lower SES groups remains unclear. It might be speculated, however, that numerous factors believed to contribute to high blood pressure may be more represented among lower SES groups (e.g., inadequate nutrition, social stress, etc.). It is important to realize, of course, that not all individuals of lower

SES develop hypertension. Other factors might interact with SES to make some individuals more susceptible to the development of hypertension than others. Socioecologic stress and social disorganization are factors that have been hypothesized to contribute to hypertension morbidity and mortality among blacks living in low-SES environments.

Socioecologic Stress and Social Disorganization

Ernest Harburg and colleagues at the University of Michigan, and Sherman James and associates at the University of North Carolina at Chapel Hill, have conducted some of the most notable studies on the role of socioecologic stress on blood pressure among blacks (76–78). Harburg, Erfurt, Chape, Hauenstein, Schull, and Schork (76) hypothesized that while individuals living in low-SES neighborhoods would have higher resting blood pressure levels than those living in high-SES areas, the highest blood pressure levels should be observed in those individuals who reside in low-SES areas that are high in social instability (SIS). Socially unstable neighborhoods were defined as those characterized by high adult and juvenile crime rate, a high marital instability rate (e.g., high divorce and separation rate), and a high residential transiency rate. Thus, a highly socioecologically stressful neighborhood was defined as one that is both low in SES (low income, high unemployment) and high in SIS. Low-stress areas were defined as those that are high SES and low SIS. It was discovered that black males residing in high-stress areas had significantly higher age- and weight-adjusted blood pressures than those living in low-stress areas (67). This high stress/blood pressure relationship was also found for white females, but not for white males. Although black females exhibited higher blood pressure levels if they resided in a high-stress neighborhood, this relationship was not maintained after adjusting for age and weight. Black males in high-stress areas also had a significantly higher percentage of borderline and hypertensive blood pressure values than other male race-area groups.

Although the above results were found while controlling for the effects of age and weight, Harburg and associates (76) also examined the interaction between stress areas, age, and weight on blood pressure. For black males only, there was a significantly higher percentage of borderline and hypertensive individuals in high-stress compared to low-stress areas *in persons less than 40 years old*. Among black males between 40 and 59 years of age, stress area did not predict the prevalence of hypertensive disease. Reasons for the greater prevalence of hypertension among the younger high-stress black males remains unclear. Syme (66) has suggested that this effect may be due to increased efforts to gain control over difficult life circumstances in the younger subjects. Indeed, the John-Henryism personality style discussed earlier, which epitomizes such an orientation to coping with difficult situations, is in fact related to higher blood pressure levels. Another explanation for the lack of high-stress and hypertension association among the older age group is that with advancing age, biological factors might begin to play a more important role in hypertensive disease, exerting their effects on blacks in general regardless of stress area. This could be one reason why such social factors as education seem to have less of a modulating affect on hypertension among older blacks.

Another concept closely related to socioecologic stress is that of social disorganization. Nesser, Tyroler, and Cassel (79) investigated the relationship between social disorganization and stroke mortality during a 9-year period in North Carolina counties. The authors defined social disorganization as (1) family instability (percent of primary families with only one parent present), (2) percentage of illegitimate births, (3) rate of males sentenced to prison road camps, (4) percentage of population separated or divorced, and (5) percentage of children under age 18 not living with both parents (79). The results of the study supported Nesser and colleagues' contention that the higher the level of social instability in a county, the higher the stroke mortality rate. As with the data on socioecologic stress, the effects of social instability appeared most striking among the middle-aged subjects. The relationship between social disorganization and stroke mortality was strongest among black males and females aged 35 to 44. No relationship between social disorganization and stroke mortality among whites was found. Importantly, this effect of social disorganization was unrelated to county poverty level, since no relationship was found between county poverty index and stroke mortality rates for any of the age or sex groups.

Another area of research relating to social factors in hypertension is the role of social support in modulating susceptibility to the disorder. In recent years, there has been an increase in research attention focusing on the role of social networks and social support in alleviating the effects of stress, promoting health behaviors, and enhancing health outcomes (80–82). Since social support and extended family relationships are thought to play significant roles in the lives of minority group members (83), exploration of the effects of social support systems on hypertension in blacks is a critical area for future research.

TREATMENT CONSIDERATIONS

Given the high mortality rate from hypertension-related diseases in the black elderly, identifying methods of reducing blood pressure in this group is clearly an important research area. It might be argued that the dimensions of hypertension previously reviewed in relation to the etiology of the disorder (biological, behavioral, nutritional, and social) are also relevant to the treatment of hypertension in the black elderly. The purpose of this section is to present an overview of potential treatment modalities for hypertension in the black elderly. With the possible exception of pharmacologic therapy, evaluations of the efficacy of these approaches have not used black hypertensives as subjects. As will become apparent in the following discussion, caution must be taken in drawing generalizations on treatment efficacy gained from studies conducted on white patients to black hyptertensives. Four areas related to the treatment of hypertension will be discussed: pharmacologic therapy, diet modification and weight reduction, behavioral treatment, and compliance.

Pharmacologic Therapy

Pharmacologic therapy is the most frequently utilized treatment modality for hypertension regardless of race or age. Drug therapy has been shown through epidemiologic studies to significantly reduce blood pressure and hypertension-related mortality (84). Although drug therapy is generally effective in both races, studies have demonstrated racial differences in the effectiveness of particular pharmacologic agents. Hall (85) recently summarized the literature on the therapeutic efficacy of a number of drugs with black patients. These various therapies included: diuretics, beta-blockers, combined diuretic and beta-blockers, alpha-blockers, combined alpha- and beta-blockers, slow channel calcium entry blockers, direct vasodilators, central and peripheral sympathetic inhibitors, and angiotensin-converting enzyme (ACE) inhibitors.

From Hall's review, two interesting trends emerged. First of all, blacks with hypertension seem to be significantly more responsive to diuretic therapy than white hypertensives (86–88). For example, in the VA cooperative study (83), black and white hypertensives were treated with 50 to 200 mg per day of hydrochlorothiazide for a 10-week period. Black patients showed on the average a 20 mmHg drop in systolic pressure and a 13 mmHg drop in diastolic pressure; white patients exhibited a 15 and 10 mmHg drop in systolic and diastolic pressure, respectively. Hall reported that in studies comparing black and white patient response to diuretic therapy, blacks exhibited an additional decrease compared to whites of 5 to 7 mmHg systolic and 1 to 2 mmHg diastolic pressure. Secondly, in contrast to the hyperresponsiveness relative to whites with diuretics, blacks appear to be hyporesponsive to beta-blocker therapy. Though the majority of studies using beta-blockers to treat hypertension among blacks have produced decreases in blood pressure, white patients have been found to be generally more responsive to beta-blockers than blacks. In the two VA cooperative studies that evaluated the comparative effectiveness of propranolol (86) and nadolol (88), whites showed a greater decrease in systolic and diastolic pressure than blacks. The additional decrease in whites over that obtained by blacks was on the order of 5 to 11 mmHg systolic and 3 to 6 mmHg diastolic pressure.

Although it is beyond the scope of this chapter to review all of the studies of drug therapy efficacy in black hypertensives, it may be concluded that diuretics are considered the first-order pharmacologic therapy for black hypertensives (85). Although blacks are less responsive to beta-blocker therapy, Hall (85) notes that the effectiveness of beta-blockers may be improved when combined with a diuretic. At this time, it is unclear whether patient age influences the efficacy of drug therapy with black hypertensives.

Diet Modification and Weight Reduction

As discussed earlier, dietary intakes of sodium, calcium, and potassium may all be related to blood pressure levels. A high sodium intake, or a low potassium or calcium intake, have been shown to be related to hypertension prevalence. It may follow, then, that modification of a patient's intake of these ions could lead to a reduction in blood pressure. Indeed, there is indication that in some patients a reduction in sodium intake (89) or increase in potassium intake (90, 91) can lead to reductions in blood pressure. Unfortunately, data were not found that examine the effectiveness of these dietary modifications on black patients with hypertension.

With obesity, current data suggest that reductions in weight may lead to reductions in blood pressure in overweight hypertensive patients. For example, Reisin, Abel, Modan, Silverberg, Eliahou, and Modan (92) discovered that in patients who were both moderately overweight as well as those who were very obese, a weight-reduction program significantly decreased both patient weight and blood pressure. In fact, in patients who were not receiving drug therapy, 75% had normal blood pressure readings at the end of the study. The blood pressure-lowering effects of weight reduction were apparent in younger as well as older patients, although the exact age range was not reported.

Clearly the efficacy for weight reduction for blood pressure control in black elderly patients, particularly females, should be evaluated. Separate studies using black patients are warranted, since epidemiologic studies suggest that changes in weight do not have the same effect on blood pressure in blacks as in whites (36, 37).

Behavior Therapy

Behavior therapy and behavior modification techniques, such as progressive relaxation, yoga, and various forms of biofeedback, have for years been used in the treatment of essential hypertension (93). Generally, the goal of these techniques is to reduce mental and physical stress that may contribute to elevated blood pressure.

Outcome studies evaluating relaxation and biofeedback for hypertension demonstrate moderate degrees of success (93, 94). These studies, however, have not included sizable numbers of black patients. To the degree that environmental stress contributes to blood pressure elevation in blacks (67, 68), relaxation training could play a role in attenuating these noxious effects. From a physiologic perspective, however, it is unclear whether relaxation or biofeedback will affect significantly the pathophysiology of hypertension in blacks. For example, it has been suggested that relaxation techniques work to decrease blood pressure through reducing sympathetic nervous system activity (95). As noted previously, hypertension in blacks may be characterized by an inhibition of some aspects of the sympathetic nervous system. Indeed, the fact that beta-blockers have been found to be significantly less effective in blacks compared to whites raises a question as to the efficacy of an ostensibly similar nonpharmacologic approach. Identifying pathophysiologic predictors of response to relaxation training is clearly an important area for future research.

Compliance with Treatment Regimens

A major problem with the pharmacologic, and presumably nonpharmacologic, treatment of hypertension is the issue of patient compliance. The effectiveness of any therapeutic regime is in part determined by the degree to which patients follow therapeutic instructions. Compliance with treatment regimens is considered a problem among many black hypertensives (96). This appears to be especially true among young, unemployed, and socially isolated black males (98, 99).

Numerous methods have been proposed that are designed to increase patient compliance with medical management. Cook (96) has emphasized the use of repeated motivational sessions, prompt scheduling of reappointments, the inclusion of significant others, follow-up visits, and periodic telephone contacts. Blackwell (97) noted that factors tending to increase patient adherence were patients' perceptions of the seriousness of their diseases, family stability, and close supervision of compliance behavior by physicians. Although these techniques should be effective in black and white patients regardless of age, conditions in the patient's social milieu that might promote or inhibit patient compliance should be taken into consideration. For example, studies have shown that among inner-city black patients, treatment compliance and blood pressure control were improved when assistance was provided by social workers or other health professionals concerning financial or family difficulties, employment problems, or other difficulties of daily life (100–102).

SUMMARY AND CONCLUSIONS

The purpose of this chapter was to provide a discussion of hypertension in aging blacks. Five important dimensions were highlighted: biological, behavioral, social, nutritional, and treatment. Research in each area was summarized, and recommendations for future research were given. Overall, although the body of literature on hypertension in blacks is substantial, there exist large gaps in our knowledge of age-related changes in factors related to hypertension. In order to close these gaps in knowledge, research should be directed toward addressing the following questions:

1. What physiological changes occur in the normal aging process in blacks?
2. Are these processes different in those blacks at risk for hypertension compared to those blacks at reduced risk, or compared to whites?
3. What are the physiological characteristics of hypertension in the black elderly?
4. How do black elderly with hypertension differ from those without the disorder (physiologically, psychologically, and sociologically)?
5. What are some psychosocial factors that *predict* the later onset of hypertension?
6. What is the interaction between race and age on the effectiveness of pharmacologic and nonpharmacologic treatments?

Future research should utilize designs that explore differences *within* black populations, particularly the black elderly, as well as comparisons of blacks with whites. This approach should clarify factors that may be predictive of the development, course, and treatment of hypertension in blacks that might be distinct from those found in whites.

REFERENCES

1. National Center for Health Statistics. *Final Mortality Statistics, 1982*. Hyattsville, MD: Author; 1984.
2. U.S. Department of Health and Human Services. *Report of the Task Force on Black and Minority Health*. Washington, DC: U.S. Government Printing Office; 1985.
3. Roberts J, Rowlands M. *Hypertension in Adults 25–74 Years of Age: United States, 1971–1975* (Vital and Health Statistics, Series 11, No. 221). Washington, DC: U.S. Government Printing Office; 1981.

4. Mason T, Fraumeni J, Hover R, Blat W. *An Atlas of Mortality from Certain Diseases* (NIH Publication No. 81-2397). Washington DC: U.S. Government Printing Office; 1981.
5. Shulman NB. Renal disease in hypertensive blacks. In: Hall WD, Saunders E, Shulman NB, eds. *Hypertension in Blacks: Epidemiology, Pathophysiology and Treatment.* Chicago: Year Book Medical Publishers; 1985: 106–112.
6. Saunders A, Williams R. Hypertension. In Williams RA, ed. *Textbook of Black-Related Diseases.* New York: McGraw-Hill; 1975: 333–358.
7. Anderson NB, Jackson JS. Race, ethnicity, and health psychology: the example of essential hypertension. In: G. Stone et al., eds. *Health Psychology: A Discipline and Profession.* 1987: 265–283.
8. Gillum RT. Pathophysiology of hypertension in blacks and whites: a review of the basis of racial blood pressure differences. *Hypertension* 1979; 1: 468–475.
9. Hall WD, Saunders E, Shulman N. *Hypertension in Blacks: Epidemiology, Pathophysiology, and Treatment.* Chicago: Year Book Medical Publishers; 1985.
10. Page IH. The mosaic theory of hypertension. In: Bock F, Cottier P, eds. *Essential Hypertension.* Berlin: Springer-Verlag; 1960.
11. deChamplain J, Cousineau D, Lapointe L. Evidences supporting an increased sympathetic tone and reactivity in a subgroup of patients with essential hypertension. *Clinical Experimental Hypertension* 1980; 2: 359.
12. Esler M, Julius S, Randall O, Harburg E, Gardiner H, DeQuattro V. Mild high-renin essential hypertension: neurologenic human hypertension? *New England Journal of Medicine* 1977; 296: 405–411.
13. Guyton A. *Textbook of Medical Physiology.* Philadelphia: W. B. Saunders; 1981.
14 Goldstein DS. Plasma norepinephrine in essential hypertension: a study of the studies. *Hypertension* 1981; 3: 48.
15. Goldstein DS. Plasma catecholamines and essential hypertension: an analytical review. *Hypertension* 1983; 5: 86–99.
16. Goldstein D, Lake C, Chernow B, Ziegler M, Coleman M, Taylor A, Mitchell J, Kapin I, Keiser H. Age-dependence of hypertensive-normotensive differences in plasma norepinephrine. *Hypertension* 1983; 5: 100–104.
17. Sever PS, Peart WS, Davies IB, Tunbridge RDG, Gordon D. Ethnic differences in blood pressure with observations on noradrenaline and renin. 2. A hospital hypertensive population. *Clinical Experimental Hypertension* 1979; 1: 745.
18. Guyton AC, Coleman TG, Cowley AW, Scheel KW, Manning RD Jr, Norman RA Jr. Arterial pressure regulation: overriding dominance of the kidneys in long-term regulation and in hypertension. *American Journal of Medicine* 1972; 52: 584–594.
19. Vick R. *Contemporary Medical Physiology.* Menlo Park, CA: Addison-Wesley; 1984.
20. Brunner HR, Sealey JE, Laragh JH. Renin as a risk factor in essential hypertension: more evidence. *American Journal of Medicine* 1973; 55: 295.
21. Wisenbaugh PE, Garst JB, Hull C, Freedman RJ, Matthews DN, Hadady M. Renin, aldosterone, sodium and hypertension. *American Journal of Medicine* 1972; 52: 175.

22. Chrysant SG, Danisa K, Kem DC, Dillard BL, Smith WJ, Frohlich ED. Racial differences in pressure, volume and renin interrelationships in essential hypertension. *Hypertension* 1979; 1: 136–141.

23. Luft F, Grim C, Weinberger M. Electrolyte and volume homeostasis in blacks. In: Hall W, Saunders E, Shulman N, eds. *Hypertension in Blacks: Epidemiology, Pathophysiology, and Treatment.* Chicago: Year Book Medical Publishers; 1985; 115–131.

24. Grim CE, Luft FC, Miller JZ, Meneely GR, Battarbee HD, Hames CG, Dahl KL. Racial differences in blood pressure in Evans County, Georgia: relationship to sodium and potassium intake and plasma renin activity. *Journal of Chronic Diseases* 1980; 33: 87–94.

25. Luft FC, Grim CE, Higgins JT Jr, Weinberger MH. Differences in response to sodium administration in normotensive white and black subjects. *Journal of Laboratory and Clinical Medicine* 1977; 90: 555–562.

26. Hypertension Detection and Follow-Up Program Cooperative Group. Five-year findings of the Hypertension Detection and Follow-Up Program: mortality by race-sex and age. *Journal of the American Medical Association* 1979; 242: 2572–2577.

27. Luft FC, Fienberg NS, Miller JZ, Rankin LI, Grim CE, Weinberger MH. The effects of age, race and heredity on glomerular filtration rate following volume expansion and contraction in normal man. *American Journal of Medical Science* 1980; 279: 15–24.

28. Warren S, O'Connor D. Does a renal vasodilator system mediate racial differences in essential hypertension? *American Journal of Medicine* 1980; 69: 425–429.

29. Levy S, Lilley J, Frigon R, Stone R. Urinary kallikrein and plasma renin activity as determinants of renal blood flow. *Journal of Clinical Investigation* 1977; 60: 129.

30. Schachter J, Kuller L. Blood volume expansion among blacks: an hypothesis. *Medical Hypotheses* 1984; 14: 1–19.

31. Lilley J, Hsu L, Stone R. Racial disparity of plasma volume in hypertensive man. *Annals of Internal Medicine* 1976; 84: 707.

32. Messerli R, Decarbalho J, Christie B, Frohlich E. Essential hypertension in black and white subjects: hemodynamic findings and fluid volume states. *American Journal of Medicine* 1979; 67: 27–31.

33. Mitas J, Hole R, Levy S, Stone R. Racial analysis of the volume–renin relationship in human hypertension. *Archives of Internal Medicine* 1979; 139: 157–160.

34. Bonham GS, Brock DW. The relationship of diabetes with race, sex, and obesity. *American Journal of Clinical Nutrition* 1985; 41: 775–783.

35. U.S. Department of Health, Education, and Welfare. *Health: U.S., 1978* [DHEW Publications No. (PHS) 78-1232]. Hyattesville, MD: National Center for Health Statistics and National Center for Health Services Research; 1978.

36. Boyle E Jr, Griffey WP Jr, Nichaman MZ, Talbert CR Jr. An epidemiologic study of hypertension among racial groups of Charleston County, South Carolina: The Charleston Heart Study, phase II. In: J Stamler, S Stamler, TN Pullman eds. *The Epidemiology of Hypertension.* New York: Grune & Stratton; 1967: 193–203.

37. Tyroler HA, Heyden S, Hames CG. Weight and hypertension: Evans County studies of blacks and whites. In: Paul O, ed. *Epidemiology and Control of Hypertension*. New York: Stratton Intercontinental Medical; 1975: 177–204.
38. Henry JP, Cassel J. Psychosocial factors in essential hypertension: recent epidemiologic and animal experimental evidence. *American Journal of Epidemiology* 1969; 90: 171–200.
39. Charvat J, Dell P, Folkow B. Mental factors and cardiovascular diseases. *Cardiologia* 1964; 44: 124–141.
40. Obrist PA. *Cardiovascular Psychophysiology: A Perspective.* New York: Plenum; 1981.
41. Brod J, Fend V, Hejl Z, Jorka G. Circulatory changes underlying blood pressure elevation during acute emotional stress (mental arithmetic) in normotensive and hypertensive subjects. *Clinical Science* 1959; 23: 339–349.
42. Hollenberg NK, Williams GH, Adams DF. Essential hypertension: abnormal renal vascular and endocrine responses to a mild psychological stimulus. *Hypertension* 1981; 3: 11–17.
43. Fredrikson M, Engel B. Cardiovascular and electrodermal adjustments during a vigilance task in patients with borderline and established hypertension. *Journal of Psychosomatic Research* in press.
44. Hastrup J, Light KC, Obrist PA. Parental hypertension and cardiovascular response to stress in healthy young adults. *Psychophysiology* 1982; 19: 615–623.
45. Jorgensen RS, Houston BD. Family history of hypertension, gender, and cardiovascular reactivity and stereotypy during stress. *Journal of Behavioral Medicine* 1981; 4: 175–189.
46. Manuck SB, Proietti JM. Parental hypertension and cardiovascular response to cognitive and isometric challenge. *Psychophysiology* 1982; 19: 481-489.
47. Anderson NB. Ethnic differences in resting and stress-induced cardiovascular and humoral activity: an overview. In: Schneiderman N, Weiss S, Kaufman P, & Carver C, eds. *Handbook of Research Methods in Cardiovascular Behavioral Medicine*. New York: Plenum; in press.
48. Fredrikson M. Racial differences in reactivity to behavioral challenge in essential hypertension. *Journal of Hypertension* 1986; 4: 325–331.
49. Anderson NB, Lane JD, Muranaku M, Williams RB, Houseworth SJ. Racial differences in blood pressure and forearm vascular responses to the cold face stimulus. *Psychosomatic Medicine* 1987: 49.
50. Abboudd FM, Ebstein JW. Active reflex vasodilatation in man. *Federation Proceeding* 1966; 25: 1611–1617.
51. Light KC, Obrist PA, Sherwood, A., James SA, Strogatz DS. Effects of race & marginally elevated blood pressure on cardiovascular responses to stress in young men. *Hypertension,* in press.
52. Gintner G, Hollandworth J, Intreri R. Age differences in cardiovascular reactivity under active coping conditions. *Psychophysiology* 1986; 23: 113–120.
53. Bertel O, Bubler F, Krowski W, Lutold B. Decreased beta-adrenoreceptor responsiveness as related to age, blood pressure and plasma catecholamines in patients with essential hypertension. *Hypertension* 1980; 2: 130.
54. Freis ED. Salt volume and prevention of hypertension. *Circulation* 1976; 53: 589.

55. Langford HG, Watson RL. Electrolytes and hypertension in epidemiology and control of hypertension. In Paul O, ed. *Epidemiology and Control of Hypertension.* New York: Stratton Intercontinental Medical; 1978: 119–130.

56. Langford, HG, Watson RL, Douglas BH. Factors affecting blood pressure in population groups. *Transactions of the Association of American Physicians* 1968; 63: 135–146.

57. Desor JA, Green LN, Maller O. Preferences for sweet and salty in 9 to 15-year-old and adult humans. *Science* 1975; 90: 686–687.

58. Karp RI, Williams C, Grant JD. Increased utilization of salty food with age among pre-teenage black girls. *Journal of the National Medical Association* 1980; 72: 197–200.

59. Frisancho AR, Leonard WR, Bollettins L. Blood pressure in blacks and whites and its relationship to dietary sodium and potassium intake. *Journal of Chronic Diseases* 1984; 37: 515–519.

60. Grim CE, Luft FC, Miller JZ, Meneely GR, Battarbee HD, Hames CD, Dahl LK. Racial differences in blood pressure in Evans County, Georgia: relationship to sodium and potassium intake and plasma renin activity. *Journal of Chronic Diseases* 1980; 33: 87–94.

61. Cruickshank JK, Beevers DG. Epidemiology of hypertension: blood pressure in blacks and whites. *Clinical Science* 1982; 62: 1–6.

62. McCarron, DA. Calcium & magnesium nutrition in human hypertension. *Annals of Internal Medicine*, 1983; 98: 800–805.

63. McCarron DA, Morris CD, Cole C. Dietary calcium in human hypertension. *Science* 1982; 217: 267–269.

64. Alexander FG. Emotional factors in essential hypertension: presentation of a tentative hypothesis. *Psychosomatic Medicine* 1939; 1: 175–179.

65. Ostfeld AM. What's the payoff in hypertension research? (Editorial). *Psychosomatic Medicine* 1973; 35: 1–3.

66. Syme LT. Psychosocial determinants of hypertension. In: Onesti G, Klimt C, eds. *Hypertension: Determinants, Complications, Interventions.* New York: Grune & Stratton; 1979: 95–98.

67. Harburg E, Erfurt JC, Hauenstein LS, Chape C, Schull WJ, Schork MA. Socioecological stress, supressed hostility, skin color, and black–white male blood pressure: Detroit. *Psychosomatic Medicine* 1973; 35: 276–296.

68. Harburg E, Blakelock EH, Roeper PJ. Resentful and reflective coping with arbitrary authority and blood pressure: Detroit. *Psychosomatic Medicine* 1979; 41: 189–202.

69. Gentry WD, Chesney AP, Gary HE, Hall RP, and Harburg E. Habitual anger-coping styles: effect on mean blood pressure and risk for essential hypertension. *Psychosomatic Medicine* 1982; 44: 195–202.

70. Johnson EH, Broman CL. *Anger expression and health problems among black Americans: a report from the national survey of black Americans.* Ann Arbor: University of Michigan, Department of Internal Medicine. (Unpublished manuscript).

71. James SA. Psychosocial and environmental factors in black hypertension. In: Hall W, Saunders E, Shulman N, eds. *Hypertension in Blacks: Epidemiology, Pathophysiology and Treatment.* Chicago: Year Book Medical Publishers; 1985: 132–143.

72. James SA, Hartnett SA, Kalsbeek WD. John Henryism and blood pres-

sure differences among black men. *Journal of Behavioral Medicine* 1983; 6: 259–278.

73. James SA, LaCroix AZ, Kleinbaum DG, Strogatz DS. John Henryism and blood pressure differences among black men. II. The role of occupational stressors. *Journal of Behavioral Medicine* 1984; 7: 259–275.

74. Hypertension Detection and Follow-Up Program Cooperative Group. Race, education and prevalence of hypertension. *American Journal of Epidemiology* 1977; 106: 351–361.

75. Keil JE, Tyroler HA, Sandifer SH, Boyle E Jr. Hypertension effects of social class and racial admixture: the results of a cohort study in the black population of Charleston, South Carolina. *American Journal of Public Health* 1977; 67: 634–639.

76. Harburg E, Erfurt JC, Chape C, Hauenstein LS, Schull WJ, Schork MA. Socio-ecological stressor areas and black–white blood pressure: Detroit. *Journal of Chronic Diseases* 1973; 26: 595–611.

77. Erfurt J, Harburg E, Rice R. A method for selection of census tract areas differing in ecologic stress. *(multilith report)* 1970.

78. James SA, Kleinbaum DG. Socioecologic stress and hypertension-related mortality rates in North Carolina. *Journal of Public Health* 1976; 66: 354–358.

79. Neser WB, Tyroler HA, Cassel JC. Social disorganization and stroke mortality in the black population of North Carolina. *American Journal of Epidemiology* 1971; 93: 166–175.

80. Berkman LF. The relationship of social networks and social support to morbidity and mortality. In: Cohen S, Syme L, eds. *Social Support and Health.* New York: Academic Press; 1985: 241–262.

81. Hamburg DA, Elliott GR, Parron DL, eds. *Health and Behavior: Frontiers of Research in the Biobehavioral Sciences* (IOM Publication No. 82-01). Washington, DC: National Academy Press; 1982.

82. Baum A, Singer JE, Taylor SE, eds. *Handbook of Psychology and Health, Vol. 4: Social Psychological Aspects of Health.* Hillsdale, NJ: Erlbaum; 1984.

83. Jackson JJ. Urban black Americans. In: Harwood A, ed. *Ethnicity and Medical Care.* Cambridge, MA: Harvard University Press; 1981: 37–129.

84. Hypertension Detection and Follow-Up Program Cooperative Group. Five-year findings of the Hypertension Detection and Follow-Up Program. II. Mortality by race-sex and age. *Journal of the American Medical Association* 1979; 242: 2572–2577.

85. Hall WD. Pharmacologic therapy of hypertension in blacks. In: Hall WD, Saunders E, Shulman N, eds. *Hypertension in Blacks: Epidemiology, Pathophysiology, and Treatment.* Chicago: Year Book Medical Publishers; 1985; 182–208.

86. Veterans Administration Cooperative Study Group on Antihypertensive Agents. Comparison of propranolol and hydrochorothiazide for the initial treatment of hypertension. I. Results of short-term titration with emphasis on racial differences in response. *Journal of the American Medical Association* 1982; 248: 1996–2003.

87. Moser M, Lunn J. Responses to captopril and hydrochlorothiazide in black patients with hypertension. *Clinical Pharmacologic Therapy* 1982; 32: 307–312.

88. Veterans Administration Cooperative Study Group on Antihypertensive Agents. Efficacy of nadolol alone and combined with bendroflumethiazide and hydralazine for systemic hypertension. *American Journal of Cardiology* 1983; 52: 1230–1237.

89. Kawasaki T, Delea CS, Bartter FC, Smith H. The effect of high-sodium and low-sodium intakes on blood pressure and other related variables in human subjects with idiopathic hypertension. *American Journal of Medicine* 1978; 64: 193–198.

90. Holly JMP, Goodwin FJ, Evans SJW, Vandenburg MJ, Ledingham JM. Re-analysis of data in two *Lancet* papers on the effect of dietary sodium and potassium on blood pressure. *Lancet* 1981; 2: 1384–1387.

91. MacGregor GA, Smith SJ, Markandu ND, Banks RA, Sagnella GA. Moderate potassium supplementation in essential hypertension. *Lancet* 1982; 2: 567–570.

92. Reisin E, Abel R, Modan M, Silverberg DS, Eliahou HE, Modan B. Effects of weight loss without salt restriction on the reduction of blood pressure in overweight hypertensive patients. *New England Journal of Medicine* 1978; 298: 1–6.

93. Shapiro AP, Schwartz GE, Ferguson DCE, Redmond DP, Weiss SM. Behavioral methods in the treatment of hypertension: a review of their clinical status. *Annals of Internal Medicine* 1977; 86: 626–636.

94. Seer P. Psychological control of essential hypertension: review of the literature and methodological critique. *Psychological Bulletin* 1979; 86: 1015–1043.

95. Lehmann JW, Benson H. Nonpharmacologic treatment of hypertension: a review. *General Hospital Psychiatry* 1982; 4: 27–32.

96. Cook CA. Antihypertensive drug compliance in black males. *Journal of the National Medical Association* 76 (Supplement); 1984: 40–46.

97. Blackwell B. The drug regimen and treatment compliance. In: Haynes RB, Taylor DW, Sackett DL, eds. *Compliance in Health Care.* Baltimore: Johns Hopkins University Press; 1979: 144–156.

98. Caldwell JR, Cobb S, Dowling M, Dejohg D. The dropout problem in anti-hypertensive treatment: a pilot study of social and emotional factors influencing a patient's ability to follow antihypertensive treatment. *Journal of Chronic Disease* 22; 1970: 579–592.

99. Nelson E, Stason W, Neutra R, Solomon H. Identification of the noncompliant hypertensive patient. *Preventive Medicine* 1980; 9: 505–517.

100. Kasl, SV. A social-psychological perspective on successful community control of high blood pressure: a review. *Journal of Behavioral Medicine* 1978; 1: 347–381.

101. Morisky D, Bowler M, Finlay J. An educational and behavioral approach toward increasing patient activation in hypertension management. *Journal of Community Health* 1982; 7: 171–182.

102. Syme L. Drug treatment of mild hypertension: social and psychological considerations. *Annals of New York Academy of Sciences* 1978; 304: 99–106.

10

Dementing Illness and Black Americans

F. M. Baker

The changing demographic profile of the United States population has led to an increased emphasis on the older American. As life expectancy and longevity have increased, the causes of death in the United States have changed from influenza and pneumonia, tuberculosis, gastroenteritis and heart disease in 1900, to heart disease, malignant neoplasms, and vascular lesions of the central nervous system in 1980 (1). Changes in cognitive function also have a higher prevalence in older populations, whether the cause is a dementing illness (2), the transient, reversible changes of deliria of whatever etiology (3), or the decompensation of a medical condition (4). With the initial warning by Plum in 1979 of an approaching epidemic of dementia (5), epidemiologic studies focused on the patterns of prevalence of dementing illness in different populations and case-control studies were implemented to identify risk factors (6).

Afro-Americans comprised 12% of the 1980 U.S. population, or approximately 22 million people (7). Eleven percent, or 2.4 million black Americans, are aged 60 or older according to the 1980 census (Table 10.1). What is the prevalence of cognitive impairment among older Afro-Americans? What are its causes? Are there specific risk factors that are preventable? To date there are few studies in black populations that have attempted to answer these questions. The purpose of this chapter is to review briefly issues involved in studying cognitive impairment, the existing literature, and the available information on cognitive impairment in older black Americans.

TABLE 10.1 Percentage Distribution of the Black U.S. Population by Age and Sex
(Total Population = 26,495,025, or 12% of total U.S. population)

Age group	% of total black males	% of total black females	% of total black population
60–64	3.08	3.48	3.29
65–74	4.52	5.54	5.02
75–84	1.82	2.57	2.22
85 +	0.42	0.76	0.60

Source: U.S. Census, 1980. Detailed Population Characteristics, U.S. Summary, Section A.

BACKGROUND

An initial concern of researchers was the establishment of a definition of
Alzheimer's disease (AD), one form of dementing illness. Although the
initial case description by Alois Alzheimer of the neurofibrillary tangles and
senile plaques in 1907 (8) remains a standard, the diagnosis of Alzheimer's
disease (AD) remains a diagnosis at necropsy. If studies of the disease in
living populations were to be implemented, the *clinical* definition of the
disease would need to be standardized so that studies of the disease in
different populations would be comparable. A work group on the diagnosis
of Alzheimer's disease, composed of representatives from the National
Institute of Neurological and Communicative Disorders and Stroke
(NINCDS) and the Alzheimer's Disease and Related Disorders Association
(ADRDA), compiled such a definition in 1984 (9). Folstein defined AD as a
brain disorder characterized by a progressive dementia in a clear sensorium
that occurs in middle and/or later life (10). Advancing beyond this definton,
the work group established specific criteria that range from a definite
diagnosis to a possible diagnosis based on the available *clinical data*. Thus
criteria for a *clinical diagnosis* of AD were established (Table 10.2).
Although several texts have been written that review the known clinical
course of the various types of dementing illness—for example, AD, multiinfarct dementia, mixed dementia, Parkinson's disease, alcoholic dementia,
Creutzfeldt-Jakob disease, and Huntington's chorea (11, 12, 13)—and report on the current neurochemical (14), immunologic (15), and genetic
research (16), few studies report data from black patients. Following the
publication of *The Epidemiology of Dementia* by Mortimer and Schuman
(17) in 1981, increased interest in epidemiologic studies of dementia occurred.

International studies of dementing illness in the United States (18, 19),
Japan (20, 21), England (22), and, most recently, Finland (23) have demonstrated an increasing prevalence of dementing illness with advancing age

and a higher prevalence in women (Table 10.3). Although studies of the prevalence of neurologic disease, including dementia, are under way in Nigeria and some results have been published (24, 25), specific data on the prevalence of dementing illness in black populations are not readily available. In the United States the Epidemiologic Catchment Area (ECA) studies (26) funded by the National Institute of Mental Health have studied the incidence and prevalence of mental illness in five cities. In three sites—Baltimore, Maryland; New Haven, Connecticut; and Durham, North Carolina—an oversampling of the elderly occurred. Further analysis of these data, particularly from the Durham site, with its larger percentage of black persons, may provide further specific information concerning the types of cognitive impairment present in older black populations. The ECA studies used a screening instrument, the Folstein Mini-Mental State examination (27), to identify persons with cognitive dysfunction. At the Baltimore site persons who screened "positive" by evidencing cognitive impairment in their screening test were referred for a more thorough evaluation of the identified cognitive impairment in order to determine its cause, reversibility, course, and indicated interventions. Thus a person with cognitive impairment may be delirious, a transient state, or demented, a fixed deficit. The results from the ECA sites will report on the *screening* for cognitive impairment *only*. A determination of the cause of the identified impairment awaits future follow-up studies.

The Baltimore site of the Epidemiologic Catchment Area (ECA) study selected a probability sample of East Baltimore households; $N = 3,626$. *All* persons aged 65 and over were selected from *each* household roster for interview by the ECA study. This resulted in the planned oversampling of the elderly. Of the 1,185 elders identified, 923 were interviewed. Of the 191 elders who screened positive for cognitive impairment on the Folstein Mini-Mental State examination, all were referred for a detailed psychiatric interview. As a result of that interview, 43 persons aged 65 and older were referred for a complete dementia workup funded by NINCDS to determine the cause of the confirmed cognitive impairment (28). Only 36 elders completed the dementia workup; 18 elders were black. These black East Baltimore residents had the following diagnoses: dementing illness = 10, multiinfarct dementia = 4, and no dementia = 4. Of the 10 subjects with a diagnosis of dementia, 6 subjects met the NINCDS–ADRDA clinical criteria for a diagnosis of *definite* AD and 4 subjects met the NINCDS–ADRDA criteria for *possible* AD. These data should not be interpreted as suggesting that 78% of the black elderly in this probability sample were demented. As estimations of the prevalence of dementing illness in East Baltimore residents were reported by Mini-Mental State score only (28), specification of the prevalence of the different dementias by age and sex categories is not possible from the published data.

Although the National Institute on Aging has funded the Baltimore

TABLE 10.2 Criteria for Clinical Diagnosis of Alzheimer's Disease

I.   The criteria for the clinical diagnosis of PROBABLE Alzheimer's disease include:
dementia established by clinical examination and documented by the Mini-Mental Test, Blessed Dementia Scale, or some similar examination, and confirmed by neuropsychological tests;
deficits in two or more areas of cognition;
progressive worsening of memory and other cognitive functions;
no disturbance of consciousness;
onset between ages 40 and 90, most often after age 65; and
absence of systemic disorders or other brain diseases that in and of themselves could account for the progressive deficits in memory and cognition.

II.   The diagnosis of PROBABLE Alzheimer's disease is supported by:
progressive deterioration of specific cognitive functions such as language (aphasia), motor skills (apraxia), and perception (agnosia);
impaired activities of daily living and altered patterns of behavior;
family history of similar disorders, particularly if confirmed neuropathologically; and laboratory results of:
normal lumbar puncture as evaluated by standard techniques,
normal pattern or nonspecific changes in EEG, such as increased slow-wave activity, and
evidence of cerebral atrophy on CT with progression documented by serial observation.

III.   Other clinical features consistent with the diagnosis of PROBABLE Alzheimer's disease, after exclusion of causes of dementia other than Alzheimer's disease, include:
plateaus in the course of progression of the illness;
associated symptoms of depression, insomnia, incontinence, delusions, illusions, hallucinations, catastrophic verbal, emotional, or physical outbursts, sexual disorders, and weight loss;
other neurologic abnormalities in some patients, especially with more advanced disease and including motor signs such as increased muscle tone, myoclonus, or gait disorder;
seizures in advanced disease; and
CT normal for age.

IV.   Features that make the diagnosis of PROBABLE Alzheimer's disease uncertain or unlikely include:
sudden, apoplectic onset;
focal neurologic findings such as hemiparesis, sensory loss, visual field deficits, and incoordination early in the course of the illness; and
seizures or gait disturbances at the onset or very early in the course of the illness.

V.   Clinical diagnosis of POSSIBLE Alzheimer's disease:
may be made on the basis of the dementia syndrome, in the absence of other neurologic, psychiatric, or systemic disorders sufficient to cause dementia, and in the presence of variations in the onset, in the presentation, or in the clinical course;
may be made in the presence of a second systemic or brain disorder sufficient to produce dementia, which is not considered to be *the* cause of the dementia; and

should be used in research studies when a single, gradually progressive severe cognitive deficit is identified in the absence of other identifiable cause.

VI.   Criteria for diagnosis of DEFINITE Alzheimer's disease are:
the clinical criteria for probable Alzheimer's disease and
histopathologic evidence obtained from a biopsy or autopsy.

VII. Classification of Alzheimer's disease for research purposes should specify features that may differentiate subtypes of the disorder, such as:
familial occurrence;
onset before age of 65;
presence of trisomy-21; and
coexistence of other relevant conditions such as Parkinson's disease.

Source: McKhann LG, Drachman D, Folstein M, et al. Clinical diagnosis of Alzheimer's disease: Report of the NINCDS–ADRDA Work Group under the auspices of the Department of Health and Human Services Task Force on Alzheimer's Disease. *Neurology* 1984; 34:939–944.

Longitudinal Study of Aging, which is in its 25th year, this was an all-white, all-male, college-educated group. In 1979 a group of white females, the spouses of the study participants, were added to this study. The National Institute on Aging (NIA) has funded, recently, four longitudinal studies of aging that include black samples. Specific data from these studies will be available in the next few years.

Why be concerned with cognitive impairment in black populations? Although the loss of younger black persons aged 18–35 due to homicide and suicide has been documented by several authors (29–33) and, most recently, by the Secretary's Task Force on Black and Minority Health (34), the causes of death and morbidity for black persons aged 60 and over are less well studied. Throughout the life cycle of too many black Americans, alcohol misuse, abuse, and/or dependence is common (35, 36). Given the data on deaths due to cirrhosis (37), the possibility of the presence of alcoholic dementia at a younger age in the black population seems a reasonable assumption. To date there are few population-based studies that have looked specifically at dementing illness (alcoholic dementia, multi-infarct dementia, and AD) in a geographically defined sample of older black persons in comparison to a sample of older whites.

I posit that black females may be at increased risk for multiinfarct dementia due to a higher incidence of obesity, hypertension, and differential survival compared to black males (38, 39, 40). The prevalence of hypertension in the black population has several suggested etiologies: heredity, obesity, dietary, and psychosocial factors (41). Adams, Savage, Watkins, and colleagues (42) and Kumanyika and Savage (43) have reviewed the risk factors for ischemic heart disease in this population. The prevalence of hypertension in black persons increases the risk for a cerebrovascular accident and multiinfarct dementia. Hasegawa (44) reported a

TABLE 10.3 Worldwide Prevalence of Severe Dementia

Study	Location	Sample		Severe cases of dementia / 100		
			Overall	60–69	70–79	80+
Schoenberg, Anderson, & Haerer, 1985	Copiah County, U.S.A.	Rural	2.2	1.2	2.55	6.81
Sulkava, Wikstrom, Aromaa, et al., 1985	Finland	Rural & urban	1.8	4.2 (65–74)	10.7 (75–84)	17.3 (85+)
Karasawa, 1980	Tokyo, Japan	Urban	4.8	1.2 (65–74)	3.9 (mean) 3.1(70–74) 4.7(75–79)	18.25 (mean) 13.1(80–84) 23.4(85+)
Hasegawa, 1974	Tokyo, Japan	Urban	4.5	1.2 (65–69)	4.35 (mean) 2.6(70–74) 6.1(75–79)	20.25 (mean) 13.7(80–84) 26.8(85+)
Hasegawa, 1982	Tokyo, Japan	Urban	4.8	1.8 (65–69)	4.4 (mean) 3.8(70–74) 5.0(75–79)	15.8 (mean) 10.8(80–84) 20.8(85+)
Kay, Bergman, Foster, et al., 1970	Newcastle-on-Tyne, England	Rural	6.2	2.3 (65–69)	4.15 (mean) 2.8(70–74) 5.5(75–79)	22.0

NB: Gender Differences—
Copiah County : Female to male rates, 2:1 for severe dementia in blacks and whites.
Newcastle-on-Tyne: Female to male rate of 2:1.
Tokyo: Female to male rates for severe Alzheimer's disease were 3:1 and for cerebrovascular dementia, 3:2

higher prevalence of multiinfarct dementia (1.7 per 100 population in 1980) in a Tokyo sample of older Japanese compared to a prevalence rate of 0.6 per 100 for AD in the same population of all older Japanese. Further, the prevalence rate of dementia was higher in females than males, a ratio of 3 : 1. Thus, by analogy, it may be that different racial groups may have different patterns of dementing illness, which may result from diet, environment, genetic factors, or all of these in weighted combination.

AVAILABLE STUDIES OF DEMENTING ILLNESS IN BLACK POPULATIONS

Schoenberg, Anderson, and Haerer completed a descriptive study of severe dementia in Copiah County, Mississippi, a rural county in south-central Mississippi (45). Although the county contained a population that was 49% black and 51% white in January 1978, the age distribution was not uniform between the races. The black population contained a large number of persons in the younger age groups. Thus, the Copiah County population age 40 and older contained 39% black and 60% white persons. This study involved a door-to-door census as well as an institutional survey. All institutions serving Copiah County, including all Mississippi state hospitals, were surveyed. Each person identified in either setting as a suggested case of *severe* dementia was evaluated by a board-certified neurologist.

The prevalence rates of severe dementing illness established in this sample were similar to the prior studies of Kay, Beamish, and Roth (46), Hasegawa (47), Karasawa (48), and Sulkava, Wilstrom, Aromaa, and colleagues (49), with the prevalence rates of severe dementia increasing with increasing age (Table 10.3). Further, prevalence rates were higher for both black and white females in comparison to black and white males (Table 10.4). In this study

TABLE 10.4 Prevalence Rates of Clinically Diagnosed Dementia by Age, Race, and Sex per 100 Inhabitants in Copiah County, Mississippi

| | Age groupings | | |
	60–69	70–70	80+
White males	.538	1.265	5.882
White females	.266	1.401	7.246
Black males	.718	2.069	3.158
Black females	.000	2.549	9.449
Total	.351	2.550	6.807

Source: Schoenberg BS, Anderson DW, Haerer AF. Severe dementia. Prevalence and clinical features in a biracial U.S. population. Archives of Neurology 1985; 42: 740–743.

the largest number of institutionalized cases of severe dementia were white females. Black females had the lowest number of institutionalized cases, probably reflecting the strength of the black families and the availability of alternative caregivers from the extended family network (50, 51, 52).

In this sample the rates of severe dementia for blacks were higher than the rates for whites, particularly in the 70–79 age groups, where the prevalence rate for black females was 1.82 times the rate for white females and the rate for black males was 1.64 times the prevalence rate for white males in this age group. In the 60–69 age group the prevalence rate for black males was 1.36 times the prevalence rate for white males (Table 10.4). Although an increasing prevalence of severe dementia with increasing age was not unexpected, given the data from previous studies, specific factors in this population contributing to the higher rates in blacks compared to whites were unclear. Although mortality rates are higher in blacks throughout the life cycle, particularly for black males, there is some evidence that once black persons reach age 75, their survival rates equal whites, with black females living longer than black males. This has been termed the "crossover" phenomenon (40). Although the increase in survival of black persons over age 75 has been noted, the importance of this observation to dementing illness in black persons is unknown.

The majority of black persons in this sample were poor. There was a wider range of socioeconomic status, however, among whites. Potential risks from environmental exposure, differences in access to health care, and constitutional factors could all contribute to the observed differences. Further studies, specifically case-control studies, are needed to specify with greater precision the risk factors for dementia in this sample. Although the observed racial differences in prevalence rates could be explained on the basis of differential survival by blacks, it seems unlikely that poor, elderly black persons would have a survival advantage. Throughout the years, the U.S. mortality statistics (38) have shown increased survival for females (white greater than black) compared to males (white greater then black). Further studies are needed to clarify its significance and factors contributing to it.

The Copiah County study was completed in 1978, before the 1984 publication of the NINCDS–ADRDA standards for the clinical diagnosis of dementia. Screening criteria used to identify potentially severely demented persons included individuals over age 40 who required constant supervision and who were unable to perform their usual job or household duties because of mentation difficulties not previously present, evidence of nocturnal disorientation, and an abnormal mental status on both the screening test and a more formal neurologist's examination (with symptoms present for at least 4 months). In this study a definite diagnosis of dementia required that functional psychosis or depression or both were ruled out and that mentation difficulty was the only reason for supervision. If these requirements were not met, a diagnosis of possible dementia was made by these authors. Although the majority of these cases were identified as "either primary, chronic, progessive dementia (presumably AD) or secondary dementia resulting mainly from stroke alone or stroke in the presence of another precipitating condition" (p. 741), a specific separation of these categories by sex and race was not done due to the small number of identified cases.

Another study that provided some information concerning dementia in black populations focused on death certificate data. As is known, death certificate data are limited by the accuracy of the recording of the cause of death (53). This coding of the immediate, underlying, and associated or contributory cause of death is complicated further by the changes in the structural categories in the International Classification of Disease in different years. The numerical code that specifies a given diagnosis in one year may not be consistent for that diagnosis across a span of years (54). Finally, the person coding the cause of death may code incorrectly, the physician recording the cause of death may not know the complete medical history of the patient and be unaware of specific illnesses, and the necropsy results may return after the death certificate has been completed. These factors are of particular concern in patients with AD whose immediate cause of death may be listed on the death certificate as an infection (e.g., pneumonia) but whose underlying cause of death is AD (55).

Chandra, Bharucha, and Schoenberg (55) reviewed death certificates for the years 1971 and 1973–1978. Data from 1972 was eliminated because the National Center for Health Statistics (NCHS) had processed only a 50% systematic sample of all death certificates for that year. NCHS had recoded all diseases on each death certificate using the eighth revision of the International Classification of Diseases adopted for use in the United States (ICDA), which linked or modified each entity on the death certificate to all other entities listed on the same death certificate. Because AD could be coded in any category, all categories of cause of death were reviewed, including immediate, underlying, contributory, or associated. Based on the diagnoses enumerated on the death certificate, two broad ICDA numeric codes were used: 290 (senile and presenile brain disease) and 794 (senility). Each numeric code included conditions not related to dementia, for example, "senile exhaustion" is included in the 794 code. Again, the study results are presented recognizing these limitations.

The sample was divided into whites and nonwhites. The nonwhite group, both sexes, had an average annual age-adjusted mortality rate for death due to senility greater than whites. For the category senile and presenile dementia, nonwhite females had higher average annual mortality rates than white females in the age groups of 45–49, 65–69, and 70–74. These authors noted that nonwhites had senility listed more frequently as the underlying cause of death. In the past, death statistics had been based only on the underlying cause of death. Recognizing that nonwhites and whites might not have the same quality of medical care, the authors noted that the condition chosen as the underlying cause of death depended on knowledge of other conditions in the individual. Without a thorough medical evaluation in comparison to whites due to a differential in the quality of care, a nonwhite person could have the underlying cause of death assigned to senility. Thus, these authors caution, the higher mortality rate for deaths due to senility in nonwhites should *not* be considered as "proof" that senility is more "malignant" and more frequently fatal in nonwhites than in whites.

Although these mortality data have several limitations, they do confirm the presence of diseases of cognitive impairment in older black Americans. Minimally, these results argue for study of this population with a recognition that dementing illnesses may present in younger (age 40 and older) age groups. These mortality data raise, again, the issue of quality of care and access to medical treatment for black Americans.

A third study, which contained a population of black patients and looked at issues of cognitive impairment, was completed at the Johns Hopkins Hospital by Roca, Klein, Kirby, and colleagues (56) in 1984. These investigators addressed the question of how accurately dementia was diagnosed among medical inpatients on three medical units by interns using the Folstein Mini-Mental State (27, 56) as a screening instrument. Study subjects were all consenting admissions, older than 40, who said they had learned to read and write and who were not deaf, blind, or gravely ill. The diagnostic criteria for dementia were those of the Third Edition-Revised of the *Diagnostic and Statistical Manual* of the American Psychiatric Association (57) and from McHugh in the Cecil-Loeb Textbook of Medicine (58) (see Table 10.5).

Two hundred and eighty-five of the 380 patients who participated or 75% of the study sample were black: 56% were female, and 46% were older than 66. Interns and investigators agreed that 45 persons (14%) were considered demented and 259 (86%) were not demented. Investigators considered 12 patients demented who were judged nondemented by the interns. When characteristics of age (<65), race (black), sex (male), and education (<12) were reviewed, only age—younger than 65—was found to be significant ($p < .027$). Thus errors in diagnostic sensitivity appeared to be related to age. On the other hand, interns diagnosed 64 patients as demented who did not meet diagnostic criteria. In this case 36 patients had insufficient cognitive impairment to warrant a diagnosis of dementia, 9 lacked a history of decline, and 19 displayed disruptions of consciousness that precluded the assignment of a new diagnosis of dementia. These authors noted that the diagnostic specificity of these interns (80%) exceeded that reported by Williamson, Stokoe, Gray, and colleagues (59) for British general practitioners (13%) for diagnosing cases of dementia.

These authors found that errors in sensitivity and specificity were related in part to easily identifiable characteristics of the patients examined. As 75% of their patient sample was black, these findings have relevance for studies of black populations that depend upon physician screening. Three main factors emerged: (1) persons with clouded consciousness were often designated as demented despite the fact that their disturbance of consciousness precluded a new diagnosis of dementia, (2) the diagnosis of dementia tended to be overlooked in younger patients, and (3) the diagnosis of dementia tended to be misapplied among the poorly educated.

Issues of misdiagnosis among black psychiatric patients have gained increased attention through the work of Adebimpe (60), Bell (61, 62), and Jones (63). Without an adequate medical evaluation, due to the absence of resources, misuse of resources, or an ineffective doctor–patient relationship, the important historical and clinical data needed for a differential diagnosis may not be elicited. The importance of screening black persons for cognitive impairment from at least age 40 is suggested by the work of Robins, Murphy, and Breckenridge (64), Viamontes and Powell (65), and Maddox and Williams (66), who documented the earlier age of onset of drinking and the heavier pattern of consumption of alcohol by black males. As a black male aged 33 may have had a 20-year or longer history of heavy drinking, the possibility of alcoholic dementia occurring before age 50 seems possible. Further, issues of disparity in care as well as compliance with precribed treatment regimens for hypertension increase the risk for multiinfarct dementia. Finally, black persons aged 65 in 1986 (Table 10.6) would have entered school at age 6 in 1927. The probabilities for completion of primary education (completion of the sixth grade) would be greater for these black Americans compared to those born in 1901. The majority of schools for these age cohorts were segregated, and for the majority of the black population completion of high school, let alone college or professional school, was unusual. Thus the impact of lack of formal education through high school on instruments designed to measure cognitive impairment must be assessed before these instruments are widely applied to black populations. Although the Task Force on Forensic Issues in Geriatric Psychiatry of the American Psychiatric Association suggests a standardized test battery in its report entitled *An Overview of Legal Issues in Geriatric Psychiatry* (67), the reliability of these well-known instruments for populations of black patients with cognitive dysfunction, depression, and anxiety has not been established. This is a necessary first step before the initiation of such a study. The methodological approaches of the National Survey of Black Americans designed and implemented by Jackson, Tucker, and Bowman (68) provide an important model of an approach to survey research in black populations.

TABLE 10.5 Diagnostic Criteria for Primary Degenerative Dementia

Diagnostic criteria for dementia

A. Demonstrable evidence of impairment in short- and long-term memory. Impairment in short-term memory (inability to learn new information) may be indicated by inability to remember three objects after five minutes. Long-term memory impairment (inability to remember information that was known in the past) may be indicated by inability to remember past personal information (e.g., what happened yesterday, birthplace, occupation) or facts of common knowledge (e.g., past Presidents, well-known dates).
B. At least one of the following:
   (1) impairment in abstract thinking, as indicated by inability to find similarities and differences between related words, difficulty in defining words and concepts, and other similar tasks
   (2) impaired judgment, as indicated by inability to make reasonable plans to deal with interpersonal, family, and job-related problems and issues
   (3) other disturbances of higher cortical function, such as aphasia (disorder of language), apraxia (inability to carry out motor activities despite intact comprehension and motor function), agnosia (failure to recognize or identify objects despite intact sensory function), and "constructional difficulty" (e.g., inability to copy three-dimensional figures, assemble blocks, or arrange sticks in specific designs)
   (4) personality change, i.e., alteration or accentuation of premorbid traits
C. The disturbance in A and B significantly interferes with work or usual social activities or relationships with others.
D. Not occurring exclusively during the course of Delirium.
E. Either (1) or (2):
   (1) there is evidence from the history, physical examination, or laboratory tests of a specific organic factor (or factors) judged to be etiologically related to the disturbance
   (2) in the absence of such evidence, an etiologic organic factor can be presumed if the disturbance cannot be accounted for by any nonorganic mental disorder, e.g., Major Depression accounting for cognitive impairment
Criteria for severity of dementia:
Mild: Although work or social activities are significantly impaired, the capacity for independent living remains, with adequate personal hygiene and relatively intact judgment.
Moderate: Independent living is hazardous, and some degree of supervision is necessary.
Severe: Activities of daily living are so impaired that continual supervision is required, e.g., unable to maintain minimal personal hygiene; largely incoherent or mute.

Source: Work Group to Revise DSM-II. *Diagnostic and Statistical Manual of Mental Disorders (Third Edition-Revised).* Washington, DC: American Psychiatric Association, 1987, pp. 107, 119–122.

TABLE 10.6 Birth Year and Year of School Entry

Age in 1986	Year of Birth	Age 6 in year
65	1921	1927
75	1911	1917
85	1901	1907

CONCLUSION

The large body of literature, which initially addressed the concerns of the black aged and emphasized the double, triple, and quadruple jeopardy that they faced as old, black, poor, and female persons in our society, must be acknowledged. The numerous publications of Jacquelyne Johnson Jackson in the gerontology literature (69–74) pressed the concerns of older black Americans and stimulated geriatric researchers to address this population. The recent works of James Carter (75–77) have highlighted the importance of addressing the psychosocial context as well as the biological illness of these patients. The National Black Survey completed by the team headed by James S. Jackson has applied rigorous survey methodology to a survey of urban-resident black Americans, demonstrating that such studies can be completed with appropriate sensitivity to the population being studied. The publications from this study (78–81) are providing important data on helper networks and the subjects' perceptions of their medical and psychological health.

The initial study of first-degree relatives of necropsy-confirmed cases of AD by Heston, Mastri, Anderson, and colleagues reported an excess of Down's syndrome, lymphoma, and immune diatheses in comparison to controls (82). The report of Heyman, Wilkinson, Stafford, and colleagues (83) from their case-control study showed a higher frequency of thyroid disease and severe head trauma. A subsequent case-control study by Mortimer, French, Hutton, and colleagues (84) confirmed prior head trauma as a risk factor for dementia. These studies show that the epidemiologic knowledge base concerning the worldwide prevalence and risk factors for AD is advancing. Rocca, Fratiglioni, Bracco, and colleagues (85) provided important data on first-degree relatives as surrogate respondents for demented patients. Although neuroscientists have addressed the transmissibility of AD (86) and Creutzfeldt-Jakob disease (87), and dietary risk factors for Creutzfelt-Jakob disease have been identified from a case-control study (88), comparable data are not available in black populations. The recent research focus on the aging National Health and Nutrition Examination Survey (NHANES) sample by NIA researchers as well as the NIA and

NIMH initiatives to study nursing home populations will provide future data, though the black sample may be small.

Today, research that addresses aging in the black American population remains a virtually unexplored area. I have underscored the dearth of epidemiologic data to answer the questions of potential differences in the prevalance of dementing illness in blacks. Although the data from the Durham and New Haven ECA sites should shortly provide important *screening* data on cognitive impairment in black populations, many research questions will remain. What is the cause of the observed cognitive impairment? What are the risk factors for developing cognitive impairment? Which causes of cognitive impairment are preventable? The study of cognitive impairment in black populations has very clear public health and primary prevention implications. If multiinfarct dementia and alcoholic dementia have a higher prevalence in black populations, then these diseases are preventable and their prevalence rates can be reduced by public health education initiatives to change destructive behavior patterns in black populations. Well-designed, clearly focused studies will clarify whether these hypotheses are in fact correct.

REFERENCES

1. Mauser JS, Kramer S. Sources of data on community health. In: Mauser JS, Kramer S, eds. *Mauser and Bahn Epidemiology—An Introductory Text.* Philadelphia: Saunders; 1985: 66–78.
2. Reisberg B, Ferris SH. Diagnosis and assessment of the older patient. *Hospital and Community Psychiatry* 1982; 33 (2): 104–110.
3. Sloane RB. Organic brain syndrome. In: Birren JE, Sloane RB, eds. *Handbook of Mental Health and Aging.* Englewood Cliffs, NJ: Prentice-Hall; 1980: 554–590.
4. Posner JB. Disturbances of consciousness and arousal. In: Wyngaarden JB, Smith LH Jr, eds. *Cecil Textbook of Medicine (17th Ed.):* Philadelphia: Saunders; 1985; 1971–1979.
5. Plum F. Dementia: an approaching epidemic. *Nature* 1979; 279: 372–373.
6. Rocca WA, Amaducci LA, Schoenberg BS. Epidemiology of clinically diagnosed Alzheimer's disease. *Annals of Neurology* 1986; 19 (5): 415–424.
7. United States Bureau of the Census. Demographic aspects of aging and older populations in the United States. Current Population Reports. Special Studies. Washington, DC: U.S. Government Printing Office; 1980.
8. Alzheimer A. Uber eine Eigenartige Erkrankung der Hirnrinde. *Allg Z Psychiatrie Psychisch-Gerichtlich Med* 1907; 64: 146–148.
9. McKhann G, Drachman D, Folstein M, Katzman R, Price D, Stadlan EM. Clinical diagnosis of Alzheimer's disease: report of the NINCDS–ADRDA Work Group under the auspices of the Department of Health and Human Services Task Force on Alzheimer's Disease. *Neurology* 1984; 34: 939–944.

10. Folstein M, Anthony JC, Parhad I, Duffy B, Gruenberg EM. The meaning of cognitive impairment in the elderly. *Journal of the American Geriatrics Society* 1985; 33 (4): 228–235.

11. Stub RL, Black FW. Alzheimer's/senile dementia. In: Strub RI, Black FW, eds. *Organic Brain Syndromes: An Introduction to Neurobehavioral Disorders.* Philadelphia: Davis; 1981: 119–164.

12. Libow LS. Senile dementia and "pseudosenility": clinical diagnosis. In: Eisdorfer C, Friedel RO, eds. *Cognitive & Emotional Disturbances in the Elderly.* Chicago: Year Book Medical Publishers; 1977: 75–88.

13. Task Force on Alzheimer's Disease. *Alzheimer's Disease—Report of the Secretary's Task Force on Alzheimer's Disease.* Washington, DC: Department of Health and Human Services; 1984: 3–57.

14. Sim NR, Bowmen DM. Changes in choline acetyltransferase in acetycholine synthesis. In: Reisberg B, ed. *Alzheimer's Disease—The Standard Reference.* New York: Free Press; 1983: 88–92.

15. Walford RL, Fortoul T. Histocompatibility locus antigens and Alzheimer's disease. In: Reisberg B, ed. *Alzheimer's Disease—The Standard Reference.* New York: Free Press; 1983: 166–169.

16. Sinex WE, Merril CR, eds. Alzheimer's disease, Down's syndrome, and aging. *Annals of the New York Academy of Sciences* 1982; 396: 3–199.

17. Mortimer JA, Schuman LM, eds. *The Epidemiology of Dementia.* New York: Oxford University Press; 1981: 3–187.

18. Kokmen E, Okazaki H, Schoenberg BS. Epidemiologic patterns and clinical features of dementia in a defined U.S. population. *Transactions of the American Neurological Association* 1980; 105: 334–336.

19. Schoenberg BS, Anderson DW, Haerer AF. Severe dementia. Prevalence and clinical features in a biracial U.S. population. *Archives of Neurology* 1985; 42: 740–743.

20. Hasegawa K. Epidemiologic studies on the age-related dementia in Japan. Paper presented at the National Workshop Epidemiologic Study, Mental Health Problems in Aging Populations, Beijing, China; 18–24 July 1985.

21. Karasawa A, Karashima K, Kasahara H. Epidemiological study of the senile in Tokyo metropolitan area. In: Ohashi, H, ed. *Proceedings of the World Psychiatric Association Regional Symposium.* Tokyo: The Japanese Society of Psychiatry and Neurology; 1982: 285–289.

22. Roth M. The natural history of mental disorder in old age. *Journal of Mental Science* 1955; 101: 281–301.

23. Sulkava R, Wikstrom J, Aromaa A, Raitasalo R, Lehtinen V, Lahtela K, Palo J. Prevalence of severe dementia in Finland. *Neurology* 1985; 35: 1025–1029.

24. Osuntokun BO, Schoenberg BS, Nottidge VA, Adeuja A, Kale O, Adeyeta A, Bademosi O, Olumide A, Oyediran ABO, Pearson CA, Bolis CL. Research protocol for measuring the prevalence of neurologic disorders in developing countries—the results of a pilot study in Nigeria. *Neuroepidemiology* 1982; 1: 143–155.

25. Osuntokun BO, Schoenberg BS, Nottidge VA, Adeuja A, Kale O, Adeyefa A, Bademosi O, Bolis CL. Migraine headache in a rural community in Nigeria: results of a pilot study. *Neuroepidemiology* 1982; 1: 31–39.

26. Eaton WE, Kessler LG, eds. *Epidemiologic Field Methods in Psychiatry.* New York: Academic Press; 1985:3–373.

27. Folstein MF, Folstein SE, McHugh PR. Mini-Mental State: a practical method for grading the cognitive state of patients for the clinician. *Journal of Psychiatric Research* 1975; 12: 189–198.

28. Folstein M, Anthony JC, Parhad I, Duffy B, Gruenberg EM. The meaning of cognitive impairment in the elderly. Journal of the American Geriatrics Society 1985; 33 (4): 228–235.

29. Hendin H. Black suicide. *Archives of General Psychiatry* 1969; 21: 407–422.

30. Poussaint AF. Black suicide. In: Williams RA, ed. *Textbook of Black-Related Diseases.* New York: McGraw-Hill; 1975: 707–713.

31. Pederson AM, Awad GA, Kindler AR. Epidemiologic differences between white and nonwhite suicide attempters. *American Journal of Psychiatry* 1973; 130 (10): 1071–1076.

32. Christian ER. Black suicide. In: Hatton CL, Valente SM, Bink A, eds. *Suicide: Assessment and Intervention.* Appleton-Century-Croft; 1977: 143–159.

33. Baker FM. Black suicide attempters in 1980: a preventive focus. *General Hospital Psychiatry* 1984; 6: 131–137.

34. Task Force on Black and Minority Health. Subcommittee on Homicide, Suicide, and Unintentional Injuries. In *Task Force Report on Black and Minority Health, Vol. I: Executive Summary.* Washington, DC: Department of Health and Human Services; 1985:157–169.

35. Viamontes JA, Powell BJ. Demographic characteristics of black and white male alcoholics. *International Journal of Addiction* 1974; 9: 489–494.

36. Task Force on Black and Minority Health. Subcommittee on Chemical Dependency. In *Task Force Report on Black and Minority Health, Vol. I: Executive Summary.* Washinton, DC: Department of Health and Human Services; 1985: 129–147.

37. Herd D. We cannot stagger to freedom. A history of blacks and alcohol in American politics. In: Brill L, Winick C, eds. *The Yearbook of Substance Use and Abuse* (Vol. III). New York: Human Sciences Press; 1985: 141–186.

38. United States Bureau of the Census. Demographic aspects of aging and the older population in the United States. Current Population Reports. Special Studies. Washington, DC: U.S. Government Printing Office; 1980.

39. United States Bureau of the Census. Demographic aspects of aging and the older population in the United States. Current Population Reports. Special Studies. Washington, DC: U.S. Government Printing Office; 1980.

40. Task Force on Black and Minority Health. Subcommittee on Cardiovascular and Cerebrovascular Disease. In *Task Force Report on Black and Minority Health, Vol. I: Executive Summary.* Washington, DC: Department of Health and Human Services; 1985: 107–127.

41. Saunders E, Williams RA. Hypertension. In: Williams RA, ed. *Textbook of Black-Related Diseases.* New York: McGraw-Hill; 1975: 333–358.

42. Adams LL, Savage DD, Watkins LD, LaPorte RE, Kuller LH. Analysis of cardiovascular risk factors in upwardly mobile black males and females. Background paper for the Department of Health and Human Services' Task Force on Black and Minority Health, 1985.

43. Kumanyika S, Savage DD. Ischemic heart disease risk factors in U.S. blacks. Background paper for the Department of Health and Human Services' Task Force on Black and Minority Health, 1985.
44. Hasegawa K. Epidemiologic studies on the age-related dementia in Japan. Paper presented at the National Workshop Epidemiological Study, Mental Health Problems in Aging Populations, Beijing, China; 18–24 July 1985.
45. Schoenberg BS, Anderson DW, Haerer AF. Severe dementia. Prevalence and clinical features in a biracial U.S. population. *Archives of Neurology* 1985; 42: 740–743.
46. Kay DWK, Beamish P, Roth M. Old age mental disorders in Newcastle upon the Tyne: a study of prevalence. *British Journal of Psychiatry* 1964; 110: 146–158.
47. Hasegawa K. Epidemiologic studies on the age-related dementia in Japan. Paper presented at the National Workshop Epidemiological Study, Mental Health Problems in Aging Populations, Beijing, China; 18–24 July 1985.
48. Karasawa A, Karashima K, Kasahara H. Epidemiological study of the senile in Tokyo metropolitan area. In *Proceedings of the World Psychiatric Association Regional Symposium* edited by H Ohashi. Tokyo: The Japanese Society of Psychiatry and Neurology, 1982, pp 285–289.
49. Sulkava R, Wilstrom J, Aromaa A, Raitasalo R, Lehtinen V, Lahtela K, Palo J. Prevalence of severe dementia in Finland. *Neurology* 1985; 35: 1025–1029.
50. Martin EP, Martin JM. *The Black Extended Family*. Chicago: University of Chicago Press; 1978: 1–114.
51. Baker, FM. The black elderly: biopsychosocial perspective within an age cohort and adult development context. *Journal of Geriatric Psychiatry* 1982; 15 (2): 227–239.
52. Hines PM, Boyd-Franklin N. Black families. In: McGoldrick M, Pearce JK, Giordano J, eds. *Ethnicity and Family Therapy*. New York: Guilford Press; 1982: 84–107.
53. Lilienfeld AM, Lilienfeld DE. Mortality statistics. In: *Foundations of Epidemiology* (2nd ed.). New York: Oxford University Press; 1980: 66–83.
54. Warshauer ME, Monk M. Problems in suicide statistics for whites and blacks. *American Journal of Public Health* 1978; 58 (4): 383–388.
55. Chandra V, Bharucha NE, Schoenberg BS. Patterns of mortality from types of dementia in the United States, 1971 and 1973–1978. *Neurology* 1986; 36: 204–208.
56. Roca RP, Klein LE, Kirby SM, McArthur JC, Vogelsang GB, Folstein MF, Smith CR. Recognition of dementia among medical patients. *Archives of Internal Medicine* 1984; 144: 73–75.
57. Work Group to Revise DSM-III. *Diagnostic and Statistical Manual of Mental Disorders (Third Edition—Revised)*. Washington, DC: American Psychiatric Association; 1987: 107, 119–122.
58. McHugh PR. Dementia. In: Beeson PB, McDermott W, eds. *Cecil-Loeb Textbook of Medicine*. Philadelphia: Saunders; 1971: 102–107.
59. Williamson J, Stokoe IH, Gray S, Fisher M, Smith A, McGhee A, Stephenson E. Old people at home: their unreported needs. *Lancet* 1964; 1: 1117–1120.

60. Adebimpe VR. Hallucinations and delusions in black psychiatric patients. *Journal of the National Medical Association* 1981; 73 (6): 517–520.
61. Bell CC, Thompson JKP, Lewis D, Redd J, Shears M, Thompson B. Misdiagnosis of alcohol-related organic brain syndrome: implications for treatment. In: Brisbane FL, Womble M, eds. *Treatment of Black Alcoholics*. New York: Haworth Press; 1985: 45–65.
62. Bell CC, Mehta H. The misdiagnosis of black patients with manic-depressive illness. *Journal of the National Medical Association* 1979; 72 (2): 141–145.
63. Jones BE, Gray BA, Parson EB. Manic-depressive illnesses among poor urban blacks. *American Journal of Psychiatry* 1981; 138 (5): 654–657.
64. Robins LN, Murphy GE, Breckenridge MB. Drinking behavior of young Negro men. *Quarterly Journal of Studies on Alcohol* 1968; 29: 657–684.
65. Viamontes JA, Powell PJ. Demographic characteristics of black and white male alcoholics. *International Journal of Addiction* 1974; 9: 489–494.
66. Maddox GK, Williams JR. Drinking behavior of Negro collegians. *Quarterly Journal of Studies of Alcohol* 1968; 29: 117–129.
67. Baker FM, Perr IN, Yesavage JA. *An Overview of Legal Issues in Geriatric Psychiatry*. Washington, DC: American Psychiatric Association; 1986: 1–45.
68. Jackson JS, Tucker MB, Bowman PJ. Conceptual and methodological problems in survey research on black Americans. In: Liu W, ed. *Issues in Minority Research*. Chicago: Pacific/Asian American Mental Health Center; 1982:11–40.
69. Jackson JJ. Social gerontology and the Negro: a review. *Gerontologist* 1967; 7 (3): 168–178.
70. Jackson JJ. Negro aged and social gerontology: a critical evaluation. *Journal of Social and Behavioral Sciences* 1968; 13: 42–47.
71. Jackson JJ. The blacklands of gerontology. *Aging and Human Development* 1971; 2: 156–171.
72. Jackson JJ. Sex and social class variation in black aged parent–adult child relationships. *Aging and Human Development* 1971; 2: 96–107.
73. Jackson JJ. Negro aged: toward needed research in social gerontology. *The Gerontologist* 1971; 11: 52–57.
74. Jackson JJ. Plight of older black women in the United States. *Black Aging* 1975; 1: 12–20.
75. Carter JH. Psychiatry and aging. *Journal of the American Geriatrics Society* 1972; 20: 343–345.
76. Carter JH. The black aged: a strategy for future mental health services. *Journal of the American Geriatrics Society* 1978; 26 (12): 553–556.
77. Carter JH. Treating black patients: the risks of ignoring critical social issues. *Hospital and Community Psychiatry* 1981; 32 (4): 281–282.
78. Jackson JS, Chatters LM, Neighbors HW. The mental health status of older black Americans: a national study. *The Black Scholar* 1982; 1: 21–35.
79. Chatters LM, Taylor RJ, Jackson JS. Size and composition of the informal helper networks of elderly blacks. *Journal of Gerontology* 1985; 40 (5): 605–614.
80. Neighbors, HW. Ambulatory medical care among adult black Americans: the hospital emergency room. *Journal of the National Medical Association* 1986; 78: 272–282.

81. Neighbors, HW. Socioeconomic status and psychologic distress in adult blacks. *American Journal of Epidemiology* 1986; 124: 779–793.
82. Heston LL, Mastri AR, Anderson VE, White J. Dementia of the Alzheimer's type. *Archives of General Psychiatry* 1981; 38: 1085–1090.
83. Heyman A, Wilkinson WE, Stafford JA, Helms MJ, Sigmon AH, Weinberg T. Alzheimer's disease: a study of epidemiological aspects. *Annals of Neurology* 1984; 15 (4): 335–341.
84. Mortimer JA, French LR, Hutton JT, Schuman LM. Head injury as a risk factor for Alzheimer's disease. *Neurology* 1985; 35: 264–267.
85. Rocca WA, Fratiglioni L, Bracco L, Pedone D, Groppi C, Schoenberg BS. The use of surrogate respondents to obtain questionnaire data in case-control studies of neurologic diseases. *Journal of Chronic Diseases* in press.
86. Goudsmit J, Marrow CH, Asher DM, Yanagihara RT, Masters CL, Gibbs CJ, Gajdusek DC. Evidence for and against the transmissibility of Alzheimer's disease. *Neurology* 30 (9): 945–950.
87. Davanipour Z, Alter M, Sobel E, Asher D, Gajdusek DC. Creutzfeldt-Jakob disease: possible medical risk factors. *Neurology* 1985; 35: 1483–1486.
88. Davanipour Z, Alter M, Sobel E, Asher M, Gajdusek DC. A case-control study of Creutzfeldt-Jacob disease—dietary risk factors. *American Journal of Epidemiology* 1985; 122 (3): 443–451.

PART IV
Social and Behavioral Processes among Older Black Adults

11

Subjective Well-Being among Older Black Adults: Past Trends and Current Perspectives

Linda M. Chatters

Subjective well-being (SWB) research has had a long history within the field of gerontology and represents work on a broad array of related concepts, such as adjustment, morale, life satisfaction, and happiness. The proliferation of work on SWB has resulted in considerable variability in its conceptualization and measurement, with the attendant problems of lack of conceptual and methodological clarity (1). Similarly, differences in the procedures employed across studies (e.g., samples, age ranges, and analysis procedures) have hampered comparative efforts (2).

Despite these problems, recent critical assessments of the state of the literature (1, 3) suggest a growing base of commonality in efforts to define and measure SWB. Current definitions emphasize that subjective well-being is an overarching construct that is characterized by a focus on subjective experience (as opposed to objective conditions), the explicit incorporation of positive measures, and the use of an overall assessment of life (3). Gerontological conceptions of SWB often incorporate specific references to age or time of life and include an ideological component (1, 3, 4).

Diener's (3) general treatment of subjective well-being encompasses research among both elderly and nonelderly samples (see also 5). Reviews of research and thought on SWB within the field of gerontology provide a general orientation to this work, as well as discussions of conceptual and methodological concerns, major correlates, and psychometric and structural properties (1, 6–9).

The present chapter is concerned with SWB theory and research as they pertain specifically to older black adults. The direction and form of SWB research among older blacks has been influenced by work among majority samples of the elderly. Somewhat less apparent is how the experiences of older blacks have influenced theoretical and research models of SWB and contributed to general efforts to understand these phenomena. The relationship between these literatures is ultimately mutually reinforcing and interdependent. The use of a variety of models and approaches to the problem, which are executed within diverse groups of elderly, provides a fuller understanding of SWB and aging processes in general (10).

The chapter begins with a brief review of the research on SWB, including a discussion of the major postulated components and correlates of well-being evaluations and a summary of relevant research findings. The next section reviews SWB research among older black adults. Trends in SWB, work addressing overall racial differences, and research on the correlates of SWB among older black adults are summarized. Following this, a general discussion of SWB and of the various explanatory models of well-being is provided. Work that emphasizes the concerns and life experiences of older black adults, thus imparting a broader understanding of SWB, is incorporated into the discussion of these models. The chapter concludes with a discussion of areas for further research and investigation.

MEASURES, COMPONENTS, AND CORRELATES OF SUBJECTIVE WELL-BEING

Although this selected review of the literature on SWB examines work from distinctly different research traditions, these varied constructs and measures of SWB are conceptually and empirically related to one another (3, 7). This should not obscure the fact that much work needs to be completed to understand more fully the conceptual and empirical relationships between these divergent approaches.

Measurement of Subjective Well-Being

Prominent among the SWB scales for use in older groups are the Life Satisfaction Indices (11, 12), the Philadelphia Geriatric Center Morale Scales (13, 14), the Kutner Morale Scale (15), and the Affect Balance Scale (16). George (1) and George and Bearon (8) provide detailed discussions of these scales, including their psychometric properties and a review of research efforts that have utilized them.

Single-item measures of SWB for general population applications (17–19) have been investigated among older groups. Investigations of the relationships between single-item and more traditional and detailed measures of subjective well-being report moderate correlations (20, 21). Single-item SWB items are examples of a general class of measures known as subjective social indicators. Subjective social indicators are focused on various facets of life and represent underlying psychological states, such as satisfactions, aspirations, values, and the quality of life experience generally (22). In contrast to objective social indicators, which are based on statements of fact, subjective social indicators reflect individuals' evaluations or perceptions of their lives. The demonstrated disparities between objective and subjective evaluations suggest that they provide different and complementary information on life quality (22–24).

Cognitive and Affective Components of SWB

Current work on the structure of SWB measures suggests three distinct components (17, 23). The cognitive component (i.e., judgmental or evaluative) represents the rational, thinking processes that are involved in forming an overall evaluation. Positive and negative affective components, on the other hand, reflect the emotional or mood aspects of SWB (16). Recent work has investigated the relationship between the positive and negative affect components of SWB. Research focusing on the development and analysis of multi-item SWB scales has attempted to address the issue of the independence of affective components, as well as to examine the role of affective frequency, duration, and intensity in SWB evaluations (3).

Some evidence indicates that while older respondents report more satisfaction with their lives, they exhibit less overall happiness than do younger persons (22, 25). In partial explanation, it is suggested that older persons experience a flattening of affect, resulting in fewer periods of strong emotion (22, 26). Happiness evaluations are accordingly depressed among older groups, whereas life satisfaction, which involves cognitive processes (22), does not evidence a similar pattern with age. Research on the cognitive and affective components of SWB may be useful in understanding these observed age differences in well-being.

Correlates of Subjective Well-Being

Research on the correlates of subjective well-being reveals several consistencies, notably the significance of health, socioeconomic status, and social interaction and activity for well-being (e.g., 6, 21, 27–33). Less consistent findings have been observed for age, gender, marital status, employment, housing and residence, and religion (e.g., 21, 22, 27, 34–41).

Despite apparent consistencies in the literature, the interpretation of these results is problematic because of variation in the methodologies employed in individual investigations. In particular, variability in the definition and measurement of independent variables (e.g., self-reports vs. objective measures), as well as differences in the samples, age ranges, and analysis procedures utilized (i.e., bivariate vs. multivariate techniques), place serious restrictions on comparative efforts (2, 3, 7). Further, there is evidence that for several of these relationships (e.g., health and social interaction), the strength of association may vary by subgroup membership, suggesting more complex models of these relationships (7). Specialized reviews of the literature, focusing on particular groups of independent factors such as health (42–44) and social activity (45), provide an overview of relevant studies and address many of the conceptual and methodological differences apparent in this work.

SUBJECTIVE WELL-BEING AMONG ELDERLY BLACKS

Subjective well-being research has focused almost exclusively on samples of the majority aged or of the general elderly population in which older blacks represent a small proportion. The studies among elderly black adults suffer from many of the conceptual and methodological limitations found in the general literature. Despite these problems, research on the black population and aging blacks in particular has begun to outline some of the relevant questions and issues regarding subjective well-being within this population group.

Comparative Trends and Racial Differences in SWB

Overall, reports of life satisfaction and happiness indicate that blacks view their lives less positively than do whites (2, 17). Jackson, Chatters, and Neighbors (46) examined trends in SWB for blacks and whites using data from a number of national surveys of the general population, nonnational surveys, and a national survey of the black population. Reports of life satisfaction and happiness indicated that evaluations of life satisfaction for blacks and the population generally were roughly similar in 1965. Subsequent years witnessed a decline in satisfaction for blacks, followed by an upturn in reports of satisfaction for the year 1978. This trend culminated in 1980 with the highest reported levels of both satisfaction and dissatisfaction for the black population. Reports of life satisfaction for the general population, on the other hand, remained fairly constant during this period. Jackson and colleagues (46) suggest that the trends for satisfaction evaluations possibly reflect an increasing polarization among particular demographic subgroups of the black population. With regard to happiness ratings, blacks reported lower levels of happiness in comparison to the general population in 1957. Both groups evidenced first a decline in reports of being very happy, followed by an upswing in subsequent years. While admittedly declining over the years, reports of being unhappy among black Americans were consistently higher than for the general population.

Early studies of SWB among aged blacks were primarily concerned with documenting racial similarities and differences (47). The collection of studies revealed that black elderly scored both lower (48–52) and higher (22, 53–56) than white elderly on SWB measures. Other studies (21, 34, 36, 57–59) report no differences between black and white elderly when socioeconomic status and other factors are controlled.

On the whole, work on racial differences has focused on the exploration of main effects of race status. Less frequent are those studies of racial differences in SWB addressing the question of whether it is race per se, other factors that are differentially distributed within racial groups (e.g., socioeconomic status, health, social activity), or possible interactions involving race that explain observed differences. Further, because samples of black elderly are typically small and unrepresentative, the full range of variability on sociodemographic and other factors is often not available for these analyses. Other advanced work (60, 61) has examined whether discrete structural models of SWB can be identified for different racial and ethnic groups.

Correlates of SWB among Older Black Adults

Research on the correlates and predictors of SWB among elderly blacks displays some consistency with the general literature. Health is a preeminent concern in relation to SWB, and better health is consistently and positively related to reports of well-being (2, 34, 62–68). Marital status (being married) emerges as an important predictor of well-being as well (2, 46, 64, 65, 67, 68). Social interaction factors are related to higher SWB levels among older black adults (59, 62). However, work examining voluntary association participation and interaction with family and friends indicates no independent effect on morale for older blacks, while solitary activities were a significant predictor (34).

Measures of socioeconomic status have been inconsistently related to SWB among older blacks. Education has been found to positively predict SWB in several studies (63, 65), although in others education bears no independent relation to well-being (2, 34, 46, 67, 68). Negative findings for income are reported for several investigations (2, 34, 46, 64, 65, 67, 68).

Employment status was found to be a significant predictor of SWB among elderly blacks (2). There is little support for gender differences in SWB among elderly blacks (34). Jackson and colleagues (67) report a significant bivariate finding for gender and life satisfaction, but subsequent multivariate analyses indicate no independent effect for gender (68). Regional differences in reports of SWB favoring older southern respondents have been noted in a national study of black adults (46).

Age of respondent and its association with SWB is second only to health with regard to the pervasiveness and consistency of observed positive effects (22, 25, 26), although negative findings for the relationship between age and SWB have been reported as well (34, 61). Witt, Lowe, Peek, and Curry (69) note that the reported trend over several years in the relationship between age and SWB (from negative to weak positive) can be explained by the introduction of important control variables that occurred during that time. However, research among older blacks and the general black population (in which relevant sociodemographic factors have been controlled) suggests that age and SWB are positively related (2, 46, 60, 62, 67, 68).

THEORETICAL MODELS OF SUBJECTIVE WELL-BEING

Within the field of gerontology, progress toward theoretical explanations of SWB has been limited and research efforts have been criticized as being fragmented and largely atheoretical (1, 2). Although social gerontological models of SWB commonly have lifespan themes and implications, these have remained relatively unexplored (9). Theoretical models of SWB have been advanced in several disciplines (1, 9, 70), however, the task of clearly elaborating these approaches (e.g., development of explicit theoretical propositions, construct definition) remains to be completed (3).

Minority scholars and researchers have long argued that research on diverse samples of elderly adults enriches conceptualizations of aging phenomena generally (10, 71). A predominant emphasis in the literature on simple racial comparisions has effectively precluded the investigation of important within-group differences and a clearer understanding of the significance of racial status for well-being. Despite this, research on SWB among the elderly of racial minority groups has made important contributions to the development of theory and models of SWB (10). Specifically, three important influences on aging processes have received attention in work on minority elderly: (1) social system forces, (2) cultural factors, and (3) life-span issues.

The impact of social system conditions and forces (e.g., racial discrimination) on patterns of socioeconomic resources, the social status of the elderly of minority groups, and available opportunities in the social structure have comprised a prominent theme in aging research. According to one model, the social status of minority elderly should predict decreased levels of SWB. However, the inefficiency of social-status factors in predicting SWB among minority elderly challenged investigators to explain and incorporate these differences within the framework of existing theory (59).

The second major theme in this research has been the influence of cultural factors on attitudes toward aging and the aged and the nature of social institutions (e.g., family) and roles (e.g., worker, parent) within which older adults interact. Researchers attempted to identify and examine those unique aspects of minority status that potentially have a positive influence on well-being evaluations. Finally, a lifespan perspective on aging phenomena was a clear and early influence on research on minority groups. In particular, the availability of resources in earlier life stages was seen as shaping one's status in old age. Lifelong patterns of disadvantage potentially require unique adaptations as reflected in a variety of behaviors and attitudes related to one's sense of well-being.

Social system, cultural, and lifespan themes in aging research on minority and black populations advanced work on SWB by broadening theory development to include other relevant factors and suggesting important modifications on expected relationships. However, the applicability and theoretical implications of these ideas were not readily generalized and incorporated into existing theories of SWB. In particular, few studies distinguish between effects on SWB that are due to cultural vs. resource (i.e., socioeconomic status) factors or are able to examine age effects in any detail.

Disengagement and Activity Theories

The debate between disengagement and activity theories of aging highlights two general explanations of SWB (1). According to the disengagement perspective, the coming of old age witnesses a reversal in the trend of increasing involvement in societal roles throughout the middle years. The experience of aging involves a mutual withdrawal of the individual and society to establish a new equilibrium predicated on relinquishing or disengaging from social roles and obligations. Older individuals, faced with declining opportunities to obtain satisfaction from social roles, progressively disengage from them and invest in other goals (i.e., intrapsychic ones).

The notion that activity (specifically social activity and interaction) promotes SWB has a long historical tradition and has been most recently and widely popularized by gerontologists (3, 72). Activity is a central concept in several theories of social adjustment (e.g., continuity, role, and activity) and has been defined broadly to include both social behaviors and interaction and solitary activities. In contrast to disengagement, an activity perspective suggests that SWB is achieved by maintaining levels of activity and social involvement that were characteristic of middle age. Summarizing the empirical evidence for these models, the propositions of disengagement theory generally fail to stand empirical test, and although activity theory found wider empirical support, it requires significant modification and qualification. Both theories as originally formulated, however, are oversimplifications of aging processes (1, 9).

Examinations of aging in racially and ethnically diverse groups provide evidence disputing the proposed universality of the disengagement process and its normative basis. Research on older black adults demonstrates the variability of aging processes and the operation of a different set of cultural values and normative expectations for aging. Researchers suggest that black Americans possess a corpus of values and attitudes toward the aged that is different from that of the majority culture. In particular, it is suggested that blacks as a group hold more positive attitudes toward their own aging (53, 73) and regard the elderly with respect (48, 74). Further, positive attitudes toward the elderly are manifested in a variety of behaviors, including family structure and interaction patterns.

Research addressing the relationship between activity and SWB among elderly blacks focuses on the number, diversity, and rates of participation in a variety of social and leisure activities. Profiles of the activities of elderly blacks indicate extensive participation in voluntary associations (e.g., church and civic) and leisure pursuits (75), as well as involvement in a variety of social roles (64). Race differences in these behaviors indicate that black elderly have generally higher rates of participation in social (76) and religious activities (77) than whites, but lower levels of social integration in formal organizations (53). Information on living arrangements demonstrates that elderly blacks are less likely than whites to live alone (58). Socioeconomic status (SES) differences among elderly blacks indicate that higher SES means higher rates of social activity and membership in voluntary associations (77–79).

From the perspective of social roles, the condition of rolelessness in old age and its attendant problems (i.e., lowered morale) is counteracted by identifying and investing in roles and sources of satisfaction other than those that were relinquished. Several writers suggest that minority elderly are unique because specific cultural values provide for alternative roles, allow greater breadth and depth of existing roles, and/or provide more explicit behavioral expectations and norms for roles generally thought of as secondary (e.g., grandparent).

Prominent among work on elderly blacks is the significance attached to active participation in the roles of family elder and grandparent. Rather than a deemphasis on parental behaviors and the loss of a functional parent role, black elderly are portrayed as being an integral component of black family life. In addition to performing an important advisory function, older blacks (women in particular) are often directly involved in caretaking responsibilities for minor grandchildren and other relatives (80).

With regard to the work role, a history of labor-market experiences marked by limited and unsatisfactory participation (i.e., under- and unemployment and discriminatory practices) can be expected to modify elderly blacks' retirement experiences and attitudes (81). Specifically, attachment to the work role is likely more tenuous, and under certain circumstances its relinquishment is met with relief.

Research on primary and secondary group relations and formal social organizations such as the church suggests that they facilitate the social integration of older blacks and contribute to their personal well-being (59, 82). The role of church in the lives of older blacks has been described as a pseudo-extended family mimicking many of the functions of the extended family (59). Emergent work (83–85) on the role of the black church in the lives of older black adults suggests that the church performs a variety of material, emotional, and spiritual functions. Primary and secondary group relations and social institutions such as the church provide elderly blacks with an additional potential source of social status and an enduring context for the performance of important social roles.

Resource Models of Subjective Well-Being

Studies of the correlates of SWB became prominent as research began to focus on the objective circumstances of old age and their relationship to subjective evaluations of life quality (1). Resource models of SWB suggest that personal and economic resources (e.g., income, health) are important in maintaining SWB (9). However, resource models that propose a one-to-one correspondence between socioeconomic resources and SWB demonstrate generally weak relationships (23). Satisfactions with particular life domains (e.g., satisfaction with income) and overall SWB produce higher correlations than those between objective status indicators (e.g., actual reported income) and overall well-being (3, 26). In explanation of this, subjective judgments of life domains are thought to be closer in the causal sequence to overall SWB (3) and, further, to incorporate subjective factors that mediate the relationship between objective conditions and SWB (9, 86).

The relationship between domain satisfactions and overall SWB, in turn, suggests two different models of how evaluations of well-being are formulated. The "top-down" approach to SWB suggests that a general predisposition toward positivism influences evaluations in specific domains of life; the "bottom-up" view states that one's overall evaluation is based on accumulated judgments across areas of life (5). Support for both interpretations is found in the literature (17, 22).

Multiple-jeopardy hypotheses (87, 88) of various forms suggest that older people who possess a devalued status on several social status characteristics (i.e., race, gender, income) occupy a precarious position in terms of social and economic resources. Early applications of the notion of double jeopardy (i.e., race and age) incorporated an explicit lifespan perspective (89). Specifically, for older blacks the problems of old age are accompanied and compounded by a life history of racial discrimination within the wider society. A competing theory of the relationship between age and race status suggests that advancing age functions to diminish racial inequities that existed in earlier periods of the life cycle (82). The age-as-leveler hypothesis, in effect, states that the elderly of different racial groups become more alike as they approach old age due to the overriding importance of age effects. A corollary hypothesis suggests that adjustment to aging has a diminished impact on the elderly of minority groups because the status differentials before and after reaching old age are less acute (59).

Conceptualizations of double and multiple jeopardy and the competing age-as-leveler hypothesis focus on both objective conditions and subjective experience (i.e., life satisfaction). As reflected in a general sense of well-being and adjustment to aging, older persons with several jeopardizing characteristics should fare worse than their more advantaged counterparts. Several investigators have failed to find significant racial differences in life satisfaction for older adults (90, 91), while others (48, 92) indicate lower satisfaction among older blacks. Jackson's review (89) of research on the double-jeopardy hypothesis suggests several areas needing attention. Among them is the need for adequate theoretical development, the lack of clearly defined and testable hypotheses, and the need to employ appropriate methodologies to distinguish between age differences, age changes, and cohort and historical-period effects in SWB (93).

Judgment Theories of Subjective Well-Being

Judgment theories of SWB suggest that a sense of well-being derives from the comparison of one's status with important reference points (3, 86). The relevant reference points can be other people (i.e., social comparison), aspirations for one's situation, past life circumstances, or adjustments and adaptations to present events and circumstances. Judgment theory explanations of SWB are often utilized to explain the observed positive relationship between age and SWB (36, 49, 94). One model, based on a proposed decline in aspiration level and expectations with increasing age (22), suggests that the comparison of one's current situation using these reduced aspiration/expectation levels results in a smaller discrepancy between relevant reference points and thereby enhances SWB. A related class of judgment theories, based on adaptational or accommodative processes, suggests that, over time, exposure to events and conditions tends to produce satisfaction with those circumstances (3, 9).

Explanations of well-being among the black population frequently utilize the concept of judgments or comparisons of status position both between and within societal groups (e.g., relative deprivation and status inconsistency). In particular, the discrepancy between the advancement of blacks as a social group and noted trends in SWB reports suggests that significant gaps exist between expectations and actual achieved progress (46). Others (95) suggest that perceptions of societal inequities, as reflected in differentials in social status position, may be more predictive of SWB than the discrepancies between individual aspirations and achievements. In relation to the subjective well-being of older black adults, similar processes have been posited, involving comparisons between one's status in relation to age peers as well as self-comparisons of one's life at earlier stages in the life cycle (aspirations vs. achievements).

The expectation of differences between major age groups or cohorts in the determinants of SWB is based in part on the notion that the choice of relevant reference points for comparisons may be influenced by life history and experiences. Sociodemographic factors, in particular, may have a differential influence on the SWB evaluations of blacks of various age groups (2, 46). For older blacks, who have experienced lifelong disadvantage in these areas, income and education (and the implied comparisons along these dimensions) are less central determinants of well-being. For younger cohorts of blacks, who have witnessed widening opportunities in these areas, the role of income and education may be more important and assume a more central role in predicting well-being (2). Glenn (96) suggests that difficulties in actualizing expected occupational and economic gains is a possible explanation for lowered reports of happiness among younger cohorts of the general population. In a related vein, Veroff, Douvan, and Kulka (25) suggest that having achieved a particular level of social or economic status, the impact of income on well-being is diminished among middle-aged persons. For younger individuals who are still achieving in these areas, income plays a more central role in well-being evaluations.

Aging and Psychosocial Stress

Notions of stress are implicit in much of the writing on aging, suggesting that there are particular, identifiable life events or occurrences in aging that convey presumptive stress (e.g., widowhood, retirement, declining health). Research interests focus on whether the physical changes associated with aging may constitute risk factors for poor health outcomes and whether social and psychological factors are important in resisting (i.e., buffering) the effects of stress (97). Tentative findings on stress and adaptation document several age differences and variations. Older persons have been found to report fewer life events than younger persons, and the attendant disruption or stress is less severe (98). Other work, which examines responses to identical events (e.g., natural disasters), suggests that older persons have less severe reactions and experience lower levels of distress (99, 100). Research on stress and coping among older populations has been criticized (97, 101, 102) for its failure to reflect the events of later life in terms of general representativeness, content validity, and appropriate weighting systems. Emergent work on stress and adaptation focuses on events that are less traumatic in nature than life events. These approaches examine stress and adaptation in relation to role strains, chronic problems, the timing and scheduling of normative life transitions, and daily hassles (97, 102).

Stress, coping strategies, and resources have been important themes in gerontological writings on black elderly and their adjustment to aging. Large segments of the older black population face obvious disadvantage in socioeconomic status, health, and housing (103, 104). Despite these disadvantages, older blacks have been variously portrayed in the literature as survivors and effective copers with life's exigencies (73, 105). Advancement to old age is itself viewed as an accomplishment, given the typical life histories of older black Americans.

Several coping strategies and resources have been identified in the literature as being particularly important to older blacks. Research on family networks suggest that living arrangements, interaction and exchange patterns, and support relationships are conducive to the provision of aid to older family members. Family networks have been cited as providing assistance to older blacks for personal problems and worries (105), material and socioemotional assistance (106), and health concerns (107, 108).

Historically, religion and religious institutions have played a vital and primary role in the black community (103, 109). Research among older blacks indicates that religion and religious behaviors of many forms are a prominent feature of their lives (see 84). Religious beliefs and values are a valuable resource for coping (73), and prayer is an important coping strategy (105, 110). Further, new work suggests that, in addition to spiritual and religious functions, the church is the focal point of supportive networks for older blacks involving the exchange of material goods and services and emotional aid (83). Others have noted the significance of the church as a social institution and a context for primary group relations (111) and the role of church friendships in bolstering the personal well-being of elderly black adults (59).

Lifespan Issues in Subjective Well-Being Models

The final orientation to be considered is not a theory of well-being processes per se but a perspective on the development of SWB. The issue of age itself has had an important influence on gerontological treatments of SWB, and a lifespan orientation to well-being is inherent in much of the theorizing concerning SWB among older groups (9). The exclusive focus on older adults within the gerontological literature, however, has overlooked the question of whether the identified processes are applicable to younger groups. One lifespan orientation to SWB suggests that personal adjustment in old age is a reflection of developments that occur over the lifetime of the individual. Prominent among these are lifespan conceptualizations that emphasize a life-course patterning of social roles and obligations (112, 113) and their subsequent effect on adjustment in old age. Specifically, the loss of major life roles (e.g., spouse, worker), as well as the absence of roles regarded as socially important, result in a dearth of meaningful outlets for older individuals. Lacking appropriate and socially valued roles, older persons assume a roleless state, with concomitant ambiguity regarding normative behaviors and expectations. Further, there is an inability to draw upon roles and their fulfillment as sources of satisfaction and well-being in old age (69).

A different lifespan approach focuses on both current levels of resources and the availability of socioeconomic and personal resources over the life course. The double-jeopardy hypothesis suggests that lifelong patterns of social and economic resources associated with particular social status categories (e.g., racial minority, women) are important determinants of adjustment in old age. In contrast, the age-as-leveler hypothesis states that lifelong disadvantage facilitates adjustment to old age because of a smaller discrepancy between middle-age and old-age levels of these resources. A marked difference between resources prior to and those available in old age (e.g., pre- and postretirement income) results in poorer adjustment (59, 82).

Lifespan issues have played a prominent role in research and writing on older black adults (i.e., double-jeopardy and age-as-leveler hypotheses). Early exposure to disadvantaged life conditions is viewed as having definite and identifiable consequences for the well-being status of current cohorts of older black adults. Specifically, for older blacks who have experienced lifelong disadvantage, social status factors (i.e., income and education) may be less central determinants of well-being. For younger cohorts of blacks who have witnessed widening opportunities in these areas, the role of status factors may be more important and assume a pivotal role in predicting well-being.

Age cohort influences are expressed through a number of factors that directly bear on SWB as well as condition the relationships between SWB and other variables. Age subgroup analyses of the general black population explore possible differences in the structure and correlates of SWB. This work is limited in its ability to address the several potential influences (i.e., cohort, period, and aging) on SWB evaluations. Nonetheless, it provides the preliminary work on several interesting hypotheses concerning age and cohort differences.

Campbell, Converse, and Rodgers (22) compare the well-being evaluations of young (18 to 34), middle-aged (35 to 54), and older (55 years of age and above) blacks. Older blacks demonstrate higher levels of both happiness and life satisfaction than did younger groups. On the whole, blacks score lower than whites on SWB; however, older blacks are more positive about their lives than are older whites. Recent work by Herzog, Rodgers, and Woodworth (9) confirms that younger blacks are less happy than other age–race groups, while older blacks and whites demonstrate comparable levels of happiness. Jackson and colleagues' work (2, 46) on age-cohort analyses (18–34 years, 35–54 years, and 55 years and above) indicates limited support for the differential impact of achieved status factors on well-being among these age cohorts. Income and education appear to have a limited role in reports of well-being among young and middle-aged cohorts of blacks, while having no effects among older adults. Taken together, this work suggests that age cohort may represent a fundamental organizing theme in research on the structure and correlates of well-being.

DIRECTIONS FOR FUTURE RESEARCH

The thesis of this chapter has been that research issues and themes in minority aging in general, and that of black elderly in particular, have made important contributions to gerontological theories of SWB. A major impetus for work on the subjective well-being of older blacks has been to explain their uniqueness vis-à-vis majority elderly and to incorporate these differences into existing models. Social system factors, cultural values, and lifespan issues have been identified as having mutually reinforcing and combined influences on aging and SWB. The consideration of these factors among elderly blacks, and minority elderly generally, has contributed important insights into aging processes and provided new research directions in social gerontology (10).

A failure to fully appreciate these contributions, however, resulted in a situation in which investigations of race effects on well-being were largely confined to simple comparative analyses. Race effects (similar to gender) were more often controlled for than investigated in their own right. Researchers are becoming increasingly aware that race status represents a surrogate for a range of phenomena that in many cases are related to and co-vary with the behavior(s) under investigation. Investigations comparing diverse samples of both minority and majority elderly will provide the opportunity to partial out the effects of factors that tend to be highly related (e.g., race and socioeconomic status). Similarly, research conducted within minority groups of elderly can shed light on phenomena that are little understood but have the promise of contributing to SWB theory generally.

Given the expanse of topics and issues that are organized under the rubric of SWB and the paucity of existing data on older black adults, recommendations for future research are necessarily voluminous. Three general areas of research—the qualitative meaning of SWB evaluations, age differences in structure and components, and the role of personality factors—are in particular need of further exploration. Research on the qualitative meaning of SWB evaluations should be focused on methodological studies in which respondents are queried as to the meaning of their responses to SWB items and scales. Work such as this will provide valuable information concerning the validity of these items. While face validity has often been an assumed feature of these measures, researchers should be aware that the underlying rationale for responses may vary in predictable ways as a function of membership in particular social status groups. Further, the use of structured probes for SWB measures may reveal the nature of judgmental evaluations (or other processes) and the relevant reference points that are used.

Emergent experimental work examining mood states and their relationships to overall evaluations can determine whether age differences in affective states can be documented. Work on age differences should explore the existence of possible period and cohort effects in shaping outlook and generalized feelings of well-being. The possible adaptive features of religion (e.g., prayer as a coping strategy), aside from the social functions of religious institutions and its relationship to aging, has received little systematic attention in the literature. Finally, the work on personality suggests that individuals may have characteristic ways of interacting and viewing their worlds that exert a pervasive influence on their sense of well-being. Age differences in personality traits and dimensions may shed light on observed variations in well-being evaluations.

The juxtaposition of varied theoretical approaches allows researchers to explore areas of commonality and divergence in their work. A broadening of perspective is required to include a consideration of the possible mechanisms by which membership in particular social status categories (e.g., age, race, and gender) impacts on well-being. Particular aspects of social status position (i.e., age and race) have demonstrated important influences on well-being evaluations. What has been less apparent and generally lacking is an understanding of the mechanisms that underlie these differences. Research on SWB among aging black populations prompted important qualifications on the relationships between status indicators and well-being, but more work needs to be devoted to examining these and related hypotheses. In particular, cohort differences in life experiences may operate to modify the role of social status and other factors as determinants of well-being. The next step in gerontological approaches to SWB should explicitly examine and develop the inherent lifespan implications of these theories and models and study the patterns of concerns that comprise SWB across the life cycle and among different cohorts of elderly.

Finally, comparative research on elderly blacks and whites should be conducted among samples in which sufficient numbers and variability on background factors within each group allow meaningful comparisons and the ability to separate out the effects of race and socioeconomic status. Such an approach will begin to determine racial and socioeconomic status similarities and differences in the processes underlying SWB and provide a greater appreciation of their effects on well-being in later life.

REFERENCES

1. George L. Subjective well-being: conceptual and methodological issues. In: Eisdorfer C, ed. *Annual Review of Gerontology and Geriatrics* (Vol. 2). New York: Springer; 1981:345–382.
2. Jackson JS, Herzog AR, Chatters LM. The meaning and correlates of life satisfaction in older (and middle-aged) blacks: a secondary analysis. Final Report AOA Grant No. 90-A-1025. Ann Arbor: University of Michigan; 1980.
3. Diener E. Subjective well-being. *Psychological Bulletin* 1984; 95: 542–575.
4. Stones MJ, Kozma L. Issues relating to the usage and conceptualization of mental health constructs employed by gerontologists. *Journal of Aging and Human Development* 1980; 11: 269–281.
5. Diener E, Griffin S. Happiness and life satisfaction: bibliography. *Psychological Documents* 1984; 14.
6. Adams DL. Correlates of satisfaction among the elderly. *The Gerontologist* 1971; 11: 64–68.
7. Larson R. Thirty years of research on the subjective well-being of older Americans. *Journal of Gerontology* 1978; 33: 109–125.
8. George LK, Bearon LB. *Quality of Life in Older Persons: Meaning and Measurement*. New York: Human Sciences Press; 1980.
9. Herzog AR, Rodgers WL, Woodworth J. *Subjective Well-Being Among Different Age Groups*. Ann Arbor: Institute for Social Research, The University of Michigan; 1982.
10. Moore JW. Situational factors affecting minority aging. *The Gerontologist* 1971; 11: 88–93.
11. Neugarten BL, Havighurst RJ, Tobin SS. The measurement of life satisfaction. *Journal of Gerontology* 1961; 16: 134–143.

12. Wood V, Wylie ML, Sheafor B. An analysis of a short self-report measure of life satisfaction: correlation with rater judgments. *Journal of Gerontology* 1969; 24: 465–469.
13. Lawton MP. The Philadelphia Geriatric Center Morale Scale: a revision. *Journal of Gerontology* 1975; 30: 85–89.
14. Morris JN, Sherwood S. A retesting and modification of the Philadelphia Geriatric Morale Center Scale. *Journal of Gerontology* 1975; 30: 77–84.
15. Kutner B, Fanshel D, Togo A, Langer TS. *Five Hundred Over Sixty*. New York: Russell Sage Foundation; 1956.
16. Bradburn N. *The Structure of Psychological Well-Being*. Chicago: Aldine; 1969.
17. Andrews FM, Withey SB. Developing measures of perceived life quality: results from several national surveys. *Social Indicators Research* 1974; 1: 1–26.
18. Cantril H. *The Pattern of Human Concerns*. New Brunswick, NJ: Rutgers University Press; 1965.
19. Gurin G, Veroff J, Feld S. *Americans View Their Mental Health*. New York: Basic Books; 1960.
20. Bell BD. Cognitive dissonance and the life satisfaction of older adults. *Journal of Gerontology* 1974; 29: 564–571.
21. Spreitzer E, Snyder EE. Correlates of life satisfaction among the aged. *Journal of Gerontology* 1974; 29: 454–458.
22. Campbell A, Converse PE, Rodgers WL. *The Quality of Life: Perceptions, Evaluations and Satisfactions*. New York: Russell Sage Foundation; 1976: 377–419.
23. Andrews FM. Subjective social indicators, objective social indicators, and social accounting systems. In: Juster FT, Land KC, eds. *Social Indicators and Social Accounting Systems*. New York: Academic Press; 1982.
24. Rossi RJ, Gilmartin KJ. *The Handbook of Social Indicators: Sources, Characteristics and Analysis*. New York: Garland; 1980.
25. Veroff J, Douvan E, Kulka RA. *The Inner American*. New York: Basic Books; 1981.
26. Campbell A. *The Sense of Well-Being in America: Recent Patterns and Trends*. New York: McGraw-Hill; 1981.
27. Edwards J, Klemmack D. Correlates of life satisfaction: a reexamination. *Journal of Gerontology* 1973; 28: 497–500.
28. Markides KS, Martin HW. A causal model of life satisfaction among the elderly. *Journal of Gerontology* 1979; 34: 89–93.
29. Phillips DL. Social participation and happiness. *American Journal of Sociology* 1967; 72: 479–488.
30. Tissue T, Wells L. Antecedents lifestyles and old age. *Psychological Reports* 1971; 29: 1100.
31. Palmore E, Luikart C. Health and social factors related to life satisfaction. *Journal of Health and Social Behavior* 1972; 13: 68–80.
32. Lemon BW, Bengtson VL, Peterson JA. An exploration of the activity theory of aging: activity types and life satisfaction among in-movers to a retirement community. *Journal of Gerontology* 1972; 27: 511–523.

33. Pihlblad C, Adams D. Widowhood, social participation and life satisfaction. *Aging and Human Development* 1972; 3: 323–330.
34. Sauer W. Morale of the urban aged: a regression analysis by race. *Journal of Gerontology* 1977; 32: 600–608.
35. Bortner RW, Hultsch DF. A multivariate analysis of correlates of life satisfaction in adulthood. *Journal of Gerontology* 1970; 25: 41–47.
36. Clemente F, Sauer WJ. Racial differences in life satisfaction. *Journal of Black Studies* 1976; 7: 3–10.
37. Medley ML. Life satisfaction across four stages of adult life. *International Journal of Aging and Human Development.* 1980; 11: 193–209.
38. Palmore E, Kivett V. Change in life satisfaction: a longitudinal study of persons aged 46–70. *Journal of Gerontology* 1977; 32: 311–316.
39. Streib G, Schneider C. *Retirement in American Society.* Ithaca, NY: Cornell University Press; 1971.
40. Schooler K. Effect of environment on morale. *Gerontologist* 1970; 10: 194–197.
41. Cutler SJ. Membership in different types of voluntary associations and psychological well-being. *The Gerontologist* 1976; 16: 335–339.
42. George LK, Landerman R. Health and subjective well-being: a replicated secondary data analysis. *International Journal of Aging and Human Development* 1984; 19: 133–156.
43. Okun MA, Stock WA, Haring MJ, Witter RA. A quantitative synthesis of the social activity/subjective well-being relationship. *Research on Aging* 1984; 6: 45–65.
44. Zautra A, Hempel A. Subjective well-being and physical health: a narrative literature review with suggestions for future research. *International Journal of Aging and Human Development* 1984; 19: 95–109.
45. Okun MA, Stock WA, Haring MJ, Witter RA. Health and subjective well-being: a meta-analysis. *International Journal of Aging and Human Development* 1984; 19: 111–131.
46. Jackson JS, Chatters LM, Neighbors HW. The subjective life quality of black Americans. In: Andrews F, ed. *Research on the Quality of Life.* Ann Arbor, MI: Institute for Social Research; 1986.
47. Jackson JJ. The blacklands of gerontology. *Aging and Human Development* 1971; 2: 156–167.
48. Register JC. Aging and race: a black–white comparative analysis. *The Gerontologist* 1981; 21: 438–443.
49. Alston JP, Lowe GD, Wrigley A. Socioeconomic correlates for four dimensions of self-perceived satisfaction. *Human Organization* 1974; 33: 99–102.
50. Donnenwerth GV, Guy RF, Norvell MJ. Life satisfaction among older persons: rural–urban and racial comparisons. *Social Science Quarterly* 1978; 59: 578–583.
51. Lipman A. *Responsibility and Morale.* Proceedings of the 7th International Congress of Gerontology. Wien: Wiener Medizinische Akademie; 1966.
52. Youmans EG. Aging patterns in a rural and an urban area of Kentucky. *University of Kentucky Agricultural Experimental Station Bulletin.* University of Kentucky; 1963; 681.

53. Messer M. Race differences in selected attitudinal dimensions of the elderly. *Gerontologist* 1968; 8: 245–249.
54. Kivett VR. The importance of race to the life situation of the rural elderly. *The Black Scholar* 1982; 13: 13–20.
55. Bengtson VL. Ethnicity and aging: problems and issues in current social science inquiry. In: Gelfand DE, Kutzik AJ, eds. *Ethnicity and Aging: Theory, Research and Policy;* 1979: 9–31.
56. Linn MW, Hunter KI, Perry PR. Differences by sex and ethnicity in the psychological adjustment of the elderly. *Journal of Health and Social Behavior* 1979; 20: 273–281.
57. National Council on the Aging. *The Myth and Reality of Aging in America.* Washington, DC: Author; 1979.
58. Rubenstein DI. An examination of social participation found among a national sample of black and white elderly. *International Journal of Aging and Human Development* 1971; 2: 172–188.
59. Ortega ST, Crutchfield RD, Rushing WA. Race differences in elderly personal well-being: friendship, family, and church. *Research on Aging* 1983; 5: 101–118.
60. Janson P, Mueller KF. Age, ethnicity, and well-being. *Research on Aging* 1983; 5: 353–367.
61. Vaughan DA, Kashner JB, Stock WA, Richards M. A structural model of subjective well-being: a comparison of ethnicity. *Social Indicators Research* 1984; 16: 315–332.
62. Ball RE. Marital status, household structure, and life satisfaction of black women. *Social Problems* 1983; 30: 400–409.
63. Himes J, Hamlett M. The assessment of adjustment of aged Negro women in a southern city. *Phylon* 1962; 23:139–147.
64. Ehrlich IF. Toward a social profile of the aged black population in the U.S.: an exploratory study. *Aging and Human Development* 1973; 4: 271–276.
65. Jackson JS, Bacon JD, Peterson J. Life satisfaction among black urban elderly. *Aging and Human Development* 1977; 8: 169–180.
66. Chatters LM. The influence of selected attitudinal and personality variables on life satisfaction among urban black elderly. Ann Arbor: University of Michigan; 1977. (Unpublished manuscript).
67. Jackson JS, Chatters LM, Neighbors HW. The mental health status of older black Americans: a national study. *The Black Scholar* 1982; 13: 21–35.
68. Chatters LM. A causal analysis of subjective well-being among elderly blacks. Ann Arbor: University of Michigan; 1983. (Unpublished doctoral dissertation).
69. Witt DD, Lowe GD, Peek CW, Curry EW. The changing association between age and happiness: emerging trend or methodological artifact? *Social Forces* 1980; 58: 1302–1307.
70. Kozma A, Stones MJ. The measurement of happiness: development of the Memorial University of Newfoundland Scale of Happiness (MUNSH). *Journal of Gerontology* 1978; 35: 906–912.
71. Jackson JS. Science, values and research on racial/ethnic groups. Ann Arbor: University of Michigan; 1986. (Unpublished manuscript).

72. Horan PM, Belcher JC. Lifestyle and morale in the southern rural aged. *Research on Aging* 1982; 4: 523–549.
73. Taylor SP. Mental health and successful coping among aged black women. In: Manuel RC, ed. *Minority Aging: Sociological and Social Psychological Issues.* Westport, CT: Greenwood Press; 1982: 95–100.
74. Wylie FM. Attitudes toward aging and the aged among black Americans: some historical perspectives. *Aging and Human Development* 1971; 2: 46–58.
75. Hearn HL. Career and leisure patterns of middle-aged urban blacks. *The Gerontologist* 1971; 11: 21–26.
76. Clemente F, Rexroad PA, Hirsch C. The participation of black aged in voluntary associations. *Journal of Gerontology* 1975; 30: 469–472.
77. Heyman DK, Jeffers FC. Study of relative influence of race and socioeconomic status upon the activities and attitudes of a southern aged population. *Journal of Gerontology* 1964; 19: 225–229.
78. Lambing ML. Social class living patterns of retired Negroes. *The Gerontologist* 1972; 12: 285–288.
79. Lambing ML. Leisure-time pursuits among retired blacks by social status. *The Gerontologist* 1972; 12: 363–364.
80. Mitchell JS, Register JC. An exploration of family interaction with the elderly by race, socioeconomic status and residence. *The Gerontologist* 1984; 24: 48–54.
81. Jackson JS, Gibson RC. Work and retirement among the black elderly. In: Blau Z, ed. *Current Perspectives on Aging and the Lifecycle.* Hartford, CT: JAI Press; 1985: 193–222.
82. Dowd JJ, Bengtson VL. Aging in minority populations: an examination of the double jeopardy hypothesis. *Journal of Gerontology* 1978; 33: 427–436.
83. Taylor RJ, Chatters LM. Church-based informal support networks of elderly blacks. *The Gerontologist* 1986; 26: 637–642.
84. Taylor RJ. Religious participation among elderly blacks. *The Gerontologist* 1986; 26: 630–636.
85. Taylor RJ, Thornton MC, Chatters LM. Black Americans' perceptions of the socio-historical role of the church. *Journal of Black Studies* in press.
86. Michalos AC. Satisfaction and happiness. *Social Indicators Research* 1980; 8: 385–422.
87. National Council on the Aging. *Employment Prospects of Blacks, Chicanos, and Indians.* Washington, DC: Author; 1971.
88. Lindsay I. *Multiple Hazards of Age and Race: The Situation of Aged Blacks in the United States.* Special Committee on Aging, U.S. Senate. Washington, DC: U.S. Government Printing Office; 1971.
89. Jackson JJ. Race, national origin, ethnicity, and aging. In: Binstock RH, Shanas E, eds. *Handbook of Aging and the Social Sciences* (2nd ed.). New York: Van Nostrand; 1985: 264–303.
90. Jackson JJ, Walls BE. Myths and realities about aged blacks. In: Brown MR, ed. *Readings in Gerontology* (2nd ed.). St. Louis, MO: C.V. Mosby; 1978:95–113.
91. Ward RA, Kilburn H. Community access and satisfaction: racial differences in later life. *International Journal of Aging and Human Development* 1983; 16: 209–219.

92. Jackson M, Kolody B, Wood JL. To be old and black: the case for double jeopardy on income and health. In: Manuel RC, ed. *Minority Aging: Sociological and Social Psychological Issues.* Westport, CT: Greenwood Press; 1982: 77–82.

93. Schaie KW, Orchowsky S, Parham I. Measuring age and sociocultural change: the case of race and life satisfaction. In: Manuel RC, ed. *Minority Aging: Sociological and Social Psychological Issues.* Westport, CT: Greenwood Press; 1982: 223–230.

94. Czaja SJ. Age differences in life satisfaction as a function of discrepancy between real and ideal self-concepts. *Experimental Research on Aging* 1975; 1: 81–89.

95. Carp FM, Carp A. Test of a model of domain satisfactions and well-being: equity considerations. *Research on Aging* 1982; 4: 503–522.

96. Glenn ND. Values, attitudes, and beliefs. In: Brim OG Jr, Kagan J, eds. *Constancy and Change in Human Development.* Cambridge, MA: Harvard University Press; 1980: 596–640.

97. House J, Robbins C. Age, psychosocial stress and health. In: Riley MW, Hess BB, Bond K, eds. *Aging in Society: Selected Reviews of Recent Research.* Hillsdale, NJ: Erlbaum; 1983: 175–197.

98. Masuda M, Holmes TH. Life events: perceptions and frequencies. *Psychosomatic Medicine* 1978; 40: 236–261.

99. Bell B. Disaster impact and response: overcoming the thousand natural shocks. *Gerontologist* 1978; 18: 531–540.

100. Huerta F, Horton R. Coping behavior of elderly flood victims. *Gerontologist* 1978; 18: 541–545.

101. Chiriboga DA, Cutler L. Stress and adaptation: life span perspectives. In: Poon LW, ed. *Aging in the 1980's: Psychological Issues.* Washington, DC: American Psychological Association; 1980: 347–362.

102. Lazarus RS, DeLongis A. Psychological stress and coping in aging. *American Psychologist* 1983; 38: 245–254.

103. Hill R. A demographic profile of the black elderly. *Aging* 1978; 278: 297–303.

104. Taylor RJ, Taylor WH. The social and economic status of the black elderly. *Phylon* 1982; 43: 295–306.

105. Gibson RC. Blacks at middle and late life: resources and coping. *Annals of the American Academy of Political and Social Science* 1982; 464: 79–90.

106. Taylor RJ. The extended family as a source of social support to elderly blacks. *The Gerontologist* 1985; 25: 488–495.

107. Chatters LM, Taylor RJ, Jackson JS. Size and composition of the informal helper networks of elderly blacks. *Journal of Gerontology* 1985; 40: 605–614.

108. Chatters LM, Taylor RJ, Jackson JS. Aged blacks' choices for an informal helper network. *Journal of Gerontology* 1986; 41: 94–100.

109. Billingsley A. *Black families in white America.* Englewood Cliffs, NJ: Prentice-Hall; 1968.

110. Neighbors HW, Jackson JS, Bowman PJ, Gurin G. Stress, coping and black mental health: preliminary findings from a national study. *Prevention in Human Services* 1983; 2: 4–29.

111. Lindsay IB, Hawkins BD. Research issues relating to the black aged. In: Gary LE, ed. *Social Research and the Black Community: Selected Issues and Priori-*

ties. Washington, DC: Institute for Urban Affairs Research, Howard University; 1974: 53–65.
112. Rosow I. Status and role change through the life cycle. In: Binstock RH, Shanas E, eds. *Handbook of Aging and the Social Sciences* (2nd ed.). Van Nostrand Reinhold: New York; 1985: 62–93.
113. Hagestad G, Neugarten BL. Age and the life course. In: Binstock RH, Shanas E, eds. *Handbook of Aging and the Social Sciences.* New York: Van Nostrand Reinhold; 1985: 35–61.

12
Aging and Supportive Relationships among Black Americans

Robert Joseph Taylor

The concept of the informal support network has particular salience for older blacks as well as the elderly of other racial and ethnic minority groups. On a variety of sociodemographic indicators, older blacks represent one of the most severely disadvantaged groups in our society (1). Given this situation of apparent need and restricted access to formal resources, it is critical to investigate the nature and functioning of the informal support networks within which elderly blacks are embedded.

Historical (e.g., 2, 3) as well as anthropological research on black families (4–8) documents the existence of viable three-generation family structures that contribute to childrearing and family stability. In these studies, elderly blacks are found to have significant and varied roles within the family (9). Recent surveys of elderly blacks and the nature of their family relations indicate that older blacks have extensive contact with their children and grandchildren (10–13). Extensive family and friend networks, characterized by the frequent exchange of goods and services, as well as socioemotional support, are also noted among blacks (14–17).

A number of small, primarily qualitative studies on the family life of blacks have pointed to the importance and critical nature of the family for the functioning of elderly blacks and, reciprocally, the importance of the

This work was supported in part by a grant (R23 AG06356) from the National Institute on Aging.

black elderly to the survival of black families. Although somewhat meager, the quantitative data also indicate that black elderly interact extensively within family and friend networks and that these networks provide the basis for reciprocal exchanges of goods and services (13, 17). Despite these efforts, recent reviews of the literature on the family life of minority elderly (18, 19) highlight the paucity of quality research in this area. Clearly, we presently know very little about the nature and functioning of the support networks of elderly blacks.

Methodological approaches to research on the support networks of the elderly in general, and elderly blacks in particular, are dominated by descriptive statistics. The majority of the available knowledge on the support networks of elderly blacks is derived from ethnographic literature (4–9, 14, 20, 21). Quantitative studies of the support relations of elderly and nonelderly blacks are typically based on small nonprobability samples (15, 16, 22) and rely on an examination of percentage differences (10, 13, 15, 16, 22–25). With few exceptions (11, 12, 26–29), research on the familial relationships of elderly blacks is not based on probability samples, and the utilization of multivariate techniques is practically nonexistent. Few studies that investigate racial differences in familial relations utilize multivariate techniques (11, 12, 26, 27).

OVERVIEW

The present chapter reviews the literature on the support networks of elderly blacks, with an emphasis on recent research. Both familial and nonfamilial (i.e., friend, neighbor, and church member) support relationships will be examined. A separate model of family supportive relationships is presented and provides the framework and organizing themes of the chapter. Embedded in the theoretical model of familial support is a series of relationships between familial and sociodemographic factors on assistance. For each of the relationships (e.g., gender differences in support exchanges), a brief review of the literature is presented. In addition, across the issues presented in the chapter, specific attention is given to reviewing literature that examines (1) general differences among the aged, (2) racial differences across the life course, (3) racial differences among the elderly, (4) differences among the general black population, and (5) differences evident among elderly blacks.

A MODEL OF FAMILY SUPPORT RELATIONSHIPS

Research on social support networks of the elderly suffers from the lack of a clear theoretical framework within which to couch the body of empirical findings. The majority of research is narrowly focused on the impact of a single independent variable on support (e.g., 30, 31), resulting in a fairly voluminous yet fragmented body of literature. Residential proximity, interaction with family members, sociopsychological measures of familialism, and mutual support have all been studied in connection with kinship structure and relationships (32, 33). There is, however, only limited discussion of the causal relationships among these variables. For instance, in some research support is used to predict attachment behaviors (34), while other work reverses the ordering of the relationship, with attachment predicting supportive behaviors (35). The works of Mutran and Rietzes (36), Cicerelli (35), and Bengtson, Olander, and Haddad (37) are notable exceptions in that they propose explicit models of family support.

Mutran and Rietzes (36) propose a model of family support in which intergenerational support activities are predictive of psychological well-being. Demographic factors, having children, and having an adult child confidant(e) are predictors of both receiving and providing support. Receiving/providing support further influences psychological well-being (i.e., positive affect and negative affect). Negative affect is, in turn, viewed as reciprocally influencing the receipt of support. Although this work represents an important improvement on other efforts, the failure to include several of the major correlates of intergenerational support (e.g., family interaction, subjective closeness) poses a serious limitation.

Cicerelli's (35) model suggests that attachment behaviors (i.e., residential proximity and family interaction), feelings of attachment (i.e., psychological closeness, value consensus, behavior consensus), and parental dependency are related to an adult child's present helping behavior. This model, however, does not explore the influence of demographic variables on these relationships. Consequently, previously reported effects for gender and marital status on helping behaviors cannot be confirmed. Bengtson and Cutler (38) proposed a model of familial relationships based on the concept of family solidarity. They argue that both intragenerational (horizontal) and intergenerational (vertical) family solidarity are comprised of several elements: associational solidarity (i.e., interaction with family members), affectional solidarity (i.e., degree of sentiment or closeness between family members), and consensus solidarity (i.e., agreement in values or opinions). Filial responsibility, type of sex linkages (e.g., having an adult daughter), residential propinquity, and the dependency needs of the elderly are proposed to have positive associations with helping behavior. In turn, helping behavior is purported to be positively related to family solidarity. A comparison of Cicerelli's (35) and Bengtson and Cutler's (38) models highlights several of the conceptual differences that have yet to be fully addressed in this field. Within Cicerelli's model, attachment behaviors and feelings of attachment are analogous to Bengtson and Cutler's associational and affectional solidarity. Further, in the Cicerelli model these factors are predictors

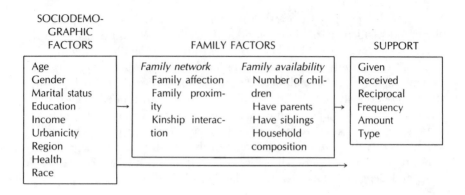

FIGURE 12.1 Family support relationships.

of support, while in Bengtson and Cutler's model they are support out-comes.

The theoretical model (Figure 12.1) of family support relationships that is proposed here hypothesizes that both sociodemographic and family factors are precursors of support. Previous analyses of the support networks of black Americans indicated that both demographic and family variables were significantly related to the probability of receiving support among black adults generally, and elderly blacks in particular. Although linear relationships are expected for many of these factors, the presence of interactions should be explored. Indeed, previous research using the National Survey of Black Americans (NSBA) data indicated that interactions were important in correctly specifying models of support (28, 29).

INDIVIDUAL RELATIONSHIPS COMPRISING
THE FAMILY SUPPORT MODEL

Embedded within the proposed model of family support are a series of relationships among the sociodemographic, family, and support factors. This section of the chapter provides a review of the existing literature on those issues.

Support

Support Relationships in the General Aging Population

It is generally acknowledged that the elderly in the United States are not isolated from their kinship networks, but rather are members of modified extended families (39, 40). The modified extended family is characterized by frequent interaction, close affective bonds, and the exchange of goods between family members (32, 38, 40, 41). Members of modified extended families typically live within visiting distance, interact by choice, and are connected to one another by means of mutual aid and social activities.

Social support is provided to the elderly in a variety of forms, including the provision of instrumental or material aid (e.g., food, money, transportation, running errands), cognitive aid (e.g., advice counseling), and emotional assistance (e.g., visiting, companionship) [see Antonucci (42) for a discussion of the definitions and measurement of social support]. Due to the diversity of types of support, face-to-face interaction and close proximity of family members are not prerequisities for receiving support (43).

Racial Differences in Support Across the Lifespan

The evidence for racial differences in the receipt of support across the lifespan is mixed. An analysis of support patterns of families with minor children found no racial difference in giving money to relatives, but blacks were less likely to receive money from relatives (44). In an analysis of the same data set (i.e., Panel Study of Income Dynamics), Morgan (45) expanded the investigation to include families with children under 18 years of age and instituted a crucial control for income level. The relatively low socioeconomic status of blacks vis-à-vis whites, coupled with the fact that the measures for money exchanges involved sums of over $500 a year, suggested that controlling for income was important in understanding racial differences in support exchanges. During emergencies, blacks were more likely to give and receive from others, but less likely to receive financial assistance. Blacks were also 4.3% more likely to report that emergency help was available from distant relatives or friends. On a regular nonemergency basis, blacks were (1) 3.5% more likely to report giving $500 or more in the last year to relatives outside the household; (2) 5.5% less likely to have received $500 or more from friends and relatives; and (3) 10.4% more likely to provide housing for others.

Gibson's (46) investigation of racial differences in the use of informal helpers in coping with psychological distress revealed that blacks utilized a more diverse pool of helpers than did whites. In both middle and late life, blacks tended to be more versatile in utilizing both family and friends. In contrast, whites were more likely to limit help seeking to spouses in middle life and to replace spouses with a single family member with the onset of old age.

Racial Differences in Support Networks of the Elderly

Research findings on racial differences in support exchanges among elderly adults are also mixed. Shanas (13) found that a higher proportion of white elderly reported that they gave help to their children and grandchildren, whereas elderly blacks were more likely than whites to receive help from children. Although Cantor (12) failed to find racial differences in the amount of support that elderly received from children, both black and Hispanic elderly provided greater amounts of help to children than did white elderly. Mindel, Wright, and Starrett (47) found that, controlling for income, elderly blacks received more formal support than elderly whites, whereas the amount of informal support received was similar. Utilizing the Myth and Reality of Aging data, Mitchell and Register (26) found that, controlling for socioeconomic status, aged blacks received more assistance than aged whites, but no racial differences in giving aid were evident. An examination of the type of social support exchanged between the elderly and their children and grandchildren (17) revealed only one racial difference: among higher-income aged, black elderly were much more likely than white aged to give childrearing assistance and financial help to their children and grandchildren.

Mutran's (27) study of intergenerational family support is superior to other work on racial differences because it utilized multivariate analysis and had the benefit of a national sample. Overall, black families were more involved in exchanges of help across generations. In comparison to aged whites, elderly blacks gave more help to children and grandchildren. Elderly black parents were also more likely to receive help from adult children, but this effect was reduced when controlling for socioeconomic status. Disaggregating racial and socioeconomic effects, elderly blacks tended to receive more help from their children by virtue of their lower income and educational levels. Mutran argues that both cultural and socioeconomic status factors are important in understanding racial differences in support transactions.

Support Relationships of Blacks

Ethnographic research provides a rich source of information on the supportive networks of blacks (5–9, 14, 20). Collectively, this research indicated that the primary social unit was the extended family, which frequently involved several households. Although each household was a separate economic unit, on a functional level extensive cooperation and support was evident among households. Support networks were characterized by general responsibility for childcare, joint cooperation for household tasks (e.g., meal preparation, grocery shopping), financial assistance, and the provision of care for aging parents and grandparents. The characteristics of informal support networks, such as elastic household boundaries, lifelong bonds to three-generational households, and an elaborate exchange network, were viewed as adaptive responses to socioeconomic conditions of chronic poverty and unemployment. Further, because of adverse economic conditions, extended families were viewed as the most enduring family form among lower-class blacks (7, 8).

McAdoo (15) found that the majority of the respondents in her sample were involved in reciprocal support networks comprised of both family and friends. The amount of help received from family was unaffected by socio-economic status and mobility patterns; both affluent and nonaffluent respondents received similar amounts of assistance. Childcare, financial help, and emotional assistance tended to be the more prevalent types of support exchanged within families.

The impact of demographic factors and familial factors on the receipt of support from extended family members was investigated in two separate analyses (29, 48). The majority of respondents reported receiving assistance from extended family members. Persons with relatively lower incomes were less likely to receive support from family members than those with higher incomes. Positive relationships between family variables (i.e., family close-ness and contact and proximity of relatives) and the receipt of aid speak to the importance of the quality of kin relations, the frequency of interaction, and having an available pool of relatives as arbiters of informal support transactions.

Neighbors and Jackson (49, 50) examined the use of informal support, in conjunction with professional help, in response to an identified personal problem. Using NSBA data, they found that the majority of respondents utilized either informal help only (43%) or both informal and professional help together (44%). Four percent of respondents used professional support solely, while 8.7% did not receive any outside assistance for their problems. Gender, age, income, and problem type were related to the four patterns of informal and professional help seeking.

Support Networks of Aging Blacks

In a cross-cultural study of minority aging, Stanford (16) found that 7 of 10 elderly blacks indicated providing assistance to others. The type of help given by older blacks was physical help or normal household chores (19.8%), help during an illness (16.8%), financial help (12.9%), transportation (10.9%), talking/counseling (4%), and foods/meals (1%).

Analyses of NSBA data reveal that elderly blacks are firmly imbedded in familial and nonfamilial support networks (28, 51, 52). Two out of three elderly blacks indicated receiving assistance from extended family members (28). Multivariate analyses revealed that gender, income, education, geographic region, familial interaction, proximity of relatives, and having an adult child were all significant predictors of the frequency of support.

Two sets of analyses by Chatters, Taylor, and Jackson (51, 52) examined the impact of sociodemographic, health, and family factors on the size and composition of the informal helper networks of elderly blacks. Respondents were asked to choose from a list of 12 informal helpers who would help them if they were sick or disabled. The majority of the sample (56%) reported that there were three people who would help them if they were ill. Twenty-two percent chose two individuals, 18% identified one person only, and 3% indicated that there was no one on the list of potential helpers who would be of assistance to them in the event of an illness. The majority of respondents (56%) had helper networks that were comprised exclusively of immediate family members. Approximately 33% of the sample had networks that were a mixture of immediate family and others, whereas the remaining 11% of respondents had networks comprised of relatives and nonkin. Analysis of the rate of nomination of specific categories of helpers indicated that daughters were nominated to the helper network most often, followed by son, spouse/partner, sister, brother, friend, neighbor, mother, and father.

Intergenerational Support Networks

The relationship between parent and adult child is thought to be the most important kin relationship for the elderly (53). Research indicates that, when in need, the elderly are more likely to seek help from their children as opposed to siblings and other relatives (54). Although adults maintain frequent contact with their siblings (13, 54, 55), relations with parents have a higher degree of emotional intensity (53). Consequently, much of the research on the family lives of the elderly emphasizes the importance of the presence of a child (13) or the presence of a functional child (12, 24).

Recent analyses of NSBA data reveal the critical importance of the elderly parent–adult child bond among blacks. Elderly blacks with children had a greater likelihood of receiving support from extended family members (28, 29). Having children was also an important determinant of the configuration of the helping networks of elderly blacks (51, 52) (i.e., the presence of children was related to larger helper networks comprised of immediate family only). The association between being a parent and having large, immediate family networks in part reflects that these elderly adults had at least one immediate family member (i.e., child) to nominate to their helper networks. Conversely, given the absence of children, substitutions of other kin and nonkin were made. In particular, childless elderly were more likely to rely upon brothers, sisters, and friends. Despite these compensations, however, childless elderly were still at a disadvantage with reference to helper network size. In addition, for childless elderly, having an available pool of relatives was the only significant predictor of the frequency of support from extended family (28).

Helper Availability

Having a pool of available helpers is considered an important determinant of the receipt of support. Analyses of the NSBA data have incorporated the availability of support providers as important predictors of support. As previously indicated, the presence of an adult child is a crucial determinant of the receipt of support from family (28, 29), as well as the size and composition of informal helper networks (51, 52). Marital status, as an indicator of helper availability, was also a strong influence on both the size and composition of helper networks (51, 52). Having neither a best/close friend nor living parents was a significant determinant of the size and composition of helper networks (51, 52).

Living Arrangements and Household Composition

The majority of elderly adults prefer to maintain independent living situations (41, 56). Widowhood, declining health, and decreasing income, however, are compelling reasons for an elderly person to move in with an adult child (32, 40, 41). Despite a strong desire to maintain independent and separate households, elderly adults are not isolated from their children and most have a child in close proximity with whom they have frequent contact (38, 41).

A consistent finding in the family literature is that blacks of all ages are more likely than whites to reside in extended households (44, 45, 57–60). These racial differences are maintained when socioeconomic status is controlled. Research on living arrangements among elderly adults also indicates that aged blacks are more likely to reside in extended households than aged whites. Although older blacks are less likely than older whites to live with a spouse, they are less likely to live alone and more likely to live with more than one person (61). Elderly blacks are more likely than older whites to reside with children and grandchildren (13, 26) and to take children and grandchildren, nieces and nephews into their households (26). Among spouseless elderly, blacks have more children living with them (62). Similarly, aged blacks are more likely to raise the children of others (10).

Absent from the aging literature, however, is a recognition that extended family arrangements are an effective mechanism for pooling limited resources, mitigating economic deprivation, and consequently, creating more viable economic units. Economic research on intrafamily transfers (63, 64) highlights the economic benefits of extended households. Joint residency of two or more nuclear families in an extended family household represents one of the most significant forms of sharing limited resources. "Doubling up" in extended households has an important bearing on the economic welfare of the family and, when compared to direct cash transfers, is generally a less expensive method of providing for needy relatives. In a study of the economic benefits of extended households, Morgan, David, Cohen, and Brazen (63) found that three out of four nonnuclear adults (i.e., extended kin) improved their economic situation by residing with relatives, while only 5% were adversely affected.

Angel and Tienda (58) found that black families rely on immediate relatives and nonnuclear members within the household for monetary support when social and economic demands are great. The relative contributions of wives, adult children, and nonnuclear relatives constituted a greater share of the total household income for blacks than for whites. Apparently, the lower earnings of black heads of households require supplemental income sources from other family members to achieve a desired standard of living or, in many cases, simply to meet daily needs.

In addition, there are other important supportive benefits of extended living arrangements. The presence of nonnuclear adults within the household allows for a reallocation of employment and domestic responsibilities. For example, the permanent presence of another adult in the household, who assists with daycare and other household duties, may enable a single parent with a young child to obtain employment outside the home (60). Similar types of support benefits of extended family households are reported in research on black families. Ladner (4) and Aschenbrenner (5, 6) indicated that many blacks resided in three-generational households where, among other things, grandparents babysat grandchildren while their own adult children worked. In some instances, black grandparents informally adopted grandchildren and assumed primary care for them into adulthood (4). This pattern (in which grandparents are the primary agents of socialization of grandchildren) was more prevalent among blacks than whites (26).

Due to the methodological focus of survey research efforts (e.g., 13, 44, 45, 58, 60), the degree of extendedness present in black families is likely to be underestimated. Ethnographic studies are able to examine extended relationships across households. Several nuclear families may reside in the same neighborhood and fully cooperate in the daily tasks of living (e.g., share meals, assist in household chores) (6). Survey research efforts, which are based on household samples, generally fail to obtain information on these types of fluid living arrangements.

Proximity of Relatives and Immediate Family

A limited body of research examines the predictors of the residential propinquity of relatives and immediate family members and, further, the influence of proximity on the receipt of support. Taylor (28, 29) found that the receipt of support from one's extended family, while unrelated to the proximity of immediate family members, was significantly predicted by the proximity of relatives for both elderly and nonelderly blacks.

Family Interaction

Frequency of interaction is a critical determinant of participation in a supportive relationship and provides an assessment of the availability of family members for companionship, daily assistance, and help during emergencies (65). In general, the elderly interact on a fairly frequent basis with their children and grandchildren (13, 24). Racial differences in familial interaction patterns among the elderly are inconsistent. Dowd and Bengtson (11) concluded that, in terms of interaction with children and grandchildren, older Mexican-Americans, and to a lesser extent aged blacks, are in a relatively advantageous position vis-à-vis white respondents. Similarly, studies have reported that black elderly interact more frequently than white elderly with children (13) and grandchildren (10). In contrast, other work fails to find a substantial race difference in interaction with children (12, 26) and grandchildren (26). In addition, Lopata (62) found that among widows generally, black widows had less contact with children than did white ones. Among widows who did have contact with children, however, blacks had more frequent contact than whites.

Research on black samples indicates that blacks across the life cycle interact with family members on a frequent basis (23, 66–68). Elderly blacks have also been found to interact with family on a frequent basis. Stanford (16) found that over 60% of the elderly blacks in his sample had at least monthly contact with relatives. Similarly, Jackson's (22) examination of older black women found that 6 out of 10 respondents reported face-to-face contact with adult children at least once a month. A study of urban black elders revealed frequent contact with children and relatives and that distance had a negative impact on the frequency of interaction (65).

Analysis of the National Survey of Black Americans (NSBA) data substantiates the findings that blacks frequently interact with extended family members. For both elderly blacks (28) and black adults of all ages (29), 6 out of 10 reported interacting with family members at least once a week. Frequency of interaction is an important determinant of the receipt of support from family members and is positively associated with the frequency of receiving support among elderly blacks (28) and the probability of receiving support among adult blacks (29). Affective bonds (i.e., family closeness), however, were more important than contact for determining the size and composition of the helper networks of elderly blacks (51).

Family Closeness and Satisfaction

Studies involving NSBA data indicate that blacks report strong affective ties with extended family members. Three of five elderly (28) and adult blacks (29) reported being very close to their families. Further, affective ties were important predictors of receiving support among blacks generally (29), but were unrelated to receiving support for elderly blacks (28). However, in a study of informal supports, black elderly who were closer to their families had larger helper networks (51).

Blacks also expressed a high degree of satisfaction with family life (28). Fifty percent of black adults and seven of ten elderly blacks reported being very satisfied with their family life. Among elderly blacks, family satisfaction had a significant bivariate association with the frequency of support, but this relationship was not maintained in the multivariate model. In addition, among blacks of all ages, family satisfaction was not significantly associated with receiving support (29).

Gender

Research examining gender differences in the nature and form of support transactions between elderly parents and adult children has established several consistent relationships. Probably the most pervasive finding is that older women have larger support networks and are more supportive than older men (41, 69–71). Women are more involved in kinship networks than men and are, additionally, more likely to maintain contact with family members over the course of the life cycle (53, 72). Additionally, Mutran (27) found that among aged blacks, women were more likely than men to receive assistance from children.

Ethnographic research on black extended families emphasizes the important role that women play in the kinship network. Martin and Martin (9) report that an elderly woman is often the dominant family figure in black extended families. This person tends to take the responsibility for directing family celebrations, arbitrating family disputes, and helping socialize the children. Aschenbrenner (5, 6), Stack (7, 8), and Shimkin, Shimkin, and Frate (14) also point out the prominence of women in maintaining the kinship networks of black extended families.

Previous analyses of the National Survey of Black Americans data set reveal an inconsistent pattern concerning gender differences and the receipt of support from family. Among blacks of all ages, gender was not significantly related to either the probability of receiving support (28) or the frequency of receiving support (48). Analysis of help seeking during a serious personal problem, however, indicated that women were more likely than men to receive both informal and formal assistance (50). Among black elderly, gender was significantly related to the frequency of receiving support (28); older women had a greater probability of receiving support than older men. In terms of support in response to an illness, older women had larger networks than men (51). Overall, daughters were most frequently mentioned as providers of assistance. Reflecting a general preference for women, daughters were mentioned more frequently than sons, sisters were chosen more often than brothers, and mother more frequently than father (52). The mother–daughter bond among elderly blacks seems to be particularly salient; older black women were more likely to have daughters in their helper networks than were older black men (52).

Age

Previous work indicates that age is inversely related to the frequency of interaction with kin (73–76). A Canadian study indicated that the percentage of respondents receiving economic support from relatives declines through the life cycle, with the elderly receiving the least support (77).

Among adult blacks, the elderly may be the most disadvantaged age group in terms of receiving support. Age was negatively related to (1) the receipt of support from extended family members (29); (2) receiving informal support during a serious personal problem (50); and (3) receiving assistance from church members (78). Collectively, this research suggests that the informal support needs of elderly blacks may not be adequately addressed. These negative age effects are mitigated to some degree by the presence of an adult child. Elderly blacks with at least one adult child are more likely to receive assistance from extended families (28, 29), have larger helper networks comprised exclusively of immediate family members (51), and are more likely to receive assistance from church members (78).

The oldest of elderly blacks (i.e., the old-old), with presumably fewest kin resources, reported networks comprised of distant relatives and nonkin. The apparent absence of close kin resources did not, however, affect the size of their helper networks (51). In addition, age was positively related to receiving assistance from adult children (27).

Marital Status

Marital status differences in support provided to the elderly reflect the "principle of substitution" (13). The principle suggests that an individual will use, in serial progression, remote kin and, in some cases, nonkin in support relationships when other alternatives are unavailable. Consistent with this principle, married couples tend to rely on one another for support (79, 80), and in the absence of a spouse, widowed individuals tend to rely on children and siblings (13, 62, 81, 82). Among never-married and unmarried childless elderly, siblings and more distant kin such as nieces and nephews are relied on (13, 79) and there is a tendency to use formal supports (83, 84).

The principle of substitution is useful in explaining the composition of the helper networks of elderly blacks (51, 52). Among married respondents there was a tendency to rely on spouses for assistance and to have larger helper networks comprised exclusively of immediate family members. The relationship between having larger, immediate family networks and being married partly reflects the availability of at least one family member for the helper network (widowed and never-married respondents had smaller helper networks than their married counterparts). Unmarried elderly blacks compensated for the absence of a spouse by using relatives and nonkin in their helper networks. In comparison to married persons, divorced respondents were more likely to report the use of friends and neighbors as helpers, widowed respondents were more likely to utilize friends, and never-married respondents were more likely to select neighbors.

Surprisingly, there are no marital status differences among blacks in the receipt of support (28, 29). Bivariate analysis indicated that widowed respondents were less likely to receive support from extended family members, but this effect was ameliorated in the presence of multivariate controls, in particular, age (29).

Socioeconomic Status

Research indicates that lower socioeconomic status, lower income, and fewer years of education are related to small support networks that consist primarily of family members. Respondents of higher socioeconomic status with higher incomes and more education generally have larger networks with a more diverse membership consisting of both family and friends (42). However, the influence of socioeconomic status on kinship interaction and informal support networks is not clear. Research findings on socioeconomic status and kinship patterns are inconclusive (33).

Socioeconomic status differences in the receipt of support indicate that income is positively associated with receiving support from family members for blacks in general and older black adults (28, 29, 48) in particular. It was anticipated that those respondents who exhibit greater objective need (e.g., low income and education, advanced age) would receive the greatest amount of assistance from family members. The obtained results challenge the assumption that "need" is of overriding importance for supportive relationships. Further, support is not unusually prominent among lower-income black Americans but instead seems to be associated with higher SES strata. Among elderly blacks, socioeconomic status was inconsistently related to support; income exhibited a positive association, but education was negatively related to the frequency of receiving assistance (28). Findings from other research reveal that among blacks, education was negatively associated with receiving assistance from adult children (27), and socioeconomic status was unrelated to both giving and receiving help from family and friends (15).

Urbanicity and Region

Very little research addresses urbanicity or regional differences in support networks. Harbert and Wilkenson (85) found that rural communities have elaborate support systems. Kahn and Antonucci (69) indicated that elderly residing in rural areas had larger networks than elderly in urban areas. Our research (28, 29) does not indicate any urban–rural or regional differences in the probability of receiving support among older blacks or blacks of all ages. However, rural black elderly were more likely than their urban counterparts to rely on immediate family helper networks when they were ill (51).

Regional differences in support networks indicate that elderly blacks who reside in the South are generally in a more advantageous position than those who reside in other regions. Southerners received support from extended family on a more frequent basis than those who resided in the Northeast (28) and tended to have larger helper networks comprised of both kin and nonkin (52). Reflecting differences in helper choice, Southerners were more likely than those in the Northeast to utilize sisters and more likely than persons in the north-central region to utilize sisters, friends, and neighbors (52).

Health Factors

One of the most important forms of support that elderly persons receive is help during an illness. The major providers of assistance during illness are typically relatives who are in close proximity (40). However, in the event of a critical or long-term illness, relatives who are more distantly located may relocate temporarily to assist the elderly person (39, 40). Female relatives are typically responsible for an elderly family member who is ill, regardless of whether they reside in close proximity or not and irrespective of the social class or family relationship (e.g., cousin, aunt) (40).

Health factors were unrelated to the size and composition of support networks of older black adults (51, 52). This is in contrast to work on older whites in which increasing levels of disability are associated with increases in network size (86, 87) and a broadening of the scope of the support network to include distant relatives and nonkin (87, 88). The absence of effects for health factors among aged blacks may indicate that other factors related to the nature of preexisting relationships and statuses (e.g., parental status) are more important for these network characteristics.

KIN AND NONKIN SOURCES OF SUPPORT

Emergent research has begun to examine nonfamily sources of support. Work by Lopata (82) and Johnson and Catalano (79) suggests that, for various segments of the older population, support is provided by individuals other than immediate family and, in some cases, by unrelated persons. Emergent work has investigated the role of siblings (89), friends and neighbors (24, 90), and others, such as church members (78, 91), in providing assistance to the elderly.

Friendship Networks of Blacks

Ethnographic research on black families emphasizes the integral role of nonkin in informal support networks (5–9, 14, 20). Ladner (4) and Liebow (21), in fact, argue that for certain subpopulations in black communities (i.e., Ladner's adolescent girls and Liebow's street corner men), friends tend to be the more dominant and influential members of the support network. Reflecting the fact that friendships often took the form of kinship, it is not uncommon for unrelated older individuals to be given the appellation "aunt" or "uncle" or to be referred as a "play mother or father." Friends referred to in kinship terms tend to intensify bonds of mutual obligation in a normally casual relationship (5). Persons designated as fictive or pseudo-kin, though unrelated by either blood or marriage, are regarded in kinship terms and accorded many of the associated rights and statuses. Generally, pseudo-kin fully participated in the informal support network. For instance, Kennedy (20) found that regardless of whether family membership was based on blood, marriage, or mutual consent, remaining in the family was based on the completion of expected duties.

The importance of friends as support providers has also been noted (15, 46, 92). Utilizing data from two national probability samples, Gibson (46) found that friends and neighbors were integral components of the support networks of middle- and late-life blacks. Data collected in 1957 indicated that blacks at both life stages were twice as likely as whites to utilize friends and neighbors in coping with psychological distress. These differences were not as large in the 1976 data set, although the racial difference in use of friends and neighbors was maintained. McAdoo's work (15, 92) also highlights the importance of the friendship role. Although kin generally had the more dominant role, one of five blacks and, more specifically, one of four black mothers indicated that friends provided the most support.

Little research has investigated the role of friends in the support networks of elderly blacks. A recent analysis found that urban black elders interacted on a frequent basis with friends (65). Research on the NSBA data indicates that nonkin in the form of friends and neighbors are integral members of the support networks of older blacks (91) and are particularly important for both childless and spouseless elderly blacks (51, 52).

Churches as a Supportive Network

Historical and present-day evidence suggests that black churches are extensively involved in the provision of support to their members. Church members exchange material, emotional, and spiritual assistance with one another, as well as providing information and advice. Other examples of more formal supportive relationships within churches are found in the various organizations designed to assist church members and others in the community (e.g., food and clothing programs, visiting programs to the sick). Finally, the church is particularly prominent in the role it plays in the positive appraisal of self (i.e., self-worth and self-esteem) and the affirmation of shared beliefs and attitudes held by the congregation.

A recent analysis of church members as a source of informal social support to elderly blacks (78) found that frequency of church attendance was a critical indicator of both frequency and amount of assistance received. Findings for the type of support received indicated that church members provided a variety of assistance. Although it is not surprising that a large percentage of respondents indicated that they received help in a spiritual or religious manner (e.g., "we pray together"), it was unexpected that almost one out of five of those who received church support reported receiving either financial assistance, goods and services, or total support. These findings suggest that the church may be a more integral component of the support networks of elderly blacks than has been previously thought (78).

Similar to familial support networks, adult children were an important link to receiving assistance from church members (78). For elderly blacks with children, as age increased the frequency of assistance from church similarly increased. For childless elderly, however, increases in age were associated with dramatic decreases in the frequency of support. It is significant to note that the presence of a child is especially important in advanced age; the old-old without children were in the most disadvantageous position in terms of receiving support from church members. These findings demonstrate that adult children apparently facilitate linkages to church support networks for their elderly parents.

DIRECTIONS FOR FUTURE RESEARCH

The emerging body of literature reviewed in this chapter indicates the critical importance of family and nonkin in the informal social support networks of aging blacks. Despite the existence of these research efforts, a comparison with similar work on whites reveals that there still remains a paucity of quality research on the support networks of blacks across the life course. Many basic support issues have yet to be investigated among the black population. In particular, there is little published research on the supportive relationships of such important subgroups of the black population as the widowed, childless elderly, and grandparents. In addition, few studies examine intergenerational support exachanges and reciprocal support relationships. Further, although research on the familial networks of aged blacks is limited, work on siblings, friends, neighbors, and church members as sources of informal support is only beginning to emerge.

With regard to future directions for this field of study, the lack of quality work indicates many areas of needed research and investigation. Research should address the nature of intergenerational transfers across three- and four-generation families. More work needs to be conducted on reciprocal support relations utilizing important familial (e.g., filial obligation, family affection, family interaction) and demographic (e.g., age, marital status, socioeconomic status, household composition, region) predictors of support. Additionally, research should examine the role of siblings, nonimmediate family members (e.g., cousins, aunts, nephews), and nonkin (e.g., friends, neighbors, church members) as sources of assistance. Methodologically, more work needs to be conducted that utilizes both survey and ethnographic approaches. Ethnographic studies, in particular, should be undertaken to comprehend the dynamic and multifacted aspects of exchange processes as they occur within both single- and multiple-household extended families. An increase in research of the type proposed will enhance our knowledge of the informal social support networks of elderly black Americans.

REFERENCES

1. Taylor RJ, Taylor WH. The social and economic status of the black elderly. Phylon. 1982; 43: 295–306.
2. Gutman H. *The Black Family in Slavery and Freedom: 1750–1925.* New York: Pantheon; 1976.
3. Genovese E. *Roll, Jordan, Roll.* New York: Pantheon; 1974.
4. Ladner J. *Tomorrow's Tomorrow: The Black Woman.* Garden City, NY: Doubleday; 1971.

5. Aschenbrenner J. Extended families among black Americans. *Journal of Comparative Family Studies* 1973; 4: 257–268.
6. Aschenbrenner J. *Lifelines: Black Families in Chicago.* New York: Holt, Rinehart & Winston; 1975.
7. Stack CB. Black kindreds: parenthood and personal kinreds among urban blacks. *Journal of Comparative Family Studies* 1972; 3: 194–206.
8. Stack CB. *All Our Kin.* New York: Harper & Row; 1974.
9. Martin E, Martin J. *The Black Extended Family.* Chicago: University of Chicago Press; 1978.
10. Hirsch C, Kent DP, Silverman SL. Homogeneity and heterogeneity among low-income Negro and white aged. In: Kent DP, Kastenbaum R, Sherwood S, eds. *Research Planning and Action for the Elderly: The Power and Potential of Social Science.* New York: Behavioral Publications; 1972: 400–500.
11. Dowd JJ, Bengtson VL. Aging in minority populations: an examination of the double jeopardy hypothesis. *Journal of Gerontology* 1978; 33:427–36.
12. Cantor MH. The informal support system of New York's inner city elderly: is ethnicity a factor? In: Gelfand DE, Kutzik AJ, eds. *Ethnicity and Aging: Theory, Research and Policy.* New York: Springer; 1979: 153–174.
13. Shanas E. *National Survey of the Elderly.* Report to Administration on Aging. Washington, DC: Department of Health and Human Services; 1979.
14. Shimkin D, Shimkin E, Frate D. *The Extended Family in Black Societies.* Chicago: Aldine; 1978.
15. McAdoo HP. Factors related to stability in upwardly mobile black families. *Journal of Marriage and the Family* 1978; 40: 762–78.
16. Stanford EP. *The Elder Black.* San Diego, CA: Campanile; 1981.
17. Jackson JJ. *Minorities and Aging.* Belmont, CA: Wadsworth; 1980.
18. Markides KS. Minority aging. In: Riley MW, Hes BB, Bond EK, eds. *Aging in Society: Selected Reviews of Recent Research.* New Jersey: Erlbaum; 1983: 115–137.
19. Mindel CH. The elderly in minority families. In: Brubaker TH, ed. *Family Relationships in Later Life.* Beverly Hills: Sage; 1983: 193–208.
20. Kennedy TR. *You Gotta Deal With It: Black Family Relations in a Southern Community.* New York: Oxford University Press; 1980.
21. Liebow E. *Tally's Corner: A Study of Negro Streetcorner Men.* Boston: Little, Brown; 1967.
22. Jackson JJ. Black aged: in quest of the phoenix. In: *Triple Jeopardy: Myth or Reality.* Washington, DC: National Council on the Aging; 1972: 27–40.
23. Martineau W. Informal social ties among urban black Americans. *Journal of Black Studies* 1977; 8: 83–104.
24. Cantor MH. Neighbors and friends: an overlooked resource in the informal support system. *Research on Aging* 1979; 1: 434–463.
25. Cantor MH, Rosenthal K, Wilker L. Social and family relationships of black aged women in New York City. *The Journal of Minority Aging* 1979; 4: 50–61.
26. Mitchell JS, Register JC. An exploration of family interaction with the elderly by race, socioeconomic status and residence. *The Gerontologist* 1984; 24: 48–54.

27. Mutran E. Intergenerational family support among blacks and whites: response to culture or to socioeconomic differences. *Journal of Gerontology* 1985; 40: 382–89.
28. Taylor RJ. The extended family as a source of support to elderly blacks. *The Gerontologist* 1985; 25: 488–495.
29. Taylor RJ. Receipt of support from family among black Americans: demographic and familial differences. *Journal of Marriage and the Family* 1986; 48: 67–77.
30. Lopata HZ. *Widowhood in an American City.* Cambridge, MA: Schenkman; 1973.
31. Petrowsky M. Marital status, sex, and the social networks of the elderly. *Journal of Marriage and the Family* 1976; 38(3): 749–756.
32. Troll L. The family of later life: a decade review. *Journal of Marriage and the Family* 1971; 33: 263–290.
33. Lee GR. Kinship in the seventies: a decade review of research and theory. *Journal of Marriage and the Family* 1980; 42: 923–934.
34. Walker AJ, Thompson L. Intimacy and intergenerational aid and contact among mothers and daughters. *Journal of Marriage and the Family* 1983; 45(4): 841–850.
35. Cicerelli VG. Adult children's attachment and helping behavior to elderly parents: a path model. *Journal of Marriage and the Family* 1983; 45(4): 815–826.
36. Mutran E, Rietzes D. Intergenerational support activities and well-being among the elderly: a convergence of exchange and symbolic interaction perspectives. *American Sociological Review* 1984; 49: 117–130.
37. Bengtson VL, Olander E, Haddad E. The generation gap and aging family members: toward a conceptual model. In: Gubrium JF, ed. *Time, Roles and Self in Old Age.* New York: Human Sciences Press; 1976: 237–263.
38. Bengtson VL, Cutler NE. Generations and intergenerational relations: perspective on age groups and social change. In: Binstock RH, Shanas E, eds. *Handbook of Aging and the Social Sciences.* New York: Van Nostrand Reinhold; 1976: 130–159.
39. Dono JE, Falke CM, Kail BL, Litwak E, Sherman RH, Siegle D. Primary groups in old age: structure and function. *Research on Aging* 1979; 1(4): 403–434.
40. Sussman MB. The family life of old people. In: Binstock RH, Shanas E, eds. *Handbook of Aging and the Social Sciences.* New York: Van Nostrand Reinhold; 1976: 218–243.
41. Troll L, Bengtson VL. Generations in the family. In: Burr W, Hill R, Reiss I, Nye I, eds. *Handbook of Contemporary Family Theory.* New York: Free Press; 1979: 127–161.
42. Antonucci TC. Personal characteristics, social support and social behavior. In: Binstock RH, Shanas E, eds. *Handbook of Aging and the Social Sciences* (2nd edition). New York: Van Nostrand Reinhold; 1985: 94–128.
43. Adams BN. Isolation, function, and beyond: American kinship in the 1960's. *Journal of Marriage and the Family* 1970; 32: 575–597.
44. Hofferth SL. Kin networks, race, and family structure. *Journal of Marriage and the Family* 1984; 46: 791–806.

45. Morgan JN. The redistribution of income by families and institutions and emergency help patterns. In: Duncan GJ, Morgan JN, eds. *Five Thousand American Families—Patterns of Economic Progress, Volume X: Analyses of the First Thirteen Years of the Panel Study of Income Dynamics*. Ann Arbor, MI: Institute for Social Research; 1983: 1–43.
46. Gibson RC. Blacks at middle and late life: resources and coping. *Annals of the American Academy of Political and Social Science* 1982; 464: 79–90.
47. Mindel CH, Wright R, Starrett RA. Informal and formal health and social support systems of black and white elderly: a comparative cost approach. *The Gerontologist* 1986; 26: 279–285.
48. Taylor RJ, Jackson JS, Quick AD. The frequency of social support among black Americans: preliminary findings from the national survey of black Americans. *Urban Research Review* 1982; 8(2): 1–4.
49. Neighbors H, Jackson JS, Bowman PJ, Gurin G. Stress, coping and black mental health: preliminary findings from a national study. *Prevention in Human Services* 1982; 2: 5–29.
50. Neighbors H, Jackson J. The use of informal and formal help: four patterns of illness behavior in the black community. *American Journal of Community Psychology* 1984; 12: 629–644.
51. Chatters LM, Taylor RJ, Jackson JS. Size and composition of the informal helper networks of elderly blacks. *Journal of Gerontology* 1985; 40: 605–614.
52. Chatters LM, Taylor RJ, Jackson JS. Aged blacks' choice for an informal helper network. *Journal of Gerontology* 1986; 41: 94–100.
53. Adams BN. *Kinship in an Urban Setting*. Chicago: Markham; 1968.
54. Shanas E. *The Health of Older People: A Social Survey*. Cambridge, MA: Harvard University Press; 1962.
55. Bultena GL. Rural–urban differences in the familial interaction of the aged. *Rural Sociology* 1969; 34(1): 5–15.
56. Shanas E. A note on restriction of life space: attitudes of age cohorts. *Journal of Health and Social Behavior* 1968; 9: 86–90.
57. Allen WR. Class, culture, and family organization: the effects of class and race on family structure in urban America. *Journal of Comparative Family Studies* 1979; 10: 301–313.
58. Angel R, Tienda M. Determinants of extended household structure: cultural pattern or economic model? *American Journal of Sociology* 1982; 87: 1360–1383.
59. Sweet JA. *Women in the Labor Force*. New York: Seminar Press; 1973.
60. Tienda M, Angel R. Headship and household composition among blacks, Hispanics, and other whites. *Social Forces* 1982; 61: 508–531.
61. Rubenstein DI. An examination of social participation found among a national sample of black and white elderly. *International Journal of Aging and Human Development* 1971; 2: 172–188.
62. Lopata HZ. *Women as Widows*. New York: Elsevier; 1979.
63. Morgan JN, David M, Cohen W, Brazen H. *Income and Welfare in the United States*. New York: McGraw-Hill; 1962.
64. Moon M, Smolensky E. Income, economic status, and policy toward the aged.

In: Tolley GS, Burkhauser RV, eds. *Income Support Policies for the Aged.* Cambridge, MA: Balinger; 1977: 45–60.

65. Wolf JH, Breslaw N, Ford AB, Ziegler HD, Ward A. Distance and contacts: interactions of black urban elderly adults and family and friends. *Journal of Gerontology* 1983; 38: 465–471.

66. Blumberg L, Bell RR. Urban migration and kinship ties. *Social Problems* 1958; 6: 328–333.

67. Feagin J. The kinship ties of Negro urbanites. *Social Science Quarterly* 1968; 69: 600–665.

68. Meadow K. Negro–white differences among newcomers to a transitional urban area. *Journal of Intergroup Relations* 1962; 3: 320–330.

69. Kahn RL, Antonucci TC. Convoys over the life-course: attachment, roles and social support. In: Baltes PB & Brim, OG, eds. *Life-Span Development and Behavior.* New York: Academic Press; 1980: 253–286.

70. Antonucci TC, Depner CE. Social support and informal helping relationships. In: Willis TA, ed. *Basic Processes in Helping Relationships.* New York: Academic Press; 1981: 233–254.

71. Bengtson VL, Kasschau PL, Ragan PK. The impact of social structure on aging individuals. In: Birren JE, Schaie KW, eds. *Handbook of the Psychology of Aging.* New York: Van Nostrand Reinhold; 1977: 327–354.

72. Hill R, Foote N, Aldous J, Carlson R, MacDonald R. *Family Development in Three Generations.* Cambridge, MA: Schenkman; 1970.

73. Anspach D, Rosenberg GS. Working-class matricentricity. *Journal of Marriage and the Family* 1972; 34: 437–442.

74. Booth A. Sex and social participation. *American Sociological Review.* 1972; 37: 183–192.

75. Croog SH, Lipson A, Levine S. Help patterns in severe illness: the role of kin network, non-family resources, and institutions. *Journal of Marriage and the Family* 1972; 34: 32–41.

76. Drabek TE, Key WH, Erickson PE, Crowe JL. The impact of disaster on kin relationships. *Journal of Marriage and the Family* 1975; 37: 481–494.

77. Kennedy L, Stokes D. Extended family support and the high costs of housing. *Journal of Marriage and the Family* 1982; 44: 311–318.

78. Taylor RJ, Chatters LM. Church-based informal suport among elderly blacks. *The Gerontologist* 1986; 26: 637–642.

79. Johnson CL, Catalano DJ. Childless elderly and their family support. *The Gerontologist* 1981; 21: 610–618.

80. Treas J. Family support systems for the aged: some social and demographic considerations. *The Gerontologist* 1977; 17: 486–491.

81. Johnson CL. Dyadic family relations and social support. *The Gerontologist* 1983; 23: 337–383.

82. Lopata HZ. Contributions of extended families to the support systems of metropolitan area widows: limitations of the modified kin network. *Journal of Marriage and the Family* 1978; 40: 355–364.

83. Gubrium JF. Being single in old age. *International Journal of Aging and Human Development* 1979; 6: 29–41.

84. Ward R. The never married in later life. *Journal of Gerontology.* 1979; 34(6): 861–869.
85. Harbert A, Wilkenson C. Growing old in rural America. *Aging* 1970; 291–292: 36–40.
86. Branch LG, Jette AM. Older's use of informal long term care assistance. *The Gerontologist* 1983; 23: 51–56.
87. Stoller EP, Earl LL. Help with activities of everyday life: sources of support for the noninstitutionalized elderly. *The Gerontologist* 1983; 23: 64–70.
88. Lowenthal MF, Robinson B. Social networks and isolation. In: Binstock RH, Shanas E, eds. *Handbook of Aging and the Social Sciences.* New York: Van Nostrand Reinhold; 1976: 432–456.
89. Cicerelli VG. Sibling relationships in adulthood: a life span perspective. In: Poon L, ed. *Aging in the 1980's: Psychological Issues.* Washington, DC: American Psychological Association; 1980: 455–462.
90. Chappell NL. Informal support networks among the elderly. *Research on Aging* 1983; 5: 77–99.
91. Taylor RJ, Chatters LM. Patterns of informal support to elderly black adults: the role of family, and church members. *Social Work* 1986; 31: 432–438.
92. McAdoo HP. Black mothers and the extended family support networks. In: Rodgers-Rose LF, ed. *The Black Woman.* Beverly Hills, CA: Sage; 1980: 125–144.

13

Health-Seeking Behavior of Elderly Blacks

Tyson Gibbs

ILLNESS DEFINITIONS

In general, older persons suffer from more chronic illnesses and diseases than younger persons. Over 55% of older blacks in the 1982 National Health Interview Survey reported their health as fair or poor. These data raise questions regarding individual assessment of sickness or ill health and the decision process involved in consulting a health professional or health facility.

In an intensive anthropological study of 30 older blacks in rural north-central Florida (1), black men and women were found to differ in their subjective views of health and well-being. When questioned about their health, men reported seldom being bothered by health problems, while women indicated that they were more often sick than well. In this instance, sick is defined as the state of being that severely reduces activities of daily living. Over 83% of the men, but only 63% of the women, stated that they were seldom sick.

Campbell (2) reported on a study that involved the data collected on older people from senior citizen centers in 25 selected cities across the country. He found that only 34.6% of the women but over 50% of the men rated their health as excellent. The remainder, 61.1% of the women and 44.4% of the men, reported that their health was fair or poor. Verbrugge (3) related similar findings. She examined the data from the Health Interview Survey from 1957 to 1972 and found that women subjectively reported their health as poor more often than did men. She attributed her findings to the following possibilities: (1) that females are generally more cooperative during health interviews, have a higher recall of their physical symptoms and health activities, or can better verbalize their physical ailments; (2) that females may more often be sensitive to body discomforts and more willing to report these symptoms to others; and (3) that females are actually exposed to greater physical risks of disease and injury and thus may report more health problems.

Other possibilities, however, do exist for male–female differences in the reporting of health problems. Men may wish to appear strong, productive, and independent and therefore will not report every ache or pain, while the women are "expected" to report all health problems. As Estes (4) indicated:

> A questionable symptom or sign may be ignored until pain or other symptoms force a medical consultation, or until concern by other family members (and close friends) leads to the same results. (p. 109)

Rosenstock (5) discussed the concepts of perceived susceptibility and perceived seriousness of a health problem. His contention was that individuals vary in their perception or acceptance of their vulnerability in terms of a given condition. In the same manner, individuals vary in their belief that a given condition is serious or not. In terms of seriousness, he stated that:

> the degree of seriousness may be judged both by the degree of emotional arousal created by the thought of a disease, as well as by the kind of difficulties the individual believes a given condition will create for him (or her). (p. 99)

One important question that emerges from these studies is the degree to which race and ethnicity play a part in the individual's perception of the extent to which a given illness or disease requires medical attention from a formal system of health care. Indications are that there is a difference by ethnicity in the effect of health and diseases in old age. For example, if the adage is true that old age does not kill but disease and illness cause death, then figures in the mortality tables suggest that black males (6), whose life expectancy is lower than that of whites and black females, must succumb to particular, killing diseases or illness at younger ages. Data on hospital visits further suggest that there are differences in illness and disease perceptions by blacks and whites; the rates and percentages of hospital visits are different for each racial group. Among older black and white women there are different rates of office visits to physicians in all major disease categories, particularly for osteoarthritis, hypertension, ischemic heart disease, symptomatic heart disease, and neuroses. There are also ample data indicating that blacks have a higher number of restricted days of activity. Some research (7) has found a 13% differential between blacks and whites. Data from the National Center for Health Statistics (8) show a 28-day difference per 100 persons per year.

Although there are questions about the perceptions that older blacks have about their state of illness or disease, certain facts are clear: (1) older black females report their health as fair to poor more often than whites; (2) older black males indicate that they are seldom sick; (3) older blacks have more restricted days per person per year; (4) black and white females have different hospital visit rates, but black females in 1981 made more visits to physicians for such problems as essential hyertension, diabetes mellitus, arthritis, and unspecified; and (5) mortality rates for older black males are much higher than for older black females, but older black females have a lower mortality rate than both older black and white males.

THE DECISION TO SEEK HEALTH CARE

Statistics indicate a higher prevalence rate of fatal diseases among blacks (hypertension, ischemic heart disease, and stroke). Additionally, blacks are usually diagnosed at later stages of their illnesses than whites and have a higher mortality rate for most diseases than whites. Since early detection is paramount for disease and illness prevention, these facts raise questions regarding the timing and process involved in older blacks seeking care.

Gibbs (1) found that the reasons governing whether older blacks chose to consult health care practitioners, close friends and relatives, or simply chose to take care of health care matters themselves were intricately related to their perception of change in health status. Simply put, each person defined an illness episode in terms of whether or not it could be taken care of at the dwelling unit. A subjective evaluation of this kind includes a ranking of the condition as "a not too serious illness," or an illness "requiring outside advice or attention" from a more formal health care facility, and hence constituting a "serious" health problem.

In both instances, whether an illness can be treated at home or treated at a formal health care facility, the threat of the illness or disease to whatever mobility the older individual has was of major importance. Generally, the older black person considered serious health problems to be those that retard or inhibit physical activity. Common examples provided by the interviewees included problems with the heart, stomach, or joints and problems that affect vision, skin, or feet. Health problems perceived as less serious primarily encompassed small cuts, bruises, burns, headaches, sleeplessness, some colds or fevers, "gas" in the stomach, "nature problems" or problems with sexual impotency, and stabilized chronic diseases.

On the basis of classifying an illness or disease episode as serious or not serious, the older persons in this study may or may not have considered themselves sick and may or may not have sought out health care advice immediately. In fact, the older persons' responses to the question of whom they would call if they were sick confirms the above findings. Most of the elderly stated that if the illness were serious, they would call someone at a formal institution of health care. Some of the older people also said that their doctors had asked them to call when their health had deteriorated to the point at which they felt the need for the doctor's advice. To prove their point, many showed the investigators phone numbers that they stated were the home phone numbers of their personal physicians. On the other hand, if the illness or disease episode was not incapacitating, 13 of the 30 persons said that they would initially call no one. Eight stated that they might call their physician anyway. Only 4 indicated that they would call the local clinic nurse or their pastor.

It is difficult to determine with certainty from an interview protocol whether an individual first calls a close friend or relative, or his or her personal physician. Illness episodes are being discussed in the abstract, and the individual is presented with a hypothetical "what if" situation. Since the investigator is not there at the immediate onset of a health problem (9), the causal sequence of events is very difficult to disentangle. This means that the process of how the elderly define a change in health status as a health problem that needs immediate self-treatment or the attention of a nurse or physician as well as their actual decision path taken to secure health care treatment are more a matter of conjecture than hard facts. Enough information on the health care-seeking habits of the elderly was obtained, however, through interview and responses to questions about informal networks, to propose a schematic outline of health care-seeking behavior. Table 13.1 displays the proposed outline of the health care-seeking decision process among older blacks.

The schematic outline presented in Table 13.1 is constructed to account for the decision-making process that occurs with episodes of both chronic and acute illness. Generally, individuals in this study (1) did not consider illnesses that they had lived with for many years as health problems unless there was a sudden change in the state of the illness or disease (10). Therefore, in most instances, the process or need to define a change in health as serious or not serious was relevant only to situations that were sudden, such as the onset of colds, fevers, rashes, heart problems, and situations in which a chronic illness or disease changed to further impair the older person's activities or cause considerable discomfort.

This concept of simply defining illnesses in terms of the ability to treat them at home or take them to the physician was echoed by Young and Garro (11), who indicated that:

TABLE 13.1 Schematic Outline of Health Care–Seeking Behavior of Older Rural Blacks

Phase one: *Self-address phase*	Self-perception of change in health status as problem, problem defined as serious or not serious.
Phase two: *Advice-seeking phase*	Depending on decision made in *phase one,* elderly person will either treat problem if defined as not serious, and may or may not ask the advice of a pharmacist, close friend, or relative. If the health problem is perceived as serious the older person may call a personal physician, the local clinic nurse, or a close friend or relative; on some occasions, the local pharmacist may be consulted.
Phase three: *Redefinition phase*	All advice is reevaluated to determine the next step in the health care-seeking process or to develop a plan of action. In this phase, the illness is redefined.
Phase four: *Action phase*	Based on outcome of reevaluation process, individual will do one of the following: consult his or her "medicine cabinet" or that of a close friend or relative, or go to the local pharmacist for self-treatment medication; for more serious problems, transportation may be sought from close friends or relatives, the Fire Department Rescue Unit may be called, or a private ambulance company may be contacted.
Phase five: *Redefinition phase*	After the illness or disease episode has either been stabilized by the older person at home or been treated by more formal health care practitioners, the individual will reevaluate his or her progress and redefine the state of his or her health status change. In this fashion, older persons continually monitor their state of health.

Source: Modeled after Weaver (9).

within Western societies the lower class [to which many black elderly belong], as compared with the middle class, are less likely to use orthodox medical services and more likely to use folk remedies, patent remedies, and marginal alternatives because of their medical beliefs about illness and their parochial orientation toward health services. (p. 1453)

This certainly was the case in rural Florida. Tanner, Cockerham, and Spaeted (12) presented several determinants that predict whether or not a particular individual will seek health or medical care. These include: (1) visibility and recognition of symptoms; (2) the extent to which the symptoms are perceived as dangerous; (3) the extent to which symptoms disrupt family, work, and other social activities; (4) the frequency and persistence of the symptoms; (5) the amount of tolerance for the symptoms; (6) available information, knowledge, and cultural assumptions; (7) basic needs that lead to denial; (8) other needs competing with illness responses; (9) competing interpretations that can be given to the symptoms once they are recognized; and (10) the availability and physical proximity of treatment resources, as well as the psychologic and financial costs of taking action. Closely associated with their model is the idea that behavior operates on two levels, other-defined and self-defined illness (12).

Safer and colleagues (13) discussed three stages in the process of seeking or delaying health care activities at the individual level. These included (1) appraisal delay, (2) illness delay, and (3) utilization delay. The premise is that at each stage of illness, the individual will either increase the speed of resolution of a medical problem or will continue to deliberate. The *appraisal delay* stage involves the ascertainment of the number of days that passed between symptom identification and symptom definition. At this stage the person perceives a change in body functions. During *illness delay* the patient has to decide whether the medical problem needs professional help or self-treatment. This stage is characterized by the assumption on the part of the individual that home remedies will not treat or cure physical or mental ailments. The final stage, *utilization delay,* is defined as the lapse in time between the decision to seek more formal treatment for a problem and the actual visit to a medical facility. At this stage factors such as cost and timing become crucial in confirming the resolution to confront medical problems.

In a study of 2,107 black respondents, Neighbors and Jackson (14) used the recall method to examine the issue of help-seeking behavior habits. Each person was asked if he or she had experienced a moment of great distress and to recall this moment. Further, each individual was asked to describe his or her solicitation of formal and/or informal support. The problem in time was coded into one of five serious problem categories: (1) emotional, (2) interpersonal, (3) death of a loved one, (4) economic, and (5) physical health. The findings suggest that people over 55 years of age use informal help only, or both informal and formal help. No data were presented on the timing of such activities. Of particular interest is the finding that people with physical problems are least likely to use informal help only.

Although there are many studies that focus on the issue of health care-seeking or help-seeking behavior, there is not a consensus by researchers on the appropriate model to characterize these activities. Further, there is no agreement on the study method, method of analysis, or hypotheses to be tested.

AN AGENDA FOR RESEARCH ON HEALTH-SEEKING BEHAVIOR OF OLDER BLACKS

The research on health care-seeking or help-seeking behavior is mired in discipline-bound research, which has provided very little definitive information capable of comparison or integration across disciplinary lines. For example, much research has been conducted using the Anderson and Newman (15) model of the early 1970s, which includes predisposing, enabling, and need components. Much criticism, however, has indicated that this model does not allow for psychosocial variables in the illumination of why persons seek help. As a result, there has been a proliferation of models seeking to link race, ethnicity, psychosocial variables, and attitudes, but few, if any, have been fully empirically tested (11–13, 16–18). It thus remains unclear what the implications of these models are for research on the health-seeking behavior of the black elderly.

The available data based upon the Anderson–Newman (15) model suggest that psychosocial-, racial-, and ethnic-related variables play a minor role in predicting physician utilization. The reasons for this conclusion, based upon the Anderson–Newman approach, are complex (19). Other, less well tested models suggest that race is important; but these have not been proven through repeated examination under rigid research conditions. What is left, then, is a gap in the literature and some indications for further research.

What is needed to fully examine the question of race and ethnicity and help health-seeking behavior is to explore the models that already assume that psychosocial, racial, and ethnic variables are important (11, 12, 14), as well as those that assume that race is not a strong predictor of who will or who will not visit the physician (15).

Within-race group studies of blacks (1, 14) should be performed and compared to studies of whites or other ethnics to determine where there are similarities and differences in terms of health-seeking behaviors. Rigorous studies should be conducted to examine the so-called soft variables and their role in predicting physician utilization by the black elderly. Of particular interest are (1) informal networks; (2) family living conditions, as measured by the number and mixture of household residents; (3) family versus older person's income and living arrangements; and (4) individual, control-related beliefs. Clearly, as a group, blacks do suffer more and die at a higher rate than comparable white populations for most of the fatal diseases. What has not been clearly delineated is whether the differences are related to skin color or social and economic conditions.

While skin color can predict quite accurately many societal circumstances, what is not so clear is how social behaviors affect health behaviors, particularly for the older black person. Further, the question raised is to what degree, at least for the black elderly, social programs (e.g., Medicare,

Medicaid, welfare, Social Security, and other benefit programs) mask differences in health behavior of blacks versus that of other racial and ethnic groups.

The data are consistent in showing that blacks delay seeking care much longer than do whites. Is this a learned behavior (children watch parents and in turn adopt their habits) or is such behavior somehow a cultural adaptation to prolonged poverty? Although at present few studies indicate that race or ethnicity can predict who will visit the physician, race can, when combined with income, be a powerful predictor of *not* see a physician.

In the 1981 version of *Use of Health Services by Women 65 Years of Age and Over, United States* (7), it was found that visits by older women were not as frequent for members of black and other races as they were for their white counterparts. These results were true for all visits in the National Ambulatory Medical Care Survey (NAMCS) regardless of sex. Similar results were found in the National Health Interview Survey (8).

The extent of intragroup variation between low-, middle-, and high-income blacks in health-seeking behavior has not been thoroughly investigated. The following is a list of possible questions that might be answered if more thorough research is conducted on health-seeking behavior in the black elderly.

1. Research on health-seeking behavior among blacks might answer the question of why there is a delay in physician visits for major health problems. Answers to this question may suggest key health promotion activities to be designed for and directed at the black community that may eventually eliminate or lower such behavior, thus reducing mortality rates.

2. Some answers to the question of why there are fewer visits to the physician by blacks might ultimately lead to the creation of better preventive health programs targeted at the black community.

3. A clearer understanding of the pathways of health behavior from time of disease onset to resolution can be important for physicians and public health community workers in targeting appropriate medical intervention programs. For example, if it is established that many older blacks follow a pattern of self-treatment, family/friend treatment, and formal treatment, then physicians might begin to ascertain from patients such things as medications used or exchanged, who significantly influences patient health behaviors, and patient beliefs about personal health.

4. Examining the intraracial variations with and similarities to whites might lead to a better understanding of why programs of health aimed at the entire black community, without recognition of intragroup differences, work well in some instances and poorly in others.

5. An examination of similarities and differences in black/white health-seeking behaviors might provide clues to the influence of race on health

activities. Race and ethnicity are probably more powerful predictors of variations in help-seeking within other status dimensions; for example, higher-income blacks might behave in a manner more similar to higher-income whites than to lower-income blacks or whites. The results of this kind of comparative research can lead to explanations and a better understanding of the health behavior of people in general. What this research would do is dispel myths about the nature of black American health status, belief systems, and health behaviors.

The existing data point to a need for a new generation of studies on blacks that begin to examine the complex interaction between behavior as measured through aggregate statistics (e.g., higher mortality and fewer visits to the physician) and health behaviors as measured through questionnaires and observations. To date, few studies have approached an understanding of the issues related to the role of social norms on older black health care-seeking activities.

REFERENCES

1. Gibbs T. *Rural Medical Self-Help Linkages*. Gainesville, FL: University of Florida; 1979. (Unpublished doctoral dissertation).
2. Campbell RM. Variable differences among older persons and their subjective health. *Texas Medicine* 1978; 74: 49–55.
3. Verbrugge LW. Females and illness: recent trends in sex differences in the United States. *Journal of Health and Social Behavior* 1976; 17: 387–403.
4. Estes EH. Health experience in the elderly. In: Busse EW, Pfeiffer E, eds. *Behavior and Adaptation in Late Life*. Boston: Little, Brown; 1977: 99–116.
5. Rosenstock IM. Why people use health services. *Milbank Memorial Fund Quarterly* 1966; 3: 94–127.
6. US Senate, Special Committee on Aging, and American Association of Retired Persons. *Aging in America: Trends and Projections*. Washington, DC: U.S. Government Printing Office; 1983.
7. *Use of Health Services by Women 65 Years of Age and Over, United States*. Hyattsville, MD: National Center for Health Statistics; 1981.
8. *Persons Injured and Disability Days Due to Injuries, 1980–1981*. Hyattsville, MD: National Center for Health Statistics; 1985.
9. Weaver T. Use of hypothetical situations in the study of Spanish-American illness referral systems. *Human Organization* 1970; 29:140–150.
10. Brearly P, Gibons J, Miles A, Tyliss E, Woods G. *The Social Context of Health Care*. London: The Chaucer Press; 1978.
11. Young JC, Garro LY. Variations in the choice of treatment in two Mexican communities. *Social Science and Medicine* 1982; 16: 1453–1465.
12. Tanner JL, Cockerham WC, Spaeted JL. Predicting physician utilization. *Medical Care* 1983; 21: 360–369.

13. Safer M, et al. Determinants of three stages of delay in seeking care at a medical clinic. *Medical Care* 1979;17: 11–29.

14. Neighbors HW, Jackson JS. The use of informal and formal help: four patterns of illness behavior in the black community. *American Journal of Community Psychology* 1984;12: 629–645.

15. Andersen, R, Newman JF. Societal and individual determinants of medical care utilization in the United States. *Milbank Memorial Fund Quarterly* 1973;51: 95–127.

16. Nuttbrock L, Kosberg JI. Images of the physicians and help-seeking behavior of the elderly: a multivariate assessment. *Journal of Gerontology* 1980;35: 241–248.

17. Dutton DB. Explaining the low use of health services by the poor: costs, attitudes or delivery systems? *American Sociological Review* 1978;43: 348–368.

18. Karl, F. The decision to see the physician: a clinical investigation. *The Journal of Family Practice* 1984;18: 265–272.

19. Mechanic D. Correlates of physician utilization and why do major multivariate studies of physician utilization find trival psychosocial and organization effects. *Journal of Health and Social Behavior* 1979; 20: 387–396.

14

Health Attitudes/Promotions/ Preventions: The Black Elderly

James H. Carter

Notwithstanding the fact that aged blacks constitute heterogenous group-ings, they have distinct attitudes about health, diseases, the time and methods for obtaining treatment, drugs, hospitals, and being sick. The *American Medical News* recently affirmed that there is also a profound difference in the use of medical systems between black and white patients (1). The explanation given by the *American Medical News* for utilization differences was the lack of access to medical care. However, the reality is that (1) black Americans live in a bigoted society and (2) health care is not provided in a vacuum, but in a socioeconomic milieu. For example, given our nation's long history of legally enforced racial inequality, it comes as no surprise that relatively few black Americans receive transplants, particularly heart transplants.

An obvious barrier to health care for the black aged is their wealth disparity and inadequate supplemental insurance coverages to Medicare/ Medicaid. For the past several years, care in investor-owned hospitals has markedly increased. It is estimated that half of all nursing homes and mental hospitals are now associated with the investor-owned hospital industry, and these for-profit hospitals have contributed to increased health care costs (2). Given that a third of all blacks, compared with 8% of whites, have no wealth at all, the increase in investor-owned hospitals carries drastic im-plications for aged black Americans. Today, it is considered poor manage-ment to increase the health care costs of the affluent in order to subsidize the health care of the uninsured. Consequently, we can anticipate that more black aged Americans will receive inferior care in public hospitals, where care is too often found to be relatively inferior due to inadeqate budgets to procure the most modern equipment and to attract competent staff. Providing quality health care to all citizens is a basic societal obligation, and even the American Medical Association has discontinued expressing concerns that Medicare is a step toward socialized medicine.

Perhaps the most pernicious reasons for a difference in utilization of health services is the lack of knowledge about health care, compounded by the scarcity of health care resources in black communities. An important health resource soon to be lost to black communities, due to declining enrollments in medical schools, is the black physician who has historically borne the brunt of treating most uninsured black patients. However, the findings of former Secretary Heckler of the Department of Health and Human Services confirmed that blacks and other minorities remain less healthy and die younger. I am convinced that many early deaths among minorities could be prevented by knowledge and changes in personal health habits. Thus the question is whether wellness is an attainable goal or an elusive, undefinable, antiphysician concept that is both unreachable and too costly to pursue (3). The attitudes of aged blacks toward good physical and emotional health, health maintenance, and prevention are imbued with myths and part-truths; some of these are discussed in this chapter.

EXPLORING THE MYTHS

Myth #1: Black families tolerate grossly abnormal behavior in the black elderly, and consequently blacks are not receptive to psychiatric intervention.

Fact #1: There is ample evidence that most blacks revere the aged and have the same interests as others in the psychiatric care of elderly family members; but they are continually frustrated in achieving proper care (4). Regrettably, aged blacks have few alternatives in seeking psychiatric help. Nursing homes are too frequently below standards, and many homes that service aged blacks are small, family-operated enterprises and thus do not meet minimum health or safety standards. If belligerent or boisterous, blacks are at risk of being prescribed major tranquilizers until docile for purposes of facilitating management.

Compounding the issues of pharmacokinetics and clinical response to tranquilizers are factors of race and ethnicity. Differences in racial and ethnic reactions to medications are believed to be quite common, which suggests the need for greater research to establish dose ranges that take into account not only weight, age, and sex, but also race. It has become apparent that failure to take racial differences into account when prescribing medications may have lethal consequences for the patient (5). For example, Hispanic patients are reported to require less antidepressant medication and to have greater side effects at half the Anglo therapeutic dosage (6). Similarly, Asians are reported to require lower dosages of neuroleptics than whites, and side effects are significantly higher at lower dosages (7, 8).

Aged blacks without families who are victims of deinstitutionalization from state mental hospitals are often found in the ghettos of our nation. For many black deinstitutionalized patients, regardless of age, community resources are nonexistent and the chances of creating these resources are rapidly diminishing. Because of racial bigotry, some American communities object to the presence of blacks in their midst despite the black individual's economic status, level of education, or social skills; thus community placement for the elderly black is problematic and mental health professionals cannot escape culpability. Society's current zoning regulations, which confine mentally ill patients to dilapidated inner cities, are legally sanctioned discrimination. The deinstitutionalized aged black may, however, find encouragement in the decision of *Klostermann* vs. *Cuomo,* in which the New York High Court decided that the judiciary has authority to decide matters of residential placement (9, 10). In the *Klostermann* case, the court ruled that chronic patients are entitled to appropriate residential placement, supervision, and care, including follow-up to verify that their placement was indeed appropriate.

I believe that further investigation is required to determine if all mentally disordered patients are in fact capable of reaching a level of normalization that allows them to cope successfully in society. In spite of the stereotype that blacks resist psychiatric care, it has been shown that mentally disordered blacks do seek psychiatric help and can be successfully treated when care is accessible and compatible with black culture, hopes, and aspirations (11). We cannot justifiably criticize the black aged for not availing themselves of new treatment methods of social rehabilitation, self-help groups, community interaction programs, medical education, transitional employment, and adult basic education. A major error in the past has been our making arrogant assumptions about how black senior citizens should mesh with our services without adequately evaluating the appropriateness of those services. We continue to develop programs based on the needs of the majority. Due to unpleasant past experiences with insensitive helping professionals and programs, aged blacks hesitate to accept some psychiatric services (12).

Myth #2: Black Americans are prone to abuse emergency medical/psychiatric services and are indifferent to early symptoms of diseases.

Fact #2: Given the reality that the major focus of American medicine has been the treatment of diseases, this accusation is ironic. Until the past few years, most physicians paid little attention to health as a positive concept.

Preventive medicine has not always been a prestigious discipline, perhaps because cures can be counted but the number of diseases prevented can only be deduced. Yet much of the good health we enjoy can be attributed to the application of public health principles. Preventive care with the elderly is further minimized by Medicare policies that prohibit reimbursement for most preventive services; theoretically these very preventive services would decrease the number of chronic illnesses and the institutionalization of the elderly. Federal rules today encourage hospitals to discharge elderly patients who can be managed with follow-up treatment at home. Parenthetically, the denial of Medicare claims for home health care has nearly tripled since 1983 (13). The late Hobart C. Jackson once stated that we have different attitudes toward chronic and acute illnesses. Jackson stated that acute diseases give rise to all kinds of new and innovative treatment methods in behalf of the patient, but chronic diseases, commonly seen in the black elderly, are of low priority (14).

Traditionally, the training of physicians, particularly psychiatrists, has been oriented toward disease rather than health maintenance (15). The development of a health-oriented ecology and a health-maintenance lifestyle is out of synchronization with the orientation of most physicians (16). My empirical observations are that accessibility, availability, and economics are the overwhelming reasons why blacks are seen frequently in emergency situations. Cultural beliefs about the etiology of diseases and the methods of treatment also impact emergency treatment.

Myth #3: Suicide and other self-destructive behaviors are not observed among the black elderly.

Fact #3: Contrary to popular opinions, suicide does occur among elderly blacks. For example, suicide has increased from 8.7 per 100,000 population in 1972 to 12.2 in 1980 for black males above the age of 65 (17). Even more important are (1) the failure of poor black families and coroners to obtain autopsies necessary for a definitive diagnosis in elderly blacks and (2) the absence of data about the deliberate refusal of elderly blacks to take life-sustaining medications in order to purposefully hasten their deaths.

I wish to make clear that the majority of black citizens do grow old gracefully; others resist as physical limitations occur. Most, seemingly, do not want to live forever or return to youth (18). I am struck by how often I encounter aged blacks who accept the fact that physical man is mortal, preferring to die a "natural" death. Most seem resigned to the fact that none of use will get out of this life alive. Nonetheless, their philosophical and religious views of life do not justify our disregarding suicide among aged blacks.

Myth #4: Aged blacks are prone to suffer from paranoid schizophrenia and organic mental disorders stemming from a variety of metabolic conditions, but affective disorders, particularly depressions, are rare.

Fact #4: From self-reported symptoms in two markedly different American communities—Kansas City, Missouri, and a rural Maryland county—Comstock and Helsing found that more Afro-Americans than Euro-Americans were depressed but that there was no significant difference when these findings were adjusted for income (19).

Although health care today is more accessible to all Americans than ever before in the history of this nation, the psychiatric care of black patients of all ages has remained essentially unchanged. Institutional and ideological changes may have corrected the appearance of neglect, but not the reality of this situation (20). Black patients are more likely than white patients to be rejected for dynamic psychotherapy, have higher attrition rates, and are more commonly treated with psychotropic drugs than with psychotherapy. I believe that the failure to successfully treat mentally disordered black patients in the past is intertwined with diagnostic errors.

The third edition of the *Diagnostic and Statistical Manual (DSM-III)*, published in 1980 by the American Psychiatric Association, was heralded as the instrument to correct diagnostic errors in black patients (21). Indeed, this was a major step forward, given that previous manuals arrived at a diagnosis by selecting the stereotypic profile that best described the patient (22). *DSM-III* was an improvement to the extent that multiaxial perspectives, particularly Axis IV (psychosocial stressors), provided the means for determining the relationship of culture, environment, and the debilitating effects of racism to the psychopathology of black Americans. Even psychopharmacologists, who may have believed that all emotional disorders have a biological basis, should now consider the importance of psychosocial stressors when formulating diagnoses. Nonetheless, Axis IV is optional, and some mental health professionals choose not to make full use of *DSM-III*. Vital issues such as nutrition, grief, loss of vision, and a sense of worth must no longer be ignored in medical intervention or in our psychodynamic formulations of emotional disorders.

A major criticism with *DSM-III* and the revised *DSM-III-R* (23) is that it overlooks conditions called "folk illnesses," conditions found among a significant number of black Americans. Folk illnesses are not rare or bizarre disorders, but rather common, cultural-bound syndromes. For example, the cultural-bound syndrome of "falling out" is considered to be a significant problem for southern blacks and is often seen in emergency rooms, presenting as disorders of the central nervous system or as metabolic abnormalities. Falling out is of sudden onset and without convulsions. Although there is frequent twitching of both small and large muscle groups, there is no bowel or bladder incontinence. Chewing of the tongue is extremely rare. The episode is brief and invariably appears when the patient is in a highly emotionally charged situation or environment.

The need to recognize folk illnesses also applies to other minorities.

Atwood Gaines, an anthropologist, informs me that the folk illness of "Susto" is rather common among Mexican-Americans in some areas of California (24). Susto, meaning "soul loss," is characterized by weakness, reduced sexual drives, fear, and a number of anxiety indicators, such as rapid heart beat, sweating, and diarrhea. Successful treatment of Mexican-Americans suffering Susto demands some awareness of the symptoms. Unfortunately, in medical circles folk illnesses are equated with ignorance, voodoo, and sorcery. It is inconceivable that cultural-bound behavioral patterns will soon find their way into *DSM-III-R*.

Myth #5: Because most working black elderly citizens are not industrious, when noncompliant with treatment or presenting to be with recurrent psychophysiological disorders, they are believed to be seeking early retirement and/or disability.

Fact #5: Because many physicians are not familiar with the adaptive behavior patterns of the black aged to stress and the attendant symptomatology, they are acting irresponsibly when they make far-reaching value judgments that may negatively impact the lives of working, aged blacks. Although the treatment for psychophysiological disorders of aged blacks may be beyond the training of some physicians, this does not relieve them of their responsibility to make accurate diagnoses and to seek appropriate consultation from knowledgeable colleagues.

Myth #6: All elderly blacks are assumed to be Christian and docile; and because alcoholism is thus perceived as nonexistent in this population, it is frequently misdiagnosed.

Fact #6: Alcohol may, in fact, become the primary source for relief from feelings of loneliness, uselessness, and despair. Alcohol is readily available, and it dulls emotional and physical pains. There are no reliable statistics on alcoholism among aged blacks describing the natural course of the disease and the attendant complex of medical/emotional and psychological sequelae. Alcoholism is one of the most underdiagnosed and untreated diseases in America, even though alcohol-related disorders are ranked among the leading causes of death (25).

The black church continues to play an important role in the treatment of alcoholism. A considerable amount of research has focused on how the traditional black church has historically provided a buffer to psychosocial stressors. It remains a viable institution for assisting with the development and implementation of treatment strategies. Past experience has shown that when Alcoholics Anonymous groups are organized and supported by the black church, black alcoholics who otherwise would refuse to participate in this sound treatment modality can be helped (26).

Myth #7: The elderly are in good health and are financially secure, a viewpoint based on a study of the American Council of Life Insurance taken from governmental data and the Census Bureau (27).

Fact #7: The plight of elderly blacks was omitted in the report, ostensibly because it is common knowledge that many black senior citizens must, at times, make the difficult choice between eating and/or maintaining shelter. Some suffer hypothermia in winter months and heat exhaustion in summer in spite of federal, state, and local assistance. Quite different from the image of the "wellderly" we would prefer to present to the world, there are ill, destitute, and unfed elderly black Americans (28). The black aged have benefited least from civil rights triumphs in education, jobs, and housing (29).

Myth #8: The extended black family, with its strong kinship ties, precludes out-of-home placement of elderly blacks (30).

Fact #8: These myths are emotionally devastating for black families with elderly parents or relatives who must, for good reasons, be placed outside of the family's home. Much guilt may be aroused, not due entirely to rumors about the physical abuses of the elderly in nursing homes, but to the expectations of friends and the community that the black aged will be cared for by "blood." Therefore, when placement occurs, the experience is emotionally traumatizing for all concerned. To refute the stereotype, a family may deny the black elderly the opportunity for appropriate placement. Anecdotally, a black patient of mine who found it necessary to place her mother in a nursing home describes each departing, after visiting the mother, as "painful as a funeral."

Myth #9: Aged black individuals contribute to family stability.

Fact #9: In some families the egotism of old age may be a pathological need of the aged family member to dominate the household in a destructive manner. This behavior in the elderly can contribute to constant turmoil; acts of selfishness and caprice can succeed in tyrannizing the family (31).

CULTURAL CONSIDERATIONS

Poindexter has indicated that the health of man is a product of the vicissitudes of life, including cultural variances in food, clothing, shelter, and occupation (32). Thus effective medical and psychosocial interventions should give attention to the culture and values of elderly blacks. Some aged black citizens believe there are natural diseases that plague mankind, and others believe that diseases occur as a consequence of evil influences. A sensitivity to their cultural beliefs in the supernatural and their respect for the laws of nature is a prerequisite to establishing treatment alliances.

Many black elderly patients cling tenaciously to the belief that there are medicinal properties in herbs, ointments, and lotions. Preoccupation with constipation often occurs out of fear that constipation can precipitate symptoms of intestinal obstruction, for example, "locked bowels," headaches, and deepening of skin pigmentation. These fears sometime lead to the habitual use of laxatives or oils that interfere with the absorption of the needed vitamins A, D, and E.

The use of home remedies may reflect economics as well as cultural preference. I believe that both factors have a relationship to the finding that 70% of the elderly use over-the-counter medicines, compared with 10% of the general adult population (33). Compounding the problem of the massive use of over-the-counter drugs is the tendency of physicians to prescribe excessive amounts of medication for the elderly, thus creating a situation referred to as "polypharmacy." It is reported by Vitale and Santos that 11% of the population age 65 and older receive 28% of all prescribed drugs (34). Regrettably, each drug, whether prescribed or over-the-counter, carries with it some risk or side effect; and these risks are pronounced in the elderly because of naturally occurring biological alterations associated with aging. Vitale and Santos also suggest that there is little evidence to support the role of nutrition in the *prevention* of diseases in the elderly. In fact, they believe that by the time we reach age 65, most of us will experience some degree of degenerative processes that began earlier in life. Thus marked changes in dietary habits of the black elderly for health promotion to reverse the damages caused by cardiovascular diseases, arthritis, and so forth should be balanced against the elderly individual's economic needs and happiness. Only when there are clear indications that the black elderly are not ingesting or utilizing essential nutrients is it necessary to alter dietary customs or habits. Yet I propose that wellness among the aged is a definable concept that physicians should embrace and promote in our practice and our own lives. The word *doctor* means *teacher* in its original Latin form, and the time has come for physicians to encourage their patients to give up smoking, to eat less, and to exercise more (35).

CONCLUSIONS AND RECOMMENDATIONS

It is obvious that equally as important as physical examinations and routine chemistries is the necessity to obtain a thorough psychosocial assessment, a dietary history, and knowledge about the use of alcohol. Attention should also be given to the use of prescribed and over-the-counter medicines. Because older black Americans may have a combination of chronic diseases, such as hypertension, diabetes, and arthritis, to mention a few, they may be victims of polypharmacy. The combined use of medications for these ailments is a threat to both their physical and emotional health.

From a decade of serving black patients at the Lincoln Community Health Center, Durham, North Carolina, I am convinced that health care for the ambulatory black elderly can best be achieved when provided by an accessible neighborhood comprehensive health care model (36). The black elderly are often seen with a multiplicity of health and social problems. At times, when obtaining a medical history, it is difficult to know exactly what poor, aged black patients are seeking. Therefore, we must ask whether the patient is seeking treatment for medical/psychiatric problems or assistance with housing or other socioeconomic conditions. Health programs serving the elderly are often too fragmented and nonresponsive to the comprehensive medical, emotional, social, cultural, and socioeconomic needs of the individual patient and his or her family. Too often many health programs require the elderly to be extraordinarily sophisticated in order to use complex, multiservice centers and related community support systems.

The abuse of emergency health services for crisis intervention without thorough evaluations and follow-up care is reduced in well-organized, comprehensive health care systems. The comprehensive health care milieu, such as that found at the Lincoln Community Health Center, offers the opportunity for us not only to address attitudes about mental illness and feelings about medicine, but also to examine dietary patterns and economic/social issues. More than 50,000 patients die annually from colorectal cancer, but the staff at Lincoln firmly believe that, if properly applied, screening programs for colorectal cancer could decrease this rate substantially. This is particularly relevant to persons who are over 50 years of age (37). The reason for the effectiveness of comprehensive health care with mentally ill elderly blacks is that it helps reduce the stigma associated with mental illness, a stigma shared by all of society. It has finally been accepted by the medical community that psychological and physiological well-being are inseparable. Present-day disenchantment of black families with mental health treatment occurs at a time when we can do much to halt or repair the ravages of serious mental illness. There is a critical need to educate blacks of all age groups about the capabilities of mental health professionals and to convince them that successful treatment can be achieved.

In addition to social work/mental health, dental care, health education, and medicine, pharmacy services are provided at Lincoln. Providing transportation is essential for the aged, who otherwise could not keep appointments. Health education can become a vehicle for health maintenance. Through education, the black elderly can be helped to relinquish their sense of powerlessness. Most importantly, as aged blacks learn more about such health issues as overeating and cancer detection and prevention, the relationship of lifestyles to health will be positively impacted. We have an obligation to provide aged blacks with information about their legal rights as patients, about governmental entitlements, and about procedures for appealing inappropriate hospital discharges.

By including pharmacy in comprehensive health care, (1) the patient's medications can be accurately monitored, especially where several physicians are involved in the care of the patient; (2) the use of medications that may lead to drug interactions can be prevented; and (3) addictive substances can be controlled.

To help elderly black citizens overcome feelings of alienation and suspiciousness of any health care agency, efforts should be made to involve them in the operation of the system, such as appointing them to membership on boards and persuading them to participate in volunteer services. The public is demanding health care systems that encourage the concept of provider and consumer as partners in health care. Most health care professionals acknowledge that the consumer should have greater control over health-related decisions. Such a health care system makes demands of consumers that were previously unheard of and frankly denied the black aged (38).

SUMMARY

A myriad of myths and part-truths prevail about the health attitudes of aged black Americans. The health attitudes of aged blacks reflect complex cultural and socioeconomic conditions. This chapter explored some of the myths about the health-seeking behavior of aged black Americans, the sociocultural determinants of emotional disorders, and issues of health maintenance and prevention.

It was concluded that health care for the ambulatory black aged can best be provided through an accessible neighborhood comprehensive health care system. Because aged blacks often have a multiplicity of medical and social needs, coordinated comprehensive health care decreases the frustrations associated with fragmented health care delivery systems. A particular advantage of providing psychiatric treatment with total health care is that the stigma of mental illness is minimized and, most importantly, physiological and psychological well-being are inseparable.

REFERENCES

1. Study: black surgery rate way below that of whites. *Am Med News* 1986; May 16: 27.
2. McNeinly WJ. Who Pays Health Bills for Uninsured. Raliegh, NC *News and Observer* June 15, 1986: 11A.
3. Fletcher DJ. Wellness. The grand tradition of medicine. *Postgrad Med* 1983; 73:87–92.
4. Sheer VT. Homebound geriatric care. *Am J Psychiat* 1974; 131: 104–105.
5. Lawson WB. Racial and ethnic factors in psychiatric research. *Hosp Comm Psychiat* 1986; 37:44–50.

6. Marcos LR, Cancro R. Pharmacotherapy and Hispanic depressed patients: clinical observations. *Am J Psychotherapy* 1982; 36:305–312.
7. Yamamoto J, Fung D, Lo S, et al. Psychopharmacology and Asian Americans and Pacific Islanders. *Psychopharmacology Bulletin* 1979; 15:29–31.
8. Carter JH. Psychiatry, racism and aging. *J Am Geriatr Soc* 1972; 20:343–346.
9. *Klostermann* v. *Como*, No. 87, New York Court of Appeals, March 27, 1984.
10. Federal court decides in Pl.202 housing claim titled by chronically mentally ill plaintiffs. *Disability Law Reporter* 8 (4).
11. Carter JH. The significance of racism in the mental illness of elderly minorities. In: Manuel RC, ed. *Minority Aging: Social and Sociopsychological Issues*. New York:Greenwood Press; 1982:89–93.
12. Carter JH. Deinstitutionalization of black patients: an apocalypse now. *Hosp Comm Psychiat* 1986; 37:78–79.
13. Medicare backs quick patient release but limits home care, report says. Raleigh, NC *News and Observer* August 17, 1986: 8A.
14. Jackson C. Crisis in our nursing home. *Urban Health—The Journal of Health Care in the Cities* 1975; 4:22–23.
15. Bursten B. Psychiatry and the rhetoric of models. *Amer J Psychiat* 1974; 136:661–666.
16. Fleming TC. Wellness. *Postgrad Med* 1980; 67:19–25.
17. U.S. National Center for Statistics. Hyattesville, MD. Personal Communication.
18. Poindexter HA. Meeting the needs of the older person. *J Nat Med Assoc* 1980; 68:131–134.
19. Comstock GW, Helsing KJ. Symptoms of depression in two communities. *Psycho Med* 1976; 6:551–563.
20. Mollica RF. From asylum to communtity: the threatened disintegration of public psychiatry. *New Eng J Med* 1980; 308:367–372.
21. American Psychiatric Association. *Diagnostic and Statistical Manual of Mental Disorders* (3rd ed.) Washington, DC: Author; 1980.
22. Carter JH. Sociocultural factors in the psychiatric assessment of black patients: a case study. *J Nat Med Assoc* 1983; 75:817–820.
23. American Psychiatric Association. *Diagnostic and Statistical Manual of Mental Disorders* (3rd ed., rev.). Washington, DC: Author; 1987.
24. Gaines A. Durham, NC: Duke University; 1982. Personal Communication.
25. Ewing JA. Recognizing, confronting, and helping the alcoholic. *Am Fam Physician* 1978; 18:107–114.
26. Carter JH, Thornton CI. Integrating an alcoholism program for low-income blacks in a neighborhood health center. *Alcoholism Digest* 1976; 5:6–10.
27. Medicare/Medicaid update. *Physician Financial News* 1986; 4(5):15.
28. Wilentz A. Lending a Helping Hand. *Time* June 2, 1986: 25.
29. Now, a black wealth gap. *Newsweek* July 28, 1986: 22.
30. Lyles MR, Carter JH. Myths and strengths of the black family: a historical and sociological contribution to family therapy. *J Nat Med Assoc* 1982; 74:1119–1123.
31. Carter JH. Psychological aspects of aging: the black aged. *J Nat Med Assoc* 1984; 76:271–275.

32. Poindexter HA. Health problems of older persons. *J Nat Med Assoc* 1980; 72:269–271.
33. Mandell AN. How to poison granny's brain. *Postgrad Med* 1983; 73:37–71.
34. Vitale JJ, Santos IJ. Nutrition and the elderly: the effects of diet on gastrointestinal-related diseases. *Postgrad Med* 1985; 78:93–110.
35. Davis Mostyn J. Society is the patient. *Postgrad Med* 1985; 78:34–35.
36. Delivering mental health services to an ambulatory low-income population. *Hosp and Comm Psychiat* 1977; 28: 846–848.
37. Anderson, L. Preventive maintenance of the gastrointestinal tract. *Postgrad Med* 1986; 80:106–113.
38. Rada R. The health care revolution: from patient to client to consumer. *Psycho Med* 1986; 27:276–279.

15

The Work, Retirement, and Disability of Older Black Americans

Rose C. Gibson

A new type of black retiree is emerging on the retirement scene. Three fairly new social trends—the declining labor-force participation of middle-aged and older blacks, increases in their physical disability, and the increasing availability of disability pay—are creating "the unretired-retired." These are individuals aged 55 and over who are not working but do not call themselves retired (1). This group appears to be the most deprived of the black elderly (2). A review of operational definitions used in the major retirement studies over the past 20 years suggests that because the unretired-retired do not meet traditional retirement criteria (age 65, a clear line between work and nonwork, income primarily from retirement sources, and viewing themselves as retired) they are ironically selected out of this retirement research (3–8). This group would also be excluded from the planning and policy that stem from that research. Reconceptualizing retirement to include the unretired-retired could challenge some of the major past findings and guiding paradigms of retirement research and make it necessary to alter retirement research designs, planning, and policy.

The purpose of this chapter is to summarize the research that examines

I would like to thank Dr. James S. Jackson for the use of the *National Survey of Black Americans* data; Drs. Frank M. Andrews, Jersey Liang, Ralph M. Gibson and Diane Vinokur for their helpful comments on the first draft of this chapter; Cheng Kuo for computer assistance; and Daniel Spengler for editorial assistance.

the effects of several factors on the *decisions* of older blacks to define themselves as retired: an indistinct line between lifetime and current work patterns, a large part of one's income stemming from one's own work, and the availability and attractiveness of the disability role. Before presenting the research, conceptual issues underlying older blacks' choices of work, retirement, and disability roles are briefly discussed. The chapter closes with suggestions for new retirement research and policy in behalf of older black Americans.

CONCEPTUAL ISSUES

Four primary concepts in regard to older blacks underlie the research reported in this chapter: self-defined (subjective) retirement, the constancy of disadvantaged work patterns over the life course, the source of old-age income as a determinant of subjective retirement, and the disability role as a rewarding substitute for the retirement role. These constructs are explicated in this section of the chapter.

Relationships between the Lifetime Work and Retirement Experiences of Older Blacks

Black Americans have disadvantaged work experiences across the life course. They are more likely to have worked in low-status jobs characterized by sporadic work patterns and low earnings (9–18). These handicapping work patterns over a lifetime have negative effects on the economic well-being of blacks as they reach old age (11). Work in old age, in the same low-status jobs, becomes a necessity for many (19). There is, therefore, a continuity of disadvantaged work patterns from youth through old age. It is this "sameness" of sporadic work patterns over the life course that may create for older blacks a certain ambiguity about work and retirement, an ambiguity that, in turn, affects the ways in which blacks define retirement for themselves.

The level and source of income for blacks in old age are also affected by their lifetime work experiences (11). Restriction to jobs characterized by instability, low earnings, and few benefits is directly related to low levels of retirement pension and Social Security benefits. Therefore, the income packages of older blacks compared to other groups contain a greater proportion of money from their own work and nonretirement sources (2, 3, 19, 20). Receiving income from one's work rather than the traditional retirement sources could also create a kind of uncertainty as to whether one is working or retired.

Greater Benefits from Disability than from Retirement

The attractiveness, availability, and appropriateness of roles alternate to retirement may also interfere with blacks' adoption of the retirement role. The identity, role theory, and sick-role theory literature lends some additional insights into reasons blacks might actually prefer the disability to the retirement role (for thorough analyses of role theory, see 21, 22). Theories of role change suggest that individuals select new roles when forced out of an old role, when an old role is no longer appropriate, or when a new role is different or offers greater benefits than the old one (23–26). Translated to work and retirement, changes in either demands or opportunities in the work sphere, or both, could encourage a search for more appropriate self-meanings, such as for the "retiree" role. Blacks, experiencing few changes in their work spheres in old age, would be less likely to search for or take on a new retiree identity. Individuals also select roles from their personal hierarchies that have the highest probabilities of being invoked across situations and of congruence between the expectations of the individual and the expectations of society in regard to the appropriate behaviors of individuals in the role (27). Extrapolated to work and retirement, when the work role is no longer available individuals choose the retirement role if (1) it is the most salient in their hierarchy of roles, (2) it is applicable across a variety of life situations, and (3) the individual and others agree to the behaviors of the retiree role. For older blacks whose work is still contributing to their income and for whom the line between work and retirement is unclear, the retiree role would not have widespread applicability across life circumstances, nor would individual and societal expectations of retirement behavior coincide. Individuals also select new roles over old ones according to the margin of benefits over costs they perceive when comparing the two roles. Extending the theory, blacks would adopt roles alternate to retirement if they perceive the benefits of that role to outweigh the benefits of the retirement role. The disability role is a case in point. Compared to the retirement role the disability role may have greater benefits for the present generation of older blacks. The special payoffs of the disability role for blacks might be explained by "nouveau" sick-role theory. These recent interpretations of sick-role theory suggest that the secondary *economic* gains of illness encourage adoption and maintenance of sick role behavior (28–31). Chirikos and Nestel (31) in fact show that reports of disability are related to economic need. Individuals with lower *expected* future wage rates are more likely than others to say they are work-disabled; and the influence of expected income on self-reported disability is greater for blacks than whites. The study suggests further that for disadvantaged workers the sick role has a better psychological "fit" and greater economic profits than the retirement role. The model seems particularly appropriate for older blacks, whose low levels of retirement benefits might make disability pay greater than retirement pay. The availability of disability pay might indeed be an important factor in blacks' viewing themselves as disabled rather than retired.

Taken together, the work, retirement, and role theory literature suggests that the self-defined retirement of blacks may not be only a function of lifetime and current labor-force experiences and source of income. Rather, the availability, attractiveness, and appropriateness of the disability role, which might have greater social, psychological, and economic benefits than the retirement role, is also a consideration.

Measuring Subjective Retirement

Three studies focus specifically on factors related to subjective retirement. Murray (32) and Irelan and Bell (33), using predominantly white samples from the Retirement History Survey data (RHS), find that individuals call themselves retired if three conditions are met: they are not in the labor force, they are receiving retirement pension income, and they do not perceive themselves as work-disabled. Both studies use a three-level measure of subjective retirement—"not retired at all," "partially retired," and "fully retired." It is interesting to note that the in-between category, "partially retired," is less well predicted from objective measures of retirement than are the extreme categories, "not retired at all" or "fully retired." This suggests that subjective retirement is more effectively conceptualized as an "either–or" decision, adding to the argument that identifying oneself as retired is a matter of role choice. Age is an important predictor only among those who are not working and not receiving pensions. Age then seems to be used in self-defined retirement when other retirement criteria are in conflict. Gender is an important factor. Women and men are different on some factors determining self-definitions of retirement and similar on others. For example, while being in the labor force determines "not retired" for both men and women, the meanings of "partial" and "complete" retirement differ. If a *man* is out of the labor force, regardless of the receipt of Social Security, he calls himself completely retired. But a *woman* out of the labor force also has to be receiving Social Security to call herself completely retired. In other words, women out of the labor force and receiving no Social Security do not think of themselves as retired. This seems related to the fact that a number of these older women in the RHS sample, although not currently living with spouses, might have been lifetime housewives instead of lifetime workers. This gender difference should not exist to the same extent among blacks because black women have always been workers.

The Murray (32) and Irelan/Bell (33) studies taken together suggest that the effects of work patterns, source of income, and perceptions of disability are more accurately measured by conceptualizing subjective retirement as a decision rather than as a continuum. The researchers do not perform separate regressions by race and so do not determine whether work status, source of income, and perceptions of disability have the same relative and collective effects on the subjective retirement of blacks and whites. These studies also consider neither the special effects on subjective retirement of the ambiguity of work and retirement nor the attractiveness of the competing disability role.

This brings us to a discussion of a third study, which focuses exclusively on the subjective retirement of blacks. Jackson and Gibson (2), taking into account the uniqueness of the lifetime work and retirement experiences of blacks, examine the possibility that self-definitions of retirement among elderly blacks are complicated by an indistinct line between work patterns earlier in life and work patterns in old age and by a large part of income stemming from one's own work. They find that those who do not call themselves retired (about 40% of all blacks aged 55 and over) compared to those who do are more likely to (1) never have had a full time job in life, (2) have been lifetime part-time workers, and (3) be working currently from time to time. These unretired-retired black elderly are also more disadvantaged economically and socially than the retired. The unretired-retired are more likely to be poor, be poorly educated, have been lifetime laborers or low-level service workers, and derive a large proportion of their income from their own work. These findings move beyond the Murray (32) and Irelan/Bell (33) findings, suggesting that it is the *continuity* of disadvantaged work across the life course, not just work patterns in old age, that is related to self-views of retirement. Moreover, income from other than retirement sources may be an important contributor to ways in which older blacks define retirement for themselves. The Jackson and Gibson study is descriptive and does not determine the relative and collective effects of work histories, source of income, and the attractiveness of the disability role on subjective retirement *after* controlling for such factors as gender and class.

PRESENT RESEARCH

The research summarized in this chapter, by exploring further the apparent complexity of self-defined retirement for black Americans, extends the research of Murray (32), Irelan/Bell (33) and Jackson/Gibson (2). Specifically, this analysis determines the relative and collective effects of age, gender, an indistinct line between lifetime and current work patterns, a large part of one's income stemming from one's own work, and the availability/attractiveness of the disability role on the *decision* to call oneself retired. A description of the data set used for analysis will be useful at this point.

The National Survey of Black Americans

The NSBA sample is a multistage probability sample of the black population consisting of 2,107 respondents. The sampling design was based on the 1970 census, and each black American residing in an individual household within the continental United States had an equal chance of being selected. The sample design is similar to that of most national surveys but has unique features of primary area selection and stratification to make it responsive to the distribution of the black population. Eligibility for selection into this household sample was based on citizenship and non-institutionalized living quarters within the continental United States. Reflecting the nature of the distribution of the black population, more than half (44) of the 76 primary areas used for final selection of households were located in the southern United States. Two methods of screening were developed to guarantee inclusion of blacks (meeting selection criteria) in both high- and low-density areas (34). The sample had a 69% response rate, and all face-to-face interviewing was conducted in 1979–1980 by black interviewers trained through the Survey Research Center of the University of Michigan's Institute for Social Research.

The questionnaire used in the NSBA was developed especially for use in the black population. Two years of pretesting and refinement preceded actual use in the field. The instrument contained both open- and closed-ended items and took approximately 2 hours and 20 minutes to administer. Although our present concern is restricted to the retirement, work, and demographic sections, the questionnaire also included the broad areas of neighborhood life, health, mental health, family, social support, racial and self-identity, religious experience, and political participation. Thus the data available for analysis in the present research represent a rich, culturally relevant, and carefully collected source of information on the work, disability, and retirement experiences of the black elderly. The multivariate analyses reported here are on the 295 currently nonworking blacks from the NSBA who were aged 55 and over.

METHOD

Measures

The dependent variable is subjective retirement; the predictor variables are age, class, gender, urbanicity (whether lived in urban or rural area), work history, source of income, and subjective disability. Table 15.1 lists the study variables.

TABLE 15.1 Percentages of the Retired and Unretired in Categories of the Eight Study Variables, Blacks 55 Years Old or Older Who Are Not Now Working $N = 295$

Variables	Retired	Unretired
Age		
less than 65 years old	8.2	64.9
65 years old or older	91.8	35.1
Income (per year)		
less than $6,000	66.3	75.7
$6,000 or more	33.7	24.3
Education		
0–8 years of school	59.8	65.8
9 or more years of school	40.2	34.2
Gender		
male	39.1	25.5
female	60.9	77.5
Urbanicity		
urban[a]	73.9	63.1
rural	26.1	36.9
Work history		
did not work all years full-time[b]	57.6	77.5
worked all years full-time	42.4	22.5
Source of income		
work, self (occasional work for money or goods), family, friends	19.6	33.3
Social Security/Supplemental Security,	44.0	40.5
retirement pay, pensions, annuities,	33.2	13.5
other[c]	3.3	12.6
Is disability the main reason not now working?		
yes	14.1	65.8
no	85.9	34.2

Note: Cases with valid data on all study variables only.
[a]Includes both large and small urban areas.
[b]Never worked/worked but never full-time/worked full-time but some years part-time.
[c]Welfare, Aid to Dependent Children, Workmen's Compensation, other disability payments except Social Security and SSI, unemployment insurance, or other governmental sources was first mention.

Class

Income and education are used as social-class indicators. Earlier analyses using linear structural relationships analysis (LISREL) indicate that occupation is not a valid social-class indicator for the present generation of older black Americans. The probable reason is that racial discrimination placed a ceiling on their occupational achievements. The increasing validity of occupational status as a measure of social class among blacks will be, in effect, a gauge of widening occupational opportunities for them.

Subjective Retirement

This is a dichotomous variable because identifying oneself as retired is conceptualized as a role choice and not as a self-categorization into gradations of retirement. Therefore, the main interest is in the *decision* to call oneself retired. To construct the measure, respondents were asked to explain why they were not working. The eight fixed choices were: homemaker, physically disabled, welfare, student, retired, transportation problems, cannot find a job, and do not wish a job. Respondents could check any, all, or none of the responses. The "retired" [N = 184] are those who named "retired" among the reasons; and the "unretired" [N = 111] did not mention "retired" at all. It was therefore possible for a respondent who named retired to also name disabled. There were only 26 respondents in this category. The only difference between the retired and unretired was their subjective labels of retirement.

Work History

This was constructed from a series of retrospective questions about lifetime employment patterns: "Have you ever worked for pay?", "Have you ever had a fulltime job?", and "Were there any years (since age 18) when you did not work full-time for most of the year?" The measure was dichotomized into those who worked all years full-time versus all others; that is, those who never worked, worked but never in a full-time job, worked full-time but some years part-time.

Source of Income

This has four levels because differences in the effects of the various types of income sources on the decision to call oneself retired are of interest. The variable was constructed from the first and second responses to the question, "How are you currently supporting yourself or being supported? Anything else?" The categories are (1) work of self either first or second mention; (2) Social Security and Supplemental Security Income first mention; (3) private retirement pay, pensions, or annuities in either first or second place; and (4) other governmental pay (e.g., welfare, Aid to Dependent Children, Aid to Families with Dependent Children, food stamps). Social Security and SSI were combined for analysis because for those aged 55 to 64 these were mainly disability payments.

Subjective Disability

This is conceptualized as the individual's choice of disability over alternate choices of the *main* reason for not working. The disability variable, then, in addition to measuring perceptions of physical functional health and an inclination to view oneself as disabled rather than retired, is anchored firmly to work. Respondents were given the same checklist as for the retired/not retired measure. Disability, however, had to be in the *priority* position of reasons for not working. As mentioned earlier, few who name disability to the priority position also name retirement among their reasons. The disability variable is dichotomized into disability as or as not the main reason for not working. The important issue in this measure is that given the same nonwork status and the opportunity to say either retired or disabled as the *main* reason, certain individuals chose disabled.

Analysis

Logit regression was selected to avoid the possibility of predicted values falling outside the (0, 1) range. This could occur if ordinary least squares estimation procedures are used with a dichotomous dependent variable (35). In the present analysis, the logit (the logarithm of the odds of identifying oneself as retired) is regressed on demographic, disability, work history, and source of income variables. A useful feature of logit regression is that by undoing the arithmetic of the logarithm, the probability of subjective retirement can be estimated for any black American from his or her lifetime work history, souce of income, and perceived disability. The DREG package of the OSIRIS IV program is used for analysis.

FINDINGS

Corroborating the Jackson and Gibson (2) findings, nearly 40% of blacks aged 55 and over do not view themselves as retired. Not surprisingly, having worked discontinuous types of patterns over the lifetime, viewing oneself as disabled, and receiving income from one's own work and sources other than private retirement pensions, annuities, or assets decrease the odds of identifying oneself as retired. Table 15.1 compares distributions of the retired and unretired on the eight study variables; Table 15.2 compares their income packages; and Table 15.3 presents the logit estimates. Model 1 in Table 15.3 shows the logit estimates before the disability variable is entered into the equation, and Model 2 shows these estimates after disability is entered. The predictive power of the model is increased from .65 to .69 by adding disability. Gender, urbanicity, and social class are not important. Self-defined retirement among blacks, then, is more a matter of patterns of lifetime work experiences, source of current income, and self-views of disability than one of gender or class.

As Table 15.2 shows, Social Security is the major source of income of both the retired and unretired black elderly. The groups differ, however, in important ways: (1) The unretired are less likely than the retired to be

TABLE 15.2 Income Sources of "Nonworking" Retired and Unretired Blacks Aged 55 Years and Older

Sources of 1978 income	Retired (N = 184)	Unretired (N = 111)
Work of self or others alone	4.3	16.2
Work of self or others combined with another source[a]	13.6	17.1
Social Security alone[b]	25.5	15.3
Social Security combined with another source[c]	35.8	16.2
Retirement pay, pensions, or annuities alone	12.0	9.9
Retirement pay, pensions, or annuities combined with another source[d]	2.2	0.0
Savings, investments, or rental property combined with another source[d]	.1	0.0
SSI alone	2.7	7.2
SSI combined with another source[e]	.5	4.5
Welfare, ADC, AFDC, or other governmental pay alone	2.2	8.1
Disability pay other than Social Security/SSI	1.1	4.5
	100.0%	99.0%

Note: Failure to add to 100 due to rounding. Percentage base = the 295 cases with no missing data on the nine study variables.
[a]Social Security; retirement pay, pensions, annuities; Welfare, ADC, AFDC, other governmental.
[b]The Social Security and SSI of the unretired is mainly disability pay, while that of the retired is mainly retirement pay.
[c]Retirement pay, pensions, annuities; SSI; Welfare, ADC, AFDC, or other governmental.
[d]Welfare, ADC, AFDC, or other governmental.
[e]Welfare, ADC, AFDC, or other governmental.

receiving Social Security (31.5% vs. 61.3%). (2) The Social Security payments of the unretired are more likely to be disability payments. (3) The unretired are more likely to be *solely* dependent on work (16.2% vs. 4.3%), welfare (8.1% vs. 2.2%), and other types of disability pay (4.5% vs. 1.1%). (4) The unretired are less likely to receive pay from private retirement pensions or annuities either alone (9.9% vs. 12.0%) or in combination (0.0% vs. 2.2%). (5) Overall, the unretired are more apt to combine nonretirement sources of income. But in spite of dual sources of income, the unretired are still less well-off financially than the retired (about 76% of the unretired have incomes below $6,000, in contrast to 66% of the retired who do [see Table 15.1]). It is interesting to note that Social Security and work of self or spouse, and not welfare or children, are the main sources of income for older blacks. The black elderly do not depend on either children or welfare.

TABLE 15.3 The Probability of Calling Oneself Retired, Blacks 55 Years Old or Older Who Are Not Now Working (Logit Estimates) Models 1 and 2 ($N = 295$)

	Model 1	Model 2	
Predictive/Power			
Variables	.65	.69	
Constant	.71	.85	
Age			
less than 65 years old	−2.00	−2.30	(.32)*
65 years old or older	.83	.95	(.13)*
Income (per year)			
less than $6,000	− .25	− .14	(.14)
$6,000 or more	.58	.34	(.33)
Education			
0–8 years of school	− .15	− .19	(.16)
9 or more years of school	.25	.32	(.26)
Gender			
male	.22	.29	(.29)
female	− .11	− .14	(.14)
Urbanicity			
urban[a]	.13	.17	(.12)
rural	− .30	− .39	(.27)
Work History			
did not work all years full–time[b]	− .32	− .36	(.15)*
worked all years full–time	.58	.66	(.27)*
Source of income			
family, friends, self (occasional work for money or goods)	− .31	.24	(.30)
Social Security/Supplemental Security,	− .30	− .26	(.23)
retirement pay, pensions, annuities,	.89	.71	(.39)
other[c]	− .46	− .27	(.67)
Is disability the main reason not now working?			
yes	.00	−1.47	(.25)*
no	.00	.73	(.12)*

Note: The first figure is the estimated coefficient. The asymptotic standard error (for Model 2) is reported in parentheses.
[a]Includes both large and small urban areas.
[b]Never worked/worked but never full-time/worked full-time but some years part-time.
[c]Welfare, Aid to Dependent Children, Workmen's Compensation, other disability payments except Social Security and SSI, unemployment insurance, or other governmental sources was first mention.
*Significant at p ≤ .05.

Age

Age is the most important predictor of subjective retirement, which is not surprising in and of itself. What seems to be the case, however, is that those not characterized by the more traditional markers of retirement (i.e., clearly defined work cessation and income from retirement pensions) are using chronological age as the single marker. As mentioned earlier, Murray (32) also found that respondents use age in defining retirement for themselves when other retirement criteria are less clearcut.

Subjective Disability

This is the second most important predictor. Those who view themselves as disabled are not likely to also view themselves as retired. Focusing specifically on the group who identify themselves as disabled, distinctions between two subgroups of the disabled fit rather nicely into sick-role theory. The disabled-unretired (those who call themselves disabled but not retired) are more economically and psychologically needy than are the disabled-retired (those who call themselves both disabled *and* retired). The disabled-unretired are more likely to feel powerless over their own fate, to feel less of a sense of life accomplishment, to be less satisfied with life and less happy. Following sick-role theory, (1) these individuals might be adopting the disability role to meet some special psychological needs, (2) the role might serve to relieve them of responsibilities for themselves, and (3) the role might provide an excuse for perceived life failures. It is also possible, of course, that the unretired-disabled are simply more debilitated than the retired-disabled. This could mean there is really no option in defining oneself as disabled or retired; that is, the disability role is the only role open to them. This, however, is not the case. The unretired-disabled report poorer health stataus, but they are no more limited by their health than are the retired-disabled. The disability role might also have larger financial payoffs for the disabled-unretired because they are more likely to have disability pay as a *single* source of income—they are more dependent on disability pay. Thus self-defined disability seems more appropriate and seems to have larger economic, social, and psychological payoffs for the disabled-unretired than for the disabled-retired.

Work History

Work history is the third most important predictor of subjective retirement. Quite expectedly, those who did not work all years full-time over the life course are less likely than others to identify themselves as retired. The unretired are more likely than the retired to have worked sporadically over the lifetime and also to be currently working between 11 and 19 hours per week (the part-time workers were included in this analysis). This special group of unretired-disabled with a constancy of sporadic work from youth well into old age may in fact be the group to which Jackson (36) refers when she states that "black Americans die from rather than retire from the work force" (p. 75). The retired, in contrast, are more likely to have worked continuously over the lifetime and not to be currently working at all or to be working very little (between 1 and 10 hours per week). Thus there is a certain *sameness* of part-time work along the life course for the unretireds and more of a *decrease* in the amount of time spent in work among those who identify themselves as retired. The work history findings are curious because the oldest age cohort of elderly (aged 65 and over) and the poorly educated are *more* likely than the youngest elderly cohort (aged 55 to 64) and those with more education to have worked full-time all years.

Source of Income

Quite expectedly, those receiving private retirement pay, pensions, or annuities are more inclined than those relying on their own work, Supplemental Security Income, Social Security, or other governmental sources to call themselves retired. Source of income, however, is not a *significant* predictor of subjective retirement in its present four-category form; but it becomes significant when dichotomized into private retirement pay, pensions, and annuities versus all other sources. The weak effect of source of income on subjective retirement is therefore more statistical than substantive. The four-level variable findings are reported in order to demonstrate the similarity of effects of the three categories of income source other than retirement pensions on the log odds of identifying oneself as retired. The three nonprivate retirement income categories, in fact, have a common underlying factor—*feeling* the necessity to work in order to supplement inadequate incomes. Individuals supported mainly or in part by the work of self, family, or friends, by Social Security, by Supplemental Security Income, or by welfare income feel similarly compelled to work intermittently, while those receiving private retirement pensions, investments, or annuities (better off financially) feel less of a compulsion to work. The fact that the retirement pension group has average higher family incomes than do those in the other three groups and is the likeliest of the groups to say they do not wish to work more also lends support to the argument that there are fewer compulsions to work among those receiving private retirement pensions. The Harris (37) study also found those receiving pension benefits less likely than those not receiving benefits to say they wish to work (40% vs. 52%). Since whites predominate in the Harris sample, this might be a class rather than a race phenomenon. A related finding is that of Jackson and Gibson (2), who found lower morale among black elderly who are *in* the labor force than among those who are *out* and receiving private retirement pensions. The lower morale of the workers suggests that work is not by choice. The point to emphasize is that not only might the *source* of income be at issue with respect to calling oneself retired, but the *feeling* of being compelled to work, as well. Interpreted within our framework,

work in old age among black Americans without private retirement pensions is more economic necessity than choice, and those black elderly who feel the compulsion to work see less clearly the line between work and nonwork. They tend less, therefore, to define themselves as retired.

Gender

Gender is not related significantly to subjective retirement. This lack of importance of gender in subjective retirement is contrary to the findings of Murray (32) and Irelan/Bell (33), both of whom find significant gender differences in the predictors of subjective retirement. These contrasting findings suggest a race difference in the effects of gender on self-defined retirement.

Selected Cases of Subjective Retirement

It is instructive to note that, using the fitted Model 2 in Table 15.3, the logit of a black male who is 65 years old or older, who did not work full-time all years (since age 18), whose income is primarily from work of self, family, or friends, and who names physical disability as a reason for not now working is computed to be .02 [Log $P(Y=1)/P(Y=0) = .85 + .29 + .95 - .36 - .24 - 1.47$]. Undoing the arithmetic of the logarithmic transformation, the probability of identifying himself as retired (holding constant income, education, and urbanicity) is .50, a chance event (see Table 15.4). In contrast, the probability of calling himself retired of a black male aged 65 or over, who worked full-time all years, whose income is mainly from retirement pay, and who does not perceive himself work-disabled is .98, an almost certain event. The probabilities for their black female counterparts are .40 and .98, respectively. These small differences in the probabilities of subjective retirement dramatize further the similarity of black men and women on the issue of self-definitions of retirement. Gender alone does not change appreciably the probability of calling oneself retired among black Americans. Table 15.4 contains probabilities of subjective retirement in selected other cases.

DISCUSSION

The research summarized in this chapter indicates that the unretired-retired status among black Americans is brought about by (1) a combination of an indistinct line between work in youth and work in old age, (2) the receipt of one's income from other than private retirement pension sources, (3) a

TABLE 15.4 Estimated Probabilities of Calling Oneself Retired. Selected Cases of Blacks Aged 55 and Older

Case	Probability of calling oneself retired[a]	Sex	Age	Lifetime work history[b]	Source of income	Disabled
1	.50	male	>65	did not work all years full-time	work[c]	yes
2	.98	male	>65	worked all years full-time	retirement pay[d]	no
3	.40	female	>65	did not work all years full-time	work	yes
4	.98	female	>65	worked all years full-time	retirement pay	no
5	.92	male	>65	did not work all years full-time	retirement pay	—
6	.92	male	>65	worked all years full-time	work	—
7	.82	male	>65	did not work all years full-time	work	—
8	.97	male	>65	worked all years full-time	retirement pay	—

Note: Probabilities were calculated using the estimated coefficients reported in Table 15.3, equation 2.
[a]Considering only the variables included in the calculations.
[b]Never worked/worked but never full-time/worked full-time but some years part-time.
[c]Of family, friends, or self (occasional work for money or goods).
[d]Retirement pay, pensions, annuities.

318

realization that one must work from time to time well into old age, and (4) the greater benefits of identifying oneself as disabled over retired.

Is There a Need to Revise Definitions of Retirement?

These findings have to do not only with the inappropriateness of the prevailing procedural definitions of retirement for a large segment of older blacks, but with the penalizing and damaging aspects of these definitions as well. They allow needy groups of the black elderly to drop through the cracks in the major retirement research today. These are individuals (1) who have never had a regular job in life, (2) who are without pension benefits, (3) for whom there is no clear cessation of work, and (4) who do not choose to identify themselves as retired. Indeed, the very definitions of retirement need rethinking if this most disadvantaged group of the black elderly is to be included in future retirement research, planning, and policy. Expanding current definitions of retirement to include the unretired-retired black elderly could change some of the major past findings of research, which suggest that blacks and whites are similar in retirement experiences. Palmore, Fillenbaum, and George (4), in fact, demonstrate that alternate definitions of retirement change the findings of retirement research. Some of the guiding paradigms of retirement research could be called seriously into question.

How Temporary is the Phenomenon of the Unretired-Retired?

Particularly disturbing findings are that older cohorts, in spite of being more poorly educated, are better off than younger cohorts of black elderly in regard to more advantaged and continuous types of lifetime work patterns. These findings suggest that education did not substantially improve employment patterns among these older black Americans. Gordon, Hamilton, and Tipps (13) and Jones (38) show, in fact, that educational levels of attainment operate in negative ways on the continuity of employment for blacks. This might also mean that successive cohorts of older blacks, even though better educated, will be less and less likely to have worked full-time over the life course. It is cause for great concern that the high unemployment rates among today's black teenagers may exacerbate the problem. If no measures are taken to ameliorate the situation, millions of young blacks will be even more disadvantaged when they reach old age than the present cohort of older blacks in regard to continuous labor-force participation. The group of unretired-retired black elderly could increase substantially in the future.

This phenomenon of an increasing group of subjectively unretired blacks may be an omen for other groups of older Americans. The fact that negative social phenomena occur first in the black community and then move on to become manifest in white America (e.g., drug abuse and the high incidence of out-of-wedlock births) can be viewed as precedents (39). If these are taken as a pattern, we might even speculate that the changes in work and retirement patterns observed among blacks are a kind of forewarning of occurrences in the society at large. As work decreases for all Americans (as it is surely doing), the confusion over retirement status will increase and retirement will need eventual redefining not only for blacks but for other groups as well. The ambiguity of work and retirement will not be exclusively a black problem.

Are New Retirement Income Policies Needed?

It is unsettling to realize that when the proposed age-of-eligibility changes take place under Social Security, there will be an even longer wait for the unretired-retired than already exists between the end of their work lives and the beginning of benefits. Raising the age of eligibility also means that increasing numbers of black males simply will not live long enough to collect their Social Security benefits. In view of the extreme economic neediness of the unretired-retired, the question becomes whether they should be identified as retired, although they do not meet the traditional criteria, simply for the purpose of receiving some type of retirement benefits. The issue becomes doubly important when it is realized that this special group of black elderly may never work systematically or beneficially again.

Is Gender Less Important among Older Black than Older White Americans?

Gender is not important in the subjective retirement of black Americans. This is contrary to much of the retirement research on the majority population, in which there tend to be clear effects of gender. The striking idea here is that black men and women in the present elderly cohort, unlike their white counterparts, are remarkably alike in critical aspects of work that affect self-definitions of retirement. Both black men and women were lifetime workers with similarly discontinuous work patterns. Extensive gender analyses have been conducted on issues of work, disability, and retirement and reported elsewhere (40). The highlights of these findings follow:

1. The failure to identify oneself as retired is not a matter of "traditional" gender differences in work histories, source of income in old age, and disability reporting.
2. While women are slightly less likely to have had full-time jobs over the life course, those who did were as likely as the men to have worked sporadically.

3. Older black men and women are not only similar in work and retirement, but in other social and psychological characteristics as well. In this way they may differ from their white counterparts, among whom gender is more of a discriminating factor.

These findings imply that extrapolating white gender differences in retirement experiences to blacks will obscure important similarities of the retirement experiences of black men and women and hide important countervailing trends between blacks and whites.

Do Black Americans Age Earlier Socially?

These retirement findings can be placed in the larger context of critical life events, which generally occur earlier for blacks (e.g., birth of first child, onset of disability, loss of a spouse, and death). The differential timing of these events suggests an earlier social aging for blacks. Retirement should perhaps now be added to this list of life events that occur earlier for blacks. Placing these findings within that larger framework raises a fundamental issue. If black Americans age earlier socially than the general population, are age-based policies tied to the life course and life experiences of the majority population generally inappropriate for them? The issue is critical to the extent that benefits are provided too late in lifespans that are truncated by high death rates at midlife, or too late in work lives that are shortened by disability and early labor-force withdrawal.

Modeling Subjective Retirement for Black Americans

The model of the factors that contribute most significantly to the formation of the new type of black retiree, the unretired-retired, should be tested across national samples to see if blacks, other minorities, and whites differ in the factors that influence perceptions of retirement. Is this a class or race phenomenon? The model should also be tested with longitudinal data to determine the special effects of social change and civil rights legislation on these meanings of retirement for black Americans and to determine the causal ordering of disability and nonwork. Does disability keep a large number of older blacks from working, or does disability legitimate nonwork? The relationships among source of income, perceptions of disability, work history, and subjective retirement (involving individuals' choices) undoubtedly form a more complex social-psychological model than presented in this research. Excluded variables might be such cognitive-motivational and personality factors as (1) ways in which individuals view their world, (2) the values they have and perceive society as having about retirement, (3) external barriers (real and perceived) to carrying out a full retirement role, and (4) various other psychological costs and benefits of the retirement over the disability role. Certainly these variables would affect self-definitions of retirement directly. They would also act in intervening and mediating capacities and enter into reciprocal relationships with subjective retirement and with each other. Moreover, subjective retirement as a latent construct would be affected by other latent constructs. It becomes important, therefore, to determine the structural linkages among subjective retirement, feelings of the compulsion to work, the ambiguity of work and retirement, subjective disability, and cognitive-motivational factors. What is the process that operates in the work, disability, and retirement of black Americans? New research on the meanings of retirement for older blacks should expand the models to incorporate these latent constructs. This research should, in addition, investigate race differences in the validity of the indicators with which these constructs are measured. Carefully formulated retirement research and the policy that stems from that research will then be more effective in enhancing the lives of *all* the elderly in our society.

REFERENCES

1. Gibson RC. Blacks in an aging society. *Daedalus* 1986; *115*(1):349–371.
2. Jackson JS, Gibson RC. Work and retirement among the black elderly. In: Blau Z, ed. *Current Perspectives on Aging and the Life Cycle* (Vol. 1). New York: JAI Press; 1985:193–222.
3. Parnes H, Nestel G. The retirement experience. In: Parnes H, ed. *Work and Retirement: A National Longitudinal Study of Men.* Cambridge, MA: MIT Press; 1981.
4. Palmore EB, Fillenbaum GG, George LK. Consequences of retirement. *Journal of Gerontology* 1984; *39*(1): 109–116.
5. Morgan JN. Retirement in prospect and retrospect. In: Duncan G, Morgan J, eds. *Five Thousand American Families—Patterns of Economic Progress* (Vol. 8). Ann Arbor: Institute for Social Research, The University of Michigan; 1980.
6. Atchley RC. *The Social Forces in Later Life: An Introduction to Social Gerontology* (2nd ed.). Belmont, CA: Wadsworth; 1980:139.
7. Streib G, Schneider G. *Retirement in American Society.* Ithaca, NY: Cornell University Press; 1971.
8. Fillenbaum G, George L, Palmore E. Determinants and consequences of retirement among men of different races and economic levels. *Journal of Gerontology* 1985; 40(1):85–94.
9. Bureau of the Census. *The Social and Economic Status of the Black Population* (Current Population Reports, Special Studies P-23, No. 80). 1980.
10. Munnell AH. The economic experience of blacks: 1964–1974. *New England Economic Review* 1978;January/February: 5–18.
11. Abbott J. Work experience and earnings of middle-aged black and white men, 1965–1971. *Social Security Bulletin* 1980; 43(12):16–34.

12. Corcoran M, Duncan GJ. A sumary of part 1 findings. In: Duncan GJ, Morgan JN, eds. *Five Thousand American Families* (Vol. 6). Ann Arbor: Institute for Social Research, The University of Michigan; 1978:3–46.

13. Gordon HA, Hamilton CA, Tipps HC. *Unemployment and Underemployment Among Blacks, Hispanics, and Women* (Clearinghouse Publication No. 74). Washington, DC: U.S. Government Printing Office.

14. Anderson BE, Cottingham DH. The elusive quest for economic equality. *Daedalus* 1981;110(2):257–274.

15. Hill MS. Trends in the economic situation of U.S. families and children: 1970–1980. Paper presented at the Conference on Families and the Economy, Washington, DC: Jan 1982.

16. Montagna PD. [1978]. *Occupations and Society: Toward a Sociology of the Labor Market.* New York: Wiley;1978.

17. Cain GG. The challenge of segmented labor market theories to orthodox theory: a survey. *Journal of Economic Literature* 1976; 14: 1215–1257.

18. Gibson RC. Work patterns of older black female heads of household. *Journal of Minority Aging* 1983; 2(2):1–16.

19. Abbott J. Socioeconomic characteristics of the elderly: some black/white differences. *Social Security Bulletin* 1970;40: 16–42.

20. Gibson RC. Blacks at middle and late life: resources and coping. *The Annals of the American Academy of Political and Social Science* 1982; 464: 79–90.

21. Biddle B, Thomas E, eds. *Role Theory: Concepts and research.* New York: Wiley; 1966.

22. Sarbin T, Allen V. Role theory. In: Lindzey G, Aronson E, eds. *Handbook of Social Psychology* (2nd ed.) (Vol. 1). Reading, MA: Addison-Wesley; 1968:488–567.

23. James W. *The Principles of Psychology.* New York: Dover; 1950(original published 1910).

24. Phillips D. Self-reliance and the inclination to adopt the sick role. *Social Forces* 1965; 43:555–563.

25. Thurlow HJ. Illness in relation to life situation and sick role tendency. *Journal of Psychosomatic Research* 1971; 15: 73–88.

26. Ellison DL. Work, retirement and the sick role. *The Gerontologist* 1968; 8: 189–192.

27. Stryker S. Identity salience and role performance: the relevance of symbolic interaction theory for family research. *Journal of Marriage and the Family* 1968; 30: 558–562.

28. Lamb HR, Rogawski AS. Supplemental security income and the sick role. *American Journal of Psychiatry* 1978; 135: 1221–1224.

29. Ludwig A. The disabled society? *American Journal of Psychotherapy* 1981; 35 (1): 5–15.

30. Prince E. Welfare status, illness and subjective health definition. *American Journal of Public Health* 1978; 68:865–871.

31. Chirikos T, Nestel G. Economic aspects of self-reported work disability. Columbus, OH: Center for Human Resource Research, Ohio State University; 1983.

32. Murray J. Subjective retirement. Social Security Bulletin 1979; 42(11):20–25, 43.
33. Irelan LM, Bell DB. Understanding subjectively defined retirement: a pilot analysis. The Gerontologist 1972; 12:354–356.
34. Jackson JS, Hatchett SJ. Intergenerational research: methodological considerations. In: Datan N, Green AL, Reese HW, eds. Intergenerational Networks: Families in Context. Hillsdale, NJ: Erlbaum; 1985.
35. Hanushek E, Jackson J. Statistical Methods for Social Scientists. New York: Academic Press; 1977.
36. Jackson JJ. Minorities and Aging. Belmont, CA: Wadsworth; 1980.
37. Harris LH, and Associates. The Myth and Reality of Aging in America. Washington, DC: National Council on the Aging; 1979.
38. Jones BA. The contribution of black women to the incomes of black families: an analysis of the labor force. Ann Arbor: The University of Michigan; 1973. (Unpublished doctoral dissertation.)
39. Gibson RC. Blacks in an Aging Society. New York: Carnegie Corporation; 1986.
40. Gibson RC. Reconceptualizing retirement for black Americans. The Gerontologist 1987; 27:691–698.

PART V
Methodological Issues in
Research on
Older Black Adults

16

Survey Research on Aging Black Populations

James S. Jackson

Methodological problems in survey research on aging black populations have not been the topic of previous rigorous investigation (1). Including informal questionnaire studies conducted on conveniently available local samples, survey-research methods are probably the most commonly used data-collection techniques on black adults in the social sciences, particularly in certain disciplines (1–4). The survey-research process, however, is susceptible to several potential errors (5, 6). These errors are magnified by aging, cultural, and cohort factors, both between and within different racial groups (7–9). The extensive use of survey-research procedures (9–10) on black and other racial minorities (1, 11) and the capability of survey methods to generate large amounts of scientific and policy-relevant data make them an important methodological area of investigation.

The purpose of this chapter is to review possible sources of error in planning and conducting survey research on aging black population groups. The material reviewed here is intended to sensitize researchers to problems that can be addressed in the design, execution, analysis, and interpretation stages of sample surveys that include elderly black respondents.

This chapter was written while the author was a Ford Foundation Senior Postdoctoral Fellow at the Groupe D'Études Et Recherches Sur La Science, Ecole Des Hautes En Sciences Sociales, Paris, France.

SURVEY RESEARCH METHODS

Many definitions of the sample survey exist. In practice a sample survey can be defined as "a method of gathering information from a number of individuals, a sample, in order to learn something about the larger population from which the sample has been drawn" (12). Population probability sampling, generalization to a large population of interest from a smaller sample of elements drawn from that population in a systematic manner, distinguishes the modern sample survey from other modes of data collection in the social sciences (13–16).

Survey research methods do not differ in intent from any other data-collection procedure in the physical, natural, behavioral, or social sciences. The only differences arise in the nature of the degree of control that can be exerted over the situation and the extent of causality that can be assumed. The survey researcher is concerned with the same fundamental processes as in any other scientific endeavor; that is, collection of rigorous data (question responses) in response to carefully presented environmental manipulations (questions) that can be unambiguously replicated.

In summary, elements of the rigorous sample survey include (1) a known population; (2) a sample drawn in a systematic and statistically appropriate manner; (3) a well-designed, rigorous questionnaire that is administered; (4) well-trained, competent interviewers (or self-administered); (5) responses to items that are coded in a standard and replicable manner; and (6) analyses and interpretations of the data that are conducted appropriately, with sensitivity to nuances of the population and the topic under investigation.

SURVEY RESEARCH ON AGING BLACKS

Insufficient attention to the systematic nature of survey research is evident in studies of black human development and aging (1). Poor samples and insensitivity to differences among subgroups characterize much of the research to date. National samples of black elderly have been small and often nonrepresentative of black populations. In smaller questionnaire studies, the basis for much of the information on black adults and the elderly, all the procedures are usually violated, including lack of defined populations, nonsystematic samples, poorly constructed stimulus materials, conceptual and coding difficulties, and problems with analysis and interpretation. These problems in the misapplication of survey-research procedures make the interpretation of existing data regarding race and age extremely difficult.

Herzog and Rodgers (16) have conducted the most systematic and detailed methodological work on older persons. Much of the material reviewed in this chapter comes from their ongoing program of research. Herzog and Rodgers (16) reported few age differences. Overall, their secondary analyses of existing data suggested that older, in comparison to younger, respondents (1) have higher nonresponse, particularly in telephone sampling; (2) tend to give more "don't know" responses; (3) tend to be less productive than younger respondents in open-ended questions; (4) use stereotypic response styles, yielding more measurement and random error; and (5) are affected more by interviewers' behaviors. Herzog and Rodgers (16) were hampered in their methodological investigation of race effects for many of the same reasons that will be noted here, including small sample sizes of blacks and the lack of attention to race and cultural differences when the surveys were originally completed.

The problems that confront social scientists in conducting valid research on aging black populations have not received the same scrutiny as provided by Herzog and Rogers (16) for the general elderly population. Thus, this chapter draws heavily on my own survey research experiences in conducting the National Survey of Black Americans (NSBA) (4), the Three Generation Family Study (TGFS) (17), and the National Black Election Study (NBES) (18). The foci of these national surveys were largely nonmethodological. Because of the paucity of previous research on black populations, however, many methodological problems were encountered and addressed during the course of these studies.

In the next section of this chapter race and cultural factors in survey-research methodology are reviewed. The subsequent section discusses potential sources of errors in sample surveys, followed by a section summarizing approaches to these sources of error developed in recent national surveys of black Americans. The primary sources of error include (1) sampling errors; (2) errors related to nonresponse; (3) errors related to task factors; (4) errors related to interviewer factors; and (5) errors related to respondent factors. The final section presents a general summary, indicating the need for future methodological research on aging black populations.

RACE AND CULTURAL FACTORS IN SURVEY RESEARCH METHODS

Research approaches to the study of black human development and aging would be enhanced by a culturally pluralistic perspective (4, 19–25). The differentiation among black subgroups is assumed to contribute sufficient variability in the survey process to warrent attention. This perspective has been noticeably absent from the research literature on aging and human development (1, 9, 26). Some studies, however, suggest that black Americans may experience a very different process of development and aging within this society (1, 8, 19, 23, 27, 28). McLoyd and Randolph (28), in their review of the developmental psychology literature, suggested the importance of studying variation among blacks:

> The theoretical importance of studying intragroup variation in minority groups is illustrated convincingly by research that indicates that differences within certain minority groups in, for example, achievement are accounted for by variables that are different from those that explain between-group differences. (p. 81)

One helpful orientation for survey research methodologists' study of black aging is a cross-national or cross-cultural research framework (20, 21, 25). Jackson's (8) recent review made a related argument, suggesting that the scientific study of aging should be conducted within an "ethnogerontology model." Martin (22) made a similar observation in her critique of comparisons of subgroups in national survey studies. Levine (23) and Kraus (29) both suggested that variability within race and sex are important sources of information that are often "controlled away" in aging research (26).

Word (30) demonstrated that modified cross-cultural research techniques were effective in eliciting accurate responding from black Americans. Our own work (4) has also revealed that consideration of cross-cultural methodological issues (21, 31) can contribute a great deal to improving the quality of research and the accuracy of responding in surveys of blacks (4). Finifter (25) labeled this general orientation to research on race and ethnicity "agnostic": it seeks to determine the existence of cross-cultural differences without making errors of a Type I (specifist) or Type II (universalist) nature.

Levine (23) proposed that characteristics such as race are more than mere sources of error but are essential, substantive aspects of aging and human development:

> Gender, socioeconomic class, and ethnicity/race are more than sociological characteristics of the population of older people. . . . They afford different life experiences and condition different psychological realities that cannot be disregarded. Furthermore, any paradigm, that singles out one set of life experiences and its concomitant psychological reality as normative is unethical. It can only lead to inaccurate assessment of, and inappropriate conclusions about, the preferred life-styles, abilities, and needs of older adults. (p. 138)

Recognition of the need for a cross-cultural perspective in aging is increasing (8, 20, 32, 33). Prior research, however, has not consid-

ered race and class within national boundaries as deserving similar treatment as variables in cross-national research (14). Yet ample empirical
evidence exists suggesting that black Americans respond differentially than
whites to stimuli and research situations and that these differences might be
best construed within a cross-cultural framework (4, 28). For example,
previous research on language has indicated that blacks have a well-
developed language form that is distinctly different from that of white
Americans (34, for example). Obviously, in such a highly language-
dependent methodology as survey research, race-related language differences will be magnified. This is even more true for older cohorts of blacks
born or reared in the South, who possess distinctive language patterns in
comparison to whites and other black Americans. Similarly, a great deal of
research also points to cultural differences between blacks and whites in
style (35) and expression (both behavioral and verbal) that can affect
responding in an interview situation (36). Such style differences are heavily
influenced by the nature of the life experiences of older blacks (37).

Some survey researchers (38, for example) have suggested that value
differences among cultural groups can greatly influence the responses to
standard survey questions. Martin (22), for example, quoted the following:

> Some sociologists have rejected surveys as an appropriate tool for the analysis
> of sub-cultures, in part because surveys rely upon "publicly expressed value
> statements" and tend to overlook elements that are particularly distinctive
> about culture—customs, behaviors, shared understandings, and artifacts. [Fine
> & Kleinman, 1978, cited in 22, p. 548]

Survey research methodology undoubtedly can be used to study different
cultural and racial groups, but not without the appropriate consideration of
value, custom, and cultural variations (4, 8, 23, 25). Labouvie (39), in a
general critique of group comparisons, stated that:

> Studies of human development and aging need to consider the possibility that a
> given measure may apply to different concepts in different age/cohort pop-
> ulations and/or that formally different measures may be required to tap the
> same concept across various groups. (p. 483)

In our own work (4) we have suggested that the emphasis on measurement equivalence among Western-oriented social sciences has come at the
expense of masking legitimate differences among racial groups. If recognized and systematically understood, such differences could be operationalized and empirically investigated (1, 4, 18, 23, 25, 39).

SOURCES OF RESPONSE ERRORS
IN SURVEY RESEARCH METHODS

The survey research process contains several distinct structural and process components. These include the formulation and nature of the research objectives, population and samples, concepts and questions, administration mode (face-to-face, telephone, mail, mixed), editing/coding, and data processing, analysis, and interpretation (14, 40, 41). The potential for error resides in each of these different aspects of the survey process. It is this error, often referred to as total response error, that concerns all survey researchers and is the source of inaccuracy and invalidity in survey results (41).

> The conclusions we reach, may be subject to serious errors due to faults in the method of measurement or observation. These response errors may arise from the questionnaire, from the execution of the fieldwork or from the nature of the data collection process. The form, extent, sources and effects of these errors are the concern not only of survey design but also of survey analysis. (41, p. 183)

Bradburn (6) and his colleagues (5) have contributed a great deal to our knowledge in their conceptualization of sources of error in the total survey situation. In their model, errors in surveys can and do arise in two fundamental manners—errors in sampling and nonresponse and errors in other factors endemic to the survey interview process. Both sources of error are of central importance in the study of human development and aging among the black elderly.

Errors of sampling and nonresponse have long been thought to affect primarily estimates of population values (6, 14). Recent work, however, suggests that these types of errors have significant effects in the analysis and interpretation of data (42, 43). Sampling and nonresponse effects have received the greatest attention in the literature (14, 44–47), and modern approaches to sampling address substantially these overall statistical and methodological problems in designing and executing probability samples of known populations. Less thoroughly treated have been the problems of sampling rare populations, such as the elderly or the black elderly, which present special difficulties of distribution and identification (17, 47, 48).

The second group of errors has also received a considerable amount of attention, although not necessarily focused on the particular problems of blacks or the elderly. Research in this area has concentrated on issues of concepts and questions (e.g. wording and context), administration mode (face-to-face, telephone, etc), editing and coding, and data processing and analysis and interpretation. From a role perspective (5, 45) nonsampling errors can be construed as difficulties having to do with the nature of the task as well as the characteristics and interactions of respondent and interviewer. In the next section each of these potential sources of error is briefly reviewed and examples of approaches to these problems in recent national surveys of aging black populations are presented (1, 4, 17).

APPROACHES TO RESPONSE ERRORS IN SURVEY RESEARCH ON AGING BLACK POPULATIONS

Sampling and Nonresponse Errors

Sampling Errors

One of the major problems in previous research has been the failure to generate adequate-sized samples of black elderly in social science research. Although there have been some notable exceptions (49, 50, for example), knowledge about the black elderly has come either from small subsamples of large national studies or from small, haphazardly obtained samples of conveniently available respondents.

Over the last few years renewed efforts have been devoted to examining the nature of and methods for sampling rare populations (47). Historically, sampling minorities and blacks has been done either haphazardly or conducted under assumptions only appropriate for general population sampling. Among the more rigorous sampling approaches have been those employed by large survey centers. One technique has been to include blacks and other rare population groups in the full sample as they are distributed in the population. In even relatively large sample surveys of 1,500 respondents, blacks constitute only about 139 of the completed sample (assuming no differences in nonresponse rates by subgroups) (48). Samples of this size are not sufficient for the type of subgroup multivariate procedures needed to analyze complex social science phenomena. This approach has undoubtedly contributed to the lack of undifferentiated racial hypotheses and conceptualizations that are common in the literature (1, 26). Because the black population is not distributed as the general population, the sampling characteristics of these small subsamples of blacks are not known. The subsamples of aged blacks within these small samples do not even permit the most basic types of analyses. While this problem has long been thought largely to affect problems of external validity or generalizability, recent work suggests that biased samples have important influences on the nature of observed relationships in multivariate analyses (17, 42, 43).

Although most of the methodological work in this area has been done on face-to-face surveys, some recent work suggests that the problems may be even more exaggerated in telephone sampling and interviewing (16, 48, 51). Because the black population has a significantly lower rate of home telephone ownership (52), particularly in poorer households, obtaining national and regional probability samples of black households may be difficult using standard procedures. In their review of sampling issues, Gibson and Herzog (48) suggested that major approaches to the probability sampling of the black elderly have not addressed a combination of substantive and cost-effectiveness problems. Their telephone approach points to a major developing problem in the telephone sampling of blacks and the black elderly. Since the telephone has become the predominant mode of data collection in survey research (15), the development and utilization of appropriate and valid procedures presents a serious problem for future studies of black adult and aging populations.

A common method developed to address problems of small subgroup samples has been to oversample blacks in areas of their high geographical concentration as a supplement to general population sampling (53). Although resulting in a saving of cost and effort, this type of approach does not address the issue in black populations of, for example, their differential distribution from that of the general population. Thus this supplemental sampling process has not permitted a complete and full representation of blacks in geographical areas of interest. An examination of previous national surveys that had utilized large supplemental samples of blacks revealed unacceptably large clustering effects for black subsamples when blacks were oversampled from areas of high geographical concentration (18). The diversity that exists in the black community has not been sampled effectively using this procedure because of the tendency of geographically proximate individuals to share socioeconomic and attitudinal characteristics. This supplemental approach to sampling becomes even more problematic when the intent is to sample a rarer subgroup, such as the black elderly.

In response to problems of geographical distribution and clustering in national area surveys, Jackson, Tucker, and Bowman (4) proposed two procedures, the Wide Area Screening Procedure (WASP) and the Standard Listing and Screening Procedure (SLASP), designed to screen for blacks in both low-density and high-density black areas, respectively, in face-to-face surveys. These procedures are explained in detail in recent chapters (1, 17, 18, 54). These methodological innovations generate adequate-sized and representative samples of the black population at reduced costs. In addition, multiplicity sampling techniques for generating probability samples of older blacks and families, for example the Family Network Sampling Procedure (FNSP), have also been developed (17). This FNSP provides a methodology for obtaining new samples of older black adults from traditional cross-section samples.

Gibson and Herzog (48) proposed a variant of the FNSP for telephone sampling, Rare Element Telephone Screening (RETS). Additionally, a new disproportionate sampling scheme has been developed that permits the generation of random digit dial black telephone samples based upon the geographical distribution of black households (1). An analysis of the outcome of this method used in the 1984 National Black Election Study (55) shows it to be an effective and generally useful procedure. It has been replicated on two subsequent occasions, with similar positive results.

The procedures developed and generated by Jackson and Hatchett (17) and Gibson and Herzog (48), for example, now make it possible to generate adequate-sized, representative probability samples of black American adults and families. This work has also led to improvements in the methods by which supplemental samples of black adults (53) and black older Americans are drawn. An example of the latter is the ongoing national study of 3,000 Americans 25 years of age and older, American's Changing Lives, at the Institute for Social Research. These new approaches do not completely solve the problems of sampling black populations. When combined with other advances in sampling rare populations (47), however, and statistical procedures for addressing errors introduced by sampling difficulties (42, 43), future samples of the black elderly in both national and regional survey studies should demonstrate vast improvements over previous efforts (17).

Nonresponse Errors

Herzog and Rodgers (16) reported that in the general population older adults were somewhat more likely than middle-aged adults to become nonrespondents. They found, however, few remaining differences that distinguish respondents from nonrespondents. Their analyses on dropouts from short-term panels suggested that age plays a minor role and that across all ages these individuals tended to be disproportionately male, black, not presently married, and of lower educational background. Markides, Dickson, and Pappas (56) reported in a 4-year panel study of the elderly that dropouts were male as well as significantly older, less healthy, and less active than those remaining in the sample. Additionally, dropouts were more likely to be Anglo rather than minority. These findings are consistent with those of Herzog and Rodgers (16), who found significant substantive differences between dropouts and panel continuers. Markides and colleagues (56) also reported that dropouts who were deceased or could not be located were socioeconomically disadvantaged, while refusers tended to be disproportionately advantaged.

One of the most extensive examinations of nonresponse was completed by Hawkins (46, 57). His secondary analysis of 10 Detroit Area Study surveys spanned an approximately 19-year period. Consistent with Herzog and Rodgers (16) and Markides and colleagues (56), Hawkins (46) reported that terminal nonrespondents over this 20-year period tended to be older than respondents. His findings indicated, however, period or cohort effects during this interval; in earlier years (1950s) nonrespondents were the older, retired segment of the population, while during the 1970s nonrespondents were drawn from middle-aged groups. With regard to race, Hawkins's (46) analysis revealed a set of mixed findings. In early years blacks appeared to be overrepresented in the respondent categories and in more recent years, in the nonrespondent categories. This change to greater representation in nonresponse categories appeared to be due primarily to an increase in unavailability rather than refusals. Overall, Hawkins (46) proposed that firm conclusions regarding race could not be drawn from his analysis:

> Overall, however, the trends regarding the response of blacks in these surveys are not clear. While there is some evidence of the effects of differential callback policies on their nonresponse, other evidence supports the idea of a varying pattern of nonresponse for blacks and whites that is influenced perhaps by other, unexamined factors. (p. 85)

The lack of multivariate analyses in these studies of nonresponse makes it difficult to draw definitive conclusions. The fact that blacks tend to be disproportionately socioeconomically and educationally disadvantaged may play a significant role in their response patterns. Our research has shown large regional variations in rates of cooperation and timing of response—southern blacks being more cooperative. Similarly, Hawkins's (46) analysis raises the question of secular and cohort trends in the data, suggesting that different factors may be operative at different points in time for different age cohorts. For example, if nonresponse is a cohort phenomenon, then Hawkins's (46) findings of increased proclivity for middle-aged individuals to be nonrespondents indicate continuing problems and increasing nonresponse in studies of older black populations. The lack of multivariate analyses, however, and the simultaneous examination of the factors that may underlie nonresponse in older black respondents, make an interpretation of the available data extremely difficult (16).

Task Errors

The remaining classes of errors relate to the execution of the sample, nature of the survey interview, and subsequent data manipulation (5, 6, 14, 45). Based on the Sudman and Bradburn (5) model, these errors are related to issues of research conceptualization and research objectives, concepts, question wording, mode of survey administration, and editing and coding errors, as well as errors that occur during data processing, analysis, and interpretation. Hardly any work has focused on issues of conceptualization and research objectives relative to the study of black aging. This is an area, however, where errors may have important consequences for the nature of the subsequent research endeavor (4). Similarly, the analysis and interpretation are also points at which large errors are possible because of poor conceptualization of the research problem and the failure to adequately operationalize a role for race in aging-related phenomena (8, 23). Errors in these domains are of a fundamental nature but as of yet have not received the same type of scrutiny as other statistical sampling and survey execution errors.

Major research emphasis has been directed to errors in interviewer and respondent roles and the nature of the survey task (14, 45). In our work we have attempted to address task issues by developing more race-appropriate survey instruments, question presentations, and data-collection procedures. As Sudman and Bradburn (5) suggest:

> The task variables are primarily determined by the interview schedule or questionnaire. The questionnaire content, independent of the formulation of the questions will have some influence, particularly on the variables of saliency and self-presentation. The formulation of the questions, however, play an important role because they determine the degree of structure in the questionnaire, can radically affect the perceived saliency of the requested information and can exacerbate or modify problems of self-presentation. Thus we believe that questionnaire construction and question formulation lie at the heart of the problem of response effects. (p. 13)

We have concentrated attention on questionnaire construction that is sensitive to research objectives and conceptualizations of constructs responsive to the unique nature of black adult behavior (4). In recent reviews of the response-effects literature, Bradburn (6) and Schuman and Kalton (14) both pointed to the relative lack of good methodological research on variables related to the survey task. They concluded with regard to race issues that only saliency of the questions themselves have clearly demonstrated negative effects and that these occur largely through interactions of interviewer and respondent characteristics.

In general, the available research shows that longer questions related to health can indeed result in more and seemingly better reports of health conditions (58). In work with black elderly we have found that long questions tend to lead to respondent restlessness and inattention to the interviewers' questions. Similarly, research on question specificity has shown that a small change in wording can have profound effects on the distribution of responses. Schuman and Kalton (14), however, noted that these effects are often not substantial.

With regard to sensitivity, Schuman and Kalton (14) reported that these issues are often assumed to be more important than has been demonstrated in empirical research. When attention is focused on various subgroups of the population, however, it may be that certain questions will be of a more sensitive nature for some groups than for others. For example, we found it very difficult during the pretest of the National Survey of Black Americans (NSBA) to ask older blacks questions of a sexual nature. Less direct items had to be substituted to address issues of sexual functioning. The same level of aversion was not noted in younger black respondents. Similarly, the very nature of racial identity had to be addressed in the questionnaire. For example, we gave black respondents the opportunity to racially self-designate by any label they desired (colored, Negro, nigra, black, Afro-American). Not surprisingly, many of the older blacks in our sample preferred to be called colored or Negro. Again, lack of attention to this and other seemingly "small" issues could lead to respondent resentment and noncooperation.

The research on open- and closed-question responding revealed that older respondents give a significantly greater proportion of "don't knows" in response to questions (16). Similarly, Herzog and Rodgers also reported that older individuals tend to be less productive in response to open-ended probes and that they tend to use stereotypic responses more often than younger respondents. Besides the finding that older blacks tend to be disproportionately involved in nonresponse, Herzog and Rodgers (16) reported few race-by-age effects. These effects, however, were not systematically assessed.

Schuman and Kalton (14) reported that question-order experiments demonstrate few systematic and replicable effects. While some notable studies have demonstrated significant effects of context on responding to questions (6), other parametric studies of these effects have not produced clear results. Schuman and Kalton (14) suggested the need for more research on the topic.

In creating the instrument for our first national survey (NSBA), nearly 2 years were spent in developing questions, ascertaining the best location of items within the questionnaire, and constructing individual items that were comprehensible and meaningful to the respondents. Additionally, in order to increase the meaningfulness and saliency of the questions, we initially used modified cross-cultural procedures (4, 30) in an attempt to validate the concepts and questions for blacks. Months were spent in black communities talking to and tape recording the open-ended responses of small groups of black Americans from all walks of life and from major regions of the country. These tape-recorded sessions were transcribed and questions written reflecting their content. In certain cases we found that many concepts defied the use of closed-ended response formats. Although closed-ended formats are preferable for ease of coding and analyses (14), we found that approximately one-third of the questionnaire content had to be open-ended. This is consistent with the literature demonstrating that open-ended questions may be superior when little is known about the topic. For the study of black elderly, we found the use of open-ended questions highly appropriate. Herzog and Rodgers (16), however, reported that older adults may respond in less productive manners to open-ended questions. Whether this lowered production reflects less quality or whether there were differential effects by race was not available from their report. In our own work we have discovered that older blacks were less talkative in response to specific probes but that it seemed, in comparison to younger blacks, not to affect the quality of their responses. This, however, is an area in need of further investigation.

At present the research seems clearly to indicate that task effects, particularly question wording, order, and context, mode of administration, and open versus closed questions produce the largest task effects. The small amount of research on this topic with older populations seems to suggest that the open–closed dimension is the most important in terms of differential responding, although some effects for the greater use of "don't know" response categories and stereotypic responding also appear to exist. The lack of research attention to issues of race-by-age interactions in prior studies leaves issues of response errors in black adults and the elderly in question. If the use of tasks (questions) of little intrinsic interest results in a lack of motivation in older people generally, then this is a problem that is truly confounded among black Americans—since the type of questions asked in most surveys may be of questionable relevance, interest, or concern to older black people. Our work suggests that careful attention to the development of a meaningful questionnaire, extensive pretesting, and the use of modified cross-cultural procedures (30) can contribute a great deal to the development of survey instruments that are responsive to many of the task problems that have been identified in the literature.

Interviewer Errors

Bradburn (6) concluded in his review that interviewer variables are only a small source of error in the total survey situation. Research results have been nondefinitive regarding the effect of interviewer characteristics, and, as Bradburn (6) indicated, the definitive studies are yet to be done. The most consistent effects have been on sex and race of interviewers and their degree of experience and training. Recent research on interviewer expectations and interviewer behavior revealed few if any effects on the content of responses (14). On a positive note, Cannell, Miller, and Oksenberg (58) have consistently demonstrated that positive contingent reinforcement during the course of the interview by the interviewer can positively affect responding.

The major finding, however, is that race and, to a less certain degree, sex can affect interviewee responding, particularly for those questions related to racial or sexual topics. The majority of the work has been conducted on race-of-interviewer effects (6). In a study of perceived race-of-interviewer effects within the NBES telephone study (1, 17), it was found that black respondents gave much more pro-black responses to racial attitudes and civil rights items when they perceived the interviewer to be black. Similar effects on other domains unrelated to racial topics were also found. While this research is consistent with the face-to-face literature, it suggests that subtle cues in the telephone interaction may influence perceptions of race and subsequent responding, regardless of the actual race of the interviewer. The identification of these factors is crucial, since telephone interviewing has become the predominant mode of data collection in survey research. While race-of-interviewer effects can be controlled through interviewer assignment in face-to-face surveys, perceptions are much more difficult to manipulate on the telephone. We have even experimented with providing actual cues as to race in our three-generation telephone study (1, 17). In this case the interviewer indicated early in the interview through a standardized identification statement that she was of the same race as the respondent (black). Obviously one can envision situations where this manner of informing the respondent may have boomerang effects.

In our own work we have been very concerned with clearly defining the demands of the interviewers. Extensive training was conducted with all black, indigenous community interviewers, and they were included as much as possible as integral members of the research team. These procedures dealt directly with the major issues identified in the literature as affecting response errors—interviewer motivation, race characteristics, and training (6, 14). We have been particularly sensitive to interviewer issues, since Herzog and Rodgers (16) reported that older adults seem to be affected by interviewer variations more than younger adults. In our studies we have attempted to sex-and-age match interviewers and respondents whenever possible. In sum, extensive training, race matching, and close supervision all tend to reduce interviewer bias effects (6).

Respondent Errors

The major topic investigated under this rubric has been response sets (e.g., acquiescence or social desirability generally). The literature is somewhat equivocal; some findings support response-set interpretations (6) and others have rejected them (14). Herzog and Rodgers (16) did seem to find greater use of response sets among older respondents. A great deal of research has investigated the role of different response sets in item responding. Some work suggests that response sets may be important sources of variability among older Americans (16) and perhaps even greater sources of variation among older black Americans.

For example, Bachman and O'Malley (59, 60) reported that young adult blacks tend to use self-esteem response scales differently than do young adult whites, preferring extreme styles of responding to Likert-like items.

Their work suggested that it is this responding variation, as much as anything else, that has contributed to mean population differences found on self-esteem scales over the years. While Bachman and O'Malley (60) attributed their findings to the nature of group-level differences in response styles, an equally likely explanation may be culturally determined race-group differences in perceptions and responses to the nature of the stimulus questions (61, 62). I expect that the Bachman and O'Malley (59, 60) findings would be even more strongly supported in an examination of older blacks, although these differences may be offset by increased similarity among aged individuals more generally (63).

In conducting our studies these issues were addressed through extensive pretests, as described earlier. It was our belief that many of the questions, response scales, and basic concepts may not be appropriate or meaningful for black respondents. Thus a combination of approaches was employed, including random probes (64) to assess the meaning of closed-ended responses. For example, one set of findings indicated that, in the case of older black respondents, the use of traditional satisfaction-with-health scales may be inappropriate (1, 18). In examining the random probes for this item from the NSBA, it seemed clear that respondents were not using the scales in the comparative sense that its designers envisioned. Our results indicated a more religious and transcendental interpretation to the individual responses. Black respondents were most likely to attribute their health and health satisfaction to divine intervention.

Finally, some research has noted the existence of respondent motivation and memory factors in respondent behavior (6, 14, 45). Herzog and Rodgers (16), however, reported no essential differences among age groups in memory factors in their work. Similarly, they did not report any differences by race.

SUMMARY AND CONCLUSIONS

Survey research methodology provides a powerful set of tools for conducting social science research on aging black populations. The scope of possible topics to be covered, the use of precise statistical methods for defining and sampling from populations, and sets of well-worked procedures for eliciting relevant information make it an ideal vehicle for studying a broad range of social science phenomena. The broad applicability of survey procedures does not lessen the value and importance of other methods, for example, anthropological approaches (32, 33). It does suggest, however, that survey research methodology is an encompassing, flexible, and scientifically precise technology for research purposes in black populations (1, 4).

Unfortunately, much of what transpires as survey research on aging black adults does not have the rigor and precision associated with the true sample

survey. Most of the literature is based on loosely drawn convenience samples and questionnaires and other procedures that do not address the types
of task, interviewer, and respondent problems reviewed here and in the
major sources on this topic (5, 6, 14, 41, 45). The recent move to telephone
surveys as the predominant mode of data collection in survey research (15)
makes it even more imperative that scientifically acceptable procedures for
conducting survey research on blacks be developed and employed.

Large numbers of black Americans in all age cohorts also suffer from
some of the same types of educational and income deficiencies shown to be
correlated with differential survey responding in older Americans generally
(e.g., 16). Thus it might be expected that the types of problems leading to
unreliability and invalidity in survey research on older black Americans
might continue to be problems over the next few decades. Just as Schuman
and Kalton (14) indicated, however, regarding the general state of knowledge on errors in surveys, more research is needed on the topic among adult
blacks.

Our survey work has been predicated on the belief that salient questions,
meaningful response scales, well-trained indigenous interviewers, carefully
designed questionnaires, and opportunities for respondent self-expression
during the course of the interview would contribute the most to reducing
interviewer and respondent errors (1, 4, 18). I am also of the opinion that
sensitivity to the cross-cultural aspects of research on black American adults
can contribute positively to the development of superior survey-research
products. Thus we have directed attention to issues of sampling errors
through the development of new screening procedures in face-to-face and
telephone surveys. These procedures were designed to give *all* black Americans in designated populations (national, regional, local) known probabilities of inclusion in properly drawn samples. In this manner we have contributed to the better definition of the populations of interest as well as to the
development of better samples of these populations (54). With regard to the
nonsampling errors, we have attempted, through the introduction of novel
cross-cultural techniques, to develop relevant and salient sets of instruments
for older black Americans that are sensitive to their lifestyles and concerns.
The use of black indigenous interviewers, extensive training, and an emphasis on the motivation of both interviewers and respondents have been
effective in improving the nature of the survey-research product in studies
on aging black populations.

REFERENCES

1. Jackson JS. Methodological issues in survey research on older minority adults.
   In: Lawton MP, Herzog AR, eds. *Research Methods in Gerontology.* Farming-
   dale, NY: Baywood Press; in press.

2. Presser S. The use of survey data in basic research in the social sciences. In: Turner CF, Martin EF, eds. *Surveying Subjective Phenomena* (Vol. 2). New York: Russell Sage; 1984:93–114.
3. Cutler SJ. Survey research in the study of aging and adult development: a commentary. *The Gerontologist* 1977; 19:217–219.
4. Jackson JS, Tucker MB, Bowman PB. Conceptual and methodological problems in survey research on black Americans. In: Liu WT, ed. *Methodological Problems in Minority Research*. Chicago: Pacific/Asian American Mental Health Center; 1982:11–40.
5. Sudman S, Bradburn N. *Response Effects in Surveys*. Chicago: Aldine; 1974.
6. Bradburn N. Response effects. In: Rossi PH, Wright JD, Anderson AD, eds. *Handbook of Survey Research*. New York: Academic Press; 1983: 289–329.
7. Schaie WK, Orchowsky S., Parham IA. Measuring age and social change: the case of race and life satisfaction. In: Manuel RC, ed. *Minority Aging: Sociological and Social Psychological Issues*. Westport, CT: Greenwood; 1982: 223–230.
8. Jackson JJ. Race, national origin, ethnicity, and aging. In Binstock RH, Shanas E, eds. *Handbook of Aging and the Social Sciences* (2nd ed.). New York: Van Nostrand Reinhold Company; 1985:264–303.
9. Montero D. Research among racial and cultural minorities: an overview. *Journal of Social Issues* 1977; 33:1–10.
10. Myers V. Survey methods for minority populations. *Journal of Social Issues* 1977; 33:11–19.
11. Becerra RM, Shaw D. *The Hispanic Elderly: A Research Reference Guide*. New York: University Press of America; 1984.
12. Ferber R, Sheatsley P, Turner A, Waksberg J. *What Is a Survey?* Washington, DC: American Statistical Association; 1980.
13. Kish L. *Survey Sampling*. New York: Wiley; 1965.
14. Schuman H, Kalton G. Survey methods. In: Lindzey G., Aronson E, eds. *Handbook of Social Psychology* (Vol. III). New York: Wiley; 1985:635–697.
15. Rossi PH, Wright JD, Anderson AB, eds. *Handbook of Survey Research*. New York: Academic Press; 1983.
16. Herzog AR, Rodgers WL. *Surveys of Older Americans: Some Methodological Investigations*. Final report to the National Institute on Aging. Ann Arbor: Institute for Social Research, The University of Michigan; 1982.
17. Jackson JS, Hatchett SJ. Intergenerational research: methodological considerations. In: Datan N, Greene AL, Reese HL, eds. *Intergenerational Relations*. Hillsdale, NJ: Erlbaum; 1986:51–76.
18. Jackson JS. The program for research on black Americans. In: Jones RL, ed. *Advances in Black Psychology*. Berkeley, CA: Cobb and Henry Publishers; in press.
19. Allen WR. The search for applicable theories of black family life. *Journal of Marriage and the Family* 1978; 40: 117–129.
20. Palmore EB. Cross-cultural research: state of the art. *Research On Aging*. 1983;5: 45–57.
21. Brislin RW, Lonner WJ, Thorndike RM. *Cross-Cultural Research Methods*. New York: Wiley; 1973.

22. Martin E. Cultural indicators and the analysis of public opinion. In: Turner CF, Martin EF, eds. *Surveying Subjective Phenomena* (Vol 2). New York: Sage; 1984:547–564.

23. Levine EK. Old people are not alike: social class, ethnicity/race, and sex are bases for important differences. In: Sieber JE, ed. *The Ethics of Social Research*. New York: Springer-Verlag; 1982:127–144.

24. Triandis HC. Some dimensions of intercultural variation and their implications for community psychology. *Journal of Community Psychology* 1983; 11:285–302.

25. Finifter BM. The robustness of cross-cultural findings. *Annals of the New York Academy of Sciences* 1977; 285:151–184.

26. Jackson JS. *Science, values and research on ethnic and racial groups*. Unpublished manuscript, University of Michigan; 1986.

27. Spencer MB, Brookens GR, Allen WR, eds. *Beginnings: The Social and Affective Development of Black Children*. Hillsdale, NJ: Erlbaum; 1985.

28. McLoyd VC, Randolph SM. Secular trends in the study of Afro-American children: a review of Child Development, 1936–1980. In: Smuts AB, Hagen JW, eds. *History and Research in Child Development. Monographs of the Society for Research in Child Development* 1985; 50:78–92.

29. Kraus IK. Between- and within-group comparisons in aging research. In: Poon LW, ed. *Aging in the 1980's*. Washington, DC: American Psychological Association; 1980:542–551.

30. Word CO. Cross-cultural methods of survey research in black urban areas. *The Journal of Black Psychology* 1977; 3:72–87.

31. Warwick DP, Lininger CA. *The Sample Survey: Theory and Practice*. New York: McGraw-Hill; 1975.

32. Fry CL, Keith J, eds. *New Methods for Old Age Research*. Chicago: Center for Urban Policy, Loyola University of Chicago; 1980.

33. Fry CL. Culture, behavior, and aging in the comparative perspective. In: Birren JE, Schaie WK, eds. *Handbook of the Psychology of Aging* (2nd ed.). New York: Van Nostrand Reinhold; 1985:216–244.

34. Labov W. *Sociolinguistic Patterns*. Philadelphia: University of Pennsylvania Press; 1972.

35. Gynther MD. White norms and black MMPI's: a prescription for discrimination. *Psychological Bulletin* 1972; 78:386–402.

36. Kochman T. *Black and White: Styles in Conflict*. Chicago: The University of Chicago Press; 1981.

37. Burton LM, Bengtson VL. Research in elderly minority communities: problems and potentials. In: Manuel RC, ed. *Minority Aging: Sociological and Social-Psychological Issues*. Westport, CT: Greenwood Press; 1982:215–222.

38. Rodgers TB. Some thoughts on the "culture fairness" of personality inventories. *The Canadian Psychologist* 1972; 13:116–120.

39. Labouvie EW. Identity versus equivalence of psychological measures and constructs. In: Poon LN, ed. *Aging in the 1980's*. Washington, DC: American Psychological Association; 1980:493–502.

40. Alwin DF. Making errors in surveys: an overview. In: Alwin DF, ed. *Survey Design and Analysis*. Beverly Hills, CA: Sage; 1977:7–26.

41. O'Muircheartaigh CA. Response errors. In: O'Muircheartaigh CA, Payne C, eds. *The Analysis of Survey Data* (Vol 1). New York: Wiley; 1977:193–239.

42. Berk RA. An introduction to sample selection bias in sociological research. *American Sociological Review* 1983; 48:386–398.

43. Berk RA, Ray SC. Selection biases in sociological data. *Social Science Research* 1982; 11:301–340.

44. Alwin DF, Jackson DJ. Measurement models for response errors in surveys: issues and applications. In: Schuessler KF, ed. *Sociological Methodology*. San Francisco: Jossey-Bass; 1980:68–119.

45. Tanur JM. Methods for large scale surveys and experiments. In: Leinhardt S, ed. *Sociological Methodology*. San Francisco: Jossey-Bass; 1983:1–71.

46. Hawkins DF. *Non-Response in Detroit Area Study Surveys: A Ten Year Analysis* (Working Papers in Methodology). Chapel Hill, NC: Institute for Research in Social Science, University of North Carolina at Chapel Hill; 1977.

47. Sirkin MG. *Discussion: Survey Methods for Rare Populations.* Proceedings of the fourth conference on health survey methods. Washington, DC: Department of Health and Human Services, 1984:347–349.

48. Gibson RC, Herzog AR. Rare element telephone screening (RETS): A procedure for augmenting the number of black elderly in national samples. *The Gerontologist* 1984; 24:477–482.

49. Shanas E. *National Survey of the Elderly.* Report to the Administration on Aging. Washington, DC: Department of Health and Human Services; 1979.

50. Watson WH. Mental health of the minority aged: selected correlates. In: Manuel RC, ed. *Minority Aging: Sociological and Social-Psychological Issues*. Westport, CT: Greenwood Press; 1982:83–88.

51. Herzog AR, Rodgers WL, Kulka RA. Interviewing older adults: a comparison of telephone and face to face modalities. *Public Opinion Quarterly* 1983; 47:405–418.

52. Thornberry OT, Massey JT. *Correcting for Undercoverage Bias in Random Digit National Health Surveys*. Proceedings of the Survey Research Section Washington, DC: American Statistical Association; 1978.

53. Tourangeau R, Smith AW. Finding subgroups for surveys. *Public Opinion Quarterly* 1985; 49:351–356.

54. Hess I. *Sampling for Social Research Surveys: 1947–1980*. Ann Arbor: Institute for Social Research, The University of Michigan; 1985:98–106.

55. Inglis KM, Groves RM, Heeringa SG. *Telephone Sample Designs for the Black Household Population*. Proceedings of the Survey Section. Washington, DC: American Statistical Association; 1985.

56. Markides KS, Dickson HD, Pappas C. Characteristics of dropouts in longitudinal research on aging: a study of Mexican-Americans and Anglos. *Experimental Aging Research* 1982; 8:163–167.

57. Hawkins DF. *The Reluctant Respondent: Two Views* (Discussion Paper Series). Chapel Hill, NC: Institute for Research in Social Science, University of North Carolina at Chapel Hill; 1977.

58. Cannell CF, Miller PV, Oksenberg L. Research on interviewing techniques. In: Leinhardt S, ed. *Sociological Methodology*. San Francisco: Jossey-Bass; 1981:389–437.

59. Bachman JG, O'Malley PM. Black-white differences in self-esteem: are they affected by response style. *American Journal of Sociology* 1984; 90:624–639.
60. Bachman JG, O'Malley PM. Yea-saying, nay-saying, and going to extremes: black–white differences in response styles. *Public Opinion Quarterly* 1984; 48:491–509.
61. Nobles WW. Psychological research and the black self-concept: a critical review. *Journal of Social Issues* 1973; 29:11–32.
62. Semaj LT. Afrikanity, cognition and extended self-identity. In: Spencer MB, Brookens GR, Allen WR, eds. *Beginnings: The Social and Affective Development of Black Children.* Hillsdale, NJ: Erlbaum; 1985:173–183.
63. Bengtson VL, Morgan LA. Ethnicity and aging: a comparison of three ethnic groups. In: Sokolovsky J, ed. *Growing Old in Different Societies.* Belmont, CA: Wadsworth; 1983:157–167.
64. Schuman H. The random probe: a technique for evaluating the validity of closed questions. *American Sociological Review* 1966; 41:224–235.

17

The Design and Conduct of Case-Control Studies in Research on Aging Black Populations

Jerome Wilson

The case-control design is a potentially useful research approach for investigating health problems in black populations. This is not to suggest that this approach is solely and uniquely suited for black subjects. This chapter, however, presents strengths and weaknesses of the case-control approach when applied to the black elderly. Finally, a discussion of the need for epidemiologic research among the black elderly is presented.

The limitations imposed on epidemiologic research by its nonexperimental nature are particularly burdensome in case-control studies. A case-control (case-referent, case-comparison, retrospective) study is defined as an investigation of the exposure frequencies of at least two groups of subjects selected on the basis of their status with respect to a particular disease entity or physical and mental state of health (1).

There is an increasing need for understanding the health problems of the elderly population in general and the black elderly in particular. While the black elderly represent a relatively small percentage of the total population, their health problems may be overrepresented among the population at large. Since disease prevention and health promotion is a goal of public health, the disease patterns that reflect the health status of blacks are needed for developing preventive health strategies. The black population suffers significantly greater morbidity and mortality than the white population in the United States. Studies must be designed to identify the biological and environmental risk factors associated with these differences.

BASIC PRINCIPLES OF CASE-CONTROL STUDIES

The case-control study is one of the most important tools currently available to the chronic disease epidemiologist. New cases of disease occurring in a defined population are compared to a control group with respect to exposures to certain environmental factors, biomarkers, and other putative risk factors. Mantel and Haenszel (2) noted in their now-classic paper on the case-control study, "A primary goal is to reach the same conclusion . . . as would have been obtained from a forward study, if one had been done" (p. 722). In a prospective study, the probability of disease development is related to each individual's exposure history.

Quantitative studies of risk factors and disease require a measure of exposure to the risk variables, as well as one of disease occurrences, and a method of associating the two. Risk factors may be difficult to measure precisely, since individual histories differ with respect to the onset, duration, and intensity of exposure, and whether it was continuous or intermittent.

Selection of Cases

Cases can be selected from hospitals, ambulatory-care practices, clinics, nursing homes, tumor registries [such as the Surveillance, Epidemiology and End Results (SEER) program], or bureaus of vital statistics; in defined geographic areas, record linkage systems can be used. Each of these approaches to case finding has limitations. These include potential biases that must be explored before initiating the study.

In hospital-based case-control studies, cases may be selected from admission logs, surgery lists, and lists of discharge diagnoses. Cases can be selected from tumor registries (hospital- and population-based). Cases can be selected from surveys, such as the National Center for Health Statistics (NCHS) Health Interview Survey. The usefulness of such surveys, however, is often compromised by the relatively small numbers of blacks that are included. In most major urban centers, blacks obtain medical care in a few large hospitals or hospitals located in the community. All cases should be confirmed by microscopical/pathological examinations. When this is not possible or appropriate, the best clinical documentation should be gathered to support the diagnosis. If personal interviews are to be conducted as part of the study, a rapid case-reporting system may be necessary for two reasons. First, the disease may be associated with low survival. Second, patients may be too ill for an interview. Such a reporting system includes obtaining consent for an interview and may include sample collection (e.g., blood, urine, etc.). In dealing with an elderly population, it may be necessary to interview a surrogate respondent or have the respondent assisted because of the illness or the mental status of the patient.

Control Population

A central problem is the choice of controls. In most early studies as well as recent ones, controls have been patients in the same hospitals as the cases. It is possible that the selection factors that influence one patient's plan of hospitalization for treatment of the disease under study will also operate to direct other patients to the same hospital. This is especially true in black communities, which may have more homogeneous levels of low economic status than is true in white communities. Multiple control groups can be selected to avoid some of these potentially biasing factors. Types of control-group populations that should be considered include (1) neighborhood residents, (2) retirement communities, (3) nursing home residents, or (4) Health Care Finance Administration (HCFA) System members. Health Care Finance Administration controls can be selected at 6-month intervals over the case-ascertainment period of the study (from the most recently updated tapes that are available). The files can be systematically selected (after a random start) for individuals with the appropriate age, race, sex, and geographic-area designations.

Advantages and Disadvantages

Advantages

The case-control method is more efficient than other primary data-collection procedures, such as surveys, in requirements of manpower, cost, and time. The number of subjects needed is comparatively fewer, and no follow-up is needed. The latter advantage is especially important for studies of the black elderly, where the numbers are relatively small. Case-control studies can be done to complement prospective studies. They permit careful examination of a wide array of factors. Moreover, the case-control method allows consideration of differences in the amount of exposure over time, up to the onset of the disease. In diseases with long latency periods (e.g., cancer), this method permits one to take into consideration exposures throughout the subject's life. The prospective method would have to continue for 20 to 30 years before such risks might become apparent.

An innovative adjunct to the case-control design is the addition of a biochemical/laboratory component. The primary objective is to develop a multidisciplinary biochemical and cellular component by combining epidemiological and experimental approaches. Laboratory components can be used to determine whether differences in nutritional, genetic, and immunologic factors could explain why blacks are at a higher risk of developing certain cancers and other diseases. By integrating laboratory and epidemiological techniques it is possible to evaluate certain risk factors that are difficult to investigate by either experimental or epidemiological approaches. Biochemical epidemiology provides one opportunity to clarify disease risks associated with environmental exposures and to provide some insight into black–white morbidity, survival, and mortality differences. Since major advances have been made recently in laboratory technologies, epidemiological approaches can now take advantage of these new techniques. Cost is a factor to be considered, however, since some of these laboratory procedures may be expensive.

Disadvantages

The major disadvantage of case-control studies is the greater potential for bias (3, 4). The choice of a suitable control group can often be difficult. Unless the study is population-based, attributable and overall absolute risk are difficult to estimate reliably.

Sometimes it is difficult or impossible to learn the temporal sequence between the factors under study and the disease (5). An example is myocardial infarction; measurements of blood pressure made during or after the illness may bear little relation to the levels before the onset.

All evidence must be assembled and considered, and studies must be repeated before conclusions are drawn. Several types of evidence should be weighed in deciding whether an environmental factor is an etiologic agent of chronic diseases. These include strength of association, confirmation by additional studies, demonstration of a dose–response relationship, chronologic relationship, and compatibility with other types of biologic evidence (6).

CONSIDERATIONS OF SAMPLE SIZE

Sample size is often invoked as the reason for not conducting epidemiologic research among black populations. The number of subjects to be selected for a case-control study depends on the specification of the following four values:

1. The relative frequency of exposure among controls in the target population
2. A hypothesized relative risk associated with exposures to warrant its detection
3. The desired level of significance
4. The desired statistical power (7)

Black Americans are more likely than whites to experience a decline in health status at all ages. Moreover, in the age range of 65 years old and older, 43% of blacks are likely to be in poor health, compared to 29% of whites (8). This observation suggests that the frequency of disease problems may be of such prevalence among elderly blacks that only a relatively small sample size would be required to detect certain disease–risk factor associations.

In case-control studies of black persons over age 65, a sequential approach may offer advantages over a fixed sample-size design. A sequential analysis proceeds as the data become available over time, rather than waiting until a predetermined number of cases and controls have accumulated for study. Data collection continues until the null hypothesis of interest is either accepted or rejected with some preestablished values for alpha and beta. The sample sizes with a sequential test will be smaller than that required for a fixed sample-size analysis (9).

Because of imprecision in one's parameter specifications, any estimated sample size should be considered as only a guide to planning a study and not an absolute requirement. Very often, as in the case of the black elderly, little or no research has been conducted. Therefore, the parameters needed to estimate sample size will only be available after a pilot or the study itself has been completed.

NEEDS AND RECOMMENDATIONS

There are important gaps in the knowledge of disease incidence, survival, and mortality and of the risk factors among blacks in the United States, especially the black elderly. Hence, case-control studies could be important in the following situations:

1. Assessing the relative importance of various suspected determinants of chronic diseases that affect blacks disproportionately compared to whites
2. Elucidating host factors (e.g., immunologic, genetic, nutritional, hormonal) that cause blacks to be at unusually high risk for developing certain diseases
3. Defining the interrelationships of host and environmental factors
4. Determining more precisely the preclinical course of chronic disease in black populations
5. Conducting cancer and cardiovascular studies of black–white differences in conjunction with research on aging, since many types of cancer and cardiovascular diseases are mainly found in older age groups

Availability and quality of medical care are critical to the health and well-being of any population, especially the elderly. In theory, Medicare benefits are equally available to all persons over 65. In reality, there are vast inequalities in these provisions. Davis (10) showed that wide differences exist in the use of services and in the receipt of benefits by income, race, and geographic location. Under the Medicare program, poorer populations (those also with the poorest health) have had lower rates of utilization of care than more affluent groups. Elderly blacks make up a disproportionate share of such poor populations. Whites had 30% more payments for inpatient hospital care per person and 60% more payments for physician services than blacks. Whites also received more than twice the payments received by blacks for extended-care facilities.

Given the evidence of unequal availability and quality of care for the elderly, it is likely that the disease problems in this population are underestimated. For many of these disorders, case-control studies are an important complement to studies of the general population. No single approach or simple set of assumptions, however, will provide definitive answers to the health problems of the black elderly. Case-control methodology with sensitive and specific innovative biological measurements is one of several important approaches to studying health problems in aging black populations. Biochemical epidemiology approaches may provide more robust predictors of disease risk. Data from such studies could yield the objective data needed for reducing the burden of morbidity and mortality in the black elderly population.

SUMMARY

Epidemiologic studies play an important role in the elucidation of health problems in populations. There is an increasing need for understanding the health problems of the elderly population in general and the black elderly in particular. The case-control design is a potentially useful research approach for investigating health issues in aging black populations. The case-control study is one of the most important tools currently available to epidemiologists. Cases can be selected from institutions serving large black elderly populations. Controls may be selected from neighborhoods and community institutions.

The case-control method is efficient in requirements of personnel, cost, and time. Biochemical epidemiology provides an opportunity to integrate laboratory and classical epidemiologic approaches. Sample size is often invoked as a limitation in conducting epidemiologic research among black populations. A sequential design is one approach to addressing the sample-size issue. Case-control studies designed with sensitive and specific biochemical markers are likely to yield the quantitative data needed for reducing the burden of morbidity and mortality among the black elderly.

REFERENCES

1. Cole P. The evolving case-control study. *J Chron Dis* 1979;32: 15–27.
2. Mantel N, Haenszel W. Statistical aspects of the analysis of data from retrospective studies of disease. *Journal of National Cancer Institute* 1959;22: 719–784.
3. Miettinen OS. Estimability and estimation in case-reformat studies. *Am J Epidemiology* 1976;103: 226–35.
4. Cornfeld J. A statistical problem arising from retrospective studies. In: Neyman J, ed. *Proceedings of the Third Berkeley Symposium on Mathematical Statistics* (Vol. IV). Berkeley, CA: University of California Press;1979: 135–48.
5. Sartwell PE. On the methodology of investigation of etiologic factors in chronic diseases. *J Chron Dis* 1960;11: 61–63.
6. Hill AB. The environment and disease: association or causation? *Proc R Soc Med* 1965;58: 295–300.
7. Schlesselman JJ. *Case-Control Studies: Design, Conduct, Analysis.* London: Oxford University Press; 1982: 144–170.
8. Ostfeld AM. Frequency and nature of health problems of retired persons. In: Carp FM, ed. *The Retirement Process* (USPHS Publication No. 1788). Washington, DC: 1968.
9. O'Neil RT, Ancllo C. Case-control studies: a sequential approach. *American Journal of Epidemiology* 1978;108: 415–424.
10. Davis K. Equal treatment and unequal benefits: the medical program. *Millbank Memorial Fund Quarterly (Health and Society)* 1985;53: 448–488.

18

Clinical Trials and the Black Elderly: Issues and Considerations

Bettie Nelson Knuckles and Camilla A. Brooks

A review of the literature on elderly blacks as participants in clinical trials research indicates that available information is scant at best. In many large-scale studies on therapeutic interventions for chronic diseases the elderly are not included in the targeted population(s). In studies where older persons are included, the actual number of elderly is usually small and the number of black elderly is even smaller, making generalizations impossible. This is true in spite of the fact that the mortality rates of blacks aged 65 years and over are generally higher than those of older whites for most chronic diseases until age 75, when the rates for blacks tend to be lower than those for whites. Additionally, some drugs have been found to be more effective than others in treating blacks for various diseases (1–3).

The Systolic Hypertension in the Elderly Population (SHEP) study is an example of a clinical study that specifically targeted the elderly. It was designed to test the effectiveness of antihypertensive medications in persons 60 years of age or older (4). Of the 551 persons randomized in the two study groups during the pilot study, nearly 100, or 18% were black. On the other hand, the majority of large-scale clinical trials have not included elderly blacks as participants or did not provide results on older blacks included in the study. Some of these studies are listed in Table 18.1.

In several of the studies, the upper age limit was 69 years; these included the Aspirin Myocardial Study (AMIS) (5), Beta Heart Attack Trial (BHAT) (6), and the Hypertension Detection and Follow-Up Program (HDFP) (7).

TABLE 18.1 Description of Major Clinical Trials

Trial	# of centers	# of subjects	# of blacks	# of older blacks	Age range	Sex
AMIS	30	4,524	380	?	30–60	M&F
BHAT	31	3,837	333	?	30–69	M&F
CPPT(LRC)	12	3,806	?	?	35–59	M
HDFP	14	10,940	4,846	?	30–69	M&F
MRFIT	22	12,861	926	0	35–57	M
SHEP	5	551	100	100	60+	M&F
VACSGAA	7	683	388	?	21–65	M

Abbreviations and Symbols:
AMIS—Aspirin Myocardial Infarction Study
BHAT—Beta Heart Attack Trial
CPPT(LRC)—Coronary Primary Prevention Trial—Lipid Research Clinics
HDFP—Hypertension Detection and Follow-Up Program
MRFIT—Multiple Risk Factor Intervention Trial
SHEP—Systolic Hypertension in the Elderly Project
VACSGAA—Veterans Administration Cooperative Study Group on Antihypertensive Agents
?—Not reported in the results

Other studies used 65 years or younger as the upper age limit; these included the Coronary Primary Prevention Trial (8, 9), the Multiple Risk Factor Intervention Trial (MRFIT) (10), and the Veterans Administration Cooperative Study Group on Antihypertensive Agents (VACSGAA) (11).

No single, clearcut reason is provided for the lack of inclusion of older blacks in clinical trials on chronic diseases. In the CPPT, only males aged 35 to 59 were included in the trial on the premise that middle-aged males were more amenable to a reduction in cholesterol lowering than males aged 60 and older or males younger than 39 years. However, no studies were cited in the article to indicate the theory of lowered reversibility among older males.

The past experiences of today's older blacks may influence whether they will participate in clinical trials. The necessary forms and procedures in clinical trials may be confusing and overwhelming to some, while distrust of the medical profession may prohibit others from participating in a study. This chapter will examine issues such as ethics, recruitment, and statistical considerations as they relate to older blacks and their participation in clinical trials.

ETHICAL ISSUES

As a group, the elderly pose unique, but not insurmountable, considerations in the conduct of clinical trials. Issues that arise when older black persons participate in clinical trials are not substantially different from those arising when older nonblack persons are participants. There is some controversy, however, as to whether the aged need any special regulations beyond those established for the rest of the population. Hakkarainen, Hattab, and Venulet (12) suggested that prior to the initiation of clinical trials in the elderly, kinetic studies should be conducted to assess whether the data for adults under 65 years of age can be considered applicable to the elderly. The interaction of drugs should be considered when older persons are included in clinical trials, since many older persons, on average, take multiple medications.

Vestal (13) concluded that while the elderly are a heterogeneous group, physiological and pathological deterioration combine to make them especially vulnerable to many types of physical stress. Lawton (14) suggested modification of the consent process when dealing with poorly educated, culturally deprived, or isolated older subjects. On the other hand, Ostfeld (15) indicated that many of the generalizations about the elderly are untrue and that special guidelines for the elderly will simply perpetuate the myth that the elderly are a homogeneous and vulnerable group that is different from the rest of the population. Although older blacks were not mentioned in the report as a separate group, many of the comments made appear applicable. There is a need, however, to be certain that the rights of older blacks are upheld to prevent the recurrence of documented abuses that have occurred in the past.

Incidents in which the rights of patients have been abused dictate the need for continual monitoring of clinical trials. Barber (16) pointed out that several researchers were willing to subject institutionalized or retarded children to a hypothetical research proposal involving some risk for controls, whereas they would not subject "normal" children to the same procedure. Makarushka and McDonald (17) suggested that researchers are more willing to subject persons whom they feel have less "worth" than others to riskier procedures.

These attitudes could have serious consequences for the black elderly population, who may be seen as having less worth because of their race and age. The most notorious incident on record is the Tuskegee Syphilis Study, in which the treatment of syphilis was deliberately withheld from 400 black sharecroppers long after penicillin had been introduced as treatment. The study began without a defined, written protocol, and subjects were not properly informed of their rights. Although penicillin was not in use as treatment for syphilis at the beginning of the study in 1932, it became the standard treatment for syphilis in the late 1940s. Participants in the program were not made aware of or given the new treatment. Rather, they continued to be monitored and untreated under the auspices of this study until public outcry forced the study to end in 1972 (18). This study was allowed to occur and continue because the participants were black and illiterate. This study in particular underscores the need to ensure that elderly blacks are treated ethically and with dignity and fairness in clinical trials.

In conducting clinical trials, one should keep in mind the following concerns: (1) there should be an unequivocal need for the clinical trial; (2) standard treatment, if available, should be provided to the control group; (3) participants should be able to give informed consent; and (4) participants should be able to follow the treatment regimen.

According to Berkowitz (19), there are three criteria for consent to be legally effective: (1) the subject must be competent to give consent, (2) the subject must be informed of the risk, and (3) the subject must give consent voluntarily. Competence refers to an individual's ability to agree to a procedure (inherent in that agreement is that the consent form be comprehensible).

Informed consent, however, is not necessarily educated consent, and according to Ingelfinger (20), the subject's only real protection depends on the conscience and compassion of the investigator and the investigator's peers. Several studies point out that the participant's level of education will determine in large measure whether he or she will be able to comprehend the purpose and procedures of the study and will be able to give informed consent. Educational attainment for the black elderly is, on average, lower than that for whites. In 1984, the median educational level was nearly 8 years for older blacks and 12 years for older whites (21). Although the median educational level of participants in a clinical trial may be provided as a part of the results, few studies are able to determine whether participants actually comprehend the study procedures and if not, whether this is a factor in refusals, noncompliance, or dropouts.

Taub, Kline, and Baker (22) evaluated informed consent as it relates to memory and age. They compared 56 community-dwelling females, aged 57 to 83, from local senior citizen centers to younger women, aged 22 to 34, who were recruited from local welcome wagon organizations or from employees of local businesses. The study involved reading prose. The two groups could be compared for only two vocabulary levels as measured by the Wechsler Adult Intelligence Scale.

Potential study participants were given information forms explaining the study and were told to ask questions for clarification. No participants asked questions, and all signed the consent forms. Two to three weeks later, the study participants were quizzed on the main points presented in the information forms. These included the funding source of the study; the main objective of the study—to find better ways to present new information to people; that participation was voluntary; and that each volunteer would be paid $3 a session.

The results suggested that the number of correct responses from the older subjects were directly related to vocabulary and educational levels. Further, when looking at the two-by-two classification of age group and vocabulary, the older women with lower vocabulary scores had the least number correct, an average of 2.08 compared to 3.23 and 3.50 for the two other groups. The authors also evaluated the percentage of subjects who were correct on each of the five questions. Among the older adults, a large percentage, particularly those with lower vocabulary scores, were incorrect on most questions. The generalizability of the study results is unknown. For example, the racial breakdown of the comparison groups was not given. In addition, the small sample size compromised the analyses, particularly when comparison groups were stratified by vocabulary groups.

Despite the limitations of this study, it does lend support to suggestions by Taub and colleagues (22) and by Miller and Willner (23) that a two-step informed consent procedure be used. This would include testing individuals before allowing them to sign informed consent documents. To improve comprehension, the study can be explained both orally and in writing.

Similar results were found by Howard, Demets, and The BHAT Research Group (24) in a study of the adequacy of the informed consent process in the Beta Blocker Heart Attack Trial (BHAT) (6), which was a double-blind placebo-controlled trial of propranolol among approximately 4,000 survivors of an acute myocardial infarction. Special efforts were made to ensure informed and voluntary consent, since patients were recruited so soon after an attack. Included in the safeguards were the addition of a bioethicist to the staff; the development of a model consent form, which was adopted by or used as a guide by the 32 centers involved; the distribution to the patients (encouraged but not required) of a brochure describing important aspects of the research design; and outlines for obtaining informed consent as part of the protocol, along with 10 procedural safeguards to assure careful deliberation and voluntary consent.

Eleven of the 32 clinics were selected for participation, and 5 patients were randomly selected from each of these 11 clinics; subsequently, 10 more patients were added (1 refused to be interviewed). The majority of the 64 persons interviewed were male (87.5%), white (85.9%), 50 years of age or older (65.6%), with at least a high school education (70.3%). Questions concerning BHAT were open-ended and included questions on the awareness of BHAT as research rather than therapy, the existence of a control group and why, the purpose of the trial, possible side effects, the assignment process, and double-blindedness.

The authors found that a large majority were well informed; however, there were differences based on education, race, and age. The overall score of those subjects with a high school education or less was significantly lower than the score of those with at least some college education. However, when looking at individual questions, they found differences between the two groups only on the awareness of a control group. Differences between whites and blacks for most of the categories were significant, even when controlling for education alone or (when sample size allowed) education and age together. The small number of blacks in the sample precludes confidently extrapolating the results beyond that particular study. Age was an important variable for differential awareness level when education was controlled. For example, the younger subjects with no college training were significantly more aware of details in the research protocol than older subjects with no college training.

Different results were found by Stanley, Guido, Stanley, and Shortell (25), who examined the capacity of elderly patients to consent to research participation. Competency was determined through the use of hypothetical consent information assessed on three levels: (1) comprehension of consent material; (2) quality of reasoning about the decision to participate or not participate in research; and (3) reasonable choice concerning participation. Patients were recruited from three facilities in major cities, with three-fourths of those asked agreeing to participate. Eighty medical patients presented with heart problems, including myocardial infarction, or hypertension, diabetes, and/or asthma. Some 39 were elderly (62 years of age and older), and 41 were young adults (aged 22–44). Race of the subject was not given.

The results presented a mixed picture regarding the elderly medical patients' capacity to give informed consent. Both the elderly and the young were more likely to agree to participate in low-risk projects rather than high-risk procedures, thereby making reasonable decisions. The rates of participation for the young and the old did not differ except in one instance, when the elderly agreed more often to a risky project. In their quality of reasoning, the elderly showed some impairment, despite the fact that they were able to reach reasonable decisions to the same degree as the younger group.

The major differences between the younger group and the older group occurred in the comprehension scores. The elderly demonstrated poorer comprehension of each of the specific elements of informed consent. The authors concluded that although the elderly patients showed poorer comprehension than their younger counterparts in giving informed consent, they generally made equally informed decisions. Implications are that perhaps only a basic awareness of relevant information is necessary to make reasonable decisions and that this quality of decision may not be adversely affected until comprehension ability is severely impaired, as in senile dementia.

To explain the reasons for the differences, the authors examined the possible effects of intelligence and attention span, but found that neither of these variables accounted for the poorer scores obtained by the elderly. Significant differences continued to exist between the two groups after the effects of intelligence and attention span were removed separately from comprehension scores. The level of education did not differ significantly between the two groups. The authors offered as reasons for the discrepancies between their results and those of Taub and colleagues the different criterion variables (immediate comprehension in this study versus delayed recall in the study by Taub and colleagues) and the study of medical patients versus normal elderly subjects.

There is little information as to how well the elderly black subject is informed in clinical trials. If it can be assumed that the less educated are less well informed and that blacks have, on average, a lower educational attainment than whites in the same age group, then there is sufficient reason for concern about the adequacy of the approach to informed consent for the black elderly in clinical trials.

As part of the informed consent process, the possible risks and benefits to the individual should obviously be explained in detail. These should be presented with such clarity that the risks and benefits can be weighed and used in the subjects' decisions regarding participation. Berkowitz (19) suggested that a support system be provided to assist the subjects in weighing the pros and cons of participation.

Suggestions from the literature on improvement in the clinical trials process include (1) the use of oral as well as written explanations; (2) the use of group discussions of risks, benefits, and procedures of the research protocol; (3) the allowance of lagtime between the explanation of the consent process and the actual signing of forms, thereby giving the patients time to discuss the research with family and friends; (4) the use of intermittent explanations of the more important aspects of the research throughout any long-term research project; (5) the improvement of forms, separating the explanation of the consent, the risks and the benefits, and the procedures (using larger type and simple and clear language); and (6) the use of someone other than the caregiver to solicit consent. According to Weintraub (26), it is a combination of human contact, through individual and group meetings, printed information sheets, and learning aids that provides a balanced approach to informed consent.

RECRUITMENT

The recruitment of subjects in a timely and cost-effective manner is one of the most important efforts of clinical trials research. Older persons, on average, have 5 diseases and take 13 different drugs, which often makes it difficult for them to meet study criteria (27). Thus the number of persons needed to obtain sufficient numbers of subjects in a trial is large because of the restraints necessary to carry out the proposed research. According to Muench's Third Law, the number of patients promised for a clinical trial must be divided by a factor of a least 10 (28). This is evidenced by comparing the number of subjects screened and the number eligible for inclusion in some of the trials cited in Table 18.1. In the SHEP study, which recruited persons 60 years of age and older, the ratio of persons screened to persons included was approximately 10 to 1. The ratio in the MRFIT study was 28 persons screened for each participant randomized.

Maddox (29) indicated that it is difficult to recruit persons in the community into a clinic for a single examination, much less for a series of different examinations. This problem intensifies as the age of the subjects increases. One of the primary objectives of the SHEP pilot study was to estimate and compare the number of participants recruited using various recruitment methods in a variety of community groups. Several sites were used to recruit subjects, including senior social organizations, senior citizen housing sites, health fairs, shopping malls, churches, banks, and polling places. In the final analysis, successful approaches were determined by a combination of factors, including local conditions and the skills, talents, and focus of the individual clinic recruitment staffs (30). A large percentage of older blacks in the SHEP study were recruited from clinical centers in the South. Successful recruiting of older blacks, in this instance, was done largely through the use of black churches (31). No attempt was made to ensure that the recruiter and the volunteer were of the same race, and it is not known whether such pairings affect agreement to participate or comply in the clinical trial.

It is difficult to determine whether the small numbers of blacks included in clinical trials are due to refusals, ineligibility, or lack of identification. More research needs to be conducted to determine the reasons for the low numbers of older black participants in clinical trials, with attention focused on implementing innovative methods to increase these numbers. Requiring adequate numbers of black participants for analyses should be a fundamental aspect of sample design. Investigators should enlist the assistance of community persons who evoke feelings of trust to serve as ambassadors for the study. Data from the SHEP (4) study indicate that the recruiter does not have to be of the same race as the potential participant to be successful in recruiting older blacks. However, it should be determined how the issue of interviewer race affects the recruitment of older blacks.

The maintenance of persons in the trial once admitted is as important, of course, as the recruitment. Participants in the Aspirin Myocardial Infarction Study (AMIS) (5) and the BHAT (6) groups were surveyed at the end of the trial to determine their perceptions of benefits, satisfactions, and disadvantages in trials. Most participants felt that the additional medical monitoring and a second opinion, plus reassurance and peace of mind, were of the greatest importance. No information was provided on the racial makeup of the respondents.

STATISTICAL CONSIDERATIONS

Sample Size

Clinical trials are designed to test a hypothesis that two or more treatment groups are of equal value against the alternative hypothesis that the treatments are different (or that one or more treatments is better). It is usually decided *a priori* that the probability of rejecting the hypothesis of no difference when the treatments are really the same will be small—usually less than or equal to .05. This is referred to as the significance level of the test. Another probability that is often overlooked in trials with a minority of blacks is the probability of rejecting the null hypothesis (in race-specific analyses) when the alternative is true (the power of a test). Although most large-scale studies do consider power, this is not always the case. Gordan (32) highlighted this problem by discussing the large number of clinical trials published in which the results are inconclusive because they are based on too small a sample size. Further, the error is compounded when uninformed investigators then incorrectly conclude that the two or more treatments under study are the same, rather than the correct conclusion that the sample size is too small to be able to detect a difference.

The adequacy of sample size in clinical trials is of paramount importance. The adequacy of sample size for blacks in general and for older blacks in particular in clinical trials has often been inadvertantly overlooked. Of the estimated 28.0 million persons aged 65 and older in the United States in 1984, only 8.2% were black. The percentage is even smaller for older subgroups—only 7.7% for those aged 75 years and older, reflecting the shorter lifespan of blacks. In clinical trials, if blacks were recruited at the rate in which they appear in the population and only the total number of persons in a trial is considered in sample-size calculations, blacks will often not be adequately represented in statistical decisions concerning the trial. The only exception to this would be when clinical trials are conducted in areas in which blacks make up a larger proportion of the population than they do overall—as in many inner-city hospitals or when the particular condition under study is particularly prevalent in the black population.

Often in large, ethical, and well-done clinical trials no particular effort is made to recruit an adequate number of blacks. In fact, they may even be excluded altogether, because investigators may feel that adequate numbers cannot be found. This trend appears to be true for the black population overall, and particularly for the elderly black population. In the Beta Blocker Heart Attack trial (6) of middle-aged persons, blacks comprised only 8.7% of the 3,837 patients enrolled in the study. The SHEP (4) study, at least in the pilot, has a better record, with approximately 18% of the subjects being older blacks.

It is suggested that in multicenter trials, efforts should be made to include centers with a large black patient population. In addition, in centers in which the percentage of blacks is underrepresented, special efforts at recruitment should be made. This includes enlisting the assistance of black professional organizations, churches, and social organizations. To attain an adequate number of blacks, oversampling may be necessary. If the sampling scheme calls for taking every fourth patient who enters a clinic, then in centers with roughly 8% blacks (the national average for the elderly population), if one of five whites is sampled and two of three older blacks, the sample size would be approximately the same but with a larger proportion of blacks.

Loss to Follow-Up

Obviously, if too widespread, loss to follow-up in a clinical trial can invalidate the results. Loss to follow-up refers to loss of data when information on some patients is incomplete. Reasons include those that are uncontrollable, such as competing risks (i.e., when a patient dies of one disease before the study is ended or develops another condition that precludes his or her participation in the study). There may also be reasons over which the investigator, to some extent, has some control, as when the subject does not return for a follow-up visit. As part of the study design, there should be detailed follow-up procedures when a participant misses a follow-up appointment. The difficulty arises because there may be differential treatment results between persons who did not complete the study and those who did. Even when those who are lost to follow-up have the same demographic and socioeconomic characteristics as those who remain in the study, there is usually resulting bias. Those who dropped out may have done so because they experienced more side effects, or those who, on the average, respond better to treatment (or those who respond worse) may decide not to return. No evidence has been presented to indicate that this may occur more in black elderly subjects than in the white elderly. Differential dropout rates on the basis of race should be adequately assessed.

FUTURE CONSIDERATIONS

There needs to be a concerted effort to increase the number of blacks in general and older blacks in particular in well-done, low-risk, high-benefit clinical trials; at the same time, we must ensure that the poor in general and older blacks in particular do not bear a greater share of the burden of participation in trials that are not properly conducted and in which the benefits are marginal at best and the risks excessive. Along with the increase in numbers is a need to maintain the quality of the trial. With these qualifications in mind, suggestions for future clinical trials involving older blacks include the following:

1. Any clinical trial addressing a problem that impacts on the black population should include a sufficient number of blacks so that the data are adequate.

2. The Tuskegee Syphilis Study (18) should be kept in mind by researchers and review boards as a reminder of not only the gross abuses to avoid, but also of those that are more subtle and likely to be overlooked. Even with the institution of review boards, it is still possible for unethical studies to be conducted, although not in as blatant a manner. These might include conducting high-risk/low-benefit studies, using placebos when standard treatment is available, not adequately explaining the risks to minority populations, and so forth. Blacks should be adequately represented on institutional review boards.

3. The assistance of hospitals and medical schools with largely black patients should be enlisted in the recruitment for an actual conduct of clinical trials. Moreover, every effort should be made to locate a clinical center at a black institution, particularly when the treatment under investigation is for a disease that is prevalent among blacks.

4. Special efforts should be made to assure that at clinic visits, older blacks are accorded the dignity they deserve. Health personnel, including physicians, should avoid assuming instant familiarity with older black patients, which may reduce participation or compliance with the treatment regimen. Such patients should be treated with respect.

5. Transportation is often a major problem for the elderly. To improve follow-up visits, transportation should be provided to those who otherwise could not come to the center.

6. Sequential monitoring of the clinical trial should be used when possible, particularly if the treatment may be life-threatening. This would reduce the likelihood of study subjects receiving the inferior treatment any longer than necessary.

In summary, older blacks, as well as older persons in general, seem to be a forgotten minority in the conduct of clinical trials. Although no single reason exists for this lack of inclusion, more effort is required to recruit the elderly than a younger group. The inclusion of elderly black subjects dictates the need for careful supervision of the study to avoid abuses that have occurred in the past. Further, those in a position to review protocols involving elderly blacks must be particularly diligent in ensuring that the research involving this segment of the population is ethical.

Studies should be designed with a high priority of having at least one site that is located in a minority hospital or center and/or a special effort should go to the recruitment of older blacks to avoid the problem of small numbers in the interpretation of the data.

REFERENCES

1. Boyles PW. Effects of age and race on clinical response to acebutolol in essential hypertension. *American Heart Journal* 1985; 109: 1184–1192.
2. Materson BJ. Black/white differences in response to antihypertensive therapy. *J Nat Med Assoc* 1985; 77:9–13.
3. Labetalol/Hydrochlorothiazide Multicenter Study Group. Labetalol and hydrochlorothiazide in hypertension. *Clin Pharmacol Ther* 1985; 38:24–27.
4. Smith WM. Isolated systolic hypertension in the elderly. In: Gross F, Strasser T, eds. *Mild Hypertension: Recent Advances.* New York: Raven Press; 1983.
5. Aspirin Myocardial Intervention Study Research Group. A randomized, controlled trial of aspirin in persons recovered from myocardial infarction. *Journal of the American Medical Association* 1980; 243(7): 661–669.
6. Beta-Blocker Heart Attack Trial Research Group. Beta-blocker heart attack trial—design features. *Controlled Clin Trial,* 1981; 2: 275–285.
7. Hypertension Detection and Follow-Up Program Cooperative Group. Five-year findings of the hypertension detection and follow-up program. 1. Reduction in mortality of persons with high blood pressure, including mild hypertension. *JAMA* 1979; 242: 2562–2571.
8. Lipid Research Clinics Group. The coronary primary prevention trial: design and implementation. *J Chron Dis* 1979; 32:609–631.
9. Lipid Research Clinics Program. The lipid research clinics coronary primary prevention trial result 1. Reduction in incidence of coronary heart disease. *JAMA* 1984; 251(3): 351–364.
10. Grimm RH, Cohen JD, Smith WM, Falvo-Gerald L, Neaton JD, Multiple Intervention Trial Research Group. Hypertension management in the multiple risk factor intervention trial (MRFIT). *Arch Intern Med* 1985; 145:1191–1199.
11. Veterans Administration Cooperative Study Group on Antihypertensive Agents. Comparison of propranolol and hydrochlorothiazide for the initial treatment of hypertension. *JAMA* 1982; 248: 1996–2011.
12. Hakkarainen H, Hattab JR, Venulet J. Phase IV research by pharmaceutical companies. *Pharmacopsychiat* 1984; 17: 168–176.
13. Vestal RE. Do elderly research subjects need special protection: physical vulnerability, 1980. *IRB,* 2:5.
14. Lawton MP. Do elderly research subjects need special protection? In psychological vulnerability. *IRB: A Review of Human Subjects Research* 1980; 2:5–7.
15. Ostfeld AM. Older research subjects: not homogeneous, not especially vulnerable, Oct 1980, *IRB,* 2:7–8.
16. Barber B, Lally JJ, Makarushka JL. *Research on Human Subjects: Problems of Social Control in Medical Experimentation.* New York: Sage; 1973.
17. Makarushka JL, McDonald RD. Informed consent, research, and geriatric patients: the responsibility of institutional review committees. *The Gerontologist* 1979; 19 (1): 61–66.

18. Jones JH. *Bad Blood: The Tuskegee Syphilis Experiment.* New York: Free Press; 1981.
19. Berkowitz S. Informed consent, research, and the elderly. *The Gerontologist* 1978; 18(3): 237–243.
20. Ingelfinger, FJ. Informed (but uneducated) consent. *The New England Journal of Medicine* 1972;287:465–466.
21. U.S. Bureau of the Census. *Social and Economic Characteristics of the Older Population, 1978* (Current Population Reports, Series P-23, No. 85). Washington, DC: U.S. Government Printing Office; 1978.
22. Taub HA, Kline GE, Baker MT. The elderly and informed consent: effects of vocabulary level and corrected feedback. *Experimental Aging Research* 1981; 7(2): 137–147.
23. Miller R, Willner HS. The two-part consent form: a suggestion for promoting free and informed consent. *The New England Journal of Medicine* 1974; 290: 964–965.
24. Howard JM, DeMets D, BHAT Research Group. How informed is informed consent: the BHAT experience. *Controlled Clinical Trials* 1981; 287–303.
25. Stanley B, Guido J, Stanley M, Shortell D. The elderly patient and informed consent. *Journal of the American Medical Association* 1984; 252(10), 1302–1306.
26. Weintraub M. Ethical concerns and guidelines in research in geriatric pharmacology and therapeutics: individualization, not codification. *J Am Geriatr Soc* 1984; 32(1): 44–48.
27. Levy ML, Mohs RC, Rosen WG, Davis KL. Research subject recruitment for gerontological studies of pharmacological agents. *Neurobiology of Aging* 1982; 3:77–70.
28. Prout TE. Other examples of recruitment problems and solutions. *Clin Pharmacol Ther*, May 1976: 67.
29. Maddox G. Selected methodological issues in normal aging. In: Palmore E, ed. *The Duke Longitudinal Study.* Chapel Hill, NC: Duke University Press; 1970.
30. Vogt TM, Ireland CC, Black D, Camel G, Hughes, G. Recruitment of elderly volunteers for a multi-center clinical trial: The SHEP pilot study. *Controlled Clinical Trials* 1986, 7(2): 118–133.
31. Hughes GH. Personal Communication, 1986.
32. Gordan RS. The design and conduct of randomized clinical trials. *IRB: A Review of Human Subjects Research* 1985; 7(1): 1–3.

PART VI
Conclusion

19

Future Directions in Research on Aging Black Populations

James S. Jackson

This volume on aging in black populations builds upon years of research on older blacks. For the most part this research has not treated race as an important independent variable but instead as a nuisance factor to be ignored or experimentally controlled (1, 2). As indicated by several of the authors in the present volume, when race has been included as an independent variable, its use has often been restricted to fairly simple racial comparisons. This type of comparative race research on poor samples, without adequate controls for such variables as socioeconomic status, and in the absence of reasonable theories of racial differences, has resulted in a set of uninterpretable findings. These types of research findings are becoming of less value as research scientists have become more sophisticated in their understanding of the role of racial and cultural variables in the study of adult development and aging (3, 4).

All previous research has not suffered from these same problems. Notable exceptions are the writings of Jacquelyne J. Jackson (5), summarized in her book *Minorities and Aging;* Percil Stanford's (6) work, especially his monograph *The Elder Black;* an edited volume by Ron Manuel (7), *Minority Aging: Sociological and Social Psychological Issues;* Donald Gelfand and Alfred Kutzik's (8) edited book on *Ethnicity and Aging;* and an edited volume by R. L. McNeely and John Colen (9), *Aging in Minority Groups.* But aside from a few additional chapters and articles (e.g., 10), the research

This chapter was written while the author was a Ford Foundation Senior Postdoctoral Fellow at the Groupe D'Études Et Recherches Sur La Science, Ecole Des Hautes Etudes En Sciences Sociales, Paris, France.

and writings on older black populations are notable for the many problems of conceptualization, planning, execution, and interpretation reviewed in the current volume.

During the course of the National Institute on Aging Workshop, and reflected in the chapters in this volume, four consistent, overarching themes emerged regarding future directions of research on aging black populations. These themes are in the areas of theory and conceptualization, the quantity of research on older black adults, disciplinary integration, and training and research funding. In the remainder of this chapter each of these themes is briefly discussed.

MORE REFINED THEORY AND CONCEPTUALIZATIONS

One of the major hindrances to conducting research on aging black populations is the need for better conceptualizations and definitions of race. Previous research, even biological/medical research, has generally used social definitions of race. This approach is less tenable as research on blacks and theories of racial differences become more refined. Similarly, there is a need for better theories that include conceptual underpinnings of observed racial differences. Several authors noted that cultural differences, if they exist, have to be identified, operationalized, and included in research designs.

Another area that was noted in nearly all the chapters is the lack of good data on normative development over the life course among adult blacks. While this is a significant problem for whites as well, the failure to investigate the nature of this development among blacks has led to invidious racial comparisons. Appropriate theoretical knowledge of the etiology and course of development could aid in better understanding the intra- and interindividual continuities and discontinuities among blacks.

GREATER QUANTITY AND QUALITY OF RESEARCH

The need for population-based longitudinal samples was noted in most chapters. The authors recognized the emergence of recent studies that are important improvements over previous efforts. None of these new studies, however, are planned, long-term, longitudinal, population-based research projects on black older adults.

Another consistent issue raised was the need for more intragroup research on blacks outside of a strictly race-comparative framework. Several authors noted that dependence on simplistic racial comparisons has obscured important intragroup variation. This variation may be important theoretically and in the more practical issues of health care delivery. The lack of focus on intragroup variation in the design and planning of research may not permit the type of sensitive intragroup analyses needed to detect these differences.

In several chapters more sensitive and thoughtful race-comparative research was proposed. The concern in these suggested studies was to ensure not only measurement equivalence in racial-group comparisons but conceptual and meaning equivalence as well.

MORE DISCIPLINARY INTEGRATION AND COOPERATION

Perhaps because of the difficulties older blacks face, an appreciation and consensus seems to be emerging regarding the need for disciplinary integration in research and service delivery. In several of the chapters the importance of having cross-disciplinary involvement was widely accepted. For example, biomedical scientists have come to realize that hypertension and diabetes may have strong social and behavioral components related to etiology, course, and treatment; and social scientists are gaining a greater appreciation of how physiological status may affect social and behavioral interaction. This need for disciplinary integration is clearly seen in the development of practical approaches to effective health care and preventive strategies in black older adult populations.

MORE TRAINING AND RESEARCH FUNDING

Inherent in the suggestions for more and better research and disciplinary integration is the need for increased funding for research on aging black populations. While such government agencies as the National Institute on Aging are appropriate sources for this funding, several of the authors pointed to the need for more private organizations, such as the American Association of Retired Persons, co-sponser of the Workshop, to contribute greater research funding. The type of research suggested—larger inclusions of blacks in clinical trials, long-term, longitudinal, laboratory- and population-based survey samples, and large epidemiological studies of aging black adults—will be an expensive addition to current funding levels.

Finally, a need was expressed in the workshop for greater funds to locate, attract, and train black researchers. The numbers of black and other minority researchers in the biomedical, social, and public health fields remain woefully inadequate. There was a general consensus that larger numbers of black researchers may provide more sensitive perspectives on, approaches to, and interpretations of empirical research. Some of these perspectives were observed at the workshop and in the resulting chapters. Better integration of black students and researchers into ongoing and planned research is considered important for training as well as for the quality of immediate research products.

In sum, future research on aging black populations will benefit from greater attention to the development of theoretical perspectives that are sensitive to the nature of black life in this society. Better definition and classification of racial status as well as better and more sensitive research questions follow naturally from these concerns. While the race-comparative research framework was seen as valuable when conducted properly, a consistent theme echoed throughout this volume has been the need to better understand the large variability that exists in physiological functioning, behavior, and health status among black population groups.

Finally, a consensus emerged that researchers were not seeking better theory and better and more empirical research on blacks merely for their own ends, important as they may be. Rather, there was a genuine appreciation for the fact that current theories and research conceptualizations do not encompass the physiological functioning, behaviors, and health status observed in blacks. It may be that by attending to these issues within aging black populations that better theories of health and effective functioning may emerge for all older adults.

REFERENCES

1. Jackson JS. *Science, values and research on ethnic and racial groups.* Unpublished manuscript, University of Michigan; 1986.
2. Levine EK. Old people are not alike: social class, ethnicity/race, and sex are bases for important differences. In: Sieber JE, ed. *The Ethics of Social Research.* New York: Springer-Verlag; 1982:127–144.
3. Fry CL. Culture, behavior, and aging in the comparative perspective. In: Birren JE, Schaie WK, eds. *Handbook of the Psychology of Aging* (2nd ed.). New York: Van Nostrand Reinhold; 1985:216–244.
4. Jackson JJ. Race, national origin, ethnicity, and aging. In: Binstock RH, Shanas E, eds. *Handbook of Aging and the Social Sciences* (2nd ed.). New York: Van Nostrand Reinhold; 1985:264–303.
5. Jackson JJ. *Minorities and Aging.* Belmont, CA: Wadsworth; 1980.
6. Sanford PE. *The Elder Black.* San Diego, CA: Campanile; 1978.
7. Manuel RC, ed. *Minority Aging: Sociological and Social-Psychological Issues.* Westport, CT: Greenwood Press; 1982.
8. Gelfand DE, Kutzik AJ, eds. *Ethnicity and Aging: Theory, Research, and Policy.* New York: Springer; 1979.
9. McNeely RL, Colen JL, eds. *Aging in Minority Groups.* Beverly Hills, CA: Sage; 1983.
10. Bengtson VL, Morgan LA. Ethnicity and aging: a comparison of three ethnic groups. In: Sokolovsky J, ed. *Growing Old in Different Societies.* Belmont, CA: Wadsworth; 1983:157–167.

Index

Accidents, as cause of death, 19, 39, 190, 191
in adolescents, 5
Activity theory of aging, 213–214
Affect Balance Scale, 238
Affirmative action, 93
Age categories, and population statistics, 4–5
Age changes, 91
Age density, in neighborhoods, 116
Age-as-leveler hypothesis, 246, 249
Aging
  attitudes toward, black vs. white, 244
  and cancer prevention, 62
  conceptualization of, 91
  differential trends in, 6, 27–30, 31–33
  and health; see Health
  markers for, 7
  need for definition of, 62
  projections for the future, 30–31
  and psychosocial stress, 247–248
  research; see Research
  and social participation, 101–102
  statistics, 4, 18, 27–37
  and subjective well-being, 242
  systems of, 6
  theories of, 243–244
Aging Society Project (Carnegie Corporation), 73
Alcohol consumption, 40, 43, 58, 87
  and cancer, 58
  and dementia, 219, 225, 228
  and hypertension, 139

Alcoholics Anonymous, 297
Alcoholism, 297
Alexander, F. G., 200
Alzheimer, Alois, 116
Alzheimer's disease
  clinical diagnosis of, 116, 218–219
  and death certificate data, 223–224
  definition of, 116
  epidemiologic studies of, 227
  and studies of first-degree relatives, 227
Alzheimer's Disease and Related Disorders Association, 216, 217
American Council of Life Insurance, 297
American Medical News, 292
Amputation, 167, 185
Anderson, R., 288
Anemia, 141
Anger, and hypertension, 200–201
Arthritis, 179
Aspirin Myocardial Infarction Study (AMIS), 354, 355, 361
Attachment behaviors, 261

Baltimore Longitudinal Study of Aging, 219
Behavior therapy, in hypertension, 207
Beta Heart Attack Trial (BHAT), 354, 355, 358, 361, 362
Beta-blocker therapy, for hypertension, 205–206, 207
Bible Belt, 111
Biofeedback, 206–207
Black institutions, 19–21

Black institutions *(continued)*
  and affirmative action, 93
  and aging research, 21, 71
  and black elderly, 20–21
  challenges to, 19–20
  fellowships in, 22
Black national origin groups, 89
Blindness, 166, 172, 185; *see also* Retinopathy
Blood volume, and hypertension, 195
Body Mass Index, 173
Breast cancer, 53–56, 62–64
  screening for, 59, 60, 63

Calcium intake, 137, 139
  and hypertension, 199, 206
  in relation to protein, 145, 148
Calloway, Nathaniel O., 73
Caloric intake, 137, 141, 144, 176
Cancer, 9–10, 50–65
  age-adjusted rate, 51, 52, 53–54
  age-specific rate, 51–52, 55
  attitudes toward, 59, 62
  black vs. white survival, 55, 57
  control, 60, 61, 62
  and ethnic groups, 56
  excess of incidence in blacks, 50,
    52, 57, 61, 64
  and health care services, 58–59, 61
  incidence of, 7–8, 19, 51
  latency period in, 61
  major risk factors/exposure, 57–58,
    64
  male vs. female survival, 55
  mortality, 7, 39, 50, 51, 61, 64
  occupational exposure to, 58, 60
  sites; *see* Cancer sites
  survival, 8, 50, 52, 55–57, 61, 63,
    64
  therapies, 58, 60, 61, 63
Cancer sites with excess incidence in
    blacks
  bladder, 53–56, 59–60, 62, 64
  corpus uterus, 53–56, 59–60, 62–64
  esophagus, 53, 55, 56, 58
  prostate, 53–56, 62–64
  rectal, 53–56, 62–64
  see also Breast cancer, Cervical
    cancer
Carbohydrate intake, 131, 132, 135,
    136
  and diabetes, 165

Cardiovascular disease; *see* Heart disease
Caregivers, 100, 118, 119, 222
Case-control studies
  advantages, 349–350
  disadvantages, 350
  follow-up, 86
  for health care, 347, 351–352
  sample size in, 350–351
Cases, selection of, for study, 348–
    349, 352
Cerebral vascular disease
  black vs. white ratios, 42, 168
  in black women, 191
  and morbidity, 11, 168
  and mortality, 7, 39
  and social disorganization, 204
Cervical cancer
  incidence, 55
  testing for, 59, 60, 63, 64
Chromium, dietary, 166
Chronological age, 6–7
Church; *see* Religious organizations
Cirrhosis, 219
Civil rights, 110
Cognitive impairment
  East Baltimore study on, 217
  Johns Hopkins Hospital study on,
    224–225
  misdiagnosis of in blacks, 225
  screening for, 225, 228
  tests for, 217
  transient vs. fixed deficits, 217
  see also Dementing illness
Colorectal cancer, screening for, 300
Communication
  of health-related information, 145–
    146, 182
  in research, 18, 19
Congregate meals, 141, 142
Cooper, R., 76, 81, 162
Copiah County, Mississippi, study on
    dementing illness, 221–223
  screening criteria for, 222
Coping
  religion in, 251
  and social support, 101
  styles, 201, 248
Coronary Primary Prevention Trial
    (CPPT), 355, 356
Creatinine clearance, 194
Creutzfeldt–Jakob disease, 227

Crossover effect, 5–6, 41–42, 73, 86, 95, 222
  male vs. female, 84
  see also Oldest-old
Cultural patterns
  and illness, 296–297, 298
  and obesity, 87, 175
  and racial differences, 105
  and Southern-born blacks, 3
  and subjective well-being, 12, 243

Dade County, Florida, nutritional study, 141
Death certificate data, 223–224
Deinstitutionalization, 294
Dementing illnesses, 11, 215–228
  among blacks, 219–225
  diagnostic criteria for, 226
  epidemic in, 215
  NINCDS-ADRDA standards for, 222
  prevalence of, 220, 221
  and prior head trauma, 227
  studies of, 217–218, 219, 221–225, 227
  types of, 216
Denial, of illness, 287
Denominations, religious, 111
Depression, 295–296
Diabetes mellitus, 59, 82, 150–172
  age of onset in blacks, 152
  diagnosis of, 152
  gestational, 151
  J-type, 152
  noninsulin-dependent; *see* Non-insulin-dependent diabetes
  types of, 150–152
Diagnosis-related groups, limitations of, 58
Diagnostic Interview Schedule (DIS), 121
Diagnostic and Statistical Manual (DSM-III, DSM-III-R), 296
Diet
  in diabetes, 184
  food frequency, 130, 166, 176
  in hypertension, 206
  lack of information on, 129–130
  preferences, 132–133, 140, 144, 182
  recommendations, 135–137, 139, 144

and weight reduction, 184, 185
Dietary recommendations, 135–137, 139, 144
Disability
  black–white ratio, 169
  and diabetes, 169–171
  payments, 306, 311, 315
  vs. retirement, 297, 306, 308, 311–312, 315–316, 321
  subjective, 311–312, 315, 317
Disengagement theory of aging, 243, 244
Diuretic therapy, for hypertension, 205, 206
Divorce, 111, 112
Duke University Center for Aging and Human Development, 86
Duncan Socioeconomic Index, 81

Education
  and diabetes incidence, 160
  and health knowledge, 79, 183
  and hypertension, 202
  and income level, 45–46
  and misdiagnosis of cognitive impairment, 225
  and nutrition, 140
  and obesity, 175
  patient, 183–184
  and subjective well-being, 247
  and support networks, 273
Eggs, in diet, 140, 166
Employment; *see* Labor force, participation in
Employment status, as predictor of subjective well-being, 242
Epidemiologic Catchment Area program, 10, 11, 77–78, 120–121
  goals of, 120
  methodology of, 120–121
  participants in, 120
  studies on mental illness, 217
Epidemiologic studies; *see* Case-control studies
Epidemiology of Dementia, The (Mortimer & Schuman), 216
Established Populations for Epidemiologic Studies of the Elderly (EPESE), 10, 120, 121–122
  goals of, 121
  methodology of, 121–122

Established Populations for
    Epidemiologic Studies of the
    Elderly (EPESE)*(continued)*
    participants in, 121
Ethical issues, in clinical trials, 355–
    360
Ethnic groups; *see* Minority groups
Evans County, Georgia, epidemiologic
    study, 86, 196
Excess deaths
    causes of, 190, 191
    concept of, 72, 89, 90, 172
    in diabetes, 172

Family
    frequency of interaction in, 269
    impact of illness on, 8, 273–274
    and income level, 45
    and life satisfaction, 270
    modified extended, 92, 259, 262–
        263
    racial differences in, 269
    as social group, 101
    solidarity, 261, 270
    as support system, 117–118, 222,
        248, 260–274, 276, 298
    see also Household composition;
        Marital status
Family Network Sampling Procedure
    (FNSP), 334
Fat consumption, 58, 133, 135,
    141
    in diabetes, 166
    reducing, 136, 144
Feet, care of, 185
Fiber, dietary, 165–166
Financial planning, 46
Folacin, in diet, 141–142, 148
Folk illnesses, 296–297
Follow-up procedures, 86, 363
Folstein, M., 216
Folstein Mini-Mental State examina-
    tion, 217
    errors in sensitivity and specificity,
        224–225
Food frequency profiles, 130, 166,
    176
Food selection patterns, 140, 182
    core items, 132–133, 144
Formal groups, participation in, 100,
    106–115
    benefits of, 101

impact on blacks vs. whites, 114–
    115, 244
vs. informal groups, 101
loss of roles in, 102, 244
and quality of life, 114–115
types of, 106
Friendship networks, 101, 115–117,
    259–260, 274–275
    class differences in, 116–117
    and life satisfaction, 116
    obstacles to, 115–116
    regional differences in, 116

Glomerular filtration rate, 194
Gout, 179
Grandparents, 268
Grant applications, improving, 71, 94
Great Society legislation, 26, 44, 45

Harburg, Ernest, 200, 201, 203
Health, of elderly blacks, 7–8, 37–43,
    47, 284
    attitudes toward, 12–13, 293–298
    behavioral determinants of, 86–87
    male vs. female perceptions of, 282–
        283, 284
    and marital status, 111
    models of, 75–76
    myths concerning, 293–298
    needs, 40, 43
    racial differences in, 283–284
    and self-treatment, 284–286, 289,
        298–299
    social determinants of, 69–95; *see
        also* Social determinants of
        health
    and social participation, 105
    and socioeconomic factors, 10, 79
    and subjective well-being, 241
Health care
    accessibility of, 40, 43, 47, 58, 63,
        64, 80–81, 183
    biases in, 17
    categorical nature of, 58–59, 63, 64
    challenges to, 17
    comprehensive, 13, 300–301
    continuity of, 58–59, 63, 64
    cost containment, 183
    factors in, 58–59, 63
    network resources for, 8
    preventive, 87, 295
    seeking, 284–290

Health Care Finance Administration, 77, 349
Health care professions
  blacks in, 19–22, 183
  training in, 295
Health data
  collecting, 78
  cross-sectional, 79, 91, 93, 94
  self-reported, 75–76, 94, 120
Health Examination Survey, 164
Health practices
  black vs. white, 40, 43, 47
  promoting, 46, 182, 300
Health-disparities model, 76
Heart disease
  black vs. white ratio, 7, 19, 39, 42
  in black women, 191
  and diabetes, 168–169, 172, 179
  mortality, 7, 11, 39, 190
  and smoking, 61
  and social status, 90
Heckler, Margaret, 293
Hispanic national origin groups, 89;
    see also Minorities
Home health care, 295
Home remedies, 298
Homicide, 19, 39, 42, 190, 191
  in adolescence, 5
  research on, 81, 219
Hospitals, 292, 293
Household composition, 106, 112–114, 267–268
  black–white differences in, 113, 244, 267–268
  and diabetes incidence, 160
  intergenerational, 113–114
  and life satisfaction, 114
  nonnuclear adults in, 268
  and socioeconomic factors, 113, 267
Howard University, 20
Hyperglycemia, 150, 167
Hypertension Detection and Follow-up Program, 196, 354, 355
  Cooperative Group, 202
Hypertension, essential, 11, 59, 190–208
  black vs. white findings, 76, 168, 191, 202
  causes of, 82, 172
  definition of, 191
  and diabetes, 167, 168, 182
  diet modifications in, 206

  incidence of, 11
  male–female ratio, 191
  and multiinfarct dementia, 219, 225
  and nutrition, 197–199
  and obesity, 179, 182, 196, 219
  personality factors in, 200–202
  prevalence of, 191
  research on, 21, 76, 82, 354–355
  screening for, 182
  social factors in, 202–204, 219
  and social support, 204, 207–208
  treatment of, 204–208
  and treatment compliance, 207–208, 225

Illiteracy, 79
Illness
  chronic vs. acute, 82, 282, 295
  definitions, 282–287
  delay in seeking help for, 287
  denial of, 287
  folk, 296–297
  phases of evaluation, 286
  research on, 74–75
  seeking care for, 284–290
  symptoms, evaluating, 287
  see also specific illnesses
Income level, 26, 43–46
  black–white ratio, 44–45
  and education, 45–46
  determining, 92
  and diabetes incidence, 161
  and health, 79
  and obesity, 195
  and social participation, 105
  and subjective well-being, 241, 247
  and support networks, 272
  see also Retirement
Infant mortality, 5, 6, 19, 42, 190
Informal groups, participation in benefits of, 101
  vs. formal groups, 101
  and quality of life, 118–119
  types of, 115
Informal support networks
  and age, 271
  health factors in, 273–274
  intergenerational, 266, 268
  kinds of help given/received, 265
  and nonnuclear-family adults, 268
  and proximity, 267, 268–269
  and psychological well-being, 261

Informal support networks (*continued*)
  racial differences in, 263–264, 267
  regional differences in, 273
  sociodemographic factors in, 261–
    262, 265
  see also Family, as support system
Informed consent, 357–360
  explaining risks and benefits, 360
  younger vs. older adults, 359
Institutional racism, 72
Insurance, health, 40, 43, 79
Intergenerational households, 113–114
International Classification of Dis-
    eases, 223
Interviewing, 339–340, 342
Irelan, L. M., 307–308
Iron, nutritional, 139, 141, 144, 145,
    148
  deficiency, 141

Jackson, Hobart C., 295
James, Sherman, 200, 201, 203
Job stress, 201
John Henryism, 201, 203
Judgment theories, of subjective well-
    being, 246–247

Kallikrein-kinin system, 194–195
Kansas City, Kansas, nutritional study,
    142
Ketoacidosis, 168
Kidney
  disease, 167, 172, 182, 185
  function, in hypertension, 193–195
Kin support; *see* Family
Klosterman vs. Cuomo (New York),
    294
Kutner Morale Scale, 238

Labor force, participation in, 102,
    106, 107
  black–white differences in, 107
  declining, in blacks, 304
  and life satisfaction, 114, 115, 245
Language styles, 3, 331
Liang, J., 75
Life expectancy
  blacks vs. whites, 5, 19, 38, 41, 47,
    84–85, 190
  in cancer, 62
  changes in, 7, 42, 215
  and income, 43

male vs. female, 7, 38, 41, 84–85
  and obesity, 172
Lifespan continuity, 5–7
  and informal support networks, 263
  and morbidity, 8
  and subjective well-being, 243, 249–
    250
  in work experience, 305, 308, 311,
    315, 320
Lincoln Community Health Center
    (Durham, North Carolina), 299–
    300
Linoleic acid, 134, 135
Literature reviews
  benefits of, 74
  funding for, 88
  misclassifications in, 75
  need for, 70, 73, 88
  scope of, 73
  and topical indexes
  updating, 88, 93
Longitudinal research, 18, 86, 91, 94
  in ECA program data base, 121
  in EPESE program, 122
  exclusion of blacks in, 86, 219
  in mental health, 219
  needed for diabetes, 181

Male–female ratio, in age groups, 36–
    37
Malignant neoplasm; *see* Cancer
Marital status, 106, 107, 111–112
  black–white differences in, 111,
    112
  and diabetes incidence, 159–160
  gender as predictor of, 111–112
  and helper availability, 267, 271–
    272
  and life satisfaction, 114
  and subjective well-being, 241
Meals, skipping, 135, 136, 137, 146
Measurement strategies, 106, 120
Medicaid, 292
Medicare, 40, 43, 47, 292, 293, 352
  and home health care, 295
  and preventive care, 295
Medications, 296, 298–299, 300–301
  over-the-counter, 299
  psychotropic, 293–294
Meharry Medical College, 20–21
Metropolitan Life Standard Weights,
    173

Middle age, 5
  and diabetes risk factors, 181
  and marital stability, 112, 113
  and obesity, 181
Minority groups
  and aging policy, 47, 78
  and folk illnesses, 297
  and food selection patterns, 140
  health data on, 78, 80, 89
  lifespan continuity in, 6
  in oldest-old group, 34
  and responses to psychotropic
      drugs, 293–294
  and social participation, 102–103
Mobility, reduced, 58, 184, 284
Mood states, in subjective well-being,
    251
Morbidity rates, 8
  and DRG limitations, 58
  and environmental factors, 76
  and hypertension, 11
  paucity of information on, 80
Mortality rates, in blacks, 4, 5, 10,
    47, 80, 283–284
  and age, 82
  cancer, 7, 39, 50, 60, 61, 62, 64
  by cause, 7, 39
  changing patterns in, 95
  in diabetes, 171–172
  differential, 39, 42, 171, 222
  and environmental factors, 76
  male vs. female, 38, 82–84, 283–
      284
  and multiple-jeopardy hypothesis, 5,
      246
  and obesity, 180
Mortimer, J. A., 216
Multiinfarct dementia, 219
  male–female ratios, 221
  prevalence of, 221
  risk for in black population, 219,
      225, 228
Multiple Risk Factor Intervention
    Trial (MRFIT), 355
Multiple-jeopardy hypothesis, 5,
    246
Multivariate models, 104–106, 122
Mutran, E., 264, 270
Myth and Reality of Aging in America
    (Harris), 104, 264
Myths, of health care in black elderly,
    293–298

National Ambulatory Medical Care
    Survey (NAMCS), 289
National Black Election Study, 329,
    335, 340
National Cancer Institute, 51, 61, 78
National Center for Health Statistics,
    74, 284
  and death certificate data, 223
  and life expectancy, 190
  mortality data, 51, 54, 77, 80, 86
  National Health Interview Survey,
      89
National Diabetes Advisory Board,
    169
National Diabetes Data Group, 150,
    175
National Health Interview Survey
    (NHIS), 89, 282, 289
  and diabetes, 152, 153, 155, 162
National Health and Nutrition Ex-
    amination Surveys (NHANES),
    130–131, 139, 145, 146
  and aging, 227
  diabetes testing in, 152, 162, 163–
      164, 166, 169
  and food frequency profiles, 130,
      166, 176
  and obesity, 173
  and 24-hour dietary intake, 130,
      131, 137, 166, 198
National Institute on Aging, 9, 21, 22,
    217–218, 227
  and affirmative action, 93
  grants from, 71–72, 75, 88, 93
National Institutes of Health, 21, 94
National Institute of Mental Health,
    74, 77, 228
  and ECA studies on mental illness,
      217
National Institute of Neurological and
    Communicative Disorders and
    Stroke (NINCDS), 216, 217
National Survey of Black Americans,
    225, 227, 309, 329, 338
  and support networks, 262, 265–
      266, 267, 269, 270
Nationwide Food Consumption Sur-
    vey, 131, 145
Nephropathy, diabetic, 167, 168
Networks; *see* Friendship networks,
    Informal support networks
Newman, J. F., 288

Nigeria, studies of neurologic disease in, 217
Noninsulin-dependent diabetes, 11, 150, 151, 152
   black–white ratios, 155–156, 159
   complications of, 166–171
   costs of, 171, 172
   dietary risk factor in, 165–166
   diets for, 184
   disability connected with, 169–171
   familial patterns in, 162
   genetic risk factors in, 163
   incidence of, 157
   metabolic risk factors, 163
   mortality, 171–172
   and obesity, 163–165, 179, 180
   prevalence of, 152–157, 158
   screening for, 182
   sociodemographic characteristics of, 156, 158–161
Nonkin support, 12, 271, 272, 276
   sources of, 274–275
   see also Friendship networks, Religious organizations
Nursing homes
   black elderly in, 298
   diabetes in, 169
   for-profit, 292
   psychiatric, 293
Nutrition, 10, 129–148
   black–white differences, 132–135, 137–138
   and cancer, 58, 60, 61, 64
   cross-sectional surveys of, 130–139
   and dietary changes, 143–144, 299
   environmental determinants of, 140
   and food selection patterns, 140
   inadequacies in, 137
   inner-city descriptive studies, 141–143
   lack of information on, for blacks, 129–130, 147
   profile, 137
   risk factors, 142

Obesity, 11, 43, 172–180, 181, 185
   in black females, 11, 58, 87, 138, 147, 163, 174, 194–195
   and body type, 164
   and cancer, 58
   childhood, 174

   complications associated with, 178–179, 184–185, 206
   and diabetes, 163–165
   dietary factors in, 175–176
   genetic factors in, 178
   and hypertension, 179, 182, 196, 206, 219
   metabolic factors in, 176–177
   and mortality, 180
   and nutrition, 138
   prevalence of, 173–174
   psychological factors in, 176–177
   risk factors for, 172, 174–178
   and sociocultural factors, 87, 175, 181
   tests for, 173, 181
Occupations, of blacks, 80, 81
   and diabetes, 160–161
Older Americans Act, 47
Oldest-old age group
   changing mortality patterns in, 84
   and church, 275
   dependence of, 34
   growth in, 5, 30, 34
   misreporting in black cohorts, 5
   physical and psychological health in, 6
   racial crossover phenomenon in, 5–6, 84, 222
   and support networks, 271, 275
   women in, 37
   and work experience, 310
Oleic acid, 134, 135
Osteoporosis, 145
Over-the-counter medicine, 299
Oversampling, 104, 120, 180, 334
Overview of Legal Issues in Geriatric Psychiatry (Baker, Perr, & Yesavage), 225
Overweight vs. obesity, 173

Pap smears, 59, 63
Para-kin, 117
Pensions, 311, 313
Peripheral vascular disease, 167–168
Peripheral vascular reactivity, 197
Pharmacists, black, 20
Pharmacologic therapy, for hypertension, 205–206
Philadelphia Geriatric Center Morale Scales, 238
Plan for Academic Renewal (PAR), 20

Plasma norepinephrine, 192–193
Plasma renin, 193–194
Poindexter, H. A., 298
Political parties, 100, 106, 107–109
  affiliation, racial differences in, 108
  leadership in, 108, 109
  see also Voting patterns
Polypharmacy, 299
Population, U.S.
  composition by gender, 36–37
  distribution of blacks in, 34–35, 116
  statistics on, 27–37
Potassium intake, 138, 144, 198–199
  in assessing obesity, 173
  black–white differences, 198
  in hypertension, 206
  ratio with sodium, 198–199
  in relation to protein, 145, 148
Poverty, 5, 19, 26
  and educational attainment, 45–46
  and family size, 45
  in the unretired-retired, 308
Poverty ratio, 45
President's Council of Economic Advisors, 25
Prevention and Treatment of the Complications of Diabetes, The, 169, 180
Preventive medicine, 87, 295
Primary degenerative dementia, diagnostic criteria for, 226
Progressive relaxation, 206–207
Protein intake, 131, 132, 135, 145, 148
  and diabetes, 166
  reducing, 136
Psychiatric care
  in a comprehensive health care system, 301
  medication in, 293–294, 296
  myth of abuse of, 294
  new treatment methods in, 294
  and psychosocial stressors, 296
  training in, 295

Questionnaires, research, preparation of, 336, 372
Quetelet Index, 173

Race vs. minority status, 89–90

Race-of-interviewer effects, 339–340, 342
Rare Element Telephone Screening (RETS), 334
Ratio-standards model, 72, 76
Recreational groups, 101
Recruitment, for clinical trials, 360–361, 362
Religious organizations, 100–101, 106, 110–111
  and alcoholism, 297
  and civil rights, 110
  denominations, 111
  and quality of life, 114, 244, 245, 248
  and regional differences, 111
  as support system, 248, 275
Research, 13–14, 18, 91–92, 328–365
  barriers to, 19
  cancer, 60–61, 62–64
  and data availability, 77–80
  in diabetes, 181–184
  funding for, 21, 71, 92–93
  and grant applications, 71
  on health-care seeking behavior, 288–290
  intraminority, 41, 89
  longitudinal; *see* Longitudinal research
  methodology, 91–92, 268, 276; *see also* Survey research methods
  need for integration in, 18, 19, 21
  on nutrition, 146–147
  for retirement years, 46
  on subjective well-being, 250–252
  time analyses in, 82–86
  see also Literature reviews; Study design
Retinopathy, diabetic, 166–167, 168, 182, 184–185
Retirement, 12, 13, 102, 114, 308–322
  and age, 314–315
  benefits vs. disability benefits, 306–307
  and class, 310
  criteria, 304, 307
  definition of, 319
  early, 107, 297
  financial planning for, 45
  male vs. female concept of, 307, 317, 320–321

Retirement (*continued*)
  self-definition of, 307, 308, 311,
    314, 317, 318, 321–322
  and Social Security, 310, 311, 312,
    316, 320
  source of income in, 311, 313, 316–
    317, 321
  welcomed, 245
  see also Disability
Retirement History Survey, 307

Sadowsky, J., 72
Salt, use of, 130, 136, 138, 144
Sample, 104, 309
  errors in, 333–335
  size of, 334, 350–351, 362
  see also Oversampling
Schuman, L. M., 216
Screening programs
  for breast cancer, 59, 60, 63
  for cervical cancer, 59, 60, 63, 64
  for diabetes, 182
  for hypertension, 182
Seaberry, Jane, 25
Senior citizens centers, 109, 110
  accessibility of, 110
Sick-role theory, 306
Social class
  and diet, 140
  and obesity, 87
  and retirement, 310
  and social participation, 109
  vs. socioeconomic status, 90
Social determinants of health
  available data on, 79, 80
  vs. behavioral determinants, 86–87,
    95
  conceptualization of, 77, 88, 89–91,
    92, 94
Social disorganization, 204
Social instability, neighborhood, 203
Social Security; *see* Retirement
Social Security Act, 47
Social Security Administration, 74
Social status
  and heart disease, 90
  and subjective well-being, 242–243,
    247, 249, 251–252
Socioeconomic factors
  and family support, 263, 272–273
  and friendship networks, 116, 263
  and household composition, 113
  and hypertension, 202–203

and obesity, 175
and racial differences, 105
and social participation, 108, 109
and subjective well-being, 240, 244,
  245
and the unretired-retired, 308
and voting patterns, 108
Sodium
  excretion, 194
  and hypertension, 198, 206
  intake, 138, 144, 145, 198, 206
  relationship to protein, 148
  retention, 194, 195
Sodium-potassium pump, 177
Standard Listing and Screening Procedure (SLASP), 334
Stress
  and behavior therapy, 207
  and coping styles, 201, 248, 297
  and hypertension, 196–197, 201,
    203–204
  physical reactivity to, 196–197
  and social support, 101
  socioecologic, 203–204
  studies of, 248
Stroke; *see* Cerebral vascular disease
Study designs, 13, 104, 309
  case-control, 347
  control population in, 349
  errors in, 332–341
  and health problems, 347, 351–352
Subjective well-being (SWB), 12, 237–
  252
  and age, 242
  and age-cohort influences, 249–250,
    251
  components of, 239
  definition of, 237
  gerontologic concepts in, 237
  judgment theories of, 246–247
  measurement of, 238–239
  racial differences in, 240–241
  and regional differences, 242
  and social participation, 100
Substance abuse, 19, 87; *see also*
  Alcoholism
Suicide
  increase of in black elderly, 295
  rates, black vs. white, 8, 72, 219
Surveillance, Epidemiology, and End
  Results (SEER) program, 9, 51,
  52, 55, 56, 78
Survey research methods, 328–342

errors in, 332–341
race and cultural factors in, 250–251, 329–331
Syme, Leonard, 200, 203
Sympathetic nervous system activity, 192–193
in stress response, 196–197, 207
Systolic Hypertension in the Elderly (SHEP) study, 354, 355, 361, 362

Task errors, 336–339
Task Force on Black and Minority Health, 19, 74, 76, 78, 88, 89, 190, 219
and relative risk, 172
report of, 70, 74, 180
Task Force on Forensic Issues in Geriatric Psychiatry, 225
Telephone surveys, 332, 334, 335, 342
Thermoregulation, 176–177
Three Generation Family Study (TGFS), 329
Tobacco use, 40, 43, 87
and cancer, 57, 58, 60, 61, 62, 64
and heart disease, 61
Transportation, and health care accessibility, 183, 300, 364
Tuskegee Syphilis Study, 356, 364

Unretired-retired; *see* Retirement
Use of Health Services by Women 65 Years of Age and Over, United States, 289

Vanderbilt University, 20–21
Variables, in research on aging, 3–4
demographic, 104, 262
in family support system, 262, 265
interviews, 339
intraracial, 10, 208
racial, 78, 81
in socioeconomic status, 92
in study of retired/unretired, 310
Vasoconductor responses, racial differences in, 197, 207
Veterans Administration Cooperative Study Group on Antihypertensive Agents, 355

Vitamin intake, 137, 138, 141, 144, 166, 299
Voluntary organizations, participation in, 100, 106, 109–110, 244
and health, 115
problems in studying, 109–110
recruitment in, 110
and socioeconomic status, 109
Voting patterns, 106
black–white differences in, 108

Weight reduction, 184, 185
in hypertension, 206
Weight Watchers, 184
West, Kelly, 164
Wide Area Screening Procedure, 334
Widowhood, 112, 113, 267
Willie, Charles V., 73
Women
and cancer survival, 55, 57, 62
and diabetes mortality, 171
and family-based support systems, 117, 270–271
and friendship networks, 116
and heart disease/stroke, 191
higher prevalence of dementing illness in, 217, 219
increase in elderly black, 30, 34
and infant mortality, 42
life expectancy of, 38, 41, 42
and marital status, 111–112
and nutrition, 147
and obesity, 11, 58, 87, 147, 163, 195
predominance of, in age groups, 37
prevalence of diabetes in, 155, 159, 166
and subjective perceptions of health, 282–283
Work experience, 305, 308; *see also* Labor force, participation in; Retirement

Younger-old age group
physical and psychological health in, 6
work experience in, 316

Zinc, dietary, 141, 142